D1714374

JX 5437.8
M 37/3

Werner Maser

NUREMBERG
A Nation on Trial

Translated from the German
by Richard Barry

Charles Scribner's Sons
New York

SEP 2 1981
'SEP
SEP 1981

211399

Nürnberg: Tribunal der Sieger first published by
Econ Verlag, Düsseldorf, 1977
This translation first published 1979

Copyright © Econ Verlag GmbH, Düsseldorf, 1977

Translation copyright © Richard Barry, 1979

All rights reserved. No part of this book may be
reproduced in any form without the permission
of Charles Scribner's Sons

1 3 5 7 9 11 13 15 17 19 I/C 20 18 16 14 12 10 8 6 4 2

Printed in Great Britain

Library of Congress Catalog Card Number 79-63242
ISBN 0-684-16252-0

Contents

List of Illustrations

Photographs courtesy: Zeitgeschichtliches Bildarchiv Heinrich Hoffmann;
Bildarchiv Preussischer Kulturbesitz; Archiv Dr Kempner;
Keystone Press Agency

Author's Foreword

The page footnotes and Notes indicate where personal information has been given by the Nuremberg prosecutors, US officers, defence counsel, the defendants, witnesses and the dependants of those condemned to death. My special thanks are due to Dr Robert M. W. Kempner, Otto Kranzbühler, Ralph Varady, Karl Dönitz, Frau Luise Jodl and former US officers who were on duty in Mondorf and Nuremberg in 1945/6. I also owe thanks to Frau Elizabet Kinder of the Federal Archives, Koblenz, to Richard Bauer of the US Document Center, Berlin, to Dr Anton Hoch of the Institut für Zeitgeschichte, Munich, to Dr Robert Wolfe of the National Archives, Washington, and to Dr Alfred Wagner of UNESCO.

Circumstances have unfortunately compelled me not to give the names of certain important informants and holders of original documents. Among them is the man from Tahiti who discovered the location of documents sent to America during the main trial.

My very special thanks are due to Gerhard Beckmann. He it was who convinced me in London in 1971 that it was 'essential' that the results of my research into the Nuremberg trial be published.

Werner Maser

Part One

The Victor's Preparations

Before the End of Hostilities

On Wednesday, 16 October 1946, under the eye of Major Rex S. Morgan, head of the US Army's Burial Service, American soldiers scattered some human ashes into the little ten-foot-wide Conwentz brook running 200 feet below No. 25 Heilmannstrasse, Munich-Solln. The men were on the staff of the US mortuary which was housed in No. 25 and for them this was routine work. Inevitably they assumed that the ashes were those of American servicemen who had been killed in some accident.

The names of the dead men meant nothing to them. One was registered as 'Georg Munger', another under the Jewish name 'Abraham Goldberg', a well-known name in the football team of the University of Pennsylvania, where Major Morgan had graduated. They had no inkling that these ashes were the last mortal remains of the major German war criminals, hanged shortly after midnight in the gymnasium of Nuremberg prison.

They did not suspect that 'Georg Munger's' ashes were in fact those of the Reich Marshal Hermann Göring, who had committed suicide, or 'Abraham Goldberg's' those of Julius Streicher, the ex-Gauleiter, fanatical anti-semite and editor of *Der Stürmer*. The others registered under fictitious names were: Field Marshal Wilhelm Keitel and Colonel-General Alfred Jodl, Reich Ministers Alfred Rosenberg, Hans Frank, Wilhelm Frick and Joachim von Ribbentrop, SS-Obergruppenführer Ernst Kaltenbrunner, Head of the Reichssicherheitshauptamt (Reich Central Security Department) Fritz Sauckel, Hitler's Plenipotentiary for the Employment of Labour, and Arthur Seyss-Inquart, Reich Commissar for the Occupied Netherlands.

In newspaper articles and radio reports the general public was informed that the ashes of the Hitler Reich's high-ranking officers and politicians, condemned to death as major war criminals and executed by hanging, had been scattered in 'a river somewhere in Germany'[1] on 16 October. Neither the 'criminals'' relatives nor the surviving defendants in the Nuremberg Trial were ever told where it was. Even Dr Ludwig Pflücker, the German doctor responsible under the American authorities for the medical care of the major defendants up to the time of their execution, was told nothing, though he was on good terms with influential American officers and officials. Six years after the executions he wrote: 'Probably the bodies were cremated and the ashes scattered. The intention was to leave no trace.'[2]

The fears harboured by the victorious Allied powers in 1946 lest 'a shrine be made of this place at any time'[3] were definitely not based on some mistaken idea about the attitude of the Germans, as has often been maintained.[4] In Germany neither gallows nor graves have been turned into memorials, as happened in Japan after the execution of the seven officers and politicians condemned to death there as war criminals; nevertheless plaques and gravestones for Wilhelm Keitel and Alfred Jodl, for instance, have been in existence for years – though not alongside the gallows nor where their ashes were scattered in 1946.

In Japan, in contrast to Nuremberg, friends of the men tried as war criminals in Tokyo, hanged as war criminals in Sugamo and cremated in Yokohama contrived to obtain possession of the ashes; these they initially hid but later buried beneath a mighty memorial on the summit of Mount Sangana. In 1952, when the Americans handed over to Japanese control the prison in Sugamo where the gallows had been, a garden of remembrance was laid out with oaks (the 'symbolic tree' to the Germans) and tea bushes; even the holes in which the five gallows stood have taken on the 'character of a memorial'. The memorial tablet on the 'graves of the seven martyrs' on Mount Sangana pays tribute to men who throughout their trial tacitly agreed to take upon themselves all responsibility for the crimes laid against them and refused to involve their Emperor Hirohito in any way.[5] Even on their way to the gallows they stubbornly maintained that 'The Tenno' had had no influence on policy and was therefore in fact innocent of anything connected with war crime. Whether this influenced the victors – two years after Nuremberg – to tolerate the memorials and the martyr cult in Japan can only be conjectured.

Admittedly the party line laid down by Göring in Nuremberg, 'not a word against the Führer', had been basically in line with the stand taken by the main Japanese defendants; from the viewpoint of the main German defendants, however, it had soon proved to be such an unprofitable instruction that, as time went on, not even Göring himself had kept to it. In Germany, two years before the executions in Sugamo, everything had to be expunged; everything reminiscent of the men who had been hanged had to disappear. Even the hoods they had worn and the ropes which had strangled them had to be burnt – a decision which may well have been influenced by the fact that American souvenir collectors had 'early on' offered the hangman, their fellow-countryman John C. Woods, up to $2,500 a time for a hangman's rope.

Shortly after the Germans had been executed the *New York Times* wrote: 'The ashes of the innocent and the ashes of unspeakable criminals are composed of the same elements, blown by the same winds, dissolved in the same waters. And in the midst of our dark day we must now hope and pray for the growth of a new world.'[6] After the Nuremberg Trial ended, however, both the ashes of the Germans condemned to be hanged as war criminals and hopes for the emergence of a new world vanished. At the end of the war some of the principal defendants had expected to be let off lightly, like the Germans tried as war criminals after the First World War; by mid-summer 1945, however, any such hope had vanished. They found themselves all lumped together by the prosecution as 'Hermann Göring et al.';[7] in the witness-box they were often addressed merely by name – without rank or title. With the possible exception of Göring none of them had expected that, after the Reich's catastrophic defeat, their victorious enemies would treat them with the consideration shown each other some three hundred years earlier by the ex-combatants of the Thirty Years War; still less, however, did they expect what actually happened to them after capitulation.[8] The warlords of the Treaty of Osnabrück had been referred to as '*serenissimum et potentissimum principem ac dominum*';[9] in Nuremberg the accused were not even addressed as 'Mr'.

Both sides had meanwhile written a definite 'Finis' to the era of 'chivalrous' battles and peace treaties, of 'perpetual oblivion and amnesty for all that has been done since the beginning of these troubles in what place or in what manner soever hostilities may have been exercised by the one or the other Party'.[10] The partners to the peace treaties of Osnabrück and Münster in 1648 had explicitly refused to list misdeeds or crimes committed during the war, to demand reparations, to raise questions of war guilt, to name or try war criminals; even in 1918, however, the Germans named as war criminals by the victor powers could no longer count on such treatment. In 1648 it had been laid down that 'officers and soldiers, counsellors and judges ... of what name and condition soever they be ... who have fought, whether with the Sword or the Pen, from the highest to the lowest, without any difference or exception, no hurt shall be done to their Persons or Goods';[11] that no proceedings be taken against these categories of persons, 'far less shall they suffer any punishment or damage under any Pretext whatsoever'.[12] The Treaty of Osnabrück did, however, contain explicit warnings to future peace-breakers – based on international law. The very first Article stated that peace must be 'christian, universal and perpetual' and that any future disturber of the peace would be subject to punishment.[13]

Not until after the end of the war did the men arraigned in 1945 learn of the Allied intention to punish certain Germans as war criminals. Some of them were extremely surprised that they should be among those so accused. The charges which the majority found themselves facing under a code of law totally foreign to them were brought against former ministers, officers and officials who – initially at any rate – felt themselves innocent. Shortly before his execution, for instance, Wilhelm Keitel wrote of the period immediately following his arrest: '... in those two unguarded hours I could have put an end to my life and nobody could have stopped me. The thought never occurred to me, as I never dreamed that such a *via doloris* lay ahead of me, with this tragic end in Nuremberg.'[14]

Even in Nuremberg the remarkable effect of Hitler's style of leadership was still apparent; the defendants had been moulded by it for years. He had been responsible for creating and fostering an atmosphere not only of uncertainty but also to some extent of 'ingenuousness'. Although a Nazi Party programme had been public property since 1920, although *Mein Kampf* had been published in 1925 and translated into numerous languages, and although Hitler had repeatedly emphasized its validity in face of criticism from abroad and had given vent to a flood of subsequent statements, much of what happened while they were working under Hitler may well have been incomprehensible to these defendants – Göring excepted. Hitler was always determined to pursue his 'might is right' policy, whatever the cost, and he presented it not only as the *ultima ratio* but as fundamentally 'correct' in principle; he obviously required a well-oiled machine for his purposes but in 1933 he could not, with a flick of the fingers, do away with the foreign policy organization which he had inherited and which was rooted in the Weimar constitution, international obligations and internal political practice. In the early days after Hindenburg's death, though determined to impose his own autocratic will, he was forced to take account of the influence of certain circles in the old ruling hierarchy and of certain social groupings; he was accordingly compelled to make many concessions, at least of a tactical nature, and to pretend even to his ministers, officers and functionaries that things were the precise opposite of what he was planning or doing. In the last analysis, therefore, each of the defendants had played a part in an 'orchestra' of which Hitler was sole conductor. The fact that hardly any of them knew in detail what any other was doing or being allowed to do resulted naturally from Hitler's policy of preventing anyone knowing more than he, Hitler, considered necessary for the performance of his duty. Moreover only at Nuremberg did it emerge that after 1933 individual ministers were in increasing competition for the Führer's favour, were intriguing or defending themselves against intrigue, spying on what their colleagues were doing and eyeing their standing with Hitler. Both documents and witnesses testified that spies had been used to attend and take notes at their rivals' meetings.

Without Hitler all the defendants were blind, dumb and paralysed, a fact which the International Military Tribunal in Nuremberg, however, refused to accept; they were puppets on strings held and pulled – or cut when he thought fit – by Hitler alone; he simply made use of them. Take Alfred Rosenberg, for instance; according to his lights he gave Hitler two decades of faithful service, but Hitler always ridiculed him; or Hans Frank – he was used for years as personal legal adviser[15] and led to believe that he was the Führer's 'right-hand man'; yet Hitler treated him coldly and impersonally and deceived him unscrupulously.

While awaiting indictment the erstwhile rivals for Hitler's favour and confidence[16] could at least suppress or allay their own feelings of guilt, if they had any, by reference to the Führer's orders and directives as the reason or cover for their activities. The provisions of the IMT Charter of 8 August 1945, however, deprived them of the defence that they were mere obedient servants of the Hitler regime, simple executors of orders, innocent people without responsibility.

Finally a contributory factor to the defendants' 'astonishment' at being tried was that they did not consider themselves and the Reich to be the only guilty parties. Every one of them could have cited facts which, in their view, must incriminate the Allies equally with themselves and the Reich. All of them could point out, for instance, that, in accordance with a secret supplementary protocol to the Non-Aggression Pact of 28 August 1939 between the Reich government and the Soviet Union, the Red Army had invaded Poland in September 1939 simultaneously with the German Wehrmacht. They equally knew that the Russians, not the Germans, were responsible for the massacre of Polish officers in Katyn Forest. They either did not know or turned their backs on the fact that in the relatively early stages the Allies had promised them a sticky end in the event of the Reich's defeat. All of them must have realized that, since Hitler's declaration of war on the United States on 11 December 1941, Allied warnings had sounded nothing like so 'harmless' as those issued by Roosevelt and Churchill on 14 August 1941 from the battleship *Prince of Wales*; at that time, in the light of Hitler's highly favourable strategic position, the Atlantic Charter had merely expressed 'hopes' – for example: 'After the final destruction of Nazi tyranny they [USA and Great Britain] hope to see established a peace which will afford to all nations the means of dwelling in safety within their own boundaries.'[17]

Subsequent protests by Allied statesmen and politicians against crimes committed by Germans in Poland and Czechoslovakia had fallen on deaf ears. In October 1941, before the US entry into the war, Roosevelt had condemned German shootings of hostages; Churchill had supported him in the name of the British government in December 1941; the Soviet Union had sent corresponding notes to various powers. In December 1941, some six months after the German attack on the Soviet Union, Churchill and Roosevelt had drafted the Washington Pact, which came into force a month later; this was a sort of Allied Grand Coalition and ultimately, as more and more nations adhered to it, became the germ of UNO.[18]

This United Nations Pact, described as 'historic' even at the time, was followed on 13 January 1942 by the St James's Declaration signed by representatives of the nine European countries occupied by Hitler (Belgium, Czechoslovakia, France, Greece, Holland, Luxemburg, Norway,

Poland and Yugoslavia). The Declaration called for international solidarity 'to avoid ... acts of vengeance on the part of the general public and in order to satisfy the sense of justice of the civilized world'; it set out as one of the most important Allied war aims 'the punishment through the channel of organized justice of those guilty and responsible for these crimes, whether they have ordered them, perpetrated them or in any way participated in them'.[19] It stated explicitly that 'in the spirit of international solidarity' the persons guilty or responsible 'whatever their nationality' (!) should be sought, handed over to justice, tried and 'the sentences pronounced carried out'.[20]

In the Anglo-Soviet treaty of alliance of 26 May 1942 the parties undertook to afford each other military 'and other' assistance in the war against Germany and her allies, not to enter into any negotiations with 'the Hitlerite Government' or 'any other government in Germany that does not clearly renounce all aggressive intentions' and not to conclude an armistice or peace treaty with Germany or her allies without the agreement of the other party.[21]

In July 1941 Roosevelt included the Soviet Union in the list of countries to which the USA would provide aid. On 11 June 1942 the USA concluded an agreement on principles for mutual assistance in prosecuting the war.[22] On 7 October 1942 Roosevelt and Viscount Simon, the British Lord Chancellor, agreed with other Allied governments to set up a United Nations Commission 'to examine war crimes'; nothing was actually done, however, until after the resounding Allied victories in North-West Africa and on the Eastern Front.

Representatives of the seventeen nations forming the United Nations War Crimes Commission (UNWCC) – Australia, Belgium, Canada, China, Czechoslovakia, France, Greece, Holland, India, Luxemburg, New Zealand, Norway, Poland, South Africa, United Kingdom, United States and Yugoslavia – did not meet until October 1943, eleven months after the Allied landing in North Africa and when the subsequent victors' military superiority over the Axis Powers was becoming ever clearer. Stalin, all public pronouncements notwithstanding, was not best pleased at the threat of punishment for German war criminals, his erstwhile companions in arms, and he adroitly ensured that Russia was not represented on the Commission; he demanded representation for each of the sixteen Soviet republics and this the seventeen nations simply could not accept. He was merely informed of the results of the Roosevelt–Churchill conference in Casablanca on 14 and 15 January 1943, which he did not attend despite repeated invitations. At this conference Roosevelt and Churchill together with their Chiefs of Staff and selected high-ranking officers (Eisenhower on Roosevelt's side, for instance) drew up agreed strategic plans for co-ordinated attacks on Germany, Italy and Japan and for the planned invasion in the West; all this was fixed without direct co-operation from Stalin. He was not even a co-signatory of the Casablanca declaration that the war could be ended only by Germany's un-conditional surrender. This uncompromising demand, which undoubtedly cost many lives, was the result of an initiative by Roosevelt who, it must be remembered, was by this time a sick and ageing man with rigid ideas.

Despite the demand for unconditional surrender the men who were later to be the principal German defendants underestimated the results of Casablanca because of the absence of Stalin; after further German reverses on the eastern front, however, they were quickly undeceived. In the Three-Power Declaration by the governments of the USA, Great Britain and the Soviet Union signed by Roosevelt, Churchill and Stalin on 30 October 1943 after the Moscow Conference German officers and political leaders were told unequivocally: 'At the time of the granting of any armistice to any government which may be set up in Germany, those German officers and men and members of the Nazi Party who have been responsible for or have taken a consenting part in atrocities, massacres or executions, will be sent back to the countries in which their abominable deeds were done in order that they may be judged and punished according to the laws of these liberated countries and of the free governments which will be elected therein. Lists will be compiled in all possible detail from all these countries, having regard especially to the invaded parts of the Soviet Union, to Poland and Czechoslovakia, to Yugoslavia and Greece including Crete and other islands, to Norway, Denmark, the Netherlands, Belgium, Luxem-burg, France and Italy.'[23]

Equally there could be no further uncertainty after the Roosevelt–Churchill–Stalin conference of 28 November to 1 December 1943 held at Stalin's wish in Teheran. The official communiqué signed on 1 December by Stalin, Roosevelt and Churchill, in the drafting of which representatives of the respective Chiefs of Staff[24] had participated, stated: 'We express our determination that our nations shall work together in war and in the peace that will follow. As to war – our military staffs have joined in our ... discussions and we have concerted our plans for the destruction of the German forces. We have reached complete agreement on the scope and timing of the operations to be undertaken from the east, west and south. The common understanding which we have here reached guarantees that victory will be ours ... No power on earth can prevent us destroying the German armies by land, their U-boats by sea and their war planes from the air. Our attack will be relentless and increasing.'[25]

Admittedly the communiqué did not repeat the threat of punishment for German war criminals; the Germans learnt, however, what the Allied post-victory ideas for the Reich were. Roosevelt wanted to split Germany up into five states – Prussia, Hanover with north-west Germany, Saxony with the area round Leipzig, Hesse-Darmstadt and Hesse-Kassel with the area south of the Rhine, Bavaria-Baden-Württemberg. The Ruhr with its industry, the Saar, Hamburg and the Kiel Canal were to be placed under United Nations control. Churchill, on the other hand, wanted to separate

Prussia from the Reich and form a Danube Confederation of the South German states. Stalin wanted to advance the Polish western frontier to the Oder and establish strict post-war control over the Germans.

The fact that, in view of these divergent ideas, no agreement was reached in Teheran was of no help to the Germans. German propaganda made much of these differences but they were simply referred to the European Advisory Commission, formed shortly before Teheran.[26]

The Allied threats of punishment for war criminals and dismemberment of Hitler's Reich – in addition to their previous demand for unconditional surrender – proved to be boomerangs. War crimes increased to a horrifying extent. The Allies drew the consequences. On 12 September 1944 in Moscow the Soviet Union, the USA and Great Britain signed an armistice with Rumania which up to that summer, led by Antonescu (against King Michael's wishes), had been allied to Germany; it contained provisions indicating to the German forces and ministers that, on certain conditions, the Allies would be prepared to accept 'timely' surrender. Certain articles in the armistice agreement, of which the Germans must obviously have been aware, sounded very like the corresponding articles on war criminals in the Treaty of Versailles. Article 14, for instance, dealt with 'cooperation between Rumania and the High Command for the purpose of arrest and judicial investigation of persons accused of war crimes'.* From 1944 onwards at latest it must have been clear at least to Göring, Ribbentrop, Kaltenbrunner, Frank and Sauckel, if to no one else, that, as long as Hitler or a successor designated by him was at the head of the Reich, they could no longer count on lenient treatment of the 1918 type once the Reich had been totally defeated, as had long been certain.

Two factors led the Allies to insist 'early on' that after the Second World War they themselves would deal with persons named by them as war criminals: in the first place they remembered the war crimes trials after the First World War before the Reich Court in Leipzig (a German court) and its (in their view) far too lenient sentences; secondly was the fact that the Allies were agreed that after the Second World War there would initially be no German governments, certainly no all-German government. Post-Second World War conditions were to be entirely different from those after the First World War, when, despite their military victory, the Allies had not been sure that they could force the German government to hand over war criminals. The Allies were determined that no German should ever again be in a position to refuse to hand over – or refuse to punish – persons named as war criminals. On 2 February 1920, for instance, fifteen months after the end of the war, the Allies had handed Freiherr von Lersner, Chairman of the German Peace Treaty Commission in Paris, a note with a list of Germans designated as war criminals. The sequel

* In Article 15 the Rumanian government undertook to disband forthwith all 'pro-Hitler organizations ... located on Rumanian territory' and not to permit formation of similar organizations in future.[27]

was spectacular: Lersner simply sent the papers back saying that he refused to forward them to the Reich government.[28] After the January 1943 demand for unconditional surrender it was clear that this time there could be no diplomatic manoeuvres of that nature.

As the Allies moved towards victory, plans were mooted for the punishment not only of a limited number of German war criminals but also of large sections of the German population. Nearly ten million were to provide 'slave labour' in the Soviet Union and France. The Morgenthau Plan, at first rejected but then initialled by Roosevelt and Churchill in Quebec in autumn 1944, produced outrage, consternation and puzzlement not only among Germans. The Plan was presented to the President early in September by Henry Morgenthau Jr, Secretary of the Treasury; it put forward a directive to Eisenhower for the period immediately following an Allied victory; this visualized de-industrialization of Germany, division of the Reich into two autonomous independent states and internationalization of the Ruhr, which was to be totally stripped;* a programme was to be drawn up for the punishment of war criminals and similar treatment meted out to Nazi organizations.[29] The Plan was suitably embellished by Nazi propaganda; in support of its 'hold-on-to-the-end' slogans it even produced the story that Roosevelt was toying with the idea of sterilizing German men and women. The fact that Roosevelt and Churchill had veered away from the Morgenthau Plan in September was not known to potential German defendants, but this was immaterial since the change of heart did not extend to the punishment of war criminals. In an Order of the Day to the German Wehrmacht on 1 January 1945 Hitler himself said: 'Today the overriding significance of the war in which we are engaged is clear to the German people; it is a pitiless struggle for existence or non-existence ... For the aim of the world international Jewish conspiracy which we face is the extermination of our people. When I made a statement to this effect in 1939 some people perhaps thought it exaggerated. In subsequent years – because it was repeated over and over again – it may have seemed like a "propaganda gambit". Today no one can have any further doubt of our enemies' intentions. They are confirmed by the enemy statesmen we face. They are further proved by their methods of warfare and their political preparations for the post-war period. Jewish bolshevism's determination in

---

* In contrast to earlier 'Big Three' plans the Morgenthau Plan envisaged separation of East Prussia, southern Silesia and the Saar up to the Rhine–Moselle border, formation of a South German state to include Bavaria, Württemberg, Baden and certain smaller areas, creation of a North German state consisting of most of former Prussia, Saxony, Thuringia and certain small states. There was to be a customs union between the southern state and Austria (with her 1937 frontiers). Within six months from the cessation of hostilities the Ruhr and the entire Rhineland industrial area, the Kiel Canal and the whole of northern Germany were to be stripped of German industry (as reparations for the Allies) as far as possible; the whole area would then be so impoverished and so closely controlled as to make revival of industry in the foreseeable future impossible. All coal-mining equipment was to be removed and the mines closed.

the East is paralleled by Jewish capitalism's aims in the West ... Mr Churchill declares that the whole of eastern Germany should be ceded to Poland – in other words actually to Soviet Russia – and not only East Prussia and Danzig but also Pomerania and Silesia ... Then his puppet de Gaulle demands that west Germany come under French sovereignty and the remainder of Germany be split up. This corresponds ... precisely to the programme announced by Stalin's tame Jew (Ilya) Ehrenburg, who also proclaims that the German people must be destroyed and exterminated. This is again the same aim as that set out in the future plans proposed by Morgenthau, the American minister and Jew.'[30] In fact Roosevelt and Churchill had hurriedly pigeon-holed the Morgenthau Plan; nevertheless in 1945, after the end of hostilities, certain of its points were still under discussion. For instance the directive (JCS 1067) from the Joint Chiefs of Staff to the Military Governor of the US occupation zone in Germany issued on 14 May 1945 and in force until 17 July 1947 contained instructions bearing at least considerable similarity to certain points in the Morgenthau Plan.

Early in 1945 the Allied noose tightened visibly and their ultimate triumph was obviously imminent. In February 1945 Roosevelt, Stalin and Churchill met in Yalta; in pursuance of their previous agreements they decided to divide Germany into occupation zones, to set up an Allied Control Council, to bring all war criminals to justice and punish them forthwith, to disarm the Reich completely, to 'destroy German militarism and Nazism and to ensure that Germany will never again be able to disturb the peace of the world'. The fact that the decisions taken at the conference, regarded by the Allies as complementary to the agreements reached at Teheran, were to be publicized only after the final defeat of the Reich[31] was hardly calculated to set at rest the minds of those liable to be brought to justice when their period of rule was over.

Hitler already had a shrewd idea what the results of this meeting were liable to be and he reacted at once. In the Nuremberg witness-box on 20 June 1946 Albert Speer recalled: 'Early in February, a few days before the beginning of the Yalta Conference, Hitler sent for his press expert and instructed him, in my presence, to announce in the most uncompromising terms and in the entire German press the intention of Germany never to capitulate. He declared at the same time that he was doing this so that the German people should in no case receive any offer from the enemy. The language used would have to be so strong that enemy statesmen would lose all desire to drive a wedge between himself and the German people. At the same time Hitler once again proclaimed to the German people the slogan "Victory or Destruction". All these events took place at a time when it should have been clear to him and every intelligent member of his circle that the only thing that could happen was destruction.'[32]

At latest by the time the Washington Pact of January 1942 had been concluded Hitler could no longer hope for a separate armistice or peace with the individual enemies of the Reich, such as Heinrich Himmler tried to conclude in secret and behind Hitler's back towards the end of the war. Allied determination to defeat the European Axis Powers totally and in concert and to take no unilateral decisions on the subject[33] was unmistakable; even Hitler realized that it was established policy. In a speech on 30 January 1942 he reacted furiously; he did not go into the detail of the agreements reached at the Roosevelt–Churchill meeting in Washington of 22 December 1941 but used all his sarcasm and invective in referring to the Allied leaders – 'This gasbag and drunkard Churchill,' he asked, 'what has he ever achieved of lasting value, this lying creature, this high-class sluggard? If this war had not happened, then our era and I myself would have been talked of for centuries as having done great things for peace. But if Mister Churchill had not brought about this war, who would have talked of him? However he will now live on as destroyer of an empire which he, not we, shall have destroyed. He is one of the most despicable pseudo-heroic personalities in world history, incapable of creating or achieving anything positive, capable only of destruction. I do not even wish to speak about his accomplice in the White House, for he is only a miserable lunatic.'[34]

At least until 1944 occasional and more than mere tentative efforts were made by Stalin to come to some fresh agreement with Hitler and re-establish to their mutual advantage the power position of 1939–41; despite his already severe losses in Russia, however, Hitler took no stock of them. He did probe Stalin's sincerity and even allowed talks to take place between Molotov and Ribbentrop; but he was not prepared to make concessions. In June 1943, for instance, when Molotov made a secret journey to German-occupied Kirovograd to discuss with the German Foreign Minister possibilities of ending the war, he was ultimately forced to return to Stalin empty-handed. The Soviet demand for re-establishment of Russia's old western frontier was countered by Ribbentrop with a demand for the Dnieper as the future eastern frontier of the Reich; this Stalin could not accept as a subject for discussion.[35] Stalin eventually figured alongside Churchill in Hitler's bad books.

In November 1941, a few weeks before Hitler's declaration of war on the USA on 11 December 1941 followed immediately by the conclusion of the Washington Pact, Hitler was still taking a very different view of Churchill. At that time – talking to Count Ciano, the Italian Foreign Minister and son-in-law of Mussolini, for instance – he still regarded Churchill as an opponent who could only be knocked off his perch by exceptionally large-scale military victories.* The St James's Declaration and the Churchill–Roosevelt agreements of January 1942 at once turned Hitler's publicly proclaimed scorn for Churchill (of whom he nevertheless still

---

* Ciano visited Hitler on 25 October and 28 November 1941 and on one occasion was told that 'Churchill would be at his wits' end' when he, Hitler, had conquered the Persian Gulf.[36]

secretly had a high opinion*) into raging hatred; further causes of irritation were the facts that, as a result of his declaration of war on the USA, the war had turned into the Second World War from the end of 1941 and that, ever since he had taken over as Commander-in-Chief of the Army in December 1941, the war had not been going according to plan primarily owing to the situation on the eastern front.[37] This was also the period at which the 'Final Solution of the Jewish Question', a highly important point at Nuremberg, was set in motion through the Wannsee Conference;[38] the 'Final Solution' had been decided upon by Hitler before the start of Operation 'Barbarossa'† and had been delegated to Reinhard Heydrich by Göring on 31 July 1941.[39]

A week after the Three-Power Declaration in Moscow of 30 October 1943, with its threat of immediate punishment for 'those German officers and men and members of the Nazi Party who have been responsible for ... atrocities, massacres or execution'‡ Hitler made a speech on the occasion of the twentieth anniversary of his 1923 *putsch* in Munich; with complete disregard of the facts, he declared among other things: 'Our opponents believe that they can wear down the German people primarily by bluff and propaganda; meanwhile they ... act as if victory was already theirs ... As they chase from one conference to the next, trying to paper over the various cracks and discover some prospect of concerted action, they act as if they were already the victors. They assemble commissions to "fashion the post-victory world" ... By a flood of paper they attempt to give the German people, and even more the peoples of our allies, the impression not only that they have already won the war and that the future is already decided but also that there are great masses of people who are longing for such a development ... I do not know whether there are among the German people men who are really hoping for something from an Allied victory. They can only be men who think exclusively of themselves, criminals ready to act as executioners of their own people. Anyone else, however, who feels at one with his own folk, knows very well what our enemies' victory would mean. So in Germany there is no section of the people hoping for this victory. At most there are one or two criminals hoping perhaps to shape their own future better. But let there be no doubt or misapprehension about this: we shall deal with these criminals ... The Americans and the British are at present planning to reconstruct the world. I am at present planning to reconstruct Germany. But there will be a

---

* Even before this Hitler had treated Churchill with scant respect. On 4 September 1940, for instance, intoxicated by victory, he had referred to Churchill, Eden, Chamberlain and Duff Cooper in scornful terms, calling them 'gasbags' and 'pompous asses' (German Press Agency, 4 September 1940).

† In January 1941 Heydrich held a conference at Wannsee near Berlin to plan the details of the 'Final Solution' (extermination of Jews). Operation 'Barbarossa' was the German code-name for the invasion of the Soviet Union. [Translator].

‡ See p. 19 above.

difference: whereas reconstruction of the world by the Americans and British will not take place, reconstruction of Germany by National-Socialism will be carried through precisely and according to plan. To this end will be harnessed our mass organizations ... including the whole of German industry and in addition the war criminals. For the first time in their lives they will carry out some useful activity. That is the first thing I have to say on the subject and the second is this: these gentlemen may or may not believe it but the hour of retribution will come ... Our enemies' conviction that by their terror raids they can reduce the ardour of the German will to fight is based on self-deception. The man who has forfeited his possessions can only wish one thing: that the war shall never be lost since only victory in war can restore his possessions to him. So the hundreds of thousands who have been bombed out of house and home are the vanguard of vengeance ... This war may last as long as it likes but Germany will never capitulate. We will never repeat the mistake of 1918 and lay down our arms at a quarter to twelve ...'[40]

Hitler's publicly expressed threat to employ Allied war criminals on some 'useful activity' in the 'reconstruction of Germany' after the war was answered some three weeks later by Stalin in Teheran; although secretly he was still hoping that Hitler might come to terms, his counter-proposal was merciless, revanchist and savage – that following an Allied victory some fifty thousand Germans should simply be shot out of hand. He was convinced that 'the whole fighting strength of Hitler's mightiest armies' depended on 'some fifty thousand officers and technicians'; during a 'Tripartite Dinner Meeting' on 29 November 1943 he accordingly stated flatly, to everyone's consternation, that 'fifty thousand must be shot'. During the preceding discussion Churchill had remarked, basically as a counter to Stalin's proposal, that the British parliament would never tolerate mass shootings; in reply to Stalin's flat-footed demand he said that he 'would rather be taken out into the garden here and now and be shot myself than sully my own and my country's honour by such infamy'.[41] This made no particular impression either on Roosevelt or Stalin however. Roosevelt's macabre comment that 'only forty-nine thousand' should be shot[42] prevented a scene but it did nothing to show whether Stalin was seriously trying out the ground for this sort of solution of the problem. On 6 November 1943, two days before Hitler's threats, humane by comparison, directed at Allied war criminals, Stalin had told the Moscow Soviet that it had been agreed at the conference of 30 October 1943 that the 'fascist criminals' should be severely punished and revenge taken 'for all their monstrous crimes'.[43] Even in London certain prominent and influential circles considered the best solution to be the summary shooting without trial of certain named German war criminals.

The gulf between the two sides was now so deep that from the time of the Three-Power Moscow Declaration of 30 October 1943 none of the 'designated' German war criminals should have been under any illusion;

only an outline indication had been given by the Allies of who they would be but there was no prospect of them being employed on 'reconstruction work' after a German defeat.

Though Hitler was a sick man,[44] prematurely aged and visibly growing increasingly stubborn, he realized that Germany was heading for defeat earlier than his ministers, functionaries and military advisers;* he had a shrewd suspicion of what awaited him after capitulation; he was under no illusions on that score. He knew that every day the war lasted was one more day for him – ever since 1936 he had reckoned that his health would not hold out long.[46] He waved aside the idea of a German capitulation as something unrealistic; he threatened the Allies with the 'hour of retribution' and with those who had been bombed-out as the 'vanguard of vengeance'; primarily for his own sake he compelled the entire German people to 'hold on' at all costs. When it was clear to everyone that the war could no longer be won, he laid the blame on the German people who, he said, had failed in the hour of 'trial'. In the summer of 1944, for instance, he told his immediate entourage, among whom were Albert Speer and Baldur von Schirach, two of the Nuremberg defendants, that the German people had proved 'too weak', had failed to withstand the test of history and so was deservedly doomed, should the war be lost.[47]

---

* On 12 December 1942, for instance, Hitler pointed out to his military advisers that, once Stalingrad had been lost, it could never be recaptured.[45]

After the End of Hostilities

A little over two months after the Yalta Conference Hitler committed suicide. One week later the last government of the German Reich, headed in accordance with Hitler's will by Grand Admiral Dönitz, capitulated. The measures agreed by the European Advisory Commission (the USA, the Soviet Union and Great Britain) in November 1944 and confirmed at Yalta (assumption of supreme authority by the Allies, a control organization and occupation zones) were put into force, France being also included as one of the victor powers. As early as 10 May 1945 Truman, the new US President, had approved a directive, JCS 1067/6 dated 26 April 1945, which resulted among other things in the dissolution and arrest of the Dönitz government on 23 May. On 5 June the Allies assumed supreme governmental authority over defeated Germany. At least in the United States preparation for the war crimes trials had begun shortly after the St James's Declaration. Admittedly at this time the victors had no agreed concrete plans either about the location and duration of the trials or about the number of major war criminals to be indicted; the Western Allies, however, were determined that there should be a trial and not the mass shootings demanded by Stalin in Teheran. Twenty years later Robert M. W. Kempner, who worked in the USA, London, Paris, Frankfurt and Oberursel as a member of the preparatory team under Robert H. Jackson, US Chief Prosecutor, and was later himself Chief Prosecutor in the (US) Wilhelmstrasse Trial, stated that after the end of the war the Americans were initially reckoning on a trial lasting some six months. He wrote: 'The individual Allies had very different ideas as to the number of persons to be accused. In addition to the combined indictment criminal proceedings in individual countries previously occupied [by the Germans] ... had to be considered. Progress from the view once expressed that five thousand criminals should be shot at dawn to ... Robert H. Jackson's assumption in London in 1945 ... that the indictment [before the IMT] should include ... twenty to twenty-five major war criminals had entailed a long process of negotiation.'[1]

This 'long process' – with the law in the background – starting with Churchill's decisive stand in Teheran was primarily the work of Robert H. Jackson, who used all his influence in the USA. As early as December 1943 he had had confirmation from a statement by Lord Simon in the House of Lords that Churchill's protest to Stalin and Roosevelt had not fallen on deaf ears in London but was in fact supported. Lord Simon had said: 'From our point of view ... we must never fail, however deeply we are tried and however fundamentally we are moved by the sufferings of others, to do justice according to justice. There must be no mass execution of great numbers of nameless people merely because there have been mass executions on the other side. We shall never do any good to our own standards, our own reputation and to the ultimate reform of the world if what we do is not reasonably consistent with justice ... Whatever happens do not let us depart from the principle that war criminals shall be dealt with because they are proved to be criminals and not because they belong to a race led by a maniac and a murderer who has brought this frightful evil upon the world.'[2]

In the United States discussion and debate on the question of punishment of German war criminals took place in the White House, in the State Department, in the War Department, in the Department of Justice and in Congress. Diplomatic representatives of France, Great Britain, the Soviet Union and the United States conferred during the San Francisco Conference early in May 1945 and submitted plans to set up an international military court to try major war criminals from the European Axis powers.[3] On 2 May Robert H. Jackson, a Supreme Court Judge, was appointed by the President to represent United States interests; at the same time he was nominated Chief Prosecutor and authorized to negotiate with other countries as United States representative concerning establishment of an international military tribunal to try major war criminals.[4] He selected his staff and agreed on collaboration with the Army Solicitor-General and the Office of Strategic Services. After numerous discussions in occupied Germany, France and Britain, on 6 June 1945, the day after assumption of supreme authority by the Allies in Germany, he handed a provisional report to President Truman; in this he set out the basic legal principles and the plan for the proposed trials but he did not at this time mention Nuremberg as the location.[5] Jackson proposed that the international military court should not deal with Quisling, Laval or Lord Haw-Haw, who ranked as 'traitors' in the victors' eyes, but should concern itself only with major war criminals for whose crimes no particular geographical location in the sense of the Moscow agreements could be determined. The little men, those who had lynched crews of Allied aircraft who had baled out or forced-landed for instance, or those who had served as guards in concentration camps or held some subordinate position in a murder squad, should be dealt with by the existing military legal system. 'We shall accuse a large number of individuals and officials,' he advised, 'who were in authority in the government, in the military establishment including the General Staff, and in financial, industrial and economic life ... who ... are provable to be common criminals ... Our case against the major defendants is concerned with the Nazi master plan, not with individual barbarities and perversions which occurred independently of any central plan.'[6]

A simultaneous proposal made by Jackson, however, showed that he did not mean to confine himself to 'a large number of individuals'; he suggested that the nature of voluntary Nazi organizations should be examined from the viewpoint of the purposes to be achieved by the IMT. It was and still is understandable that reports on the 'Gestapo and activist units of the SS', as Jackson's report puts it, should inevitably influence decisions of this nature taken in 1945. Accordingly Jackson's proposals eventually became guidelines for the purely American follow-up trials at Nuremberg; they decided the fate of those who listened to their sentence or acquittal there under the Stars and Stripes. When the men concerned were already in prison or prisoner-of-war camps he wrote the following general directions: 'If in the main trial an organization is found to be criminal, the second stage will be to identify and try before regular military tribunals members not already personally convicted in the principal case. Findings in the main trial that an organization is criminal in nature will be conclusive in any subsequent proceedings against individual members. The individual member will thereafter be allowed to plead only personal defenses or extenuating circumstances, such as that he joined under duress.'[7]

Twenty days after Jackson had given the President his ideas, fifty-one nations, who had either signed the United Nations Declaration following the Roosevelt–Stalin–Churchill agreements in Yalta or had declared war on the European Axis powers at latest by 1 March 1945, made known their decision on the United Nations Charter at the San Francisco Conference which had been in session since 25 April.[8] On 17 July there began in Potsdam the conference of the so-called Big Three (Truman, Stalin and Churchill), intended to iron out the differences which had arisen between them meanwhile. While those accused as major war criminals were already being interrogated and Hermann Göring in Bad Mondorf was thinking that he would soon be able to appear in court as the radiant Reich Marshal and accuse the victors of their own war crimes, the latter were arguing in Potsdam about Germany, which for Stalin was no more than a geographical expression. The Soviet record of the session of 18 July 1945 is sufficiently eloquent to make further comment unnecessary:

Churchill: I want to raise only one question. I note that the word 'Germany' is being used here. What is now the meaning of 'Germany'? Is it to be understood in the same sense as before the war?[9]
Truman: How is this question understood by the Soviet delegation?
Stalin: Germany is what she has become after the war. There is no other Germany. That is how I understand the question.[10]
Truman: Is it possible to speak of Germany as she had been before the war, in 1937?
Stalin: As she is in 1945.[11]
Truman: She lost everything in 1945; actually Germany no longer exists.
Stalin: Germany is, as we say, a geographical concept. Let's take it this

way for the time being. We cannot abstract ourselves from the results of the war.

Truman: Yes, but there must be some definition of the concept 'Germany'. I believe the Germany of 1886 or of 1937 is not the same thing as Germany today, in 1945.

Stalin: She has changed as a result of the war and that is how we take her.

Truman: I quite agree with this but some definition of the concept of 'Germany' must be given.

Stalin: For example, is there any idea of establishing a German administration in the Sudeten part of Czechoslovakia? That is an area from which the Germans had expelled the Czechs.

Truman: Perhaps we shall speak of Germany as she had been before the war, in 1937?

Stalin: That could be taken formally but actually that is not so. If a German administration should put in an appearance at Königsberg, we shall expel it; we shall most certainly expel it.

Truman: It was agreed at the Crimea conference that territorial questions should be settled at a peace conference. How are we then to define the concept of 'Germany'?

Stalin: Let us define the western borders of Poland and we shall then be clearer on the question of Germany. I find it very hard to say what Germany is just now. It is a country without a government, without any definite borders, because the borders are not formalized by our troops. Germany has no troops including frontier troops; she is broken up into occupation zones. Take this and define what Germany is. It is a broken country.

Truman: Perhaps we could take Germany's 1937 borders as the starting point.*

Stalin: We could start anywhere. We have to start somewhere. In that context we could take 1937 too.

Truman: That was the Germany after the Versailles Treaty.

Stalin: Yes, we could take the Germany of 1937 but only as a point of departure. It is merely a working hypothesis for the convenience of our work.

Churchill: Only as a starting point. That does not mean that we shall confine ourselves to this.

Truman: We agree to take the Germany of 1937 as a starting point. We have not finished with the second question but we shall agree on that.[12]

The Allies were unanimous, however, on punishment of war criminals and their determination to make the German people pay for crimes committed. The communiqué stated:

'Allied armies are in occupation of the whole of Germany and the

---

* In early June 1945 the German frontiers as at 31 December 1937 had been taken as the basis for the division of the Reich into four occupation zones.

German people have begun to atone for the terrible crimes committed under the leadership of those whom, in the hour of their success, they openly approved and blindly obeyed.

'Agreement has been reached at this conference on the political and economic principles of a coordinated Allied policy towards defeated Germany during the period of Allied control.

'The purpose of this agreement is to carry out the Crimea declaration on Germany. German militarism and Nazism will be extirpated and the Allies will take in agreement together, now and in the future, the other measures necessary to assure that Germany never again will threaten her neighbours or the peace of the world.'[13]

Later (in para. V I I), the communiqué dealt with the punishment of major war criminals:

'The Three Governments have taken note of the discussions which have been proceeding in recent weeks in London between British, United States, Soviet and French representatives with a view to reaching agreement on the methods of trial of those major war criminals whose crimes under the Moscow Declaration of October 1943 have no particular geographical localization. The Three Governments reaffirm their intention to bring those criminals to swift and sure justice ... They hope that the negotiations in London will result in speedy agreement being reached for this purpose and they regard it as a matter of great importance that the trial of those major war criminals should begin at the earliest possible date. The first list of defendants will be published before 1 September.'[14]

In dealing with German problems the Germans could expect neither leniency nor conciliation either from the Americans and British or from the Soviets. The 'Big Three' had come to Berlin to eradicate once and for all the seat and source of aggression. The 'Carthaginian Peace' proposed by the victors for defeated Germany was still part of the Western Allies' programme, though differences with the Russians were increasing and fears were being voiced that the Soviets might possibly be even worse than the 'Nazis'. The Potsdam decisions were also influenced by the facts that the Western Allies still regarded defeated Germany as more dangerous than the Soviet Union and Stalin once more affected to believe that the Germans might soon be partners of the West. Not even Churchill raised objection to the practice already enforced by Stalin in Russia and recommended by him to the others at the conference of using German prisoners of war as forced labour, contrary to international law though it was.[15]

Apart from Stalin, however, leading statesmen and politicians were unwilling at this stage actually to name the Germans to be tried by the IMT as major war criminals. The question whether names should be given ahead of time at all was discussed in the Cecilienhof, Potsdam, on 1 August 1945 by Truman, Stalin, Attlee (Churchill's successor), their Foreign Ministers and senior Foreign Office officials. On this subject the Soviet record of the Twelfth Plenary Session of the Potsdam Conference reads as follows:

Byrnes: The next question is that of war criminals. The only question remaining open here is whether the names of some of the major German war criminals should be mentioned. The representatives of the United States and Britain, at today's meeting of the Foreign Ministers, deemed it right not to mention these names but to leave that to the prosecutor. They also agreed that the British text should be adopted. The Soviet representatives declared that they agreed with the British draft, provided some names are added.

Stalin: I think we need names. This must be done for public opinion. The people must know this. Are we to take action against any German industrialists? I think we are. We name Krupp. If Krupp will not do, let's name others.

Truman: I don't like any of them (*laughter*). I think that if we mention some names and leave out others, people may think that we have no intention of putting these others on trial.

Stalin: But these names are given here as examples. It is surprising, for instance, why Hess is still in Britain all provided for and is not being put on trial. These names must be given; this will be important for public opinion, for the peoples.

Bevin: Don't worry about Hess.[16]

Stalin: It's not a question of what I think but of public opinion and the opinion of the peoples of all the countries which had been occupied by the Germans.

Bevin: If you have any doubts about Hess, I can promise you that he will be put on trial.

Stalin: I am not asking for any undertakings on the part of Mr Bevin; his statement is enough to leave me in no doubt that this will be done. But it is not a question of me but of the peoples, of public opinion.

Truman: You are aware that we have appointed Justice Jackson as our representative on the London Commission. He is an outstanding judge and a very experienced jurist. He has a good knowledge of legal procedure. Jackson is opposed to any names of war criminals being mentioned and says that this will hamper their work. He assures us that the trial will be ready within thirty days and that there should be no doubt concerning our view of these men.

Stalin: Perhaps we could name fewer persons, say three.

Bevin: Our jurists take the same view as the Americans.

Stalin: And ours take the opposite view. But perhaps we shall agree that the first list of the German war criminals to be brought to trial should be published not later than in one month.[17]

Astoundingly enough the name Adolf Hitler appeared only on the fringe of the discussions concerning names of major German war criminals, although those at the conference were still doubtful whether he was dead. When Attlee, the new British Prime Minister, eventually expressed a desire to have him named, Stalin was evasive. 'We haven't got him,'[18] he said and then inquired suspiciously and reproachfully* why Rudolf Hess was being 'well cared for' in England and 'not brought to account'. Hitler was named as a major war criminal only when it had already been established that he was no longer alive.† Truman had inherited from Roosevelt a fixed policy based solely on American interests; it had not prevented him making overtures to Hitler when Britain had her back to the wall. Stalin had made common cause with Hitler in Poland in 1939, had later accused him of the Soviet crime of Katyn‡ and even as late as 1944 was still hoping for a resumption of Russo–German relations; he also had his reasons for wishing to exclude Hitler from the initial list of war criminals. It was therefore no accident that at Potsdam it was Attlee, the British First World War Major, who wished to see Hitler designated as a war criminal and not Truman or Stalin.

On 8 August, one week after the issue of the Potsdam Conference communiqué, the London Conference had already drafted the Charter of the International Military Tribunal to try German war criminals.

From June 1945 Germany was divided into four occupation zones, not (yet) into independent states as had been the earlier intention;[21] the four most senior military commanders§ formed the Control Council. To provide a uniform legal basis in all four zones the Control Council, on 20 December 1945, issued Law No. 10. This repeated once more the acts already described as criminal in the London Charter of 8 August 1945 under the following headings: Crimes against Peace, War Crimes, Crimes against Humanity and membership of a 'criminal group or organization'; the law set out punishments envisaged on conviction (death, imprisonment for life

* Stalin was primarily suspicious of the German troops still in Norway who, he maintained (in August 1945), had not yet been disarmed by the British.[19] He seriously regarded them as a pool of enemy manpower for the war to be waged by the Western Allies and the Germans against the Soviet Union which at the time was the subject of intensive rumour propaganda and was forecast as imminent.

† Twenty-three years later Lew Besymenski, a Soviet journalist, gained considerable publicity with his book *The Death of Adolf Hitler* (German translation, Hamburg, 1968). Contrary to Stalin's statement in Potsdam he maintained that in early May 1945 Soviet soldiers had found a body in a shell-hole near the Führer's bunker and that an expert Red Army Commission had identified it as that of Adolf Hitler. Besymenski states (p. 86) that the Soviets delayed publication of the results of the autopsy because they were afraid 'that someone might pass himself off as "the Führer saved by a miracle"'; this is sheer politically motivated nonsense and the story is self-contradictory. Anatomical details of the Soviet corpse 'supposedly' that of Hitler differed so noticeably from those of Hitler himself that the body cannot have been that of Adolf Hitler.[20]

‡ Shortly before his death Roosevelt forbade any accusation against Stalin on this score, although he knew better.

§ Eisenhower for the USA, Zhukov for the Soviet Union, Montgomery for Great Britain and De Lattre de Tassigny for France.

or a defined period with or without hard labour, fines, confiscation of property, return of illegally acquired property, complete or partial deprivation of civil rights); it stated that neither an official position nor an order from his government or a superior were valid as a defence.[22]

This Control Council Law, together with the Moscow Declaration of 30 October 1943 and the London Charter of 8 August 1945, were the main foundations for the IMT's jurisdiction. Hopes harboured by some defendants that, as the end of hostilities receded, increasing 'forbearance' would be shown by the law and that the less incriminated would escape scot free proved to be self-deception and wishful thinking. Wounds could not be healed in so short a time. The Control Council Law stated explicitly: 'Execution of the death sentence may be postponed should the Zone Commander have reason to suppose that the condemned man may be required as witness at a trial inside or outside his zone but postponement will not be for more than one month from the time the sentence has acquired the force of law.'

The Agreement concluded on 8 August 1945 between 'the Government of the United States of America, the Provisional Government of the French Republic, the Government of the United Kingdom of Great Britain and Northern Ireland and the Government of the Union of Soviet Socialist Republics'[23] covered the much-quoted Charter of the International Military Tribunal. In broad terms the Moscow Declaration of two years before had laid down who should be brought to justice and punished if convicted; they were to be major war criminals named by the victor powers 'whose offenses have no particular geographical location'.[24]

The main document on which the trial was based, however, was the London Charter. This was criticized by defence counsel in Nuremberg as being in violation and contempt of the traditional legal principle of division of powers; it also had one glaring defect: the Four-Power Agreement,[25] of which the Charter was the major component part, was signed, as if they were legislators, by Robert H. Jackson, Robert Falco, French alternate judge in Nuremberg and I. Nikitchenko, the Russian member of the IMT. Also regarded as misuse of their power by the victors were the facts that Sir David Maxwell-Fyfe, later British Deputy Chief Prosecutor in Nuremberg, and Francis Biddle, US Member of the IMT, had participated in working out the punishment code; Biddle, moreover, had been US Minister of Justice at the time of the Yalta Conference[26] and had been co-author of a memorandum which included the basic ideas of the London Charter. Ever since the French Revolution it had been regarded as a 'sacred' principle that, if legislators, prosecutors and judges were the same people, this constituted a gross violation of guarantees for the rights of the individual. In the case of Nuremberg this principle was 'set aside'.[27]

In 1945, moreover, the fact that the Charter for this international military court of justice was drawn up some three months after the capitulation and the arrest of those Germans accused as major war criminals contributed to the impression that this was a form for retribution rather than a court of justice. The Charter of the IMT proclaimed that it had been established 'for the just and prompt trial and punishment of the major war criminals of the European Axis';[28] the Tribunal was empowered

to try ... all persons who, acting in the interests of the European Axis countries, whether as individuals or members of organizations, committed any of the following crimes ...
CRIMES AGAINST PEACE ... planning, preparation, initiation or waging of a war of aggression or a war in violation of international treaties, agreements or assurances, or participation in a Common Plan or Conspiracy for the accomplishment of any of the foregoing;
WAR CRIMES ... violations of the laws or customs of war. Such violations shall include, but shall not be limited to, murder, ill-treatment or deportation to slave labor or for any other purpose of civilian population of or in occupied territory, murder or ill-treatment of prisoners of war or persons on the seas, killing of hostages, plunder of public or private property, wanton destruction of cities, towns or villages or devastation not justified by military necessity;
CRIMES AGAINST HUMANITY ... murder, extermination, enslavement, deportation and other inhumane acts committed against any civilian population before or during the war,[29] or persecutions on political, racial or religious grounds in execution of or in connection with any crime within the jurisdiction of the Tribunal, whether or not in violation of the domestic law of the country where perpetrated.

Article 6 then concludes: 'Leaders, organizers, instigators and accomplices participating in the formulation or execution of a Common Plan or Conspiracy to commit any of the foregoing crimes are responsible for all acts performed by any persons in execution of such a plan.'[30]

Up to mid-August the accused were held in easy-going detention in a high-class hotel in Bad Mondorf, Luxemburg; at the time they still thought that the trial would be a relatively harmless affair; only after transfer to prison in the Nuremberg Palace of Justice did they learn that, according to the provisions of the Charter, their former official positions would not save them from punishment.[31] Article 8 of the Charter read: 'The fact that the defendant acted pursuant to order of his government or of a superior shall not free him from responsibility, but may be considered in mitigation of punishment if the Tribunal determine that justice so requires'[32] – which it never once did. Finally the Charter laid down that 'the final designation of major war criminals to be tried' should be decided by a committee formed of the Chief Prosecutors of each of the signatory states;[33] the committee was also to decide on the groups and organizations to be regarded as unquestionably criminal.*

* Article 10 states: 'In cases where a group or organization is declared criminal ... the criminal nature of the group or organization is considered proved and shall not be questioned' (IMT Vol. I, p. 12).

The 'Indictment' giving the definitive list of designated defendants was now drawn up. All were called upon to answer both individually and also – primarily at Jackson's instigation – as members of criminal groups or organizations which were specified in detail in an Appendix to the Indictment.[34]

The General Secretary of the IMT made the following announcement: 'The International Military Tribunal for the trial of the major war criminals having been duly constituted and an indictment having been lodged by the Chief Prosecutors, in order to make fair provision for notice to defendants:

IT IS ORDERED that each individual defendant in custody shall receive, not less than thirty days before trial, a copy, translated into a language which he understands, of the documents set out in paragraph (a) of Rule 2 of the rules of the Tribunal in accordance with the terms of that paragraph.

There followed a 'Form of Notice to Individual Defendants':

To the Defendants above named :
You and each of you is hereby notified that an indictment has been filed against you in the International Military Tribunal. A copy of this indictment and of the Charter constituting the International Military Tribunal are attached hereto. Your trial will take place at the Palace of Justice, Nuremberg, Germany, not less than thirty days from the service of the indictment upon you. The exact date will be made known to you later. Your attention is specifically directed to your right to counsel under Article 23 and Article 16 of the Charter and Rule 2 (d) of the Tribunal, a copy of which and a list of counsel are attached hereto for your information.

An officer has been designated by the Tribunal to deliver this Notice and accompanying documents to you and to confer with you in respect to the employment and designation of counsel.[35]

A public announcement, millions of copies of which were distributed, was then issued setting out all the above in detail. It ran as follows:

Form of Notice

INTERNATIONAL MILTARY TRIBUNAL

THE UNITED STATES OF AMERICA, THE FRENCH REPUBLIC, THE UNITED KINGDOM OF GREAT BRITAIN AND NORTHERN IRELAND and THE UNION OF SOVIET SOCIALIST REPUBLICS

against

HERMANN WILHELM GÖRING, RUDOLF HESS, JOACHIM VON RIBBENTROP, ROBERT LEY, WILHELM KEITEL, ERNST KALTEN-BRUNNER, ALFRED ROSENBERG, HANS FRANK, WILHELM FRICK, JULIUS STREICHER, WALTER FUNK, HJALMAR SCHACHT, GUSTAV KRUPP VON BOHLEN UND HALBACH, KARL DÖNITZ, ERICH RAEDER,

BALDUR VON SCHIRACH, FRITZ SAUCKEL, ALFRED JODL, MARTIN
BORMANN, FRANZ VON PAPEN, ARTHUR SEYSS-INQUART, ALBERT
SPEER, CONSTANTIN VON NEURATH and HANS FRITZSCHE,
Individually and as Members of Any of the Following Groups or Organ-
izations to Which They Respectively Belong, Namely: DIE REICHS-
REGIERUNG (REICH CABINET); DAS KORPS DER POLITISCHEN LEITER
DER NATIONALSOZIALISTISCHEN DEUTSCHEN ARBEITERPARTEI
(LEADERSHIP CORPS OF THE NAZI PARTY); DIE SCHUTZSTAFFELN
DER NATIONALSOZIALISTISCHEN DEUTSCHEN ARBEITERPARTEI
(commonly known as the 'SS') and including DER SICHERHEITSDIENST
(commonly known as the 'SD'); DIE GEHEIME STAATSPOLIZEI
(SECRET STATE POLICE, commonly known as the 'GESTAPO'); DIE
STURMABTEILUNGEN DER NSDAP (commonly known as the 'SA'); and
the GENERAL STAFF and HIGH COMMAND of the GERMAN ARMED
FORCES,

Defendants

Notice is hereby given to all members of the following groups and
organizations:

1. Die Reichsregierung, consisting of persons who were:
   (a) Members of the ordinary cabinet after 30 January 1933. The term
   'ordinary cabinet' as used herein means the Reich Ministers, i.e.
   heads of department of the central government; Reich Ministers
   without portfolio; State Ministers acting as Reich Ministers; and
   other officials entitled to take part in meetings of this cabinet.
   (b) Members of Der Ministerrat für die Reichsverteidigung.*
   (c) Members of Der Geheime Kabinettsrat.*
2. Das Korps der Politischen Leiter der Nationalsozialistischen Deutschen
   Arbeiterpartei, consisting of persons who were at any time, according to
   Nazi terminology, Politische Leiter of any grade or rank.
3. Die Schutzstaffeln der Nationalsozialistischen Deutschen Arbeiterpartei
   (commonly known as the SS) and consisting of the entire corps of
   the SS and all offices, departments, services, agencies, branches, formations, organizations and groups of which it was at any time comprised
   or which were at any time integrated in it, including, but not limited to, the
   Allgemeine SS, the Waffen SS, the SS Totenkopf Verbände, SS
   Polizei Regimenter and the Sicherheitsdienst des Reichsführers-SS
   (commonly known as the SD)†
4. Die Geheime Staatspolizei (commonly known as the Gestapo) consisting of the headquarters, departments, offices, branches and all the forces
   and personnel of the Geheime Staatspolizei of Prussia and equivalent
   secret or political police forces of the Reich and the components thereof.

---

* Ministerrat für Reichsverteidigung = Ministerial Council for National Defence.
Geheime Kabinettsrat = Secret Cabinet Council.
  † Allgemeine SS = General SS. Waffen SS = fully militarized SS units. SS Totenkopf
Verbände = Death's Head Formations, originally providing concentration camp guards but
later fully militarized. SS Polizei Regimenter = SS Police Regiments.

5. Die Sturmabteilungen der Nationalsozialistischen Deutschen Arbeiterpartei (commonly known as the SA).
6. The General Staff and High Command of the German Armed Forces,
consisting of those individuals who between February 1938 and May
1945 were the highest commanders of the Wehrmacht, the Army, the
Navy and the Air Forces. The individuals comprising this group are
the persons who held the following appointments:
Oberbefehlshaber der Kriegsmarine (Commander-in-Chief of the Navy)
Chef (and, formerly, Chef des Stabes) der Seekriegsleitung (Chief of
Naval War Staff)
Oberbefehlshaber des Heeres (Commander-in-Chief of the Army)
Chef des Generalstabes der Luftwaffe (Chief of the General Staff of
the Air Force)
Oberbefehlshaber der Luftwaffe (Commander-in-Chief of the Air Force)
Chef des Oberkommandos der Wehrmacht (Chief of the High Com-
mand of the Armed Forces)
Chef des Führungsstabes des Oberkommandos der Wehrmacht (Chief of
the Operations Staff of the High Command of the Armed Forces)
Commanders-in-Chief in the field, with the status of Oberbefehlshaber
of the Wehrmacht, Navy, Army, Air Force.

THAT such groups and organizations are accused by the Chief Prosecutors for the prosecution of major war criminals of being criminal organizations and this Tribunal has been asked by the Chief Prosecutors to
declare said groups and organizations criminal.

THAT if any of such groups and organizations are found by this
tribunal to have been criminal in character members will be subject to
trial and punishment on account of their membership in accordance with
the provisions of the Charter of this Tribunal and upon any such trial the
criminal character of the group or organization shall be considered proved
and shall not be questioned.

THAT the issue of the criminal character of these groups and organizations will be tried commencing the 20th day of November 1945 at the
Palace of Justice, Nuremberg, Germany.

THAT any person who acknowledges membership in any of the said
groups or organizations may be entitled to apply to the Tribunal for leave
to be heard by the Tribunal upon the question of the criminal character of
the group or organization. Such application shall be made without delay, in
writing, and addressed to the General Secretary, International Military
Tribunal, Nuremberg, Germany.

THAT in the case of members of any of the said groups or organizations
who
(i) may be in the custody of the prosecuting powers, such applications shall
be handed to the Commanding Officer of the place where the said members are detained;
(ii) may not be in custody, such applications shall be handed to the nearest
military unit.

THAT the Tribunal has power to allow or reject any such application.

If the application is allowed, the Tribunal will direct in what manner the applicant shall be represented and heard.

THAT nothing contained in this notice shall be construed to confer immunity of any kind upon such applicants.

For the International Military Tribunal
Harold B. Willey
General Secretary.[36]

The IMT was under specific obligation to conduct 'an expeditious hearing';[37] under Article 13 of its Charter it was to 'draw up rules for its procedure';[38] its judgements were to be 'final and not subject to review'.[39] In all these matters the Tribunal followed the provisions of the Charter in so far as they accorded with the ideas and expectations of the prosecution.[40]

With the exception of Martin Bormann the persons concerned had already been under arrest for months.

Part Two
The Trial

On the Road to Nuremberg

Western Allied search parties hunting for war criminals swarmed through the countryside between Hamburg and Flensburg where Dönitz, Hitler's official legatee, had installed his government, and also between Munich and Berchtesgaden, where the victors suspected the majority of 'top Nazis' to be. A nation-wide search was made for Hans Frank, Robert Ley, Alfred Rosenberg, Julius Streicher, Joachim von Ribbentrop and other high-ranking Nazi leaders who were to be brought to trial as major war criminals. The hunt also included some one million other Germans accused of having committed war crimes. All sorts of people were herded into camps and incarcerated – anyone who wore a uniform, a smart livery or other official military-looking garb, representatives of professions or 'jobs' the title of which ended with 'Führer'. In 1945, therefore, as well as officers of all grades, the camps and prisons held lift attendants, crane drivers, railway guards, postmen and porters simply because they wore a uniform and were some sort of 'Führer'.

Hermann Göring, major war criminal No. 1, had already been arrested on orders from Hitler and, at Martin Bormann's instigation, was being treated as a traitor under sentence of death. On 12 March 1946 Colonel Bernd von Brauchitsch, senior military aide to the C.-in-C. of the Luftwaffe (together with Major Klaas), who had worked with Göring and had normally been with him, described his arrest from the Nuremberg witness-box. The relevant extract from the record reads:

Mr Justice Jackson: You were with him [Göring] on the 20th day of April 1945, when he sent the telegram proposing to take over the government of Germany himself and was arrested and condemned to death?
Von Brauchitsch: Yes, I was present at that time.
Mr Justice Jackson: And the SS seized you and the Reich Marshal and several others and searched your houses, seized all your papers and took you prisoner, did they not?
Von Brauchitsch: It is correct that on 23 April at 1900 hours we were surrounded. The Reich Marshal was led to his room and from that moment on he was kept closely guarded; later we were separated and put into solitary confinement. Finally we were separated from him altogether by SS troops stationed at the Berghof.
Mr Justice Jackson: And this occurred at Berchtesgaden?

Von Brauchitsch: It happened at Berchtesgaden.

Mr Justice Jackson: I think you have told us that you were all supposed to be shot by the SS at the time of the surrender and were supposed to approve it by your own signature. Is that correct?

Von Brauchitsch: No, that is not quite correct. I know that an order existed that the Reich Marshal with his family and his entourage should be shot in Berlin at the time of the capitulation.* The second thing you mentioned refers to something else, namely that we were to be compelled to report voluntarily to the SS. I must say, in order to be just, that this SS leader would far rather not have had us there at that time so as not to have to carry out this order. At that time we were already separated from the Commander-in-Chief.'[1]

In fact von Brauchitsch and Major Klaas were not 'separated', as von Brauchitsch puts it, from their Commander-in-Chief until one month after despatch of the Göring telegram to Hitler referred to above. The sequence of events was as follows: In the last ten days of April 1945 Göring, in the security of Berchtesgaden on the Obersalzberg, formed the opinion that Hitler in Berlin no longer had freedom of action and so he, Göring, should take over the leadership. He sent a telegram to Hitler setting out his supposition and conclusions. Martin Bormann read it in a sense in-criminating to Göring and vainly tried to persuade Hitler that Göring had carried out a *coup d'état* against him. With the arrival of Göring's telegram to Ribbentrop, however, Hitler, who was depressed and at times completely apathetic, lost his temper. Göring's phraseology seemed to lend support to Bormann's story of an intrigue; the telegram said: 'I have asked the Führer to provide me with instructions by 10 p.m. 23 April. If by this time it is apparent that the Führer has been deprived of his freedom of action to conduct the affairs of the Reich, his decree of 29 June 1941 becomes effec-tive, according to which I am heir to all his offices as his deputy. If by 12 midnight 23 April 1945 you receive no other word either from the Führer directly or from me, you are to come to me at once by air.'[2]

Bormann won the day. Hitler accused Göring of disloyalty and betrayal of National-Socialism; initially, however, he approved a reply telegram drafted by Bormann assuring Göring that he would not be punished pro-vided he resigned from all his offices for health reasons. When Göring received Hitler's telegram – 'I myself will decide time at which decree of 29 June comes into force. My freedom of action is unrestricted. I forbid any move by you in the direction indicated' – he temporarily abandoned his preparations to assume power, but this did him little good. Following an instruction from Bormann two SS officers, Frank and Bredow, arrested Göring, his family, his staff and his aides in Berchtesgaden; his house was surrounded and kept under guard by SS sentries. After an accurate RAF raid on Hitler's 'Berghof' and Göring's house in Berchtesgaden he asked

* This should undoubtedly read 'at the time of the capitulation in Berlin'.

his gaolers, who were meanwhile having second thoughts, to send a telegram to Hitler to the effect that he wished to be shot at once if the Führer thought him disloyal but asking that his wife and daughter and his immediate entourage should 'eventually' be set free.

Despite Bormann's instruction that Göring was to be executed should Berlin fall, Frank, the SS officer, was hesitant. If Berlin capitulated and Hitler and Bormann were dead, Göring's death could do no good and might only do harm, for Göring was regarded by many people as one of the few personalities who might possibly be able to negotiate with the Allies. The SS accordingly agreed to Göring's proposal that they should leave Berchtesgaden, which was partially destroyed and dangerous, and move to Mauterndorf. The cavalcade arrived there thirty-six hours later; on the way the German radio announced: 'Reich Marshal Hermann Göring is suffering from a heart disease which is now entering an acute stage. He has therefore asked to be relieved of command of the Luftwaffe and all duties connected therewith because at this moment the full harnessing of all strength is needed. The Führer has granted his request. The Führer has appointed Colonel-General Ritter von Greim to be the new commander of the Luftwaffe, promoting him at the same time to the rank of Field Marshal.'[3]

Though now relieved of all his offices and titles Göring was nevertheless in better form during these final days than he had been for some time – though his pills no doubt had something to do with it. On 1 May 1945 he heard of Hitler's suicide over the radio and this brought to an end his first 'imprisonment'. On 6 May he wrote to Dönitz in Flensburg proposing that he should meet Eisenhower, talk to him 'Marshal to Marshal' and so negotiate an honourable peace for Germany. In view of the situation Dönitz regarded this as illusory and unrealistic and initially did not even reply.[4]

Göring and his entourage meanwhile stayed at Schloss Fischhorn in Bruck bei Zell waiting for the Americans, to whom he had despatched Colonel von Brauchitsch and another officer with a white flag to hand over two letters. One was destined for General Eisenhower and contained a request to be received by him; the other was addressed to the local US commander, asking to be protected against the Gestapo and SS. An American officer, Lieutenant Jerome N. Shapiro, was detailed to arrest him, but before he could reach the castle, Göring, impatient and once more full of energy, was again on the road, cheerfully and sometimes enthusiastically hailed by German soldiers during the frequent traffic jams. When he finally met Shapiro (who saluted him) this was the final end of freedom for Göring.

He was given a friendly cordial greeting by the US General Robert J. Stack, who shook hands with him, but the American knew that it was the beginning of the end – Göring was a prisoner of war and not, as he imagined, the German Reich's plenipotentiary for armistice negotiations. On the next day, however, he was given a champagne party in the headquarters of General Patch's US Seventh Army in Kitzbühel surrounded by reporters and photographers; this could only suggest to a man as dependent on drugs as he was that his future was something very different from that prescribed for him by various Allied agreements ever since 1941. Eisenhower's order that on 'apprehension' Göring was to be treated as an ordinary prisoner of war was not the result solely of his vexation over reports of the 'party' at headquarters. Next day the vain and ostentatious Reich Marshal was taken to Seventh Army's Interrogation Center in Augsburg, thought by some high-ranking US officers to be too lavishly equipped; there he was stripped not only of his decorations, the Pour le Mérite* and the Grand Cross of the Iron Cross with Swords and Diamonds, but also of his gold Field Marshal's baton, his gold shoulder tabs and even his diamond ring.

Even Göring could now have no doubts about his situation. The Americans placed him in a working-class block in the suburbs of Augsburg, where he had a primitive living room, an adequate bedroom and an extremely small kitchen. He regarded the fact that there was neither lavatory nor bath as a deliberately planned humiliation, which was undoubtedly the American intention. Preliminary interrogations now began. Initially the Americans were specially interested in Göring's art collection, but the interrogations taught them to respect the intelligence, quick wit and cunning of the man whom they had imagined resembled a Shakespearian court jester; as far as war criminal No. 1 was concerned he now had more than a suspicion that the days of pompous autocratic ways were over. This being so he advised the Americans to secure as quickly as they could his art treasures, paintings, Gobelin tapestries and furniture; he signed a statement undertaking to assist in the recovery and return of the *objets d'art* which he had 'acquired and bought' out of the collection confiscated from the Jeu de Paume museum. Apart from articles seized by the Russians in 1945 all the works of art were found and returned;[5] Göring was invited to another champagne party by the Americans. On 21 May 1945, however, they told him that he would have to leave his working-class quarter in Augsburg and give up one of his two military aides, von Brauchitsch and Klaas. Göring decided to leave them both behind. His new temporary 'domicile' was Bad Mondorf in Luxemburg, where he finally renewed acquaintance with some of the surviving dignitaries of the late Great German Reich.

On 6 May 1945, 36 US Infantry Division had taken over two thousand prisoners whom they held in a hutted camp at Berchtesgaden. Many were without identity papers; others gave false information. The best known among them did no such thing, for the Americans knew who he was – Hans Frank, former Governor-General of Poland, *Reichsleiter* of the NSDAP and President of the Academy for German Law. American GIs had arrested

* The German equivalent of the Victoria Cross or Congressional Medal of Honor.

him on 4 May in 'Haus Bergfried', Neuhaus am Schliersee, where he had established his 'Branch of the Polish Government-General'; thence he had been taken to the municipal prison in Miesbach, where two coloured US GIs gave him a sadistic beating-up before herding him on to a lorry for transport to the camp. Under a tarpaulin thrown over him to hide the more obvious signs of ill-treatment he tried to cut an artery in his left arm. A US Army medical officer saved his life and he then showed the Americans the *objets d'art* which he had brought with him from Cracow, Poland, to his last temporary headquarters in Bavaria.* When arrested in 'Haus Berg-fried' on 4 May he had already handed over most of his official diary, running to 11,367 pages of typing. The Americans had hoped that this 'find' would enable them to hand over to their authorities not only Hans Frank himself but also valuable evidence of his participation in crime, but they were doomed to disappointment. The prosecution in Nuremberg studied the diaries, but the information they contained proved useless. Frank's staff had written up in laborious detail accounts of his speeches, travels, receptions, conferences and special instructions from 1939 to 1945, but there was nothing against Frank which the Military Tribunal could lay hold of. The diaries were no more than the would-be statesman's official record 'written in advance' as the basis for historic memoirs which he imagined himself writing later. On conclusion of the IMT they were handed over to the Polish government who stored them in the 'Central Archives for Research into Hitler Crimes'.[6]

Dr Robert Ley, formerly Reich Organizer of the German Labour Front and initiator of the 'Werwolf' partisan organization at the end of the war, was found by men of 101 US Airborne Division in a mountain hut in the Bavarian Alps south of Berchtesgaden on 16 May 1945. He was dressed in a coarse grey woollen cape, under which he wore blue pyjamas, with a green Tyrolese hat and climbing boots. Shivering with fever and shaking with terror he followed the soldiers to their divisional headquarters near Berchtesgaden. His attempt to escape arrest by passing himself off as 'Dr Ernst Distelmeyer' was a dismal failure. Xaver Schwarz, the former Reich Treasurer of the Nazi Party, had no hesitation in identifying him and Franz Schwarz, the son, confirmed to the Americans that his father had spoken the truth. Ley then hit upon the grotesque idea of offering himself to the Americans as an experienced organizer; he wrote a rambling memorandum recommending that they make use of his capabilities as a brilliant leader of the working-class masses to solve social problems. When the Americans refused his offer, which Ley in his simplicity found in-comprehensible, he spent his time wondering what they really thought of him.[7]

* Michael Frank, Hans Frank's son, gave the author details of his father's arrest both verbally and in writing on 26 September 1976; he considers it out of the question that Hans Frank should have stolen any art treasures and shown them to the Americans.

Even in his period of 'stardom' under Adolf Hitler, Ley had cut a poor figure and as a prisoner he lost all dignity. Göring was not alone in his relief at Ley's suicide before the trial opened.

Alfred Rosenberg, Reich Minister for the Occupied Eastern Territories from 1941, was arrested by British soldiers looking for Heinrich Himmler, not for him, on 19 May 1945 in the Flensburg-Mürwik hospital located in the former Naval War College. Rosenberg had taken refuge there on learning that the new Head of State did not want him as a Minister. Karl Dönitz had no wish to encumber his government with Rosenberg;[8] he had been isolated for years and ever since the 1920s had been involved in intrigue initiated against him by his Party colleagues. He was a difficult character, something of an exhibitionist with his eccentric plans for creating a better world which even Hitler had not taken seriously; even when under arrest he kept himself aloof. Only a year earlier he had been involved in an outright battle with Heinrich Himmler for the maintenance of the powers formerly granted him by the Führer and retention of his rank, offices and prerogatives as Reich Minister for the Occupied Eastern Territories. On 26 April 1944 he had written to Himmler: 'Naturally matters are not acute at the moment and I therefore reserve the right to revert to this problem again in the event of reoccupation of the Eastern territories.'[9] Gottlob Berger, Himmler's amanuensis who spied on nearly everybody including Rosenberg and Ribbentrop, reported to his master in a 'Top Secret' memorandum dated 20 December 1944 and eloquently headed 'Ref: Reich Minister for the no longer occupied Eastern Territories' as follows: 'It is established that *Reichsleiter* Rosenberg has paid eight visits since 1 December to *Reichsleiter* Dr Lammers in order to preserve his ministerial office under all circumstances. According to my information . . . Rosenberg is said also to have been received by the Führer . . . I am keeping the battle in every way on the Rosenberg–Ribbentrop level . . . I am trying to keep myself, under all circumstances, out of this power struggle so that I may be all the more active in penetrating it.'[10] Obviously such rivalries could not suddenly be forgotten either in Mondorf or in Nuremberg, particularly seeing that the contestants had previously been overshadowed by Adolf Hitler and, for the benefit of the outside world, had been forced to pretend that they were in agreement ideologically, had similar aims and were united in their desire to see them achieved. The accusation repetitiously advanced by the prosecution of a 'Common Plan' and 'Conspiracy' to initiate wars of aggression[11] was therefore to some extent based on conceptions bearing little relation to the realities of the Hitler Reich. The prosecution imagined community of interest in cases where there was no such thing. In the sense envisaged by the IMT there was no Common Conspiracy between, for instance, Alfred Rosenberg and Alfred Jodl,[12] between Jodl and Hitler (whose personal acquaintance Jodl only made in 1939 after the war had begun),[13] between Fritz Sauckel and Gustav Krupp von Bohlen und Halbach, between Julius Streicher and Albert Speer. In 1945 and 1946, however, the prosecution was not alone in thinking this theory of a conspiracy to be possible.

The story of Julius Streicher, the *Gauleiter* 'sent on leave' by Hitler in 1940,[14] is a good example. From 1940 to May 1944 he was regarded by high-level functionaries as having been 'expelled'; he had no contact with leading Nazis and lived in retirement in his country house. As he and his wife stated in Nuremberg, he had even refused Hitler's offer, transmitted by Ley and Goebbels in May and June 1944, to rejoin the ranks of the 'old fighters'.[15] The record of the IMT session of 26 April 1946 (the cross-examination of Streicher) is revealing:

Dr Marx: Adolf Hitler always spoke on the anniversary days of the Party about a sworn fellowship. What do you say about that?
Streicher: Sworn fellowship – that meant that he, Adolf Hitler, was of the conviction that his old supporters were one with him in thought, in heart, and in political loyalty – a sworn fellowship sharing the same views and united in their hearts.
Dr Marx: Would not that mean that a conspiracy existed?
Streicher: Then he would have said we were a fellowship of conspirators.
Dr Marx: Was there any kind of close relationship between you and the other defendants which could be termed a conspiracy, and were you better acquainted or did you have especially close relations with any one of these defendants?
Streicher: Inasmuch as they were old members of the Party we were one community of people with the same convictions. We met at Gauleiter meetings, or when one of us spoke in the other's Gaustadt, we saw one another. But I had the honor of getting to know the Reich Ministers and the gentlemen from the Army only here. A political group therefore – an active group – certainly did not exist.[16]

No search was instituted for Baldur von Schirach because the Americans thought him to be dead. The rumour went round in Vienna, where Schirach had been Gauleiter, Reichsstatthalter and finally Reich Defence Commissar, that Schirach had fallen in the fighting round Vienna on 12 or 13 April and that resisters had hung his body from the Floridsdorf bridge over the Danube before the Russians moved in. The Allies did not know that a week earlier Hitler had ordered his former Reich Youth Leader over the radio to 'report for service in the field in his last rank'[17] and that Lieutenant (Reserve) von Schirach had done just that.* On orders from Sepp Dietrich, who was especially apprehensive of Hitler's rage for destruction in the final days of the war,[18] Schirach, who was still Head of Civil Administra-

---

* Schirach had reported to Sepp Dietrich who had used him as liaison officer between his headquarters and his subordinate corps and divisions. See Schirach: *Ich glaubte an Hitler*, pp. 315ff.

tion, drove off during the night 1/2 May with his aide Weishofer in the direction of the Tyrol; there he was to reconnoitre 'rear positions for the army, the refugees and the wounded crowding into the narrow Danube plain'.[19] His car broke down and he was stranded in Schwaz near Innsbruck; there he was overtaken by the news of formation of a provisional government in Vienna, Dönitz's decisions regarding armistice negotiations and the fact that resistance groups had embarked on an intensive search for 'Nazis'. He threw away his uniform, now an encumbrance, called himself Richard Falk and camouflaged himself as a writer of novels. He heard the announcement from the London BBC that Schirach was dead[20] and talked quite openly to American soldiers (he spoke perfect English). He had a room in the attic of a working-class house where he worked peacefully on a novel, *The Secrets of Mira Loy*; giving his name as Richard Falk, he took books out of the Schwaz public library.[21]

His aide was the only person who knew him and helped him. On 4 June 1945, however, on hearing the radio announcement that all Hitler Youth leaders from Bannführer upwards were under automatic arrest and were to be charged, he gave himself up. He wrote a letter to the local American commander, whose office was in the 'Hotel Post' in Schwaz, stating: 'I, Baldur Benedikt von Schirach, will voluntarily give myself up to the occupation authorities today in order to answer for my actions before an international court.'[22] The Americans took this letter for a bad joke, telling the bearer of it that Schirach was 'after all dead';[23] they finally arrested him, however, when he himself appeared at the headquarters and said to the astonished and sceptical American officers (in English): 'I am Schirach.'

Joachim von Ribbentrop, foreign Minister of the Reich from February 1938, was in Flensburg when Grand Admiral Dönitz was trying to form a new government composed of the least incriminated people. Dönitz would not accept him[24] and so he went to Hamburg where he paraded about openly in a smart double-breasted suit and Anthony Eden hat renewing old contacts. An old acquaintance's son told the Allied police who arrested him in bed early on the morning of 14 June 1945 on the fifth floor of his Hamburg apartment house.

Julius Streicher had fallen into disfavour with Hitler in 1940 and in April 1945 had not even been allowed to take part in the defence of Nuremberg, his former 'seat'.[25] He was discovered by the Americans in the region of Waldring near Berchtesgaden, where he was passing himself off as an artist named 'Seiler'. Contrary to his original intention he had decided[26] not to follow the example of his last two high-ranking old-time visitors and commit suicide. He was found fortuitously by a search party from 101 U S Airborne Division. A U S Army jeep carrying four men stopped in front of the house; the 'artist' was on the terrace working on a water-colour.

His wife Adele (she had been his secretary since June 1940 and he had married her only in April 1945) told the story of his arrest.[27] Two American officers, Captain Hugh Robertson and Major Henry Blitt, appeared on the terrace, revolvers in hand. Blitt asked Streicher, now grey-bearded in a blue-striped collarless shirt and crumpled trousers: 'Do you belong to the Nazi Party?' This he did in faultless Yiddish, which Streicher, the former editor of *Der Stürmer*,* understood well enough.

Streicher, who was obviously playing for time, pretended to be deaf and asked his wife to repeat the question louder. Then he answered 'Yes.' Blitt asked: 'What's your name?' Streicher, after again getting his wife to repeat the question, replied: 'Julius Streicher.' Blitt, astonished at his 'find', ordered 'Come on.'[28] The Americans went into the house with Streicher and his wife; Streicher changed and, being lame, asked for a walking-stick which Blitt examined carefully in case it concealed some sort of firearm. Streicher was then taken to Berchtesgaden in the jeep.† There he experienced the first results of his notorious 'popularity' as editor of the incredibly crude anti-semitic weekly *Der Stürmer*.

Before eventually reaching Nuremberg by a roundabout route, Streicher later maintained that he had been humiliated, brutally tortured and beaten up by Jews. A manuscript account which he handed to Dr Hanns Marx, his defence counsel in Nuremberg, includes the following:

'At top speed to Berchtesgaden via Reit im Winkel. Jeered at by press reporters (4/5ths Jews). Film. Prison in Salzburg – "Now we've got him! That's Julius Streicher!" Jewish officers: "Cur! Swine! When I was ten years old you listed me in *Der Stürmer* for race pollution! Out with your hands!" Handcuffs on. Jeered at by Jews all night. Under heavy guard, nothing to eat. About midnight a woman's voice: "You're Julius Streicher?" I: "It is as you say." Next day in a lorry to Freising via Munich with Epp. I had been left only with shirt and trousers. I was terribly cold. In Freising put into a north-facing cell. Window was out so it was even colder. Two niggers undressed me and tore my shirt in two. I kept only my pants. Being handcuffed I could not pull them up when they fell down. So now I was naked. Four days! On the fourth day I was so cold that my body was numb. I couldn't hear anything. Every 2–4 hours (even in the night!) niggers came along under command of a white man and hammered at me. Cigarette burns on the nipples. Fingers gouged into eye-sockets. Eyebrows and chest hair pulled out. Genitals beaten with an oxwhip. Testicles very swollen. Spat at. "Mouth open" and it was spat into. When I

* A violently anti-Jewish and largely pornographic Nazi newspaper.

† An hour later the two officers returned and asked Frau Streicher where the picture was on which Streicher had been working shortly before. Frau Streicher asked Blitt to leave her this picture, which he did. Nevertheless he demanded a 'substitute', which he selected from three Streicher water-colours. Frau Streicher later saw a reproduction of it in an American newspaper in a series headed 'Famous landscape artists' but the name of the artist did not appear. (Information from Frau Streicher, 1 August 1974.)

refused to open, my jaws were prised apart with a stick and my mouth spat into. Beaten with the whip – swollen, dark-blue weals all over the body. Thrown against the wall. Blows to the head. Thrown on the floor. A heavy chain across the back. When I refused to kiss the niggers' feet kicks and whipping. When I refused to eat rotten potato skins, more blows, spittings and burns. When I refused to drink out of the chamber-pot in the latrine, fresh torments. Jewish pressmen every day. Photographed naked! Jeered at wearing an old army greatcoat which they hung round me – "Now, how long d'you think you've got to live?" No opportunity to lie down, no chair. I collapsed on the floor with my hands still handcuffed. Four days handcuffed without a break. Impossible to relieve nature. I never cried out. All the time I was thinking of my Adele. On fourth day carted off to Wiesbaden with Epp, Gaul, Bohle and a young Englishman (a Nazi). I imagined I was going to be executed and said to myself: "I would never have thought that one could be so glad to die." To Wiesbaden via Nuremberg and Frankfurt ... fifth day and still handcuffed. Deputy Prison Governor (a dentist) to Bohle: "Why is this man handcuffed?" When Bohle said that I had been handcuffed for four days, he was indignant and took the handcuffs off me at once. Blood and pus ran out of the joints. I couldn't move my hands. The feeling did not come back into them for at least a minute and I have only been able to use them since arriving in Wiesbaden. Next day interrogation by twenty Jews through the Prison Governor (a Jew). After the interrogation he came into my cell looking serious: "Do you want anything?" "I am a prisoner and have no wants." "I only meant: I like you. You are the only prisoner who has stuck to his story. All honour to you." From Wiesbaden to Mondorf camp, Luxemburg. Late August to Nuremberg.'[29]

To judge from documents and personal statements, such treatment was meted out only to Hans Frank and Julius Streicher. For two decades Streicher had reviled, slandered and insulted world Jewry, had offered them up to racial fanatics as vermin; so, eighteen months before his execution by hanging, he found himself with a personal account to square; the 'holy' wrath of his victims led them to apply the Old Testament law of 'an eye for an eye and a tooth for a tooth'.

Nowhere, however, did the victors treat the vanquished with friendship or chivalry. In 1945 they held practically every German to be a 'Nazi' who had made his contribution to the crimes increasingly publicized abroad since 1942. The victors knew that: on 10 April 1932 13·4 million German electors had cast their votes for Hitler in the presidential election; 37 per cent of the electorate had voted for him and his party on 31 July 1932 and 43·9 per cent on 5 March 1933. In addition Allied propaganda had made much of the fact that 92 per cent of the electorate had approved Hitler's policy on 12 November 1933 and 90 per cent had voted for him as 'Führer and Reich Chancellor' on 19 August 1934. All this had its effect.

Wilhelm Keitel had joined Grand Admiral Dönitz at Plön in Holstein on

30 April 1945, travelling from Dobbin via Wismar in Mecklenburg and Neustadt in Holstein. On 13 May he was made 'prisoner of war',* whereupon he issued an announcement to OKW stating that he had been 'transferred to prisoner of war status on Eisenhower's orders' and was now facing 'trial as a war criminal'.[30]

The fact that his memoirs, which he began to write a year before his execution, include accounts of the final stages not only of his own personal career but of the top-level Wehrmacht headquarters after Hitler's suicide make it seem worth quoting them at this point. They have since become known in Germany primarily through Walter Görlitz's book.[31]

'On 8 May (1945), after Jodl's return from Eisenhower's headquarters in Reims,† I was commanded by the Grand Admiral (Karl Dönitz), acting as Head of State and Supreme Commander of the Armed Forces, to fly by British transport aircraft to Berlin with the preliminary instrument as signed by Jodl and Eisenhower's Chief of Staff. Admiral von Friedeburg accompanied me as the Navy's representative, and Colonel-General Stumpff, the last C.-in-C. for Home Defence, on behalf of the Air Force. In addition to these I took with me Vice-Admiral Bürkner, Chief of OKW Military Intelligence, and Lieutenant-Colonel Böhm-Tettelbach (Air Force Operations officer in the OKW Operations Staff), because not only did he speak fluent English but he had also passed the Russian interpreter examination.

'We flew by British transport plane to Stendal first. There a squadron of civil aircraft had been mustered by the British Air Chief Marshal who was General Eisenhower's representative. After a sort of victory flight round Berlin, we all landed, with my plane last, at Tempelhof airport. A Russian guard of honour had been drawn up for the British and American parties, with a military band; from our landing area we were able to watch the ceremony from afar. A Russian officer had been detailed to accompany me – I was told that he was General Zhukov's Deputy Chief of Staff – and he drove me in one car while the rest of my party followed in other cars. We drove ... to Karlshorst, where we were put into a small empty villa ... It was about 1.0 p.m. We were left absolutely to ourselves. Presently a reporter came and took some photographs and after a while a Russian interpreter arrived; he was unable to tell me at what time the signing of the Instrument of Surrender was to take place; I had already been given a German copy of it at the airport.

'I was therefore able to compare the version initialled by Jodl with the

---

* Keitel was taken at once to the Grand Hotel, Mondorf, where the major defendants were initially 'assembled' for the war crimes trial. He was moved from Mondorf to Nuremberg on 14 August 1945 and there (after being sentenced by the IMT) on another 13th, 13 October 1946, he was awaiting execution of the death sentence.

† Colonel-General Jodl returned on 7 May 1945 from Eisenhower's headquarters near Reims where, on the evening of 6 May, he had concluded a preliminary agreement for capitulation (and had informed Keitel thereof over the radio).

wording of this new one, but I observed only minor divergencies from the original. The only basic modification was the insertion of a clause threatening to punish troops who failed to cease fire and surrender at the time stipulated. I told the interpreter officer that I demanded to speak to a representative from General Zhukov, since I would not sign this insertion unconditionally. Several hours later a Russian general arrived ... to hear my objection. I explained that I was objecting because I could not guarantee that our cease-fire orders would be received in time, with the result that troop commanders might feel justified in failing to comply with any demands to that effect. I demanded insertion of a clause to the effect that Surrender would only come into force twenty-four hours after the orders had been received by our troops; only then would the penalty clause take effect. About an hour later the general was back with the news that General Zhukov had agreed to twelve hours' grace being given instead of twenty-four. He ended by asking for my credentials as the representatives of the victorious powers wished to inspect them; I would receive them back shortly. The signing was to take place "towards evening", he added.

'At about 3.0 that afternoon we were served a magnificent meal by Russian girls. Our patience was being sorely tried. At 5.0 we were taken into another building and served afternoon tea, but nothing happened. They brought back my credentials and told me everything was in order but apparently they still did not know what time the Surrender was to be signed. At 10.0 p.m. my patience was exhausted and I officially demanded to know when the signing was going to take place; I was told it would be in about an hour. During the evening I had our modest baggage fetched from the plane as the return flight ... was now impossible.

'Shortly before midnight – the time the surrender was due to come into force – I was taken with my staff into the barrack's mess. As the clock struck the hour, we entered the great hall through a side door and were led across to the long table directly facing us, where three seats had been kept free for my two companions and myself; the rest of our entourage had to stand behind us. Every corner of the hall was packed and brilliantly lit by spotlights. Three rows of chairs running the length of the hall and one across it were crowded with officers; General Zhukov took the chair with the plenipotentiaries of Britain and America on either side of him.

'As soon as Zhukov's Chief of Staff laid the Instrument in front of me, in three languages, I asked him to explain why the qualification I had demanded to the penalty clauses had not been inserted in the text. He went across to Zhukov and, after a brief word with him, as I could see, came back and told me that Zhukov had expressly agreed to my demand for the penalty measures not to take effect for a further twelve hours.

'The ceremony began with a few introductory words; then Zhukov asked me whether I had read the Instrument of Surrender. I replied: "Yes." His second question was whether I was ready to authenticate it with my signature. Again I answered with a loud "Yes". The signing ceremony began at once and, after I had been the first to sign it, the attestation. Finally I and my party left the hall by the door close behind me.

'Now we were taken back to our small villa again; during the afternoon a table had been laid, well stocked with a cold buffet and various wines, while in the other rooms beds had been prepared – a bed per man. The official interpreter said that a Russian general was coming and that dinner would be served on his arrival. A quarter of an hour later Zhukov's Deputy Chief of Staff appeared and asked us to be seated but then excused himself. We all thought that the buffet ... was the end of this hangman's breakfast; we were all feeling very replete when we learned that there was a hot roast meat course to follow and finally came fresh frozen strawberries, something I had never eaten before in my life ... After the meal the interpreter officer left us; apparently he had stood in for the host ... We all turned in.

'Next morning, at 5.0 a.m., we were given a simple breakfast. As I was about to leave about 5.30 I was asked to wait for Zhukov's Chief of Staff who wanted to have a talk with me ... The general requested me to remain in Berlin; they would endeavour to provide me with the opportunity to issue from Berlin our cease-fire orders to the troops on the eastern front, just as I had demanded when we discussed the terms of the penalty clauses the day before. I replied that if they would guarantee radio communication I would issue a number of additional signals at once; they would have to hand over the German cyphers to me. The general disappeared again to ask Zhukov for a decision. He returned with the news that it would not be possible after all for me to despatch these signals; but General Zhukov still invited me to remain in Berlin nevertheless.

'Now I saw what they were up to. I insisted on flying to Flensburg at once, since I would have to transmit the amended surrender conditions to the troops as quickly as possible from there; otherwise I would not accept the consequences for what might happen. I said that I had signed in good faith and had been relying on General Zhukov's word as an officer.

'Ten minutes later the Chief of Staff was back again with the news that my aircraft would be ready to take off in an hour. I got quickly into my car with Bürkner, Böhm-Tettelbach and the interpreter ... We drove past the City Hall, the castle and along Unter den Linden and the Friedrichstrasse ... Numerous German and Russian tanks blocked the Friedrichstrasse at several points and the street was strewn with rubble from the tumbledown houses. We flew straight back to Flensburg, relieved when the British aircraft was in the air. We landed at Flensburg about 10.0 a.m.

'We had arranged to exchange official delegations with Montgomery and Eisenhower to facilitate business during the process of capitulation. On Saturday 12 May the American delegation arrived in Flensburg and were accommodated aboard the *Patria*, a luxury liner ... Dönitz was required to go aboard the *Patria* first to be received by the Americans while I was to make my appearance half an hour later. After Dönitz had left the ship I was received. The American general (Major-General Rooks) told me that

I was to surrender as a prisoner of war and would be flown out at 2.0 that afternoon – in two hours' time. I was to turn over my official business to Colonel-General Jodl; I was to be allowed to take with me one personal staff officer, a batman and 300 lbs of baggage. I stood up, saluted briefly with my Field Marshal's baton and drove back to headquarters with Bürkner and Böhm-Tettelbach who had both accompanied me during this "audience". I took leave of Dönitz, who had already been briefed on what was to happen, and selected Lieutenant-Colonel John von Freyend and Mönch to accompany me, thereby ensuring a considerably less arduous captivity for them. I handed my personal papers and keys to Jodl and handed Szimonski ... one or two things and a letter for my wife which were to be flown down to Berchtesgaden in the courier plane. Unfortunately the British later seized everything from the good "Schimo", even my ... bank pass-book and the letter to my wife.

'We took off for a destination not disclosed to us and, after flying right across Germany, landed that evening at Luxemburg airport; there I was treated as a prisoner of war for the first time and taken to the internment camp in the Palace Hotel, Mondorf, where Seyss-Inquart had already arrived.

'In Flensburg I had been my own master; I drove to the airfield in my own car; in those two unguarded hours I could have put an end to my life ... The thought never occurred to me, as I never dreamed that such a *via doloris* lay ahead of me, with this tragic end in Nuremberg.'[32]

After their arrest in Flensburg, Grand Admiral Dönitz with the members of his government and of OKW – Alfred Jodl, Albert Speer, Graf Schwerin von Krosigk and others – were treated like gangsters or partisans. On 23 May 1945 the government 'enclave' in which Dönitz had been living with the permission of the victors was cordoned off by two infantry battalions and a tank regiment; Dönitz was invited on board the liner *Patria*, where the Allied Control Commission was located, and informed by Allied generals that, on instructions from Eisenhower, the Acting German Government was dissolved and under arrest. After Dönitz and his entourage had left the ship, British soldiers burst into the board-room of the Foreign Ministry, where a conference was about to begin. All Germans had to strip completely and submit to humiliating physical searches which took place in different rooms, sometimes officers and female secretaries together. British soldiers seized watches, rings and other valuables from the prisoners and led them with their hands above their heads into the courtyard, where a dozen or so reporters were ready waiting for the 'big show'; the trouserless officers and ministers were then photographed. The *New York Times* of 24 May 1945 commented on this undignified scenario: 'The Third Reich died today'.

On 5 June 1945 the Allies officially assumed governmental authority in Germany.

Until mid-August 1945 the men accused as major war criminals – Göring, Dönitz, von Papen, von Ribbentrop, Rosenberg, Keitel, Kesselring and Streicher, to name only these – were 'lodged' in the smart 'Palace Hotel' in Bad Mondorf, Luxemburg, which had been cleared for the purpose. There they were under command of an arrogant, very military and overbearing US Army Colonel, Burton C. Andrus, who also acted as Prison Commandant in Nuremberg from August 1945.

Twenty-four years later Albert Speer recalled: 'Outside, through the glass doors, we could see Göring and other former members of the leadership of the Third Reich pacing back and forth. The whole hierarchy was there: ministers, Field Marshals, Reichsleiter, State Secretaries and generals. It was a ghostly experience . . .'* After the end of the war ordinary German prisoners of war – generals, colonels, staff officers, officers, NCOs and men – particularly in the POW camps in France and Germany, were suffering from real hunger, frequently had to bed down on the bare floor or do the best they could in miserable bivouacs with thin blankets and nothing to lie on but a palliasse and were subjected to many vexations; the German civil population too was hungry and in want. The victors took care, however, that the Germans who were to appear in front of the IMT footlights as major war criminals were kept 'in good form'. Speer says: 'Compared with our fellow-countrymen, who were going hungry in their freedom, we were inappropriately well off, for we received the same rations as American troops.'[33]

Speer, Hjalmar Schacht and other internees in Schloss Kransberg arranged cabarets, listened to lectures and busied themselves with all sorts of pastimes to overcome their boredom.[34]

The internees in Mondorf did not live quite so luxuriously. There were no excursions into the countryside such as Speer had been able to make in Chesnay. While Speer, cleverly articulate, vain and self-assured, though later classified as only moderately intelligent by the American psychologist in Nuremberg, was arguing with Thyssen, Schacht and Werner von Braun[35] in Schloss Kransberg,[36] some of those in Mondorf began to revive old intrigues – and start up new ones.

Hermann Göring, still much affected by Hitler's rejection of him, inevitably competed with Dönitz for the role of *primus inter pares*;† he was morbidly insistent on 'presiding' and took it upon himself to send back food he did not like with the comment that in his day he would not have given it even to his dogs. Just as in his headquarters he wore his red silk

* Albert Speer: *Inside the Third Reich*, p. 502. After a fortnight's stay in Bad Mondorf Speer was 'transferred', as he puts it, to Schloss Kransberg near Bad Nauheim im Taunus, which he had remodelled in the winter of 1939 as a headquarters for Göring. Not until the end of August did he learn that he was listed as a major war criminal. He did not reach Nuremberg until the end of September.

† According to Speer (*Inside the Third Reich*, p. 502) they avoided meeting at the hotel door. Each of them presided at one of the two tables in the dining room so that the burning question of precedence did not arise.

flowered dressing gown over a pair of black silk pyjamas. His shoes and his boots were still polished for him and his former splendid uniforms were cleaned; he was still allowed to receive visitors and 'hold court'. He could still take his morphine, enabling him to see even this crazy world through rose-coloured spectacles. He expatiated almost with glee to Dr Ludwig Pflücker, the German prison doctor, on how he would make his appearance in court. He was convinced that spotlights would be trained on him when he accused the Allies of their terror raids on German cities. In Bad Mondorf he was perhaps still justified in thinking this, for the interrogations to which the internees were subjected were mere innocent battles of words compared to the subsequent cross-examinations in Nuremberg. The interrogators simply asked ordinary questions and in general did not touch on the main problems which were to be the subject of the indictment in Nuremberg, where every question and answer was related to documentary evidence.

Some of the accused, ex-Ministers and State Secretaries, reached Nuremberg only via the interrogation centre (referred to by Speer as 'notorious')[37] at Oberursel near Frankfurt. They were interrogated – on the same lines as the others in Bad Mondorf – in the so-called 'Haus Alaska' and then taken on to Nuremberg after what was often sarcastically called 'the last sitting of the Reich cabinet'. The Americans, one of whom was Dr Robert M. W. Kempner, were at pains to decide at this stage who should be in the dock and who should be cited as a witness in order to clear away unnecessary dead wood before the IMT began to sit. Kempner had been a Prussian civil servant (deprived of all civil rights by Hitler) and was on the staff of Robert H. Jackson, the US Chief Prosecutor; he was naturally particularly well informed on all internal details and circumstances. Even at this stage he found that some of the accused were prepared to offer to pump their fellow-sufferers and inform him of the results.[38] Even in Bad Mondorf some of the accused refused to consort with certain of their co-defendants.

Along with everyone else the major defendants had long known from newspaper reports that Nuremberg was the place where the International Military Tribunal would sit and pronounce its judgements;[39] all who arrived there realized that they had reached a decisive stage. Not a few were surprised by the conditions which greeted them there.

4

The Prison

A woman witness gives this report: 'During 1945 and 1946 I was in a series of eleven internment camps under American and British guard. From September 1945 I was in the Nuremberg Court prison where, in contrast to my treatment both before and afterwards, everything was in general perfectly decent. Living conditions made life there more tolerable than in the other camps. After a humiliating acceptance procedure I was initially put into a cell in the defendants' wing where accommodation and security measures were the same as for the major defendants ... A fortnight after my arrival the so-called "witnesses' wing" was opened and I was transferred there at once. The ground floor and first floor of the building were "inhabited" by some seventy male internees. On the second floor were cells for the women prisoners, of whom for a time there were only six though numbers rose to fourteen on occasions. There was a barrier at the end of the passage but behind this we were allowed to move about freely on our floor – as were the men on theirs. Down the centre of the building – between the two narrower sides – there ran a broad light-shaft so that from the landings, which were fenced with wire netting, we could talk to the internees incarcerated with us. In the witnesses' wing were people who would normally have been prisoners of war – or who came under the automatic arrest category. Some of them had to give evidence at the trial. The IMT hoped to get from them information helpful to the prosecution. The prosecution witnesses ... were lodged in a hotel outside the court prison under much more comfortable conditions. Inmates of the witnesses' wing included Field Marshals, Army, Air Force and Waffen-SS generals, Reichsleiter and Gauleiter of the NSDAP, senior officials, members of the SD and finally Wehrmacht aides. The only foreigner among them was the Hungarian Regent, Horthy.*

'Among the women internees were the secretaries to Adolf Hitler and his ministers, members of the families of leading Nazis,† female doctors who

* Among the inmates were Field Marshals Albert Kesselring, Werner von Blomberg, Erhard Milch and Erich von Manstein, Colonel-General Heinz Guderian, ex-Army Chief of Staff Franz Halder, SS-Brigadeführer Otto Ohlendorf, Fritz Wiedemann, formerly aide to Hitler, SS-Obergruppenführer Erich von dem Bach-Zelewsky, Reichsleiter Max Amann and Gauleiter August Eigruber.

† Among the women under arrest were Frau Himmler and her daughter Gudrun Himmler. The doctor referred to in this account was Dr Pflücker, who emphasized Frau Himmler's modesty, industry and exemplary behaviour.

had worked in concentration camps and one Frenchwoman accused of
collaboration with the SD ... Most of us had had a bad time before
commitment to Nuremberg (I, for instance, had seen Italian fascists
horribly tortured in a prison in Milan). All heaved a sigh of relief in
the atmosphere of relative calm and security prevalent in Nuremberg. We
were visited daily by a German POW doctor ... Our food was brought to
us by German prisoners of war who all made much of their anti-fascist views,
which we often found amusing. The American Father Sixtus O'Connor
frequently visited us and also an American woman officer, a German-
speaking Jewess, who, however, always asked how we were and whether we
wanted anything. The woman doctor helped us as best she could.

'When we women were taken out into the courtyard for "exercise" for
the first time the American guards lined up along our path and urinated
in our direction. When we asked our women warders whether this was just
the fashion or a normal custom in the US Army, the result was a reminder
to our guards that a latrine existed ... But we had other things to think about
in Nuremberg; we had long talks to while away the time and sometimes even
played bridge. Initially we were allowed to take a shower and go for an
hour's walk once a week. Later it was even possible to play games in the
prison gymnasium. It was the place where the major defendants condemned
to death were hanged on 16 October 1946; one of them was the husband of
one of my cell-mates who had taken her exercise there. We spent much of
our time doing jobs for the men interned in the witnesses' wing. They would
shout out what they wanted from their cells and send us uniforms or laundry
for cleaning or mending via the guards or prisoners of war. Sometimes there
were requests from the defendants' wing. We often got touching little
thank-you letters as a result ... We could talk to the men in the witnesses'
wing enough to know that they were bearing up well under their imprisonment. As on the women's floor there was a very good spirit among them.
Lahousen, a member of Canaris' staff,* was the only person whom everyone obviously avoided. Most of the prisoners were at pains to set an example
to the others. Among the men the behaviour of Skorzeny and Ohlendorf[1]
was particularly exemplary. Ill-treatment suffered previously, however, had
its effect on their views and their attitude. Eigruber,[2] for instance, Gauleiter
of Upper Austria, had been terribly tortured by his fellow-countrymen at
the end of the war, being mutilated and even castrated, but he still maintained that he would gladly die for his ideas; Field Marshal von
Brauchitsch, who before commitment to Nuremberg had seen German
prisoners of war being maltreated in Dachau, said on several occasions that
he had recovered his faith in the German soldier.'[3]

Witnesses arriving in Nuremberg by train found certain double-dealing
informers waiting for them at the exit of the station. These people passed
on current phraseology, advised on ways to behave and presented them-

---

* General Lahousen, born in Vienna in 1897, appeared as a prosecution witness and
testified against a number of the accused on 30 November 1945. See IMT Vol. II, pp. 440ff.

selves as ideological blood brothers, which sometimes in fact they were. Not a few of them, however, were American secret service informers. One of them, Erich Kordt, had worked in the Foreign Ministry under Ribbentrop, had defected to the Americans in China during the war and was now posted at Nuremberg railway station where, by agreement with OSS, he extracted 'information' from the relatively inexperienced new arrivals who were unfamiliar with Anglo-American judicial methods.[4] Later, during the trial, he gave evidence for the prosecution against his former master Ribbentrop.

Factors governing witnesses' accommodation were the degree of their own criminality and the court's desire to keep them immune from outside influences. If, for instance, they arrived as prisoners, they remained under arrest. A certain category of witnesses, aristocrats, ex-diplomats and politicians – Carl Severing, for instance, the former Social-Democrat Minister of the Interior, whom the defence had summoned as a witness in the case of Erich Raeder – and certain not particularly incriminated academics lived in a so-called 'witnesses' house' in the Bülowstrasse, Nuremberg, run by a Countess. Some of the defence counsel and journalists lived there too. On occasions Dr Kempner arranged 'exclusive' accommodation if he thought it justified. He placed Crown Prince Wilhelm, for instance, with the Faber-Castell family, whom he knew and who placed their hunting lodge at his disposal.[5]

All discoverable defendants for the Nuremberg trial and many of the witnesses were incarcerated in the prison of the Palace of Justice, a star-shaped building with four wings each containing one hundred cells. Dr Ludwig Pflücker, the German prison doctor, gave the following description of it in 1952: 'Our prison was constructed on the usual lines for such institutions. Four wings of cells fanned out from a central circular building; there was a fifth, so-called church wing containing the small prison hospital on the ground floor and above it a very well-appointed chapel. Later this so-called church wing was occupied by officers from the British zone who had not yet been released from the Wehrmacht and it was then nicknamed the "Feldherrnhalle" [Valhalla]. During the first weeks we only used one wing, which was completely shut off from the central building by matchboarding; it remained so during the whole of the first trial and while the survivors of that trial were still there. After the latter had been taken to Spandau[6] all partitions were taken down. Security measures during the initial trial were especially strict ... This stemmed in the first place from the importance attached to the trial but also from the personality of the Commandant, Colonel Andrus, who was indefatigable in thinking up new security precautions – and was frequently disillusioned by the negligence of the guards. We Germans working inside were ... cut off from the outside world.'[7]

In the first wing were housed those who had not been condemned to death during the main trial. In the second wing and on the top floor of the third there were still over a hundred persons in solitary confinement in the autumn of 1946. Some were new arrivals committed for the later trials; others, who had been there for several weeks, had not even been interrogated nor did they know why they had been brought to Nuremberg in the first place. The inmates of the lower floors of the third wing were not locked in by day. The internees themselves could not understand how all these people had been categorized. Some of them were witnesses or defendants in future trials, others were prosecution witnesses at the main trial against Göring, Keitel, Jodl and the others. In some cases there seemed to be no reason why they were being held in Nuremberg at all. Confusion of names and similar errors frequently took place.

As the prisoners themselves said, periods of confinement were to be reckoned 'not in days or weeks but in months'. It was no exception for people to be kept in solitary confinement or in the witnesses' wing for six months or more.

The inmates' life was governed by the 'House Rules' issued on 11 September 1945:

HOUSE RULES FOR PRISONERS

Definitions:

A. INTERNEE In these House Rules the word 'internee' denotes any person detained here who is not required to work in connection with the administration of the prison or furnish other services.

B. PRISONER The designation 'prisoner' includes all persons detained here in imprisonment.

C. PRISONER OF WAR The designation 'prisoner of war' denotes all medical, clerical and labour personnel detained here for prison administration.

1. Internees are forbidden to speak to each other. In no case must they attempt to enter into communication with each other or other persons except as set out under A, B, C and D below:

    A. Internees may speak to guards or prisoners of war on duty matters only.

    B. They may write to their families, the Commandant, interrogating officers and the authorities only through the prison office.

    C. They may speak at will to the Commandant, the prison officer, deputy prison officers, warders, doctors, dentists and clerical assistants on all matters pertaining to these gentlemen's official duties.

    D. If necessary the conversation will be conducted through an interpreter.

2. No internee may attempt to give forbidden articles to other persons or accept such articles from other persons.

3. Guards will check the serving tables to ensure that no forbidden objects are passed to internees or received from them and that mess kit is complete and correct.

4. No internee may attempt to escape. In the event of attempted escape they will be struck down or shot down. It is their fault if they are wounded in the process. The sentry will shout 'Halt' *if time allows*.

5. The German doctor will visit each internee daily. An American interpreter will accompany him. Requests for dental treatment will be made on these occasions.
6. Hair-cutting, shaving etc. will be done by a German barber accompanied by an American guard. Conversation is forbidden on these occasions.
7. Internees may take a shower-bath once a week.
8. Reading and writing:
   A. Every internee will be given a bible on request.
   B. German books will be provided from the camp office, requests being passed via the interpreter or prison personnel. A list of available books will be provided from which choice may be made. Books will be returned in reasonable time to facilitate circulation.
   C. Writing materials will be provided in the quantity desired.
   D. The number of letters and postcards permitted for personal communications with families will be made known from time to time. Delivery of letters cannot be guaranteed until German postal services are once more in operation.
9. Internees are responsible for the cleanliness of their cells. The necessary cleaning materials will be brought to internees' cells daily.
10. Internees will be conducted to exercise daily; the following rules apply:
    A. More than one internee will exercise simultaneously.
    B. They are forbidden to approach each other closer than a distance of 10 m.
    C. An internee may walk anywhere in the courtyard but not closer to buildings or the wall than the outer edge of the sidewalk or roadway.
    D. Internees may not pick up anything or sit down.
    E. Internees may not speak to anyone or make signs to anyone except to the guard on duty.
11. Complaints regarding treatment in prison will be addressed in writing to the Commandant.
12. Formalities and compliments:
    Since it is not proposed to enter into great detail regarding the general form of compliments, the following five rules are issued for observance. They should serve as general guides for cases not specifically mentioned here. In cases of doubt it is best to observe the formalities and pay compliments on all occasions:
    A. Since exchange of military salutes between prisoners and members of the Allied forces is forbidden, the customary form of greeting of a bow is regarded as a suitable substitute for intercourse between internees and Allied officers.
    B. All members of the Allied Powers have precedence on entering a doorway, a lobby, a stairway, or other passageway. Internees and prisoners will stand aside if they approach such places simultaneously with members of the Allied Powers.
    C. Should Allied officers, officials or inspectors enter an internee's area or room for inspection, the internee will stand up, remain still and look the Allied representative in the face until otherwise indicated (except that any sick in bed or in a wheel-chair may remain there,

keep still, look at the visitor and wait until spoken to if conversation is desired).

D. If prisoners are proceeding through corridors or passageways, they will halt and stand still should the Commandant, his deputy or other visiting military or civilian dignitaries come towards them. Anyone walking in the courtyard will equally stand still and turn towards the Commandant or his deputy should they enter the courtyard, until it is indicated to him that he may continue walking.

E. In all these cases internees are free to continue their activities as soon as the Commandant or other personalities in the vicinity have returned the internee's compliments by a bow.

By order of Colonel Andrus   (signed)
                                                     Elmer W. Fox Jr
                                                     Major C A C
                                                     Operations Officer.

Newcomers' persons and baggage were thoroughly searched and they were then initially placed in solitary confinement. Albert Speer, who was committed to prison late in the day, writes: 'Before I knew it, I was locked into one of the cells ... A straw pallet, tattered and filthy old blankets, impassive, indifferent guards.'[8] Additional washing gear, shoe-laces, braces, belts, buckles on jacket or trousers, mirrors, shaving gear, knives, forks, watches, ties, collar-studs, in short everything which any prisoner would regard as essential, were removed from new arrivals. They then found themselves in a cell $2 \cdot 5 \times 4$ metres which contained: an iron plank bed with a dirty mattress which had not been cleaned for years, woollen blankets, a wash-basin, a tin plate, a spoon, a roll of toilet paper and a built-in W C. There was neither wall mirror, clothes hooks, table or chair.

One of the witnesses for the defence reports:[9] 'Having been summoned to Nuremberg in autumn 1945 I approached the Palace of Justice with a certain optimism. Having no experience of the methods of international justice, I had no forebodings and had convinced myself that a witness was entitled to humane treatment, very different from that accorded to convicted criminals. I was quickly disillusioned. No sooner had the prison doors of the Palace of Justice closed behind me than it was quickly made clear to me that, at least in the eyes of the inter-allied Military Tribunal, there was barely any difference between the treatment of witnesses, the accused, prisoners under investigation and convicted criminals. Life as a witness started with a physical examination of the most degrading kind. Shoes clacking since laces had been removed, holding up my trousers since belt and braces had been taken away, tieless and with a cardboard box under my arm, I left the examination cell to vanish into a solitary cell from which I was not allowed to emerge for the next six weeks apart from the daily compulsory walk in the courtyard. During all this time I was interrogated neither by the prosecution nor the defence. The equipment of the cell was spartan ... There was no table, chair or stool nor any means of hanging up coat, cap or towel. The contents of the cardboard box consisted of a pull-over, a sponge-bag with washing gear – but without shaving gear, tooth-paste, nail scissors or nail file etc.; all this had to be stacked on the stone floor. Cells were frequently searched – not a very difficult task. Inmates of the cells could either just stand, walk a step or two in any direction or sit on the plank bed. There was a flap in the door which was permanently open allowing the guards an unimpeded view into the cell. From dusk a light was fixed in the peep-hole and it was alight all night, lighting up the cell.' Seven years later Pflücker recalled: 'Internees were accommodated in single cells from which all furnishings and lighting had been removed. In each cell there was a WC; an iron bedstead was fixed to the wall. Each man ... had to arrange a pillow for himself using his clothing. The fastenings of the electric light leads had been pulled out very violently so that there were holes in the plaster. The whitewash was dilapidated and dirty so that the cells did not look very pretty.'[10]

The cells had obviously not been properly maintained for years; they were decaying and cold. The heating, which was turned on only two or three times a day for a few minutes at a time, was so ineffective that it hardly penetrated as far as the pipes in the cells. Windows did not shut and many panes of glass were broken; neither labour nor material were available for repairs and not even cardboard could be obtained, so the cells were draughty as well as cold. The walls, from which the plaster was flaking off, were damp and dirty; there were large cracks in which mice lived. WCs were not in working order and their stink pervaded the whole prison. The majority of cells were so badly lit that internees could generally read or write only around about midday.[11]

Pflücker says: 'Later, after the conclusion of the first trial (he means the IMT), this system of surveillance was abolished. The cells were still illuminated at night but guards were no longer posted before each individual cell and were replaced by patrols. After much effort the illumination of the cells was reduced even during the first trial, the beam no longer being directed on the internee's face at night. Nevertheless certain hardships persisted particularly when guards were changed and the new men followed their instructions too precisely and literally. In general things returned to normal after a few days when the guards were sufficiently relaxed not to interpret their instructions too strictly and had got to know the internees better. In this lamentable situation I did my best to comfort and mediate and achieved more than the internees could by complaining; most of them committed the indiscretion of quoting international law or the Geneva Convention.

'Guards' behaviour was not invariably impeccable but for any mis-behaviour they were reprimanded by the officers. Many of them talked loudly during the night and in a few instances used bad language against the internees but there was never any maltreatment. Many of the guards were good-natured, helped the internees when they could and were friendly to us who were working in the prison even during the period when fraternization was still forbidden. It was striking that Jewish guards were generally not only correct in their attitude but friendly.'[12]

The US GIs generally worked on the theory (not yet divulged to the internees) that the Germans under Hitler had disregarded and perverted traditional international and criminal law and therefore could not claim any protection thereunder.

For some inmates of the prison, food was inadequate. Figures for sixty-seven comparable inmates of the witnesses' wing showed that sixty-two of them had lost an average of 5–6 lb. in a month, one of them even as much as 13 lb.[13] The prisoners deteriorated both mentally and physically as a result of hunger and cold. Symptoms of exhaustion and general decline were the result. Workmen in dirty overalls continued to labour on the water system and WCs during mealtimes. One of them was a friend of Walter Schellenberg (head of a departmamt in the SS Reichssicherheitshauptamt from 1944 to the end of the war).[14] While working in Nuremberg he acted as undercover postman and transmitter of verbal messages which he passed from cell to cell. After his release he told Lina Heydrich, Reinhard Heydrich's wife, that he was responsible, on instructions from Schellenberg, for passing on the 'directive' that 'everything should be laid at the door' of Reinhard Heydrich, who was dead, so that 'he himself could stay alive'.[15]

Rations were changed only when the authorities began to fear prison psychosis. The prison doctor writes: 'We were given German rations. The comment will be made at this point that a large section of the German population had to make do with this ration and that for many people accommodation in the bomb-damaged cities was no better than in the prison. The answer to this, however, is that the internees were being kept in solitary confinement and that so far no case had been raised against them. The deterioration in health which I anticipated showed itself after about a fortnight in a rapid loss of weight. Even the Colonel (the Commandant) took serious note of this and asked me for the reason. I had been worried about the outcome and had been thinking over the problem for days, so I was able to give him a short report stating that this must be ascribed to various causes. In the first place the transition from easy-going detention in Mondorf to solitary confinement was a highly depressing experience. Secondly the food had become far worse.'[16] The major defendants, Fritz Sauckel for instance,[17] frequently applied to Dr Pflücker not only for sleeping tablets but also for additional food such as bread and jam. Rudolf Hess wrote to Pflücker: 'I have been given a mass of egg which I cannot eat. Could I not be given instead more bread – even black bread – and some jam?'[18]

Tobacco, razor-blades, toothpaste and other canteen articles were delivered irregularly and in inadequate quantities. Toilet soap could be obtained only on doctor's orders and shaving soap not at all. On the pretext of taking things to be washed and mended in town the guards removed almost all cotton or woollen garments and also all washing things. Each internee was allowed only one shirt. Prisoners were given an opportunity of changing their underclothes only twice between August and October 1946. Parcels from relatives were not received. There were neither washbasins nor warm water. Official prison regulations were observed only in so far as prohibitions and restrictions were concerned.

Basically the dentist was able only to do extractions; anything else simply had to be left undone, since he did not possess the necessary equipment, this despite the fact that some internees had already been in Nuremberg for over a year and, in view of their age, many of them urgently needed dental treatment. Pflücker later described the situation as follows: 'We found the atmosphere gloomy and sinister and it took some time for us to get used to these surroundings ... The dentist and I were allotted a room which must previously have been a warder's bed-sitter. It had a normal window, not the usual cell window. There was a cupboard with wooden shelves, one plain shelf, a table, chairs and two bunk beds; this was all the simple furnishing. Three others working in the prison were accommodated in a small adjoining room but they were soon given another room so that the dentist and I could use the second room as a store for medicines, bandages etc. We also used it as a washroom, since it had a tap and basin. When the staff was later reduced the dentist was given another room and then I had very tolerable accommodation given the circumstances, particularly since I managed to obtain a second table at which I could write. With its dark iron-hinged oak door, doorway of green-painted sandstone, green cupboard door and partition my room presented a picture far less gloomy than that of the normal cell. A gay lampshade and a light at the head of my bed were regarded as luxuries in this camp life.'[19]

The barber came only once between summer and autumn 1946. Since the prisoners were not allowed scissors, only once during this period did they have an opportunity of having their finger- and toenails cut or doing it themselves under supervision by an American guard.

The prescribed weekly shower frequently did not materialize. When it did the guards usually hustled everyone along to such an extent that anyone physically handicapped hardly had the time to undress. The defence witness previously quoted writes: 'The shower was a special source of amusement for the guards (less so for the prisoners). Prisoners bathed in groups of six to eight; the showers were in the cellar, generally reached at the double amid the clatter of truncheons and loud shouts from the guards; one had to undress as far as possible while on the move since, as soon as one entered the washroom, the water ran for one minute followed by one minute's pause for soaping followed by a further minute of running water for rinsing off. After barely being given time to dry and throwing on their clothes as they went the "bathers" were then herded back to the cells with "*Mak snell, mak snell*". Everyone looked forward to "shaving day" since the majority of prisoners naturally disliked going about continually with a "convict's stubble". The German barber appeared . . . accompanied by one or two guards whose obvious duty was to ensure that no information was passed from or to the barber or that a prisoner did not snatch his razor in order to commit suicide. If the guards were in bad humour it sometimes happened that they stopped the hair-cutting or shaving halfway so that the German being "dealt with" had the "pleasure" of going around with half a beard until next shaving day.'

The prison library remained closed for weeks at a time. Prisoners were allowed to write letters to relatives twice a month – eighteen lines in script using set phrases. Mail in the reverse direction, in so far as there was any, was unrestricted, but letters took two to three weeks from arrival in the prison to receipt by the prisoner. They were frequently returned marked 'Await new address'. The censor confiscated periodicals and newspapers; parcels and packets did not reach the prisoners either. Even articles considered essential by the doctor, such as spectacles and hearing aids, were not delivered. Dr Otto Meissner, for instance, the former Minister of State, who had always been short-sighted and in the semi-darkness of his badly lit cell became totally blind in the right eye and almost blind in the left, wrote to Colonel Andrus, the prison Commandant, asking for a stronger bulb in his cell since he was unable to read the documents submitted to him and so was unable to prepare his defence; his request was returned to him a few days later marked in red: 'Shit'.[20]

The prescribed daily exercise so frequently failed to materialize that in practice prisoners emerged from the stale stuffy air of the prison building only twice or three times in a week. During exercise periods talking was forbidden and prisoners had to keep five yards away from each other.

The American guards regarded all inmates of the prison, whether convicted, undergoing trial or witnesses, as criminals, a fact which they admitted unashamedly in conversation. They sometimes carried their hostility so far as to sing or whistle outside the cells during the night and bang their truncheons against the heating pipes, cell door flaps or walls.

'The guards merit a chapter to themselves. Initially they consisted of white Americans drawn from a fighting division. Admittedly those detailed as guards, mostly youngsters aged eighteen to twenty, were not malicious by nature but as a result of the orders they had obviously been given and their crude habits they were a severe trial to the prisoners. They were armed with truncheons, obviously for self-defence, and their main ambition seemed to be to train as "tough guys". Their training was always accompanied by much shouting and the clatter of their swinging truncheons against the iron gangways rang through the prison day and night. They also had a passion for singing and whistling, which was done in groups of six to eight and as loud as possible; the most varied melodies were produced and this permanent "jazz show" naturally sapped the strength of prisoners already under considerable stress. The guards thought up all sorts of ways of passing the time. One of them collected autographs. I remember my warder's fresh young countenance appearing in the trap-door of my cell saying in a sort of German–English jargon: "You sure hang; name on paper here please, so I show it at home – souvenir." This and much else was naturally a far greater trial for the older prisoners, who constituted the majority, than for the younger ones who took such aberrations as rather a joke ... When later (after the main trial) ... guard duties were taken over by coloured Americans ... and Poles, the atmosphere ... became much calmer but administration became worse. From that time prisoners, who were badly fed and languishing in unheated cells, often had no fresh air for a week ... In my view these conditions were largely the fault of the American prison Commandant who ... seemed to think it his duty to maltreat his prisoners, mentally if not physically, whenever he could. Nothing illustrates his attitude better than a remark made on the occasion of one of the frequent conducted tours of the prison for foreigners; the prisoners had just been given their tin mugsful of thin soup at midday; pointing with his cane to some German generals and Field Marshals, he said: "Here you see the German gangsters." '[21]

No difference was made between ex-prisoners of war, officers acting as witnesses after release, and other internees. Decorations and badges of rank were removed from them on entry, if not before. Accommodation, food, heating, lighting, postal arrangements, right of complaint, open-air exercise, collective punishments etc. did not conform to the provisions of the Geneva Convention and other international agreements.[22] To eliminate protests and reference to international agreements members of the German Wehrmacht had been nominally released from service and were held under arrest as civilian internees, no reasons being given.[23]

The prisoners were hermetically sealed off from the outside world. Owing to the delay in postal deliveries the news they received of events 'out there' was meagre. Inquiries and requests of all types went to the prison office, which seldom answered them and rejected them almost on principle. The International Red Cross and YMCA were not allowed entry. There was no protecting power.

'This total absence of legal status is the worst feature,' General Vormann says; 'the first implication is that the normal internee is completely in the hands of the guards and junior supervisory personnel. Although the prison rules are followed strictly as far as prohibitions are concerned, the provision that prisoners may address officers or the Commandant is seldom observed in the case of officers and in the Commandant's case never. Requests to this effect receive no answer. Even witnesses who had come to Nuremberg voluntarily were kept in prison despite the fact that in some cases the hearing of evidence had been over for months. They were kept in solitary confinement as if they were condemned criminals. In certain instances they were held for months, sometimes in solitary confinement and sometimes under collective arrest, without ever being told why they were being so treated; finally, without ever having been interrogated, they were sent back to their camps. Similar treatment was meted out even to those who had not come from an internment camp but were at liberty and had simply been asked to present themselves at the Palace of Justice on a certain day as a witness. Even when some of the inmates had been told that they were no longer required or when it had been established that they were not required at all and some muddle had simply been made, months passed before they were released. The same happened even when immediate hospital treatment was necessary and it was clear that a man was unfit to be in prison.'[24]

The Trial Opens

Early in October 1945 the members of the Tribunal, sitting in Berlin, had agreed on their rules of procedure and dress when in public session; they had decided that Nikitchenko should preside at the opening session in Berlin and Lord Justice Lawrence in Nuremberg. When the opening session eventually took place on 18 October the Western judges appeared, as agreed, in black robes, but the Russians were in uniform. After barely an hour they were once more in disagreement. In the hall in which, only a year before, Roland Freisler had pronounced sentence on the German resisters of 20 July 1944, they had sworn an oath, each in his own language, declaring: 'I solemnly declare that I will exercise all my powers and duties as a Member of the International Military Tribunal honorably, impartially and conscientiously.'[1]

Nikitchenko stated: 'The Tribunal has formulated Rules of Procedure, shortly to be published, relating to the production of witnesses and documents in order to see that the defendants have a fair trial with full opportunity to present their defense.'[2] At the conclusion of the session, the only one over which he presided, he announced: 'The Indictment having been duly lodged by the Prosecutors in conformity with the provisions of the Charter, it becomes the duty of the Tribunal to give the necessary directions for the publication of the text. The Tribunal would like to order its immediate publication but this is not possible inasmuch as the Indictment must be published simultaneously in Moscow, London, Washington and Paris. This result may be achieved, as the Tribunal is informed, by permitting publication in the press of the Indictment not earlier than 8 p.m. GMT, i.e. 2000 hours today, Thursday, 18 October.'[3]

Meanwhile the accused were in Nuremberg and there, a few hours later, each of them was handed a copy of the Indictment in their cells by Colonel Andrus, a West Pointer and caricature version of the unpleasant Prussian sergeant-major, Major Airey Neave (British) and Harold B. Willey, General Secretary of the Tribunal; they were told what rights of defence were allowed them and the place and earliest date at which their trial would open – not before thirty days.[4]

The accused's reactions were very different. When visited in his cell five days later by the American psychologist Gustav M. Gilbert, Robert Ley was indignant and considered himself innocent. He demanded 'a decent Jewish lawyer', placed himself against the wall crucifix-like and declaimed:

'How can I prepare a defence? Am I supposed to defend myself against all these crimes which I knew nothing about? If after all the bloodshed of this war some more sacrifices are needed to satisfy the vengeance of the victors, all well and good.'[5] Two days later he hanged himself in the toilet recess of his cell with the zip fastener torn from his anorak. He left behind a series of confused notes and letters to his wife, who had long been dead; on Jackson's instructions they were impounded and so are not accessible.

Karl Dönitz felt himself innocent and unconcerned.[6] On being handed the indictment Göring said: '... For me the outlook is gloomy ... I cannot imagine that there can be any legal basis for the accusation ... One does not require lawyers in this trial ... What is needed here ... is a good interpreter.'[7] Walter Funk wept. Julius Streicher looked hard at Neave and said emphatically: 'I want an anti-semite as defence counsel. A Jew cannot defend me. The names on this list all sound Jewish ... The Major (Neave) is not a Jew. He will help me find a lawyer.'[8] Alfred Jodl was taciturn. Alfred Rosenberg wanted to be defended by Hans Frank, one of his co-defendants, since he was a lawyer and had defended Adolf Hitler before 1933.

At this time Erich Raeder and Hans Fritzsche were still being held in Berlin by the Russians, who had previously attempted to brainwash them in Moscow, where Raeder had been in a comparatively comfortable house and Fritzsche in the dreaded Lubyanka; they were both visibly relieved that they would soon no longer be in Russian 'custody'. Fritzsche was intelligent and unusually quick-witted; he was not prepared to be intimidated by threats. He laughed uproariously when Soviet officers, photographers, interpreters and stenographers came to watch him as he read the indictment. Then he said: 'If I am accused of having killed a man, then I can prove the contrary ... But if I am accused of being the Devil, there is no proof against that. Tens of thousands ... have died for that reason.'[9]

With these two the Soviets did not have the success they achieved with the former Field Marshal Friedrich Paulus after his Sixth Army surrendered in Stalingrad. In 1942 Hitler had wanted to put Paulus in Alfred Jodl's place, but in Nuremberg, from March 1946, he proved to be a completely tame witness of the Russians. They failed, however, in their attempt to persuade the IMT to forgo his appearance in person and rely on written statements,[10] Lord Justice Lawrence deciding unequivocally: 'Field Marshal Paulus will be produced as a witness for the defendants' counsel to cross-examine. That meets your objection, I think, Dr Nelte.'[11]

There is no need for the historian to enter into detailed argument about Paulus, described by Göring in Nuremberg as 'a dirty swine' and a 'traitor' – he was questioned only by the Soviets and the surprised (and therefore inadequately prepared) defence counsel.[12] Paulus, who was persuaded to talk only by Dr Sauter, Funk's defence counsel, tried to confine himself to his messages of devotion to Hitler during the concluding stage of the Battle of Stalingrad; during cross-examination he generally failed to 'remember' except when his statements were of assistance to the Soviets. He attempted to incriminate his former comrades – in particular Keitel and Jodl – addressing them as 'defendants', and his attitude towards them was arrogant; both in court and outside he acted as if he had never had anything in common with the men in the dock.

The first defence counsel, selected by the accused from official lists, arrived in Nuremberg at the end of October 1945. Under the Charter the accused had the right to conduct his own defence[13] but – luckily for him – this provision was disregarded when Rudolf Hess took his stand upon it and actually prepared to act on it. Not all the defendants kept to these lists, which were handed to them together with the Indictment. Alfred Jodl, for instance, asked for the inclusion of Professor Franz Exner, whose acquaintance he had made in the house of his uncle Friedrich Jodl in Vienna;[14] this was agreed. Rudolf Hess and Julius Streicher did not accept the counsel allotted to them and initially raised complaint. Speer and the rest accepted the situation.[15]

So defence counsel during the IMT were:

Dr Otto Stahmer for Hermann Wilhelm Göring
Dr Günther von Rohrscheidt (to 5 February 1946) and Dr Alfred Seidl
   (from 5 February 1946) for Rudolf Hess
Dr Fritz Sauter (to 5 January 1946) and Dr Martin Horn (from 5 January
   1946) for Joachim von Ribbentrop
Dr Otto Nelte for Wilhelm Keitel
Dr Kurt Kauffmann for Ernst Kaltenbrunner
Dr Alfred Thoma for Alfred Rosenberg
Dr Alfred Seidl for Hans Frank
Dr Hanns Marx for Julius Streicher
Dr Fritz Sauter for Walter Funk
Dr Rudolf Dix and Professor Herbert Kraus for Hjalmar Schacht
Flottenrichter [Fleet Judge] Otto Kranzbühler for Karl Dönitz
Dr Walter Siemers for Erich Raeder
Dr Fritz Sauter for Baldur von Schirach
Dr Robert Servatius for Fritz Sauckel
Professor Franz Exner and Professor Hermann Jahreiss for Alfred Jodl
Dr Egon Kubuschok for Franz von Papen
Dr Gustav Steinbauer for Arthur Seyss-Inquart
Dr Hans Flaechsner for Albert Speer
Dr Otto Freiherr von Lüdinghausen for Constantin von Neurath
Dr Heinz Fritz and Dr Alfred Schilf for Hans Fritzsche
Dr Friedrich Bergold for Martin Bormann, who was tried *in absentia*

Defence counsel for groups and organizations were:

Dr Egon Kubuschok for the Reich Cabinet

Dr Robert Servatius for the Leadership Corps of the Nazi Party

Dr Ludwig Babel with Horst Pelckmann, Dr Carl Haensel and Dr Hans Gawlik for the SS and SD

Dr Rudolf Merkel for the Gestapo

Professor Franz Exner (to 27 March 1946) and Dr Hans Laternser (from 27 March 1946) for the General Staff and High Command of the German Armed Forces

The fact that certain defence counsel – there was talk of six – had been members of the Nazi Party[16] led the Russian members of the IMT – without success however – to vote against their acceptance. The Western members insisted on their point of view in closed session.[17]

The prisoners were now individually interrogated – generally intensively and aggressively – in rooms within the Palace of Justice. All were downcast and cut sorry figures, with their lined faces, some without ties, and the officers in faded uniforms without badges of rank or decorations.

At the end of October Andrus moved all the major defendants to the top floor and cleared the cell wing of other prisoners. Then, a few days later, they saw in black and white what awaited them.

The IMT having been constituted 'for the trial of the major war criminals' (the court's own words before opening the trial) and an Indictment having been lodged by the Chief Prosecutors, the court ordered each individual defendant in custody to be given a copy of the following: 'You and each of you is hereby notified that an indictment has been filed against you in the International Military Tribunal. A copy of this Indictment and of the Charter constituting the International Military Tribunal are attached hereto. Your trial will take place at the Palace of Justice, Nuremberg, Germany, not less than thirty days from the service of this Indictment upon you. The exact date will be made known to you later. Your attention is specifically directed to your right to counsel under Article 23 and Article 16 of the Charter and Rule 2(d) of the Tribunal, a copy of which and a list of counsel are attached hereto for your information.'[18]

The Article 16 referred to reads as follows:

'The Indictment shall include full particulars specifying in detail all the charges against the defendants. A copy of the Indictment and of all the documents lodged with the Indictment, translated into a language which he understands, shall be furnished to the defendant at a reasonable time before the Trial ... During any preliminary examination or trial of a defendant he shall have the right to give any explanation relevant to the charges against him ... A preliminary examination of a defendant and his trial shall be conducted in, or translated into, a language which the defendant understands ... A defendant shall have the right to conduct his own defense before the Tribunal or to have the assistance of counsel ... A defendant shall have the right through himself or through his counsel to present evidence at the Trial in support of his defense, and to cross-examine any witness called by the Prosecution.'[19]

The second paragraph of Article 23 read:

'The function of counsel for a defendant may be discharged at the defendant's request by any counsel professionally qualified to conduct cases before the Courts of his own country, or by any other person who may be specially authorized thereto by the Tribunal.'[20]

Rule 2(d) of the Tribunal read:

'Each defendant has the right to conduct his own defense or to have the assistance of counsel ... The Tribunal will designate counsel for any defendant who fails to apply for particular counsel or, where particular counsel requested is not within ten (10) days to be found or available, unless the defendant elects in writing to conduct his own defense ... provided that ... only one counsel shall be permitted to appear at the trial for any defendant, unless by special permission of the Tribunal and ... no delay of trial will be allowed ...'[21]

The hope harboured by most of the defendants that they would each receive an individual indictment had proved to be a naïve illusion. Each of them now realized that he was accused of all the horrors summarized in such sonorous terms in the Indictment. Gustav M. Gilbert, the American prison psychologist, immediately went from cell to cell with a copy of the Indictment in order to find out initial reactions and he asked the accused to comment on the general charges raised against them. In almost every case he met with biting scorn and icy non-acceptance. Only Speer, having read the comments of those questioned before him, wrote: 'The trial is necessary. There is a shared responsibility for such horrible crimes even in an authoritarian state.'[22]

During the preliminary investigations the accused had not been allowed to speak to each other at all; at this stage, however, there was a noticeable relaxation of the previous rules. They were now permitted to converse as they pleased both in the courtyard and inside the prison and to discuss the general lines of their defence and the attitude they would take to Hitler; under the – once more charismatic – leadership of Göring this led to certain inhibitions and hallucinations. Despite – or perhaps because of – the all-embracing nature of the indictment, no 'common plan' was ever agreed in Nuremberg, nor was there any feeling of solidarity or 'partnership in misfortune'. The generals promenaded by themselves, ostentatiously shunned by the civilians, in a 'spacious' area of garden, 6 × 6 yards. Places at lunch were allocated by the prison authorities according to a psychologically adroit order of precedence. For the trial itself a further rule came into force: the defendants must look tidy, well dressed and well nourished. Their suits and uniforms were taken out of American mothballs and they were allowed to choose what they would wear for trial after discussion with the pedantic Commandant Andrus, who wished to be informed of everything even down to cuff-links.

Before the first session of the court all the accused were conducted into the empty courtroom by white-helmeted U S soldiers; they were not hand-cuffed however; the visit was merely intended to lower their morale. Each man was allocated his place. Despite the fact that Hess had been Hitler's official deputy up to 1941 and Dönitz had acted as Head of State after Hitler's suicide, Göring ranked as No. 1 war criminal. Hess had to sit between Göring and Joachim von Ribbentrop, Hitler's Foreign Minister. It has often been said that the seating arrangement was in line with a pre-arranged 'order of precedence' in the ultimate sentences; that this is not so is shown by the fact that, for instance, Albert Speer sat next to Seyss-Inquart, who was later hanged.

When they finally appeared before the full court the accused received no form of encouragement or support except from their defence counsel and an occasional friendly nod from the interpreters' box.

Meanwhile the judges, so carefully selected by the victor powers, had prepared themselves as far as the situation permitted for their responsible and unprecedented task. Nevertheless, when they first assembled on the bench on 14 November 1945, a trivial matter almost led to a scene indicative of the perceptible atmosphere of tension. Judge John J. Parker, the American Alternate Member of the Tribunal, who was touchy and most insistent on his prerogatives and rights, felt that he had been slighted. Four of the leather chairs were lower and smaller than those allocated to the voting Members. As an alternate member he had to make do with a smaller chair and this he did not like at all. As a result of his protest eight similar chairs had been made available by the time of the first regular session of the Tribunal six days later; another result of this fracas was that, although not entitled to vote, the alternate members were permitted to put questions to witnesses in court and express divergent opinions.[23]

Preparatory sessions of the I M T took place on 14, 15 and 17 November and the first regular session on the 20th. Whereas the representatives of the Western Allies prepared themselves feverishly for the first working session, the Russians reacted with a transparent procrastinating manoeuvre. Twenty-four hours before the date set they suddenly announced that Rudenko was sick and so the opening of the court must be postponed for ten days. Jackson, however, who suspected that the Russians were afraid of possible revelations about, for instance, the secret Stalin–Hitler agreement of August 1939, the Soviet attack on Finland, the murder of Polish officers in Katyn Forest or the establishment of seventeen concentration camps in Poland, stuck to his guns.[24] Charles Dubost, the French deputy Prosecutor, wanted a postponement until Rudenko was fit again but Jackson and Shaw-cross insisted on the date fixed and this gave the Russians to think. Rudenko was suddenly well again. The case could open on the date set and with him present. On 20 November the President of Court set the tone with the firm statement:

'Before the defendants in this case are called upon to make their pleas to the Indictment which has been lodged against them, and in which they are charged with Crimes against Peace, War Crimes and Crimes against Humanity, and with a Common Plan or Conspiracy to commit those crimes, it is the wish of the Tribunal that I should make a very brief statement on behalf of the Tribunal.

'This International Military Tribunal has been established pursuant to the Agreement of London, dated the 8th of August 1945, and the Charter of the Tribunal as annexed thereto, and the purpose for which the Tribunal has been established is stated in Article 1 of the Charter to be the just and prompt trial and punishment of the major war criminals of the European Axis.

'The Signatories to the Agreement and Charter are the Government of the United Kingdom of Great Britain and Northern Ireland, the Government of the United States of America, the Provisional Government of the French Republic and the Government of the Union of Soviet Socialist Republics.

'The Committee of the Chief Prosecutors appointed by the four Signatories have settled the final designation of the war criminals to be tried by the Tribunal and have approved the Indictment on which the present defendants stand charged here today.

'On Thursday the 18th of October 1945, in Berlin, the Indictment was lodged with the Tribunal and a copy of that Indictment in the German language has been furnished to each defendant and has been in his possession for more than thirty days.

'All the defendants are represented by counsel. In almost all cases the counsel appearing for the defendants have been chosen by the defendants themselves, but in cases where counsel could not be obtained the Tribunal has itself selected suitable counsel agreeable to the defendant.

'The Tribunal has heard with great satisfaction of the steps which have been taken by the Chief Prosecutors to make available to defending counsel the numerous documents upon which the Prosecution rely, with the aim of giving to the defendants every possibility for a just defense.

'The Trial which is now about to begin is unique in the history of the jurisprudence of the world and it is of supreme importance to millions of people all over the globe. For these reasons there is laid upon everybody who takes any part in this Trial a solemn responsibility to discharge their duties without fear or favor in accordance with the sacred principles of law and justice ...'[25]

After this statement Sidney S. Alderman, Associate Trial Counsel for the United States, began the reading of the Indictment, extracts from which are as follows:[26]

'I. The United States of America, the French Republic, the United Kingdom of Great Britain and Northern Ireland and the Union of Soviet Socialist Republics by the undersigned Robert H. Jackson, François de Menthon, Hartley Shawcross and R. A. Rudenko, duly appointed to represent their respective governments in the investigation of the charges against and the prosecution of the major war criminals, pursuant to the Agreement of London dated 8 August 1945, and the Charter of the Tribunal annexed thereto, hereby accuse as guilty, in the respects hereinafter set forth, of Crimes against Peace, War Crimes and Crimes against Humanity, and of a Common Plan or Conspiracy to commit those Crimes, all as defined in the Charter of the Tribunal, and accordingly name as defendants in this cause ...: Hermann Wilhelm Göring, Rudolf Hess, Joachim von Ribbentrop, Robert Ley, Wilhelm Keitel, Ernst Kaltenbrunner, Alfred Rosenberg, Hans Frank, Wilhelm Frick, Julius Streicher, Walter Funk, Hjalmar Schacht, Gustav Krupp von Bohlen und Halbach, Karl Dönitz, Erich Raeder, Baldur von Schirach, Fritz Sauckel, Alfred Jodl, Martin Bormann, Franz von Papen, Arthur Seyss-Inquart, Albert Speer, Constantin von Neurath and Hans Fritzsche, individually and as members of any of the groups or organizations next hereinafter named.

'II. The following are named as groups or organizations (since dissolved) which should be declared criminal by reason of their aims and the means used for the accomplishment thereof, and in connection with the conviction of such of the named defendants as were members thereof:

Die Reichsregierung (Reich Cabinet); Das Korps der Politischen Leiter der Nationalsozialistischen Deutschen Arbeiterpartei (Leadership Corps of the Nazi Party); Die Schutzstaffeln der Nationalsozialistischen Arbeiterpartei (commonly known as the "SS") and including the Sicherdienst (commonly known as the "SD"); Die Geheime Staatspolizei (Secret State Police, commonly known as the "Gestapo"); Die Sturmabteilungen der NSDAP (commonly known as the "SA") and the General Staff and the High Command of the German Armed Forces. The identity and membership of the groups or organizations referred to in the foregoing titles are hereinafter ... more particularly defined.'[27]

The Indictment then set out in detail the crimes of which the defendants were accused under the following headings:

Count One: The Common Plan or Conspiracy
Count Two: Crimes against Peace
Count Three: War Crimes
Count Four: Crimes against Humanity
Appendix A: Statement of Individual Responsibility for Crimes set out in Counts One, Two, Three and Four
Appendix B: Statement of Criminality of Groups or Organizations
Appendix C: Charges and Particulars of Violations of International Treaties, Agreements and Assurances caused by the Defendants in the course of Planning, Preparing and Initiating the Wars

The text of the Indictment, running to some 25,000 words, has a ring both of sober fact and unreality, despite the atrocities described in it. The crimes enumerated, often in over-emotional phraseology, are so incredible, so monstrous, that they read like scenes from a horror film. The facts are so appalling that the occasional ridiculous statement by the prosecution strikes one merely as an admittedly effective but unimportant embellishment. To say that mere supposition carried any weight in this catalogue of crime is pure fiction. What difference would it have made, for instance, if, as the Indictment maintained, Hitler had actually forged Hindenburg's will and testament to suit his own purposes or if – as a prosecution rumour equally maintained – he had threatened to hit Chamberlain in the stomach in front of press photographers at some meeting?

In the courtroom all eyes were on the defendants, everyone trying to deduce from their attitude what each one of them might have had to do with all this crime. Some of them tried to parade their feelings, but the fact remained that for them this day was almost as momentous as 1 October 1946, the day on which they heard the sentences carrying some dozen of them to the gallows.

One of them, Wilhelm Frick, who had a shrewd idea of what the trial would bring to him, was reading the Indictment intently. Papen, on the other hand, seemed more interested in following the various translations through his earphones. Göring, occupying the position of the Führer's regent so to speak, lounged against the corner of the dock. Sometimes he folded his arms and acted as though he was only vaguely concerned in all this. He still did not believe that it would end on the gallows. Joachim von Ribbentrop, on the other hand, listened intently and slumped in his seat when the Soviet prosecutor read out the details implicating him, Hitler's last Foreign Minister, in the crimes under Counts Three and Four. Wilhelm Keitel sat there straight-backed, the Prussian Field Marshal to the last, his face totally impassive.

Rudolf Hess, the former Führer's Deputy, was staring into space; his mind seemed to be elsewhere; he looked waxen and lifeless. Defence counsel and his co-defendants thought him mentally sick. On 7 November his attorney had requested the International Court in writing for a judicial opinion as to whether Hess was mentally responsible and fit to stand trial.[28] Dr Rohrscheidt's memorandum stated that Hess was 'not in a position to give ... any information whatsoever regarding the crimes imputed to him in the Indictment.'[29] He himself admitted that he had 'completely lost his memory since a long period of time'; his attitude was 'the reverse of every natural reaction of any other defendant'.[30] It was therefore right and just, Dr Rohrscheidt maintained, that Hess be subjected to expert examination; the panel should include '*several* experts to be appointed by the Defense' from the medical faculties of the Universities of Zurich and Lausanne.[31] On 24 November Lord Justice Lawrence, President of the IMT, informed the defence that 'This application is denied.'[32] Opinions from countries other than the four victor Powers were not acceptable to the International Military Tribunal.

On 14 November Hess had to submit, at times much against his will, to examination by medical experts from the Soviet and British delegations and on 15 November to examination by French experts. On 15 and 19 November further neurological and psychological examinations were conducted by psychiatrists from Paris, Montreal and New York.[33] Hess was adjudged to be 'not insane in the strict sense'.[34] This meant that henceforth he had to take part in the proceedings. On the day of the reading of the Indictment, however, he was allowed back into his cell ahead of time. Violent stomach pains made it impossible for him to be present in court throughout the reading.

On 8 November, the day after Dr Rohrscheidt's application, Jackson and Amen, the American prosecutors, had conducted a test of their own on Hess. They had had him brought into a projection room, handcuffed to two US soldiers, and shown him a film of the 1934 Party Rally with him as one of the leading figures alongside Hitler and Göring. 'I can't remember it,' he maintained and capped his play-acting by saying: 'I must have been there because I have just seen that I was in the film, but I can't remember it.'[35]

Thirty years after the trial Florence R. Miale, the American psychologist, and Michael Selzer, the historian, from City University, New York, evaluated the original notes kept by Dr Gustav M. Gilbert, the US prison psychologist, whose task had been to observe and test the major war criminals in Nuremberg from November 1945 to October 1946. In 1975, after analysing Gilbert's material,[36] they certified that at the time of the trial Hess's personality was severely reduced and disturbed. The answer to the question which was wrong – Miale and Selzer's evaluation methods or the sentencing of Hess – is definitely in the IMT's favour. The concrete proven facts, of which Miale and Selzer have frequently failed to take account in their naïve and somewhat crude psychological disquisition, indicate that in Nuremberg, despite symptoms of paranoia and repeated periods of loss of memory, Hess was perfectly 'normal'.

In 1976 Eugene K. Bird, the American ex-Commandant of Spandau prison, who had had Hess under observation for two decades in Spandau and had talked to him frequently, stated that he considered Hess 'absolutely normal'. In his view Hess had merely been trying to throw dust in the eyes of the court in Nuremberg – where he still thought that the Western Allies would shortly instal him as head of government in the occupied Western zones.[37]

Miale and Selzer are prejudiced, judging the personality of the man who was tested at Nuremberg but whom they only 'knew' from biographies, in the light of such hallucinations. In almost every word written by Gilbert they look for a typical Freudian false conclusion, although a year after the execution of the major war criminals Gilbert had given a warning in his *Nuremberg Diary*[38] against over-estimation of the results of his tests. The fact that, as a result of prejudice, the psychological diagnoses prepared by these two inadequately informed authors describe the major defendants as psychopathic criminals in every case does not, nevertheless, render certain aspects of their personality analyses superfluous.[39] Gilbert was quick to recognize the questionable nature of his conclusions. His colleague Douglas M. Kelley, a psychiatrist who had equally been able to test the major Nuremberg defendants,[40] committed suicide on New Year's Eve, 1957 – with a cyanide capsule which he said he had found on Hermann Göring in Nuremberg.[41]

On 21 November 1945, the first day on which the accused were called upon to speak in court, the Tribunal had initially to clear up an ambiguity typical of the defence's uncertainty at the outset of the trial. Dr Rudolf Dix, Hjalmar Schacht's defence counsel, complained of inadequate contact between the defendants and their counsel and Dr Thoma, Rosenberg's counsel, asked how the accused were to answer the first question to be put to them by the President.* The record of the opening of the session and the exchange of questions and answers reads as follows:

The President : A motion has been filed with the Tribunal and the Tribunal has given it consideration, and insofar as it may be a plea to the jurisdiction of the Tribunal, it conflicts with Article 3 of the Charter and will not be entertained. Insofar as it may contain other arguments which may be open to the defendants, they may be heard at a later stage.

And now, in accordance with Article 24 of the Charter, which provides that, after the Indictment has been read in court, the defendants shall be called upon to plead guilty or not guilty, I now direct the defendants to plead guilty or not guilty.

Dr Dix : May I speak to Your Lordship for just a moment?

The President : You may not speak to me in support of the motion with which I have just dealt on behalf of the Tribunal. I have told you that so far as that motion is a plea to the jurisdiction of the Tribunal, it conflicts with Article 3 of the Charter and will not be entertained. Insofar as it contains or may contain arguments which may be open to the defendants, those arguments may be heard hereafter.

Dr Dix : I do not wish to speak on the subject of a motion. As speaker for the defense I should like to broach a technical question and voice a question to this effect on behalf of the Defense. May I do so?

The President : Yes.

Dr Dix : The Defense Counsel were forbidden to talk to the defendants this morning. It is absolutely necessary that the Defense Counsel should be able to speak to the defendants before the session. It often happens that after the session one cannot reach one's client at night. It is quite possible that counsel may have prepared something overnight which he wishes to discuss with the defendant before the session. According to our experience it is always permissible for the Defense Counsel to speak to the defendant before the session. The question of conferring between Defense Counsel and

* Lord Justice Lawrence.

clients during sessions could be dealt with at a later date. At present I request, on behalf of the entire Defense, that we be allowed to confer with our clients in the courtroom, into which they are usually brought at a very early hour. Otherwise we shall not be in a position to conduct the defense in an efficient and appropriate manner.

The President: I am afraid that you cannot consult with your clients in the courtroom except by written communication. When you are out of the courtroom, security regulations can be carried out and, so far as those security regulations go, you have full opportunity to consult with your clients. In the courtroom we must confine you to written communications to your clients. At the end of each day's sitting, you will have full opportunity to consult with them in private.

Dr Dix: I shall discuss this with my colleagues of the Defense and we should like if possible to return to this question.

Dr Thoma: May I have the floor?

The President: Will you state your name please.

Dr Thoma: Dr Ralph Thoma. I represent the Defendant Rosenberg. Yesterday my client gave me a statement as regards the question of guilt or innocence. I took this statement and promised him to talk with him about it. Neither last night nor this morning have I had an opportunity to talk with him; and consequently neither I nor my client are in a position to make a statement today as to whether he is guilty or not guilty. I therefore request that the proceedings be interrupted so that I may speak with my client.

The President: Dr Thoma, the Tribunal will be prepared to adjourn for fifteen minutes in order that you may have an opportunity of consulting with your client.

Dr Thoma: Thank you. I should like to make another statement. Some of my colleagues have just told me that they are in the same position as I, particularly Dr Sauter.

The President: I meant that all defendants' Counsel should have an opportunity of consulting their clients; but I would point out to the defendants' Counsel that they have had several weeks' preparation for this Trial, and that they must have anticipated that the provisions of Article 24 would be followed. But now we will adjourn for fifteen minutes in which all of you may consult with your clients.[42]

Dr Thoma then objected that the defence had been told only two days before that the defendants would have to answer the question whether they were guilty or not guilty solely with 'Yes' or 'No'. To this the President replied: 'The question will have to be answered in the words of Article 24 of the Charter ...: "The Tribunal shall ask each defendant whether he pleads guilty or not guilty." That is what they have got to do at this stage. Of course the defendants will have a full opportunity themselves, if they are called as witnesses, and by their counsel, to make their defense fully at a later stage.'[43]

After the adjournment came the moment for which, depending on their temperament and mental state, the defendants had prepared themselves – their confrontation with the court. For the first time they took the floor; for the first time they had to give a terse, pregnant reply to the question to which the court gave the final answer 273 days later, on 1 October 1946. The President raised the curtain on the scene for which journalists from every sovereign country had been waiting for months, declaring: ' I will now call upon the defendants to plead guilty or not guilty to the charges against them. They will proceed in turn to a point in the dock opposite to the microphone.'[44]

It should here be explained that every participant in the trial could use a simultaneous interpretation system provided free of charge by IBM; this enabled him to hear what was being said (sometimes about a sentence behind, often simplified and on occasions even distorted) in the language he wished through a set of earphones; on the dial No. 1 gave the language actually being used, No. 2 gave English, No. 3 Russian, No. 4 French and No. 5 German.

Göring was once more reading his notes; Keitel was talking to Rosenberg; Hess was gazing about, apparently not even interested. The President then called upon Göring, who rose, went to the microphone and, notes in hand, began to address the court. 'Before I answer the question of the Tribunal,' he began, 'whether or not I am guilty ...'

He got no further. The President, who had no intention of allowing the court to become a propaganda platform for the accused, interrupted him with the firm statement: 'I informed the court that defendants were not entitled to make a statement. You must plead guilty or not guilty.'[45]

Göring, who was addressed only by christian name and surname like all the other defendants, answered tersely: ' I declare myself in the sense of the Indictment not guilty.'

The record of the remainder of this ' ceremony ' is as follows:

The President: Rudolf Hess.
Rudolf Hess: No.
The President: That will be entered as a plea of not guilty (*laughter*).
The President: If there is any disturbance in court, those who make it will have to leave the court. Joachim von Ribbentrop.
Joachim von Ribbentrop: I declare myself in the sense of the Indictment not guilty.
The President: Wilhelm Keitel.
Wilhelm Keitel: I declare myself not guilty.
The President: In the absence of Ernst Kaltenbrunner, the trial will proceed against him, but he will have an opportunity of pleading when he is sufficiently well to be brought back into court. Alfred Rosenberg.
Alfred Rosenberg: I declare myself in the sense of the Indictment not guilty.
The President: Hans Frank.

Hans Frank: I declare myself not guilty.
The President: Wilhelm Frick.
Wilhelm Frick: Not guilty.
The President: Julius Streicher.
Julius Streicher: Not guilty.
The President: Walter Funk.
Walter Funk: I declare myself not guilty.
The President: Hjalmar Schacht.
Hjalmar Schacht: I am not guilty in any respect.
The President: Karl Dönitz.
Karl Dönitz: Not guilty.
The President: Erich Raeder.
Erich Raeder: I declare myself not guilty.
The President: Baldur von Schirach.
Baldur von Schirach: I declare myself in the sense of the Indictment not guilty.
The President: Fritz Sauckel.
Fritz Sauckel: I declare myself in the sense of the Indictment, before God and the world and particularly before my people, not guilty.
The President: Alfred Jodl.
Alfred Jodl: Not guilty. For what I have done or had to do, I have a pure conscience before God, before history and my people.
The President: Franz von Papen.
Franz von Papen: I declare myself in no way guilty.
The President: Arthur Seyss-Inquart.
Arthur Seyss-Inquart: I declare myself not guilty.
The President: Albert Speer.
Albert Speer: Not guilty.
The President: Constantin von Neurath.
Constantin von Neurath: I answer the question in the negative.
The President: Hans Fritzsche.
Hans Fritzsche: As regards this Indictment not guilty.

[At this point Defendant Göring stood up in the prisoner's dock and attempted to address the Tribunal.]

The President: You are not entitled to address the Tribunal except through your counsel at the present time.

I will now call upon the Chief Prosecutor for the United States of America.[46]

6

Vengeance or Justice

This scene was watched by people all over the world in their news films. Just at this time a lively discussion was going on in Great Britain as to how the Americans could have been 'taken by surprise' at Pearl Harbor on 7 December 1941 and allowed their fleet to suffer such heavy casualties when they had known of Japanese aggressive intentions for six months. The opinion was openly expressed that the USA had provoked this attack and accepted the loss of ships and crews in order to cause Hitler to declare war upon them, which he did on 11 December. Although he had encouraged the Japanese to take active military steps against the USA,[1] Hitler had been taken aback by the news – in contrast to the American leaders. When given it in his headquarters on 8 December, he had said: 'Now the British will lose Singapore. That was never my intention. We are fighting the wrong people. We ought to have the Anglo-American powers for our allies, but force of circumstances has compelled us to make an error of worldwide importance historically.'[2]

Eisenhower's remark, much-quoted at the time, that were he not a believer in world peace he would jump out of his aeroplane over the sea,[3] expressed what the whole world would have liked to believe during the Nuremberg Trial following a frightful war. Nuremberg was supposed to be a spectacular fresh start, and with the words of Jackson, the US Chief Prosecutor, that the IMT had no wish to annihilate Germany or exact vengeance but to hand over the guilty to the law and set new international standards for the future, hopes rose.

Ever since the start of preparations for the IMT Justice Jackson had been pressing for a trial based on documentary evidence.[4] This is what the defendants and their counsel heard him say on 21 November 1945:

'The privilege of opening the first trial in history for crimes against the peace of the world imposes a grave responsibility. The wrongs which we seek to condemn and punish have been so calculated, so malignant and so devastating, that civilization cannot tolerate their being ignored, because it cannot survive their being repeated. That four great nations flushed with victory and stung with injury stay the hand of vengeance and voluntarily submit their captive enemies to the judgement of the law is one of the most significant tributes that Power has ever paid to Reason.

'This Tribunal, while it is novel and experimental, is not the product of abstract speculations nor is it created to vindicate legalistic theories.

This inquest represents the practical effort of four of the most mighty of nations, with the support of seventeen more, to utilize international law to meet the greatest menace of our times – aggressive war. The common sense of mankind demands that law shall not stop with the punishment of petty crimes by little people. It must also reach men who possess themselves of great power and make deliberate and concerted use of it to set in motion evils which leave no home in the world untouched. It is a cause of that magnitude that the United Nations will lay before Your Honors.

'In the prisoners' dock sit twenty-odd broken men. Reproached by the humiliation of those they have led almost as bitterly as by the desolation of those they have attacked, their personal capacity for evil is forever past. It is hard now to perceive in these men as captives the power by which as Nazi leaders they once dominated much of the world and terrified most of it. Merely as individuals their fate is of little consequence to the world.

'What makes this inquest significant is that these prisoners represent sinister influences that will lurk in the world long after their bodies have returned to dust. We will show them to be living symbols of racial hatreds, of terrorism and violence, and of the arrogance and cruelty of power. They are symbols of fierce nationalisms and of militarism, of intrigue and war-making which have embroiled Europe generation after generation, crushing its manhood, destroying its homes and impoverishing its life. They have so identified themselves with the philosophies they have conceived and with the forces they directed that any tenderness to them is a victory and an encouragement to all the evils which are attached to their names. Civilization can afford no compromise with the social forces which would gain renewed strength if we deal ambiguously or indecisively with the men in whom those forces now precariously survive.

'What these men stand for we will patiently and temperately disclose. We will give you undeniable proofs of incredible events. The catalog of crimes will omit nothing that could be conceived by a pathological pride, cruelty and lust for power. These men created in Germany, under the "Führerprinzip", a National-Socialist despotism equalled only by the dynasties of the ancient East. They took from the German people all those dignities and freedoms that we hold natural and inalienable rights in every human being. The people were compensated by inflaming and gratifying hatreds towards those who were marked as "scapegoats". Against their opponents, including Jews, Catholics and free labor, the Nazis directed such a campaign of arrogance, brutality and annihilation as the world has not witnessed since the pre-Christian ages. They excited the German ambition to be a "master race", which of course implies serfdom for others. They led their people on a mad gamble for domination. They diverted social energies and resources to the creation of what they thought to be an invincible war machine. They overran their neighbors. To sustain the "master race" in its war-making, they enslaved millions of human beings and brought them into Germany, where these hapless creatures now wander as "displaced persons". At length bestiality and bad faith reached such excess that they aroused the sleeping strength of imperiled Civilization. Its united efforts have ground the German war machine to fragments. But the struggle has left Europe a liberated yet prostrate land where a demoralized society struggles to survive. These are the fruits of the sinister forces that sit with these defendants in the prisoners' dock.

'In justice to the nations and men associated in this prosecution, I must remind you of certain difficulties which may leave their mark on this case. Never before in legal history has an effort been made to bring within the scope of a single litigation the developments of a decade, covering a whole continent, and involving a score of nations, countless individuals and innumerable events. Despite the magnitude of the task the world has demanded immediate action. This demand has had to be met, though perhaps at the cost of finished craftsmanship. In my country established courts, following familiar procedures, applying well-thumbed precedents and dealing with the legal consequences of local and limited events, seldom commence a trial within a year of the event in litigation. Yet less than eight months ago today the courtroom in which you sit was an enemy fortress in the hands of German SS troops. Less than eight months ago nearly all our witnesses and documents were in enemy hands. The law had not been codified, no procedures had been established, no tribunal was in existence, no usable courthouse stood here, none of the hundreds of tons of official German documents had been examined, no prosecuting staff had been assembled, nearly all of the present defendants were at large and the four prosecuting powers had not yet joined in common cause to try them. I should be the last to deny that the case may well suffer from incomplete researches and quite likely will not be the example of professional work which any of the prosecuting nations would normally wish to sponsor. It is, however, a completely adequate case to the judgement we shall ask you to render, and its full development we shall be obliged to leave to historians.

'Before I discuss particulars of evidence, some general considerations which may affect the credit of this trial in the eyes of the world should be candidly faced. There is a dramatic disparity between the circumstances of the accusers and of the accused that might discredit our work if we should falter, in even minor matters, in being fair and temperate.

'Unfortunately the nature of these crimes is such that both prosecution and judgement must be by victor nations over vanquished foes. The worldwide scope of the aggressions carried out by these men has left but few real neutrals. Either the victors must judge the vanquished or we must leave the defeated to judge themselves. After the First World War we learned the futility of the latter course. The former high station of these defendants, the notoriety of their acts and the adaptability of their conduct to provoke retaliation make it hard to distinguish between the demand for a just and measured retribution and the unthinking cry for vengeance which arises from the anguish of war. It is our task, so far as humanly possible, to draw the line between the two. We must never forget that the record on which we judge these defendants today is the record on which history will judge us tomorrow. To pass these defendants a poisoned chalice is to put it to our own lips as well. We must summon such detachment and intellectual integrity to our task that this Trial will commend itself to posterity as fulfilling humanity's aspirations to do justice.

'At the very outset let us dispose of the contention that to put these men to trial is to do them an injustice entitling them to some special consideration. These defendants may be hard pressed but they are not ill used. Let us see what alternative they would have to being tried.

'More than a majority of these prisoners surrendered to or were tracked down by the forces of the United States. Could they expect us to make American custody a shelter for our enemies against the just wrath of our Allies? Did we spend American lives to capture them only to save them from punishment? Under the principles of the Moscow Declaration, those suspected war criminals who are not to be tried internationally must be turned over to individual governments for trial at the scene of their outrages. Many less responsible and less culpable American-held prisoners have been and will continue to be turned over to other United Nations for local trial. If these defendants should succeed, for any reason, in escaping the condemnation of this Tribunal, or if they obstruct or abort this trial, those who are American-held prisoners will be delivered up to our continental Allies. For these defendants, however, we have set up an International Tribunal and have undertaken the burden of participating in a complicated effort to give them fair and dispassionate hearings. That is the best-known protection to any man with a defense worthy of being heard.

'If these men are the first war leaders of a defeated nation to be prosecuted in the name of the law, they are also the first to be given a chance to plead for their lives in the name of the law. Realistically, the Charter of this Tribunal, which gives them a hearing, is also the source of their only hope. It may be that these men of troubled conscience, whose only wish is that the world forget them, do not regard a trial as a favor. But they do have a fair opportunity to defend themselves – a favor which these men, when in power, rarely extended to their fellow countrymen. Despite the fact that public opinion already condemns their acts, we agree that here they must be given a presumption of innocence and we accept the burden of proving criminal acts and the responsibility of these defendants for their commission.

'When I say that we do not ask for convictions unless we prove crime, I do not mean mere technical or incidental transgression of international conventions. We charge on planned and intended conduct that involves moral as well as legal wrong. And we do not mean conduct that is a natural and human, even if illegal, cutting of corners, such as many of us might well have committed had we been in the defendants' positions. It is not because they yielded to the normal frailties of human beings that we accuse them. It is their abnormal and inhuman conduct which brings them to this bar.

'We will not ask you to convict these men on the testimony of their foes. There is no count in the Indictment that cannot be proved by books and records. The Germans were always meticulous record keepers, and these defendants had their share of the Teutonic passion for thoroughness in putting things on paper. Nor were they without vanity. They arranged frequently to be photographed in action. We will show you their own films. You will see their own conduct and hear their own voices as these defendants re-enact for you, from the screen, some of the events in the course of the conspiracy.

'We would also make clear that we have no purpose to incriminate the whole German people. We know that the Nazi Party was not put in power by a majority of the German vote. We know that it came to power by an evil alliance[5] between the most extreme of the Nazi revolutionists, the most unrestrained of the German reactionaries and the most aggressive of the German militarists. If the German populace had willingly accepted the Nazi program, no Storm-troopers would have been needed in the early days of the Party and there would have been no need for concentration camps or the Gestapo, both of which institutions were inaugurated as soon as the Nazis gained control of the German State. Only after these lawless innovations proved successful at home were they taken abroad.

'The German people should know by now that the people of the United States hold them in no fear and in no hate. It is true that the Germans have taught us the horrors of modern warfare, but the ruin that lies from the Rhine to the Danube shows that we, like our Allies, have not been dull pupils. If we are not awed by German fortitude and proficiency in war, and if we are not persuaded of their political maturity, we do respect their skill in the arts of peace, their technical competence, and the sober, industrious and self-disciplined character of the masses of the German people. In 1933 we saw the German people recovering in the commercial, industrial and artistic world after the set-back of the last war. We beheld their progress neither with envy nor malice. The Nazi regime interrupted this advance. The recoil of the Nazi aggression has left Germany in ruins. The Nazi readiness to pledge the German word without hesitation and to break it without shame has fastened upon German diplomacy a reputation for duplicity that will handicap it for years. Nazi arrogance has made the boast of the "master race" a taunt that will be thrown at Germans the world over for generations. The Nazi nightmare has given the German name a new and sinister significance throughout the world which will retard Germany a century. The German, no less than the non-German world, has accounts to settle with these defendants.

'The fact of the war and the course of the war, which is the central theme of our case, is history. From 1 September 1939, when the German armies crossed the Polish frontier, until September 1942, when they met epic resistance at Stalingrad, German arms seemed invincible. Denmark and Norway, the Netherlands and France, Belgium and Luxemburg, the Balkans and Africa, Poland and the Baltic States, and parts of Russia, all had been overrun and conquered by swift, powerful, well-aimed blows. That attack on the peace of the world is the crime against international society which brings into international cognizance crimes in its aid and preparation which might otherwise be only internal concerns. It was aggressive war, which the nations of the world had renounced. It was war in violation of treaties, by which the peace of the world was sought to be safe-guarded.

'This war did not just happen – it was planned and prepared for over a long period of time and with no small skill and cunning. The world has perhaps never seen such a concentration and stimulation of the energies of any people as that which enabled Germany, twenty years after it was defeated, disarmed and dismembered, to come so near carrying out its plan to dominate Europe. Whatever we may say of those who were the authors of this war, they did achieve a stupendous work in organization, and our first task is to examine the means by which these defendants and their fellow conspirators prepared and incited Germany to go to war.

'In general our case will disclose these defendants all uniting at some time with the Nazi Party in a plan which they well knew could be accomplished only by an outbreak of war in Europe. Their seizure of the German State, their subjugation of the German people, their terrorism and extermination of dissident elements, their planning and waging of war, their calculated and planned ruthlessness in the conduct of warfare, their deliberate and planned criminality toward conquered peoples – all these are ends for which they acted in concert; and all these are phases of the conspiracy, a conspiracy which reached one goal only to set out for another and more ambitious one. We shall also trace for you the intricate web of organizations which these men formed and utilized to accomplish these ends. We will show how the entire structure of offices and officials was dedicated to the criminal purposes and committed to the use of the criminal methods planned by these defendants and their co-conspirators, many of whom war and suicide have put beyond reach.

'It is my purpose to open the case, particularly under Count One of the Indictment, and to deal with the Common Plan or Conspiracy to achieve ends possible only by resort to Crimes against Peace, War Crimes and Crimes against Humanity. My emphasis will not be on individual barbarities and perversions which may have occurred independently of any central plan. One of the dangers ever present is that this trial may be protracted by details of particular wrongs and that we will become lost in a " Wilderness of single instances". Nor will I now dwell on the activity of individual defendants except as it may contribute to exposition of the common plan.

'The case as presented by the United States will be concerned with the brains and authority back of all the crimes. These defendants were men of a station and rank which does not soil its own hands with blood. They were men who knew how to use lesser folk as tools. We want to reach the planners and designers, the inciters and leaders, without whose evil architecture the world would not have been for so long scourged with the violence and lawlessness, and wracked with the agonies and convulsions of this terrible war.'[6]

For the accused the initial tension was over. Now they knew, or at least suspected, what awaited them. With the presentation of the case and the opening of proceedings the hopes even of those who had thought that the IMT would be a farce and that the trial would be quickly over were gone.[7] Göring, for instance, had initially maintained that the worst would not happen to any of them, but he now reckoned that he would probably be hanged,[8] though he secretly harboured the hope that the Allies would be unable to agree among themselves.[9] Some of the defendants were unable to adjust to their unaccustomed treatment resulting in sleepless or very disturbed nights with occasional outbreaks of panic and screaming; any who became really ill were taken for treatment to a former SS hospital in Fürth near Nuremberg.[10] The German prison doctor records that he was quite frequently called to the defendants' cells at night to calm them down and ask the guards on the cell doors to leave them in peace as far as possible.[11]

Rudolf Hess, who had been brought to Nuremberg from England, suffered most. On his first encounter with Hess Dr Pflücker noted: 'I was summoned to him several times during the first night because he was having spasms. Each time I saw him he was lying in bed with his features distorted and his arms moving spasmodically. During a spasm his whole body was quivering. During a pause in the spasms I examined the patient and found nothing in the region of the stomach or gall bladder to account for the violent colic pains of which Hess complained. Other details given by Hess gave no real indication of serious illness. In the early days these spasms occurred very frequently, as often as six to eight times a day, so that I had plenty of opportunity to observe them. I could not diagnose them as anything other than a nervous disorder. The only possible psychotherapy was naturally ineffective in prison since it is impossible to produce any psychological effect under the constraints of imprisonment with their resultant resistance reaction. The American doctors agreed with my opinion and left it to me to deal with the problem.'[12]

Hermann Göring too had major problems in prison at first. Dr Pflücker recalls: 'When I visited him for the first time his morning porridge was still untouched. When I asked him why he was not eating, he replied that a person of culture could not eat with the toilet directly under his nose ... In Göring's case the agitation of the first days in Nuremberg – the defendants had to clean their cells themselves – led to attacks of tachycardia with a very high pulse rate; they eventually became so frequent that his movement had to be restricted. I frequently observed that these attacks were particularly severe on Fridays, the regulation day for cell-cleaning, and eventually an instruction was issued that Göring's cell be cleaned by an employee – a victory of which Göring was very proud.'[13]

Göring, however, soon accommodated himself to life in prison, particularly since he was now in perfect health, having been forced to follow a drug withdrawal course in Mondorf. Again the prison doctor recalls: 'One evening in Mondorf a police officer appeared in my office and asked for the patient who was provided with pills. By good luck I took him to Göring's room and it emerged that each evening Göring was given a dose of paracodin of which he had brought a large quantity with him ... After a few days Sergeant Bock was made responsible for the pill distribution instead of an officer; then, as a result of the rapid reduction in quantity and the resulting unfavourable reaction on the part of Göring, the pills were handed over to me. I discussed the problem at length with Göring and got him to give me his medical history in so far as this malady was concerned. I established that Göring had twice taken a withdrawal course but had abandoned it on each occasion allegedly for duty reasons. It was clear to me that a man in the Reich Marshal's powerful position had never accepted the authority of the doctors or followed their instructions when the critical stage of the cure, with its unpleasant consequences, had been reached. He had simply evaded the unpleasantness by breaking off the cure ... Though Göring had taken large doses of paracodin, his case could not be described as serious and withdrawal ... was completely smooth. When Göring complained of intolerable nervous pains, he was given a sleeping pill.'[14]

Keitel, Jodl, von Neurath, von Schirach and Speer accommodated themselves comparatively quickly and successfully to the hardships and irritations of prison life – unlike Sauckel and Streicher.[15] Both defendants and witnesses began to amass sleeping pills – some of them for 'the extreme case' – so that Dr Pflücker was ultimately compelled to control the issue and consumption of them.[16] As a result 'in no case was there any sleeping drug poisoning from pills issued in the prison'.[17] Rudolf Hess and Julius Streicher, who were initially ostentatiously obstinate, eventually reluctantly complied with prison discipline. SS-Obergruppenführer Wolff, who had capitulated on his own authority in Upper Italy, steadfastly refused to take nourishment until he had once more been allowed to wear his SS uniform with all his decorations; astonishingly enough this was permitted.[18]

7

The Evidence

On 22 November 1945 Robert G. Storey, an American high-school teacher and one of the US 'Executive Trial Counsel', described the process of collection of evidence for the American prosecuting authorities and its preparation for production at the trial. The Colonel told the court:

'As the United States Army advanced into German territory, there were attached to each Army and subordinate organization specialized military personnel whose duties were to capture and preserve enemy information in the form of documents, records, reports and other files. The Germans kept accurate and voluminous records. They were found in Army headquarters, Government buildings and elsewhere.* During the later stages of the war, particularly, such documents were found in salt mines, buried in the ground, behind false walls and many other places believed secure by the Germans. For example, the personal correspondence and diaries of the Defendant Rosenberg, including his Nazi correspondence, were found behind a false wall in an old castle in eastern Bavaria. The records of the OKL or Luftwaffe, of which the Defendant Göring was Commander-in-Chief – equivalent to the records of the Headquarters of the Air Staff of the United States Army Air Forces – were found in various places in the Bavarian Alps. Most of such Luftwaffe records were assembled and processed by the Army at Berchtesgaden.

'When the Army first captured documents and records, they immediately placed the materials under guard and later assembled them in temporary document centers. Many times the records were so voluminous that they were hauled by fleets by Army trucks to document centers. Finally, as the territory seized was made secure, Army zones were established and each Army established a fixed document center to which were transported the assembled documents and records. Later this material was indexed and cataloged, which was a slow process.

'Beginning last June, Mr Justice Jackson requested me to direct the assembling of documentary evidence on the continent for the United States case. Field teams for our office were organized under the direction of Major William H. Coogan, who established United States liaison officers at the

* Storey's phrase 'and elsewhere' clearly referred to the fact that houses and dwellings of suspects, defendants and persons denounced had been searched by these US specialists, many owners or occupiers arrested if still at liberty and all written or graphic material considered of importance confiscated. See pp. 98ff below.

main Army document centers. Such officers were directed to screen and analyze the mass of captured documents, and select those having evidentiary value for our case. Literally hundreds of tons of enemy documents and records were screened and examined[1] and those selected were forwarded to Nuremberg for processing. I now offer in evidence an affidavit by Major Coogan, dated 19 November 1945, attached hereto, describing the method of procedure, capture, screening and delivery of such documents to Nuremberg.

'At this time, if Your Honors please ... I believe it wise to read at least substantial portions of this affidavit ...[2]

' "I, Major William H. Coogan, o-455814, QMC, a commissioned officer of the United States of America, do hereby certify as follows:

' "1. The United States Chief Counsel in July 1945 charged the Field Branch of the Documentation Division with the responsibility of collecting, evaluating and assembling documentary evidence in the European Theater for use in the prosecution of the major Axis War Criminals before the International Military Tribunal. I was appointed Chief of the Field Branch on 20 July 1945. I am now Chief of the Documentation Division, Office of United States Chief of Counsel.

' "2. I ... am a practicing attorney by profession. Based on my experience as an attorney and as a United States Army officer, I am familiar with the operation of the United States Army in connection with seizing and processing captured enemy documents. In my capacity as Chief of the Documentation Division ... I am familiar with and have supervised the processing, filing, translating and photostating of all documentary evidence for the United States Chief of Counsel."

'I skip to paragraph 4.

' "4. The Field Branch of the Documentation Division was staffed by personnel thoroughly conversant with the German language. Their task was to search for and select captured enemy documents in the European Theater which disclosed information relating to the prosecution of the major Axis war criminals ... When the documents were located, my representatives made a record of the circumstances under which they were found and all information available concerning their authenticity was recorded ...

' "5. After receipt of these documents they were duly recorded and indexed. After this operation, they were delivered to the Screening and Analysis Branch of the Documentation Division ... which Branch re-examined the documents in order to finally determine whether or not they should be retained as evidence for the prosecutors. This final screening was done by German-speaking analysts ... When the document passed the screeners, it was then transmitted to the Document Room of the Office of United States Chief of Counsel, with a covering sheet prepared by the screeners showing the title or nature of the document, the personalities involved and its importance. In the Document Room, a trial identification number was given to each document and to each group of documents in cases where it was desirable for the sake of clarity to file several documents together.

' " 6. United States documents were given trial identification numbers . . . designated by the letters: "P S", "L", "R", "C" and "EC", indicating the means of acquisition of the documents. Within each series documents were listed numerically.

' " 7. After a document was so numbered, it was then sent to a German-speaking analyst who prepared a summary of the document with appropriate references to personalities involved . . . information as to the source of the document as indicated by the Field Branch, and the importance of the document to a particular phase of the case. Next the original document was returned to the Document Room and then checked out to the Photostating Department, where photostatic copies were made . . . One of the photostatic copies . . . was sent to the translators . . . leaving the original itself in the safe. A commissioned officer . . . is responsible for the documents in the safe. At all times when he is not present the safe is locked and a military guard is on duty outside the only door. If the officers preparing the certified translation, or one of the officers working on the briefs, found it necessary to examine the original document, this was done within the Document Room . . . The only exception to this strict rule has been where it has been occasionally necessary to present the original document to Defense Counsel for examination. In this case the document was entrusted to a responsible officer of the Prosecution staff.

' " 8. All original documents are now located in safes in the Document Room . . . until they are presented by the Prosecution to the court during the progress of this Trial.

' " 9. Some of the documents which will be offered in evidence by the United States were seized and processed by the British Army . . .

' " 10. Substantially the same system of acquiring documentary evidence was utilized by the British Army and the British War Crimes Executive as above set forth with respect to the United States Army and the Office of the United States Chief of Counsel.

' " 11. Therefore I certify in my official capacity as hereinabove stated, to the best of my knowledge and belief, that the documents captured in the British Zone of Operations and Occupation . . . have been authenticated, translated and processed in substantially the same manner as hereinabove set forth with respect to the operations of the United States Chief of Counsel.

' " 12. Finally I certify that all documentary evidence offered by the United States Chief Counsel, including those documents from British Army sources, are in the same condition as captured by the United States and British Armies; that they have been translated by competent and qualified translators; that all photostatic copies are true and correct copies of the originals and that they have been correctly filed, numbered and processed . . .

Signed: William H. Coogan, Major, QMC, 0–455814." '

Storey then continued:

'After the documents selected by the screening process outlined reached our office, they were again re-examined, re-screened and translated by expert US Army personnel...

'Finally more than 2,500 documents were selected[3] and filed here in this Court House ... They have been photographed, translated into English, filed, indexed and processed. The same general procedure was followed by the British War Crimes Executive with regard to documents captured by the British Army ...

'In order to present our case and to assist the Tribunal, we have prepared written briefs on each phase of our case which cite the documents by appropriate numbers. Legal propositions of the United States will also be presented in such briefs ... Accompanying each brief is a document book containing true copies in English of all documents referred to in this brief[*] ... Likewise copies in German have been, or will be, furnished to Defense Counsel at the time such documents are offered in evidence. Upon conclusion of the presentation of each phase or section of our case by counsel, the entire book of documents will be offered in evidence ... At the same time Lieutenant Barrett, who will sit right here all during the trial and who is on our staff, will hand to the Clerk of this Tribunal the original documents that may be offered in evidence in this form. It will have the seal of the Tribunal, will be Exhibit USA ...[4] and in turn Lieutenant Barrett will hand that original document to the Tribunal. In the same manner the document book will be passed ... to the clerk of the court, and these trial briefs for the assistance of the Tribunal will be made available to the court and to Defense Counsel. Likewise copies of documents actually introduced in evidence will be made available to the press.'[5]

So the prosecution had available documents and archives, the very existence of which was in many cases unknown to defence counsel. How complex the distinctions between documents were and how questionable their validity as evidence inevitably was on occasions is well illustrated by an extract from the cross-examination of Jodl by his defence counsel, Dr Exner, on 5 June 1946. The record is as follows:

Dr Exner: We now come to the Balkans. In your diary[6] ... on 19 March you made the following entry: 'The Balkans should and must remain quiet.' That is ... the entry of 19 March.[7] It says first: 'The Führer has returned beaming with joy and highly satisfied from the conference with the Duce. Complete agreement ... The Balkans should and must remain quiet.' What does that mean?

---

[*] The prosecution document books, separate for each trial, were arranged by specific aspects and subjects such as war of aggression, Auschwitz, extermination of Jews; they were compilations of individual documents 'brought in evidence' and were submitted to the court as 'exhibits' applicable in each case to the crimes of individual defendants. In all they comprised about 185,000 pages.

Jodl: Herr Professor, I must correct you. This is not my diary.

Dr Exner: Yes. Well then I must put in another question here. Your diary and your diaries are always being talked about. Explain just what this is – what we are dealing with here ...

Jodl: There is only one diary[8] ... which is from the year 1937 to 1938 and I used to make entries in it every evening.

Dr Exner: And now this diary[9] ... what was that?

Jodl: I kept no diary at all during the war, but, of course, I filled up dozens of small notebooks. When one of these notebooks was full I marked important passages in red on the margin, and my secretary copied them out later, as they might be important for writing the history of the war and for the official diary of the Armed Forces Operations Staff[10] ...

Dr Exner: Did you check what your secretary had compiled?

Jodl: No, I did not check it and never saw it again. It fell then into the hands of the Prosecution.

Dr Exner: Now there is still a third one which is always quoted here as a diary. That is the Diary of the Armed Forces Operations Staff.

The President: You said it fell into the hands of the Prosecution. Do you mean it was not one of the documents that you handed over to the Prosecution?

Jodl: No. I did not know at all where those extracts from my notebook had gone. The Prosecution captured it somewhere or other. The remainder are extracts, and partial extracts, from the official diary of the Armed Forces Operations Staff.

Dr Exner: And who kept this, the official Diary of the Armed Forces Operations Staff? Not you?

Jodl: No. It was always kept by a highly qualified expert of my own selection ... The final check was made by Dr Schramm, a professor at the Göttingen University.

Dr Exner: We shall hear him as a witness. Did you check the entries made in that official diary or did you not?

Jodl: I usually did not have the time; but if General Scherff read through it and discovered anything particular, he would draw my attention to it.[11]

In contrast to the defence the prosecution was able to obtain anything they thought necessary from anywhere in the world. They could provide documentary proof of numerous details and cross-connections about which the defence generally had no inkling, since, contrary to what one might have supposed from the statements of Storey and Coogan, the defence was generally allowed access only to incriminating material.[12] Defence counsel had no opportunity to make their own selection of exonerating material.

When they asked the prosecution for documents quoted, they had not infrequently 'disappeared'. Prosecution documents were made available to them only in an inadequate number of copies. They were often provided too late, in no sequence, untranslated and with parts of a series missing.[13] Documents asked for by the defence had invariably first to be submitted to the prosecution, which decided whether they should be translated; in certain definitely decisive cases this inevitably imposed considerable restrictions on the defence, since, under the Charter, only 'relevant' passages needed to be translated[14] and that only 'in general terms'.[15] Glaring mistranslations and distortions were frequent, leading to misunderstandings in court. The defence had hardly any influence on the decision as to which documents should be laid on the table. The work of defence counsel – most of whom had been appointed by[16] and were on the payroll[17] of the court – was complicated by the existence of forged documents; they were literally submerged in a flood of unaccustomed paper; they had to work in cramped conditions and were suddenly confronted with questions of which, owing to their totally inadequate facilities for orientating themselves, they frequently had not even hearsay knowledge.

Thousands of documents which seemed likely possibly to incriminate the Allies and exonerate the defendants suddenly disappeared. Since documents in Nuremberg were under the care of officers,[18] they could be removed from the safes only by officers, and they were under command of Colonel Burton C. Andrus, the Prison Commandant. At an early stage Karl Dönitz, the ex-Grand Admiral and Hitler's successor, began to suspect that Andrus had withdrawn documents from circulation and sent them to the United States.[19] Having had long experience as an officer of the rules and practices of the American military, after his release from Spandau he instituted a search for proof of this and it was eventually provided from Tahiti.[20]

There is much evidence that documents were confiscated, concealed from the defence or even stolen in 1945. An example is the case of Dr Otto Meissner,[21] Head of the Presidential Chancellery, who was held in US Army internment camps in Plattling, Hammelburg and elsewhere before being taken to Nuremberg to be prosecuted by Dr Kempner in the so-called 'Wilhelmstrasse Trial'. During this period American officers of the rank of Colonel[22] appeared on several occasions at his summer retreat in Neuhaus am Schliersee looking for documents which he might have had taken there from Schloss Bellevue, his official residence in Berlin.

His son, Dr Hans-Otto Meissner, says: 'Whether the Americans who arrived, among whom there was invariably an officer, really belonged to a search party for documents, as they alleged, or whether they merely pretended to belong to such a party for the purposes of looting, or whether they came from a combination of both motives, it was not always possible to tell. In any case, in the end my parents' house had been almost completely emptied. Some of the ... files they took were used against my father by the prosecution in the Wilhelmstrasse Trial but they did not stop him being acquitted. Of all the documents "confiscated" in our house by the

Americans covering the twenty-five years of my father's appointment as Head of the Presidential Chancellery, however, none that might have served to exonerate him ever appeared.'[23]

The defence in Nuremberg found itself facing problems of this nature from the outset. Dr Fritz Sauter, Ribbentrop's defence counsel, for instance, declared:

'On 30 October the Defendant von Ribbentrop requested that his former secretary, Margareta Blank, at that time in the Remand Prison in Nuremberg, be placed at his disposal in order that he might dictate his reply to the Indictment as well as a description of the manner in which he performed his official duties in the last seven or eight years.

'On 11 November 1945 the Tribunal allowed this request. The Defendant von Ribbentrop was therefore able to dictate for a few hours, but this was stopped for reasons unknown to him. Neither has the Defendant von Ribbentrop had returned to him the shorthand notes or the typed transcript ...

'On 15 November Ribbentrop repeated his request regarding the witness Blank but up to the present she has not been placed at his disposal again ... The Defendant von Ribbentrop has repeatedly asked that some of his former colleagues, in particular Ambassador Gaus, Ambassador von Rintelen, Minister von Sonnleitner, Professor Fritz Berber and Under State Secretary Henke be brought to Nuremberg as witnesses and that he be permitted to speak to these witnesses in the presence of his counsel. This request had in part been refused by the court on 10 November. The remaining part has not yet been decided.

'It is quite impossible for the defendant ... to give a clear and exhaustive account of the entire foreign policy for the last seven or eight years if nothing is placed at his disposal except a pencil and a block of writing paper. Even the White Books of the Foreign Office, for which he has asked, could not be placed at his disposal. In view of the fact that the data concerning Germany's foreign policy during the last seven or eight years is so extensive, the defendant ... cannot possibly recall every single date, every event, every document *et cetera* unless his memory is refreshed by his being able to speak with his former colleagues ...

'It would not be very helpful to the investigation of historical truth in a field which interests not only this Court but also, to an even greater extent, the outside world if von Ribbentrop during his examination might have to state at every turn that he could no longer recollect these details.'[24]

The President of the court simply stated:

'The Tribunal has already intimated to defendant's counsel that all applications should, as far as practicable, be made in writing and they consider that the applications which have now been made orally should have been made in writing. They will consider the facts with reference to the applications in respect of the Defendant von Ribbentrop's secretary. The other applications as to witnesses and documents, which have been made in writing, have been considered or will be considered by the Tribunal.'[25]

The President had already on several occasions ignored the fact that Dr Sauter had submitted the applications to the court in writing.

Witnesses and assistants for the defence were on occasions thoroughly intimidated; not infrequently they were either forcibly kept away or alternatively permitted entry and then, via the control system or through confiscation of their statements, turned into witnesses for the prosecution. Oswald Pohl, who was not imprisoned until May 1946, was tied to a chair during his interrogation by American and British officials, was beaten unconscious, kicked and generally maltreated until he was prepared to incriminate Walter Funk in writing. Of nineteen witnesses nominated by Alfred Jodl only four actually addressed the court, for reasons of time. Karl Wolff, the SS General, who wished to testify on behalf of Ernst Kaltenbrunner, was straightaway sent to a lunatic asylum. But when the prosecution wanted witnesses or their statements in writing, they were available. If, however, it seemed that certain prosecution witnesses were unlikely to stand up to cross-examination by the defence, the prosecution and the court contented themselves with affidavits, of which several thousand were compiled during the course of the trial.

In order to restrict the use of this procedure and reduce the large number of unverifiable 'witnesses', on 28 November 1945 Dr Egon Kubuschok, Papen's defence counsel, disputed an affidavit by a witness named Messersmith which gravely incriminated some of the accused. In Kubuschok's view the witness could have been made available; he used the following arguments:

'An affidavit of a witness who is obtainable has just been turned over to the court. The content of the affidavit offers so many subjective opinions of the witness that it is imperative we hear the witness personally in this matter.

'I should like to take this occasion to ask that it be decided as a matter of principle whether that which a witness can testify from his own knowledge may, without further ado, be presented in the form of an affidavit; or whether if a witness is living and can be reached, the principle of oral proceedings should be applied, that is the witness should be heard directly.'[26]

The President did not comment but asked Alderman, the American Prosecutor, to reply to Kubuschok's objection. Initially it sounded as if Alderman was in agreement, since he began: 'I recognize, of course, the inherent weakness of an affidavit as evidence where the witness is not present and subject to cross-examination.'

Then, however, he went on: 'Mr Messersmith is an elderly gentleman. He is not in good health. It was entirely impracticable to try to bring him here ... I remind the court of Article 19 of the Charter: "The Tribunal shall not be bound by technical rules of evidence. It shall adopt and apply to the greatest possible extent expeditious and non-technical procedure and shall admit any evidence which it deems to have probative value." '[27]

This reply showed the Germans quite clearly what the prosecution's purpose was. They wanted to get the trial over as quickly as possible and not to be hampered in this by formalities. In order not to lose face *vis-à-vis* the defence and preserve an appearance of orderly judicial procedure, Alderman stated firmly:

'Of course the court would not treat anything in an affidavit such as this as having probative value unless the court deemed it to have probative value; and if the defendants have countering evidence, which is strong enough to overcome whatever is probative in this affidavit,* of course the court will treat the probative value of all the evidence in accordance with this provision of the Charter.

'By and large this affidavit and another affidavit by Mr Messersmith, which we shall undertake to present, cover background material which is a matter of historical knowledge, of which the court could take judicial notice. Where he does quote these amazingly frank expressions by Nazi leaders, it is entirely open to any of them who may be quoted, to challenge what is said, or to tell Your Honors what they believe was said. In any event it seems to me that the court can accept an affidavit of this character, made by a well-known American diplomat, and give it whatever value the court thinks it has.'[28]

Kubuschok, however, had at once perceived the weakness of the arguments and refused to be satisfied. He raised the level of debate with:

'The representative of the Prosecution takes the point of view that the age and state of health of the witness make it impossible to summon him as a witness. I do not know the witness personally. Consequently I am not in a position to state to what extent he is actually incapacitated. Nevertheless I have profound doubts regarding the presentation of evidence of such an old and incapacitated person. I am not speaking specifically now about Mr Messersmith. I do not think the court can judge to what extent old age and infirmity can possibly influence memory and reasoning powers; so personal presence would seem absolutely indispensable.

'Furthermore, it is important to know what questions *in toto* were put to the witness. An affidavit only reiterates the answers to questions which were put to the person. Very often conclusions can be drawn from unanswered questions. It is here a question of evidence solely on the basis of an affidavit. For that reason we are not in a position to assume, with absolute certainty, that the evidence of the witness is complete.

'I cannot sanction the intention of the Prosecution in this case to introduce two methods of giving evidence of different value, namely a fully valid one through direct evidence of a witness and a less complete one

---

* Since, in view of their restricted facilities, neither the accused nor their defence counsel were in a position to provide this, Alderman could use this form of words without risk of any consequences worth mentioning from the prosecution's point of view.

through evidence laid down in an affidavit. The situation is this: either the evidence is sufficient or it is not. I think the Tribunal should confine itself to complete and fully valid evidence.'[29]

Alderman was forced to recognize that the defence was not going to allow itself to be railroaded as easily as appearances might have given him to think. He hastened to iron out the 'misunderstanding', countering Kubuschok with:

'I wish to make this correction, perhaps, of what I said. I did not mean to leave the implication that Mr Messersmith is in any way incapacitated. He is an elderly man, about seventy years old; he is on active duty in Mexico City; the main difficulty is that we did not feel that we could take him away from his duties in that post, combined with a long trip and his age.'[30]

The President immediately came to the Prosecutor's assistance and, basing himself on the 'powers of the Tribunal', came down definitely against the Germans, saying:

'The Tribunal has considered the objection ... In view of the Powers which the Tribunal has under Article 19 of the Charter, which provides that the Tribunal shall not be bound by technical rules of evidence, but shall adopt and apply to the greatest possible extent expeditious and non-technical procedure and shall admit any evidence which it deems to have probative value, the Tribunal holds that affidavits can be presented and that in the present case it is a proper course.

'The question of the probative value of an affidavit as compared with a witness who has been cross-examined would, of course, be considered by the Tribunal. If, at a later stage, the Tribunal thinks the presence of a witness is of extreme importance, the matter can be reconsidered.'[31]

The eyes of Justice remained unblindfolded.

The difficulties faced by defence counsel, who were adequately informed only in a few cases and were unfamiliar with Anglo-American legal procedure, emerged with particular clarity during the IMT's initial proceedings. The following extracts from the Record of Proceedings are especially illustrative. On 22 November 1945, for instance, Frank Wallis, Assistant Trial Counsel for the USA, prefaced his reading of the briefs and documents relating to Count One of the Indictment with the following:

'It will be my purpose to establish most of the material allegations of the Indictment ...[32] The subjects involved are:

'The aims of the Nazi Party, their doctrinal techniques, their rise to power and the consolidation of control over Germany between 1933 and 1939 in preparation for aggressive war ... This ... is history beyond challenge by the defendants ... we rely upon the Tribunal to take judicial notice of it. What we offer is merely illustrative material – including statements by the defendants and other Nazi leaders – laws, decrees and the like. We do not need to rest upon captured documents or other special sources, although some have been used ...

'I intend only to comment briefly on some of the materials and to summarize the main lines of the briefs . . .

'The charge in Count One is that the defendants, with divers other persons, participated in the formulation or execution of a Common Plan or Conspiracy to commit, or which involved the commission of, Crimes against Humanity (both within and without Germany), War Crimes and Crimes against Peace. The charge is, further, that the instrument of cohesion among the defendants, as well as an instrument for the execution of the purposes of the conspiracy, was the Nazi Party, of which each defendant was a member or to which he became an adherent.

'The scope of the proof which I shall offer is:

'First, that the Nazi Party set for itself certain aims and objectives, involving basically the acquisition of "Lebensraum", or living space, for all "racial" Germans.

'Second, that it was committed to the use of any methods, whether or not legal, in attaining these objectives, and that it did in fact use illegal methods.

'Third, that it put forward and disseminated various lines of propaganda, and used various propaganda techniques to assist it in its unprincipled rise to power.

'Fourth, that it did ultimately seize all governmental power in Germany.

'Fifth, that it used this power to complete the political conquest of the state, to crush all opposition and to prepare the nation psychologically and otherwise for the foreign aggression upon which it was bent from the outset.

'In general we undertake to outline, so far as relevant to the charge, what happened in Germany during the pre-war period, leaving it to others* to carry the story and proof through the war years.

'The aims of this conspiracy were open and notorious. It was far different from any other conspiracy ever unfolded before a court of justice not only because of the gigantic number of people involved, the period of time covered, the magnitude and audacity of it, but because, unlike other criminal conspirators, these conspirators often boastfully proclaimed to the world what they planned to do before they did it.'[33]

After Wallis had then quoted from Hitler's *Mein Kampf* and his speeches, and from the texts of Nazi oaths, the President, who was clearly somewhat taken aback, interrupted him with the question: 'Major Wallis, have you got copies of these for defendants' counsel?' Wallis's immediate reaction to this was merely to reply 'In Room 54', but there then followed this series of questions and answers:

The President: Well, they [defence counsel] will be wanting to follow them now.

* Meaning Great Britain, France and the Soviet Union for Counts Two, Three and Four.

Major Wallis: Mr President, my remarks, which I am proceeding toward, will cover an entirely different subject than in the briefs before you. The briefs cover what I have already said, Sir.

The President: Are you depositing a copy of these briefs for each of the defendants' counsel?

Major Wallis: I am informed, if Your Honor pleases, that the same procedure has been followed with respect to these briefs as has been followed with respect to the documents, namely that a total of six [for some forty defending counsel] has been made available to the defendants in Room 54. If Your Honor does not deem that number sufficient, I feel sure ... that before the close of the day an ample supply of copies will be there for use.

The President: The Tribunal thinks that the Defense Counsel should each have a copy of these briefs.

Major Wallis: That will be done, Sir.

The President: Members of the Defense Counsel: You will understand that I have directed on behalf of the Tribunal that you should each have a copy of this brief.

Dr Dix: We are very grateful for this directive, but none of us has seen any of these documents so far. I assume and hope that these documents will be given to the Defense in the German translation.

The President: Yes ...[34]

Dr Rudolf Dix, Schacht's defence counsel, found himself compelled to put forward another point which was proving a serious obstacle to the defence. He said:

'I have one request. We are here as German Defense Counsel and in face of great difficulties. These proceedings are conducted according to Anglo-American customs. We are doing our best to make our way through these principles and would be very grateful if the President would take into consideration our difficult situation.

'I have heard ... that according to these Anglo-American principles, it is necessary to prepare objections immediately, if one has any objections to the contents of a document ... This is a point on which I would like to make my request. I am convinced that both the trial brief and the documents will be made available to us and we will see if we can have a German translation of one or the other ... If the Defense Counsel needs a translation, we shall have it but ... I have one request – that we have leisure to raise an objection later when we have had a chance to discuss it.

The President: The Tribunal is glad that defendants' counsel are making efforts to cooperate in the trial. After the adjournment the Tribunal will consider the best method of providing defendants' counsel with as many translations as possible and you are right in thinking that you will be able to make objections to any document after you have had time to consider it.

Dr Dix: Thank you, Sir.[35]

After a ten-minute recess Colonel Storey, US Executive Trial Counsel, stated to the court:

'During the recess defendants' counsel and the Prosecution arrived at an agreement for the furnishing of briefs to the defendants, which I understand to be this:

'Copies of the documents offered in evidence in German will be delivered in the Defendants' Information Center, with the understanding that if any Defense Counsel needs to show the German photostatic copy to his client, he may do so in the defendants' counsel room adjacent thereto; that the briefs which we are passing to the Tribunal as an aid will likewise be passed to defendants' counsel in English, and that if any of them have trouble in the translation of any portion of the briefs, we have German-speaking officers in the Defendants' Information Center who will assist counsel.'[36]

Dr Alfred Seidl, Hans Frank's defence counsel, raised another problem:

'... The defendants were given, along with the Indictment, a list of the documents. This list contains the following preamble:

' "Each of the defendants is hereby informed that the Prosecution will use some or all of the documents listed in the appendix in order to corroborate the points enumerated in the Indictment."

'Now, the Chief Prosecutor introduced in court this morning about twelve documents and a scrutiny of that list revealed that not a single one of the documents is mentioned. Thus, already now, at the very beginning of the trial, we are confronted with the fact that not only are documents presented to the court without the defendant being acquainted with their contents but that documents are being used as documentary evidence which are not even listed ... I must confess that an adequate defense is altogether impossible under these circumstances.'[37]

On the ninth day (30 November 1945) there occurred the first sharp clash between the defence and the prosecution resulting from this sort of discrepancy. It was sparked off by Dr Otto Nelte, Keitel's defence counsel, who regarded his work in Nuremberg as a patriotic duty and had refused all remuneration. Somewhat aggressively he declared:

'As far as I know, an agreement was reached between the Prosecution and the Defense to the effect that, whenever possible, questions to be brought up in the proceedings on the following day should be announced beforehand. The obvious purpose of this very reasonable understanding was to enable Defense Counsel to discuss forthcoming questions with their clients and thus assure a rapid and even progress of the trial.

'I was not informed that the witness Lahousen[38] was to be called by the Prosecution today, nor was I told on what questions he was to be heard. It was particularly important to know this because today, I believe, the witness Lahousen was not to be heard on questions connected with the Prosecution's case as presented during the past days.'[39]

There then ensued the following argument between the President and Dr Nelte, the President's immediate reply being: 'That is the contrary of what I said. What I said was that the witness was to be confined to evidence relating to Count One, which is the Count which has been solely discussed up to the present date.'

Dr Nelte: Do you mean, Mr President, that in order to enable the Defense to cross-examine the witness, there will be a recess after the interrogation by the Prosecution, during which counsel may discuss the questions with their clients? The witness Lahousen, as far as I recall, has never until now been mentioned by the Prosecution.

The President: Is that all you have to say?

Dr Nelte: Yes.[40]

After this emphatic parade-ground reply from Nelte the President called upon the Chief Prosecutor of the United States to put an end to the discussion, saying: 'I think the Tribunal would like to hear Counsel for the United States upon the agreement which counsel for the Defendant Keitel alleges, namely, an agreement that what was to be discussed on the following day should be communicated to defendants' counsel beforehand.'[41]

Justice Jackson did not disappoint him, declaring: 'I know of no agreement to inform defendants' counsel of any witness nor of his testimony.'[42] And he then stated quite frankly: 'Nor would I want to make such.'[43]

Before the Germans had really grasped what had happened, the Chief Prosecutor continued: 'We did advise them that they would be given information as to the documentary matters and I think that has been kept. As to witnesses, however, a matter of policy arises. These witnesses are not always prisoners. They have to be treated in somewhat different fashion than prisoners*; and the protection of their security is a very important consideration where we are trying this case in the very hotbed of the Nazi organization with which some of Defense Counsel were identified.'[44]

Even the most dull-witted defendant could not fail to grasp the situation when the President pronounced: 'I think, Mr Justice Jackson, that that is sufficient. If you tell the Tribunal that there was no such agreement, the Tribunal will, of course, accept that.'[45]

The ensuing objections from the defence by Dr Stahmer on behalf of Göring and Dr Dix on behalf of Schacht were cut short by the President with the categorical statement: 'The Tribunal will consider the submissions which have been made to them on behalf of Defense Counsel with reference to what shall or what shall not be communicated to them.'[46]

In mid-November 1945 Jackson's staff was shown a confidential film said to produce particularly effective arguments and an impressive pictorial record of facts supporting the prosecution's case for a conspiracy, the planning of aggressive war and the story of a 'Nazi Plan'. It proved to

---

* In effect this applied only to witnesses for the prosecution.

be a double-edged weapon, however. The Americans were taken aback when they saw the German Wehrmacht being greeted with frenzied applause and rejoicing as it moved into Austria, the Sudetenland and the Saar territory. Unless certain scenes were cut, the film was of more use to the defence than the prosecution. Jackson was advised to take the appropriate steps.

On 29 November 1945, a fortnight after the American film experiment and a week after Colonel Storey's exposé of the origin of documents, the defendants were shown a film to which most of them reacted with horror and consternation. They saw what took place in the German concentration camps for which – depending on their position and commitment – they were here held responsible. Some of them sobbed, covered their faces and were unable to hide their revulsion. After it Jodl wrote to his wife: 'These facts are the most fearful heritage which the National-Socialist regime has left the German people. It is far worse than the destruction of German cities. Their ruins could be regarded as honourable wounds suffered during a people's battle for its existence. This disgrace, however, besmirches everything – the enthusiasm of our youth, the entire German Wehrmacht and its leaders. I have already explained how we were all systematically deceived in this matter. The accusation that we were all aware of these circumstances is false. I would not have tolerated such wrongdoing for a single day.'[47]

All the defendants except Rudolf Hess, Alfred Rosenberg and Julius Streicher attended the Sunday service in the prison chapel, hoping to escape, at least temporarily, from the pressure of events. Some of them considered suicide. While in Kransberg Albert Speer had heard from a scientist that nicotine from a cigar, crumbled and dissolved in water, could be fatal. He had kept a cigar in his kit ever since. Twenty-five years later, however, he ruminated: 'But from the intention to the deed is a very long way.'[48] Whole collections of razor blades, boot-laces, knives and other objects which might have served as 'suicide accessories' were found in the cells of those executed. None of them had made any serious attempt to use them for this purpose however.

Initially, of course, the defendants were most afraid of the mountains of documents captured by the Allies, since they could no longer remember all that they had signed or initialled over the years. Speer found this 'horrible and only to be borne because our nerves became more blunted from session to session'. In 1969 he wrote: 'To this day photographs, documents and orders keep coming back to me. They were so monstrous that they seemed unbelievable.'[49] But they also feared the witnesses' evidence, for none of them knew how their witnesses would react if, as could happen at any time, they were liable to endanger themselves by their statements.

As was inevitable with such a unique mammoth trial, a routine timetable soon developed. The morning proceedings lasted until 12 noon. Then came lunch in the upper rooms of the Palace of Justice. The proceedings then continued from 2.0 p.m. to 5.0 p.m. The defendants then returned to their cells and were allowed until 10.0 p.m. to discuss with their defence counsel in rooms specially appointed for the purpose. The IMT did not sit on Saturdays and Sundays and the defendants could use these days for exhaustive discussions with their counsel.

Hans Fritzsche, who was acquitted by the IMT, subsequently described the proceedings as monotonous except when something unusual was happening: 'Anyone entering the courtroom would see a number of men in profound silence and an attitude of gravity. He would hear someone speaking somewhere but the words sounded muffled as if in private conversation. The uninitiated visitor witnessed to all intents and purposes nothing. At best he would see a silent theatre piece with surprisingly little action. There was nothing to indicate that here the victors were pronouncing men guilty of the outbreak and conduct of World War II ... Only if he took up his headphones ... would he realize that anything at all was happening. What the speaker was saying, in such low tones that his neighbour could hardly hear him, then came to life. This was the curious picture of proceedings conducted in four languages simultaneously.'[50]

The uncertainty engendered among defence counsel by Anglo-American methods of procedure and the varying level of information provided to them was to some extent increased by statements made outside the Palace of Justice that the defence was attempting to save 'Nazis' who had been in power until 1945. This soon gave way to a sober, realistic view of things. The defendants, most of whom had not even known their counsel's name until told in Nuremberg that they had consented to defend them before the IMT, quickly became convinced that, as a result of their solid legal training, their counsel would be in a position to launch a 'counter-stroke' when the time came.

Since the end of October defence counsel had had time to become familiar with their clients, to accustom themselves to the methods of procedure, strange to most of them, and to acquaint themselves with the material to be presented not only in the arguments of the prosecutors and defendants but also in the 2,736 prosecution documents and the evidence of the twenty-nine witnesses which the prosecution presented over the seventy-two days of the proceedings. The prosecution's statements – spread over seventy-two days in all – were mostly monotonous repetitions of documents incriminating the accused, which those involved soon found wearisome, making boredom and 'a yawn the symbol of Nuremberg'[51]; they did, however, provide defence counsel with a welcome opportunity to renew their acquaintance with the material as presented by the prosecution. Nevertheless on 4 February 1946 they applied for a recess because, in their view, they were not yet adequately prepared.[52]

On 19 February the IMT replied with the decision to take up the case against groups and organizations after presentation of the prosecution's case against individual defendants and at the same time to deal with procedural questions and problems of documentation. The defence accordingly gained a further seven days.

Depending on their former positions, the particular interest of defendants was concentrated in turn on such events as, for instance, Katyn, Russian participation in the Polish campaign and Stalin's war against Finland. Obviously they awaited the statements of certain witnesses with apprehension and in some suspense, particularly those of men like Field Marshal Friedrich Paulus, who had surrendered at Stalingrad and since then had been so thoroughly coached by the Russians as a prosecution witness that he occasionally even referred to 'the defendants'. He was simply not allowed to get into the clutches of the defence; in 1951 Viktor Freiherr von der Lippe, Dr Siemers' assistant counsel, reported that the Russians had prevented all contact with their star witness Paulus and that 'rumour has it that he is to be returned by air' as soon as he had made his statement.[53]

The initial reservations of some of the defendants regarding their defence counsel rapidly disappeared. The more they became divorced from each other, the greater became their attachment to their defence lawyers. Kranzbühler, Exner, Stahmer and Kubuschok, to name only a few, quickly became very friendly with their clients, though their relationships remained within prescribed limits. Kubuschok, for instance, by means of a tit-for-tat manoeuvre – 'if you don't beat my donkey I won't beat yours' – succeeded in persuading the prosecution to withdraw a witness hostile to his client von Papen.

Between the application by the defence of 4 February and the court's decision of 19 February a subject was raised for which most of the defendants had been waiting ever since the opening of the trial – Katyn. This, they hoped, would highlight two things: first that in their view not only they but the Soviets as well should be in the dock; secondly that the IMT was assembled to judge not solely them, the representatives of the vanquished. Based on the Moscow and Yalta declarations the Soviets, who had at first looked upon the IMT purely as a piece of democratic window-dressing, had intended to include Katyn in the Indictment, but in this they had been thwarted by Jackson, a fact unknown to the defendants.

On 8 February 1946, when Rudenko accused them of responsibility for the extermination policy in Poland, his statements were greeted with biting sarcasm and studied ridicule. Göring and Hess ostentatiously took off their headphones; Schirach gave a malicious chuckle. With pious solemnity Rudenko declaimed:

'It is for the first time that criminals who have seized an entire state and made this state an instrument of their monstrous crimes, appear before a court of justice ... On 1 September 1939 the fascist aggressors invaded Polish territory in treacherous violation of existing treaties. The Polish people were subjected to mass extermination and their cities and villages were mercilessly destroyed ... Evidence will be presented of the monstrous crimes committed by the Hitlerites in Poland.'[54]

In 1946 there was no need for a Nuremberg Trial to prove that Germans had committed fearful crimes in Poland. Some of the defendants inevitably knew more about them than the prosecution. They also knew, however, that in Katyn Forest near Smolensk – long before the Germans arrived there – the Russians had murdered 15,000 Polish prisoners of war including 8,300–8,400 officers and 800 doctors posted as 'missing' during the war.[55]

The fact that General Rudenko was unable to keep Katyn out of the subsequent proceedings in the trial was one of the defence's achievements; they knew from German publications of the Hitler period – which in this instance were objective – that this was a Soviet crime; they were also able to show in Nuremberg that from August 1939 to June 1941 the National-Socialist leaders had been able to base their actions on a secret supplementary protocol to the Non-Aggression Treaty of 23 August 1939 between the Reich and the USSR.[56]

On 5 June 1946, when Alfred Jodl was testifying concerning German–Soviet agreements during the Polish campaign (regarded as a war of aggression), there was embarrassed silence in the courtroom, broken only by a request from the President to the Colonel-General that he should 'speak a little faster'.[57] Jodl stated:

'When we were still three days' march away from the Vistula, I was informed to my great surprise – by, I believe, the representative of the Foreign Office ... that Soviet Russia would occupy the Polish territories ... that the Polish territories east of an agreed demarcation line would be occupied by Russian troops at the appointed time. When we were approaching this agreed demarcation line, which was shown to me on a map – the line was the East Prussian–Lithuanian border, Narev, Vistula, San – I telephoned to our Military Attaché in Moscow and informed him that we would probably reach individual points of this demarcation line in the course of the following day ... When, the day after the next, we reached the demarcation line and had to cross it in pursuit of the Poles, I ... received news from Moscow, at 0200 hours, that the Soviet Russian divisions would take up their position along the entire front at 0400 hours. This maneuver was punctually carried out, and I then drafted an order to our German troops that wherever they had contacted the troops of the Soviet Union, and in agreement with them, they were to withdraw behind the demarcation line.'[58]

In any event, for the time being 'Katyn' became a symbol and a dirty word in Nuremberg – and not only for those who were opposed to the IMT.

World public opinion, which had been roused by press reports about German concentration camps and was consequently largely convinced that only the Germans had committed crimes against humanity and genocide during the war, reacted with horror. As early as 15 February 1946 eleven Polish senators and ten members of the Polish government-in-exile in

London had advised Robert Jackson, the American Chief Prosecutor, to exclude the question of Katyn from the IMT since it required 'its own investigation and proceedings'.[59] But by then it was already too late. The Russians had referred to the matter so explicitly that the IMT could no longer drop it. The report of the Soviet Commission accusing the Germans of the massacre[60] was already on the table.

The Soviet prosecutors, who presumably knew that their 'documentation' was a forgery,[61] were taken by surprise by the reaction and proposed that the matter be dealt with quickly without evidence of witnesses and that the Soviet 'documentation' be accepted as irrefutable proof of the Germans' guilt; this the defence rejected. They were very well informed on this point and applied for the hearing of witnesses, a request which Rudenko attempted to counter with the statement that 'this episode of criminal activity on the part of the Hitlerites has been fully established by the evidence presented by the Soviet prosecution'.[62] His efforts were unsuccessful and the court decided[63] to hear three witnesses for the prosecution and three for the defence.[64] As their witnesses the Soviet prosecution nominated Dr Prosorovsky, Professor Basilevsky and Dr Markov. Prosorovsky was a member of the Soviet Commission established to shift responsibility for this crime on to the Germans. Basilevsky's knowledge was hearsay only and he could prove nothing. The Bulgarian Professor Marko Antonov Markov had signed the German report incriminating the Russians, but he was an opportunist and recanted on everything that he had held scientifically proved in 1943 and – according to statements by the US Congress Investigating Committee – had voluntarily confirmed on several occasions[65] that this crime must have been committed by the Russians.

Markov was thoroughly intimidated; after the Soviet move into Bulgaria he had been arrested and taken to court as an 'enemy of the people' because of his participation in the International Commission of Inquiry on Katyn arranged by the Germans.[66] In Nuremberg, however, the Soviet prosecution made it easy for him to revoke his previous statements and present them as having been made under duress. Nevertheless neither the prosecutors nor the witnesses were very comfortable. On 2 July 1946, for instance, Smirnov's agitation was such that the President had to ask him not to keep interrupting Markov and thus preventing complete translation of the questions and answers – 'You are interrupting the interpreter all the time. Before the interpreter has finished the answer you have put another question. It is very difficult for us to hear the interpreter'.[67]

This witness's testimony produced little more than procedural points of this nature, as the following example from the record shows:

Mr Counsellor Smirnov: I should like to ask you to reply to the following question. On what impartial medico-judicial data did the commission base the deduction that the corpses had remained in the earth not less than three years?

The President: Will you put the question again? I did not understand the question.

Mr Counsellor Smirnov: I asked on what impartial medico-judicial data were the deductions of the protocol of the International Medical Commission based, which stated that the corpses had remained in the ground not less than three years.

The President: Has he said that that was the deduction he made – not less than three years?

The Tribunal (Mr Biddle): He has not said that.

The President: He has not said that at all. He never said that he made the deduction that the corpses remained in the ground not less than three years.

Mr Counsellor Smirnov: He did not make this deduction; but Professor Markov, together with the other members of the commission, signed a report of the International Commission.

The President: I know; but that is why I ask you to repeat your question. The question that was translated to us was: On what grounds did you make your deduction that the corpses had remained in the ground not less than three years – which is the opposite of what he said ...[68]

The President had already had to intervene during the examination of this witness and point out to the Soviet counsellor that it was not permissible to ask leading questions. The record is as follows:

Mr Counsellor Smirnov: That is to say the date and the locality which are shown on the protocol are incorrect?

Markov: Yes, that is so.

Mr Counsellor Smirnov: And you signed it because you felt yourself compelled to?

The President: Colonel Smirnov, I don't think it is proper for you to put leading questions to him. He has stated the fact. It is useless to go on stating conclusions about it.[69]

On 1 July 1946 the President of the IMT stated that he 'did not propose' to answer the question put by the defence (which felt itself on very sure ground in this instance) as to 'who is to be made responsible for the Katyn case'[70] – a striking revelation of what the IMT's object was on this particular point. As early as 28 March 1945, about a fortnight before his death, President Roosevelt had written to George Howard Earle, his former envoy in Bulgaria and Portugal, forbidding him to publish the details he had discovered about Russian responsibility for Katyn. For the sake of Russo-American relations he categorically forbade Earle to disclose his conclusions and left him in no doubt what awaited him should he fail to keep his discoveries to himself. Roosevelt's letter speaks for itself:

Dear George,
I have read your letter of 21 March to my daughter Anne and have

noted with alarm your plan to publicize your unfavourable opinion of one of our allies precisely at the moment when such publication by one of my former envoys might do irreparable damage to our war effort. As you say, you have occupied important positions of confidence under your government. Publication without proper authority of information received in such positions would be all the greater breach of confidence. You say that you will publish unless you have been told by 28 March that I do not wish it. Not only do I not wish it but I expressly forbid you to publish any information whatsoever or any views about an ally to whom you have been accredited during your service as an envoy or with the United States Navy.

Regarding your desire to continue on active service I will cancel any previous agreements under which you acted as my envoy and I will instruct the Navy Department to employ you further wherever your services can be used. I am sorry that pressure of business prevents me talking to you on Monday. I value our old relationship and I hope that one day time and circumstances will permit reestablishment of our good relations.

Sincerely yours
Franklin D. Roosevelt[71]

After the end of the war in Europe Truman was just as anxious as Roosevelt[72] not to offend the Soviets, since he too wanted Russian help in the war against Japan. Though he did not like Stalin as much as his predecessor, he avoided anything calculated to annoy him. All evidence incriminating the Russians vanished into the archives. Even in 1952 Churchill refused to say anything about Katyn,[73] despite the fact that he had already attacked the Soviets in his famous 'Fulton speech', had outlined their ideologically based expansionist policy and had urged the West to be on its guard – even militarily. But in Nuremberg the defence was fighting a losing battle. The judgement of the I M T did not include a single word about Katyn.

On 19 March 1946 two of the defence counsel, Dr Siemers and Dr Dix, started an argument in which Jackson was so clearly worsted by Göring that foreign journalists made fun of him, describing Göring as the radiant victor who had 'made a monkey' of Jackson;[74] one of them even asked Göring's assistant defence counsel sarcastically whether the Reich Marshal (who had lost 35 kilo in weight since June 1945) was prepared to accept declarations of adherence to the NSDAP.[75] The Associated Press correspondent, obviously an influential figure in the world press, had initially intended to cable only a couple of words on Göring's appearance on the scene but by 16 March he was already telegraphing 'Very clever'.[76]

Jackson had not cut a good figure on 15 March, the third day of his examination of Göring. Though he tried to adopt a lofty attitude as the principal prosecutor of the USA, he was nothing in face of Göring. The thought that he now had to cross swords with Hitler's No. 2 – as was continually being emphasized in the press – undoubtedly inhibited him to such an extent that in this phase of the proceedings he sometimes lost his proper form. He was maladroit, was continually being called to order by the

President,[77] was inept in his choice of words and occasionally actually made himself ridiculous. On many occasions Göring interrupted him in such a domineering and self-assured manner[78] that he seemed like a junior clerk of the court. He was not helped by the fact that the President of the court was bent on keeping to the letter of the Charter, made efforts to avoid prejudicing the defence and from 12 March, the day on which Göring entered the witness-box, put a stop to Jackson's interventions if they did not accord with his ideas of justice. During the first ten minutes of this verbal duel Sir Norman Birkett, the British Member of the Tribunal, sensed that 'Göring was the complete master of Mr Justice Jackson'.[79]

Over the years this verbal duel has been the subject of much exaggeration, distortion and deliberate wishful thinking – it was, and still is, maintained, for instance, that the Soviet Chief Prosecutor was so provoked that he lost his temper and shot at Göring with a revolver. There is almost a danger that it will become a new 'stab-in-the-back' legend. Accordingly the most important passages are here quoted textually with only very brief comment:

Dr Siemers: I cannot see ... why it repeatedly happens that the defence does not receive documents that are discussed in Court and that are submitted to the court ... During the last few days I have noticed that several times documents were suddenly presented by the Prosecution without any effort having been made to inform us of their existence.

Mr Justice Jackson: That is perfectly true, and I think every lawyer knows that one of the great questions in this case is credibility, and that, if we have, in cross-examination, to submit every document before we can refer to it in cross-examination, after we hear their testimony, the possibilities of useful cross-examination are destroyed.

Now, of course, he [Göring] did not know this document; and we have had the experience of calling document after document to their attention, always to be met with some explanation, carefully arranged and read here from notes ... I submit that cross-examination of them should not be destroyed by any requirement that we submit documents in advance ...

Dr Siemers: I should like to make two points. First, I am entirely agreed if Mr Justice Jackson wants to make use of the element of surprise. I should merely be thankful if the Defense then were also permitted to use the element of surprise. Yet we have been told heretofore that we must show every document we want to submit weeks ahead of time, so that the Prosecution has several weeks to form an opinion on it.

Secondly, if the element of surprise is being used ... at least we, as Defense Counsel, should not be given this surprise at the moment when the document is submitted to the court and to the witness. I have ... neither today's documents nor the documents of the previous days.

The President: What you have just said is entirely inaccurate. You have never been compelled to disclose any documents which you wished to put to a witness in cross-examination. This is cross-examination and therefore it is perfectly open to Counsel for the Prosecution to put any document without disclosing it beforehand; just as Defense Counsel could have put any document to witnesses called on behalf of the Prosecution ... in cross-examination ... The Tribunal now rules that this document may be put to the witness now.

Dr Siemers: Does the Defense also have the opportunity, now that it is known to the entire court, of receiving the document?

The President: Yes, certainly.

Dr Siemers: I should be thankful if I could have a copy now.[80]

At this point Jackson's reaction was, to say the least, inept; he said in some embarrassment: 'I am frank to say that I do not know whether we have adequate copies to furnish them to all Defense Counsel now.'

The President thereupon asked whether it was not possible to make available to the defence at least 'one or more copies'. Jackson's reaction – 'But I do not think we should furnish copies until the examination with reference to that document is completed' – led Dr Dix to interrupt Jackson and to ask:

'I should like to make one request, that at least the technical possibilities – that at least the Counsel of these defendants who are being cross-examined also be given the document that is being submitted to the defendant, so that they are in a position, just as the Tribunal is, to follow the examination.

'If Justice Jackson says that ... it would be right for the Defense Counsel ... to receive this document only after the examination – in this case of Göring – has ended, I beg earnestly, in the interest of the dignity and prestige of the Defense, to take objection to this suggestion ...

'I therefore make this request: If in the cross-examination ... in view of the altogether justified element of surprise, a document is presented to a witness that at the same time is presented to the Tribunal, that at least a copy of this document be given at the same time to ... the Defense Counsel concerned so that he can have some idea of what the witness is being confronted with, for Göring could read this document but Dr Stahmer could not. In other words he was not in a position to follow the next part of Mr Justice Jackson's cross-examination. That is certainly not intended ... and I should therefore like to ask Mr Justice Jackson to reply to my suggestion and my application, in order to arrive at an understanding and thereby to relieve the Tribunal of the decision on a question that seems to me self-evident.

The President: Mr Justice Jackson, the Tribunal is inclined to think – the Tribunal certainly thinks – that you are perfectly right, that there is no necessity at all ... to disclose the document to the defendants before you use it in cross-examination. But, at the time you use it in cross-examination, is there any objection to handing a copy of it to the Counsel for the defendant who is being cross-examined?

Mr Justice Jackson: In some instances it is physically impossible ... A good many of these documents have come to us very lately. Our photostatic facilities are limited.

The President: I am not suggesting that you should hand it to all of them, but only to Dr Stahmer.

Mr Justice Jackson: If we have copies, I have no objection to doing that, but if we do not have them in German – our difficulty has always been to get German copies of these documents.

At this point Dr Dix intervened with the question: 'May I say something else. If it is not possible in German, then it should at least be possible in English ... Furthermore, if it is a question of German witnesses, such as Göring, the document will be shown to him in German anyhow; it will certainly be shown the witness in German ...

Dr Siemers then unexpectedly approached the lectern, causing the President to say: 'We do not really need to hear more than one Counsel on this sort of point. I have already ruled upon your objection ... the Tribunal has already ruled that the objection should be denied.'

But Siemers was not to be dismissed so easily; he said: '... I am sorry. My motion was that Defense Counsel should receive these documents at the same time the Tribunal does. I am not of the opinion ... that only one defense counsel should receive it. If ... it is a document important to several defendants. One copy is therefore not sufficient, but each defense counsel must have one. I believe that Mr Justice Jackson ...

The President: But not at this moment. There are ... the very greatest difficulties in producing all these documents and extraordinary efforts have been made by the Prosecution and the Translating Division to supply the defendants ... with documents in German, and it is not necessary that every member of the Defense Counsel have these documents at the time the witness is being cross-examined. I am sure the Prosecution will do everything it can to let you have the documents in due course – any document that is being used. In the opinion of the Tribunal it is perfectly sufficient if one copy of the document is supplied to the Counsel for the witness who is being cross-examined ...

Dr Siemers: The result of that is that the Defense Counsel who is not momentarily concerned cannot understand the cross-examination ...

The President: Counsel for the Prosecution will consider what you say but no rule has been made by the Tribunal that every document should be supplied to every Counsel during cross-examination.

Göring: I should like to say again in regard to the document that this is not ...

Mr Justice Jackson: May I respectfully ask that the witness be instructed to answer the question and reserve his explanations until his Counsel takes him on. Otherwise this cross-examination cannot be successfully conducted, in the sense of being reasonable in time.

The President: I have already explained, on several occasions, that it is the duty of defendants ... to answer questions directly, if they are capable of being answered directly, in the affirmative or in the negative; and if they have any explanation to make afterwards, they can make it after answering the question directly.

Jackson now tried to play another card against Göring, but that did not make an impact either. The deductions which he thought he had made from documents proved to be only partially true, as he was soon to find out. He first tried to accuse Göring, who manoeuvred with extreme skill, of having tried to improve the Reich's critical financial position in 1938 by the fine of a milliard marks imposed on the Jews after the so-called 'Kristallnacht' of 9/10 October 1938 and by the profits accruing from the 'aryanization of Jewish enterprises'.[81] He then began to deal with a document the contents of which, he hoped, were calculated to put an end to Göring's arrogant self-assured demeanour. Full of hope he began: 'I call your attention to Document Number E C–405, minutes of a meeting of the Working Committee of the Reich Defense Council, Meeting Number 10.'

Göring began his answer, however, with an adroit reference to the President of the I M T and declared didactically: 'I understood the President to say before that when I have answered the question, I can add an explanation that seems necessary to me. Now that I have clearly answered your question with regard to the first document, I want to stress once again that this was not a meeting of the closed Reich Defense Council but a general calling together of all ministers, state secretaries and numerous other persons ... The Reich Defense Council was already, by decision of the Cabinet of 1933 and 1934, called into being but it has never met.[82] Through the Reich Defense Law of 4 September 1938 it was re-established. The Chairman is the Führer who appointed me, General Field Marshal Göring, as his permanent deputy. Concerning the Reich Defense Council of which we have been talking ... it is attested here in writing once more, as I have correctly said, that this Council never met. I have to ask the question about the second document repeated, as I have forgotten it.'

Jackson dodged the issue and faced Göring with: 'You have testified that the movement into the Rhineland had not been planned in advance.'

Göring replied reproachfully: 'Only a short time in advance, I emphasized.'

There then ensued the following verbal duel:

Mr Justice Jackson: How long?
Göring: As far as I recall, at the most two to three weeks.
Mr Justice Jackson: Now I call your attention to the minutes of the tenth meeting of the Working Committee of the Reich Defense Council ... on the 6th month, 26th day of 1935 which reads as follows ...

Jackson did not get further. Göring interrupted him as if he was a Public Prosecutor: 'May I ask what page? This document is new to me and is very long. What page please, otherwise I shall have to read the whole document.'

Jackson having read from the document, Göring enlightened him: 'This document . . . contains alternating statements of various individuals, that is, a dialogue. May I ask once more: the last paragraph contains nothing of what you have stated, apparently there must be a difference between the English and German texts. The last paragraph here is altogether irrelevant. Where, please, am I to read in the document?

Mr Justice Jackson: Do you find the third paragraph from the end? If my document is correct we have got the same document.

Göring went on playing his game to the limit, saying: 'You must tell me who was speaking, for different persons speak here.'

A member of the prosecution indicated to him the place in the document to which Jackson was referring and Jackson then quoted the following passage: 'The demilitarized zone requires special treatment. In his speech of 21 May 1935 and other statements, the Führer and Reich Chancellor declared that the stipulations of the Versailles Treaty and the Locarno Pact regarding the demilitarized zone would be observed . . . Since at present international entanglements must be avoided under all circumstances, all urgently needed preparations may be made. The preparations as such, or their planning, must be kept in strictest secrecy in the zone itself as well as in the rest of the Reich . . . These preparations include in particular – (a) and (b) are not important to my present question – (c) preparation for the liberation of the Rhine.'

This having been read, Göring again enlightened him: 'Oh, no, here you have made a great mistake. The original phrase – and this alone is the point in question – is "(c) Preparation for the clearing of the Rhine". It is a purely technical preparation that has nothing at all to do with the liberation of the Rhineland. Here it says, first, mobilization measures for transportation and communications, then "(c) Preparation for the clearing of the Rhine", that is, in case of mobilization preparations the Rhine is not to be overburdened with freighters, tugboats *et cetera*, but the river has to be clear for military measures. Then it continues: "(d) Preparation for local defense" *et cetera*. Thus you see, it figures among small quite general, ordinary and usual preparations for mobilization. The phrase used by the Prosecution . . .'

After this statement by Göring the record shows Jackson interjecting: 'Mobilization, exactly.'

Göring: That, if you remember, I stressed clearly in my statement, that in the demilitarized zone general preparations for mobilization were made. I mentioned the purchase of horses *et cetera*. I wanted only to point out the mistake regarding 'clearing of the Rhine', which has nothing to do with the Rhineland, but only with the river.[83]

Mr Justice Jackson: Well, those preparations were preparations for armed occupation of the Rhineland, were they not?

Göring: No, that is altogether wrong. If Germany had become involved in a war, no matter from which side ... then mobilization measures would have had to be carried out for security reasons throughout the Reich, in this event even in the demilitarized Rhineland; but not for the purpose of occupation, of liberating the Rhineland.

Mr Justice Jackson: You mean the preparations were not military preparations?

Göring: Those were general preparations for mobilization, such as every country makes, and not for the purpose of the occupation of the Rhineland.

Mr Justice Jackson: But were of a character which had to be kept entirely secret from foreign powers?

Göring: I do not think I can recall reading beforehand the publication of the mobilization preparations of the United States.

At this point Mr Justice Jackson lost his temper. He tore off his headphones in a fury, banged them and a bundle of files down on the table and jumped up. His face red and distorted and his voice quivering with anger, he turned to the Tribunal and shouted:

'I respectfully submit to the Tribunal that this witness is not being responsive and has not been in his examination. It is perfectly futile to spend our time if we cannot have responsive answers to our questions. We can strike these things out. I do not want to spend time doing that, but this witness, it seems to me, is adopting, and has adopted, in the witness-box and in the dock, an arrogant and contemptuous attitude toward the Tribunal which is giving him the trial which he never gave a living soul, nor dead ones either.

'I respectfully submit that the witness be instructed to make notes, if he wishes, of his explanations, but that he be required to answer my questions and reserve his explanations for his Counsel to bring out.'

Lord Chief Justice Lawrence, the British President of the IMT, was unmoved and decisive; he addressed Jackson, not Göring as the US Prosecutor had expected, saying: 'I have already laid down the general rule, which is binding upon this defendant as upon other witnesses.' Then, equally calmly, he continued: 'Perhaps we had better adjourn now at this stage.'

On the following day Jackson, who was worried about his prestige among other things, continued where he had left off on 19 March, saying: 'The last question which I asked last night was this:' He then read the relevant passages from the record and continued: 'Representing the United States of America, I am confronted with these choices – to ignore that remark and allow it to stand for people who do not understand our system; or to develop, at considerable expense of time, its falsity; or to answer it in rebuttal. The difficulty arises from this . . . that if the witness is permitted to volunteer statements in cross-examination, there is no opportunity to make objection until they are placed on the record. Of course, if such an answer had been indicated by a question of Counsel, as . . . would be the orderly procedure, there would have been objection. The Tribunal would have been in a position to discharge its duty under the Charter and I would have been in a position to shorten the case by not having that remark placed . . .'

Lord Chief Justice Lawrence, the President, calmed him down adroitly and pertinently: 'I quite agree with you that any reference to the United States' secrecy with reference to mobilization is entirely irrelevant and that the answer ought not to have been made, but the only rule which the Tribunal can lay down as a general rule is the rule . . . that the witness must answer, if possible, "Yes" or "No" and that he may make such explanations as may be necessary after answering questions directly in that way . . . As far as this particular answer goes, I think it is entirely irrelevant.

Mr Justice Jackson: I must, of course, bow to the ruling of the Tribunal . . . I cannot blame . . . this witness; he is pursuing his interests. But we have no way of anticipating . . . when these statements are volunteered they are in the record before the Tribunal can rule upon them and I have no opportunity to make objections and the Tribunal have no opportunity to rule. And it puts . . . the control of these proceedings in the hands of the defendant, if he first makes the charges and then puts it up to us to ignore them or answer them by long cross-examination in rebuttal; and I think the specific charge made against the United States of America . . . presents that.

The President: What exactly is the motion you are making? Are you asking the Tribunal to strike the answer out of the record?

Mr Justice Jackson: Well, no; in a trial of this kind, where propaganda is one of the purposes of the defendant, striking out does no good . . . and Göring knows that as well as I. The charge has been made against the United States and it is in the record. I am now moving that this witness be instructed that he must answer my questions "yes" or "no" . . . and that the explanation be brought out by his Counsel in a fashion that will permit us to make objections . . . and to obtain the rulings of the Tribunal, so that the Tribunal . . . can rule out irrelevant issues and statements of any kind whatsoever. We must not let the Tribunal degenerate into a bickering contest between Counsel and the witness. That is not what the United States would expect me to participate in . . .

The President: Are you submitting to the Tribunal that the witness has to answer every question "yes" or "no" and wait until he is re-examined for the purpose of making any explanations at all?

Mr Justice Jackson: I think that is the rule of cross-examination under ordinary circumstances. The witness, if the question permits it, must answer, and if there are relevant explanations they should be reserved until later . . . Here is an answer given which the Tribunal now rules is irrelevant. But we have no opportunity to object to it. The Tribunal had no opportunity to rule upon it ... the difficulty is that the Tribunal loses control of these proceedings if the defendant, in a case of this kind ... is permitted to put his propaganda in and then we have to meet it afterwards. I really feel that the United States is deprived of the opportunity of the technique of cross-examination if this is the procedure.

The President: Surely it is making too much of a sentence ... whether the United States makes its orders for mobilization public or not. Surely that is not a matter of very great importance. Every country keeps certain things secret. Certainly it would be much wiser to ignore a statement of that sort ...

The President's next sentence showed that he wished to bring this discussion to an end finally and unequivocally: 'I have already laid down what I believe to be the rule, and I think with the assent of the Tribunal, but I will ascertain ...'

Jackson did not allow Lawrence to finish and, clearly over-estimating the extent of his personal defeat, said: 'I agree with Your Honor that as far as the United States is concerned we are not worried by anything the witness can say about it – and we expected plenty. The point is, do we answer these things or leave them, apart from the control of the trial? And it seems to me that this is the beginning of this trial's getting out of hand, if I may say so, if we do not have control of this situation. I trust the Tribunal will pardon my earnestness in presenting this. I think it is a very vital thing.'

The President, however, still remained unmoved, saying to the US Prosecutor: 'I have never heard it suggested that the Counsel for the Prosecution have to answer every irrelevant observation made in cross-examination.'

This caused Jackson to reply in some irritation: 'That would be true in a private litigation, but I trust the court is not unaware that outside of this courtroom is a great social question of the revival of Nazism and that one of the purposes of the Defendant Göring ... is to revive and perpetuate it by propaganda from this trial now in process.'

The President, who clearly did not wish to break off the argument abruptly and categorically despite Jackson's continued repetitions, now came to the assistance of the defence. He called on Dr Stahmer, who said: 'An accusation has been made as if we intended to make propaganda here for Nazism or in some other direction. I do not think this accusation is justified. Neither do I believe that the defendant intended to make an accusation against the United States ... If instead of the USA he had said any other nation, then the remark would have been considered harmless. In my opinion the answer was quite justified. The witness should be given the possibility not only to answer "yes" or "no" ...'

The President seized upon this argument of the defence and began his summing-up with: 'The Tribunal considers that the rule which it has laid down is the only possible rule.'

Then he made a concession to Jackson, saying: 'The defendant ought not to have referred to the United States but it is a matter which I think you might well ignore.'

Jackson had obviously been worsted in this duel; he had also drawn from the President of the I M T an unequivocal pronouncement to the effect that he was not prepared to allow legal formalism to turn the Tribunal into a camouflaged drum-head court martial. Jackson's final remark, 'I shall bow to the ruling of course',[84] was not taken by the defendants or journalists solely as an acknowledgement of resignation on the part of a prosecutor worsted in a 'duel'.

Though demoted to 'detainee' by the Allies, the Reich Marshal Hermann Göring had won a battle. But he had not won the war.

The weight of documentary evidence increasingly forced Göring to admit more than he had initially believed would be necessary. Admittedly Robert M. W. Kempner had promised him that certain matters would not be mentioned; but they were mere trifles, such as proof of corruption and self-enrichment,[85] upon which it was not the province of the I M T to pass judgement. Had Göring 'merely' had to admit that he had been in a position of authority in regard to the 'Final Solution of the Jewish Question',[86] that 'alone' would have been far too much. The occasional ostentatious assistance he had given to Jewish and 'half-Jewish' inmates of concentration camps when acting the jovial country squire carried no weight in Nuremberg in face of the fact that he had been one of the authoritative instigators of a horrible case of genocide. He had no counter-argument to that. Despite his high intelligence, his studied dialectical eloquence, his cunning and his dexterity, his experience of two decades of political intrigue and his knowledge of the background, as the proceedings went on he continually came off worst. The following examples illustrate this with striking clarity:

On 21 March Sir David Maxwell-Fyfe, who on principle addressed Göring simply as 'Witness', opened his examination of him as follows: 'Witness, do you remember telling me last night that the only prisoners of war handed over to the police were those guilty of crimes or misdemeanors?'[87]

Göring side-stepped and said: 'I did not express myself that way. I said if the police apprehended prisoners of war, those who had committed a crime during the escape, as far as I know, were detained by the police and were not returned to the camp. To what extent the police kept prisoners of war, without returning them to a camp, I was able to gather from interrogations and explanations here.'[88]

The British Prosecutor, however, knew that Göring was in a position which could not be improved by evasion. He accordingly faced him with: 'Would you look at Document D–569? ... the top left-hand corner which shows that it is a document published by the Oberkommando der Wehr-macht.'

Göring: The document ... has the following heading at the top left-hand corner: 'The Reichsführer S S' and the subheading: 'Inspector of Concen-tration Camps' ...

Sir David Maxwell-Fyfe: Now look at the left-hand bottom corner, as to distribution. The second person to whom it is distributed is the ... Commander-in-Chief of the Air Force, on 22 November 1941. That would be you.

Göring: That's correct ...

Sir David Maxwell-Fyfe: I would like you to appreciate the document and then make your statement upon it ... I want you to look at the third sentence in Paragraph 1. This deals with Soviet prisoners of war ... The third sentence says: 'If escaped Soviet prisoners of war are returned to the camp in accordance with this order, they have to be handed over to the nearest post of the Secret State Police in any case.'

And then Paragraph 2 deals with the special position – if they commit crimes ...: 'at present these misdemeanors on the part of Soviet prisoners of war are particularly frequent, due most likely to living conditions being somewhat unsettled, the following temporary regulations come into force ... If a Soviet prisoner of war commits any other punishable offense, then the commandant of the camp must hand the guilty man over to the head of the Security Police.'

Do I understand this document to say that a man who escapes will be handed over to the Security Police? ... Wasn't that the condition that obtained from 1941 up to the date we are dealing with in March 1944?

Göring: I would like to read the few preceding paragraphs so that no sentences are separated from their context ...

Sir David Maxwell-Fyfe: Then I am right ... that the Soviet prisoners of war who escaped were to be, after their return to the camp, handed over to the Secret State Police. If they committed a crime, they were to be handed over to the Security Police, isn't that right?

Göring: Not exactly correct. I would like to point to the third sentence in the first paragraph. There it says: 'If a prisoner-of-war camp is in the vicinity, then the man who is recaptured is to be transported there.'

Maxwell-Fyfe, however, who had the document in front of him, countered with: 'But read the next sentence: "If a Soviet prisoner of war is returned to the camp" – that is in accordance with the order which you have just read – "he has to be handed over to the nearest service station of the Secret State Police."'

Göring: Yes, but the second paragraph which follows gives an explanation of frequent criminal acts of Soviet prisoners of war *et cetera* committed at that time. You read that yourself ... But this order was given by itself and it was distributed to the Army, the Air Force and the Navy. And I would like to give the explanation of its distribution. In this war there were ... thousands of current orders which were issued by superiors to subordinate offices and were transmitted to various departments. That does not mean that each of these thousands of orders was submitted to the Commander-in-Chief; only the most decisive and most important were shown to him. The others went from department to department ...

Sir David Maxwell-Fyfe: This order would be dealt with by your prisoner-of-war department in your ministry ... ?

Göring: This department, according to the procedure adopted for these orders, received the order ...

Sir David Maxwell-Fyfe: I think the answer to my question must be 'yes'. It would be dealt with by the prisoner-of-war department of your ministry. Isn't that so?

Göring: I would say yes.

Sir David Maxwell-Fyfe: It is quicker, you see, if you say 'yes' in the beginning; do you understand?

Göring: No; it depends upon whether I personally have read the order or not ...[89]

Göring had kept his end up fairly well with Maxwell-Fyfe, but when he came to be examined by Rudenko it soon became clear that intelligence, evasion and mendacity were of little use. Rudenko addressed him as 'Defendant Göring' and adopted an attitude of biting sarcasm. He began by asking Göring what he had meant by his statement that the German invasion of Poland had started 'after the bloody happenings in the town of Bromberg'.[90] Göring's diplomatic answer was: 'I said that the date for the attack was set due to the bloody events which included, in addition to many other incidents, also the Bloody Sunday at Bromberg.'

From this it was not immediately clear whether he was wanting to challenge Rudenko or whether the Russian's question had taken him by surprise. Rudenko was not to be diverted, however, and next asked: 'Do you know that these events happened on 3 September 1939?'

Göring was somewhat rattled and tried to gain time, saying: 'I might have made a mistake regarding the date of Bromberg; I would have to see the documents about that. I merely quoted that as one example among a lot of others.'[91]

The examination then took a most undesirable turn from Göring's point of view:

General Rudenko: ... The attack was perpetrated on 1 September and the events in the town of Bromberg, which you just mentioned ... happened on 3 September 1939. I submit to the Tribunal the document evidence issued by the High Commission for the Investigation of German Crimes in Poland ... From this testimony it is clear that the events about which the Defendant Göring is testifying here happened on 3 September 1939 ...

The President: You can put the document to the witness, if you want.
General Rudenko: I have no German text. I have it in English and in Russian
... This document ... is dated 19 March and I will submit it to the
Tribunal as conclusive evidence to prove this fact.[92]

Lord Justice Lawrence, who clearly did not like Rudenko's last proposal,
at first said: 'I do not think this is the appropriate time to put in documents
in that way.' Then he relented, however, saying: 'Very well, you can put in
the document now if you like.'[93]

Rudenko was appreciative of this concession, saying politely: 'Thank
you, Mr President.'[94]

This, however, caused Lawrence to put in a proviso at once: 'It must
be translated into German of course.'[95]

When Rudenko said that he had no German translation available, the
President again explicitly pointed out to him that the defence needed a
German translation. Rudenko did not argue, saying: 'We will do that with-
out fail.'[96]

At this point Dr Stahmer, Göring's defence counsel, intervened, saying:
'May I ask to have the document read now ... so that we can hear
immediately what it contains.'

By this time the Tribunal was becoming restive; they had already
begun to formulate their sentences even before the closing addresses and
final pleas. They regarded Göring's admissions and the vast, literally overwhelming, weight of documentary evidence as sufficient to pronounce
Göring guilty on all four Counts. Their judgement includes this: 'There is
nothing to be said in mitigation. For Göring was often, indeed almost
always, the moving force, second only to his leader. He was the leading war
aggressor, both as political and as military leader; he was the director of the
slave labor program and the creator of the oppressive program against the
Jews and other races, at home and abroad. All of these crimes he has
frankly admitted. On some specific cases there may be conflict of testimony but in terms of the broad outline his own admissions are more than
sufficiently wide to be conclusive of his guilt. His guilt is unique in its
enormity. The record discloses no excuses for this man.'[97]

The fact that no one in Nuremberg succeeded in proving that the
German Wehrmacht was prepared for a war of aggression in 1939 was
ignored. Nevertheless the following were condemned for conspiracy and
planning a war of aggression: Hermann Göring, Rudolf Hess, Joachim von
Ribbentrop, Wilhelm Keitel, Alfred Rosenberg, Erich Raeder, Alfred Jodl
and Constantin von Neurath. The I M T also condemned the following for
official participation in the responsibility for wars of aggression and crimes
against peace (the wars against Britain and France and also against the
United States not counting as wars of aggression): Göring, Hess, Ribbentrop, Keitel, Rosenberg, Frick, Dönitz, Raeder, Jodl, Seyss-Inquart and
von Neurath. On all these counts decisive influences, to which hardly any of

those concerned were immune, were prejudice, lack of expertise and the fact that neither the defendants nor defence counsel were able to prove at the time that the court was not working on provable fact but was confusing deliberately angled assertions with reality.

No one in Nuremberg apart from Joachim von Ribbentrop seriously contested the fact that Hitler's Polish 'campaign' was a German war of aggression. Inevitably, however, the IMT took no account of the fact that, though the war was provoked by the Germans, secret agreements had been concluded in Moscow on 23 August 1939 between the German and Soviet governments.[98] The prosecution did not refer to this Russo-German agreement; the defence, though continually harassed by the Russians, did so, but was nevertheless not permitted to table a certified copy of the treaty.* On 1 April 1946, however, the President did allow Seidl, Hess's defence counsel, to submit an affidavit by Gaus, the German Ambassador, concerning the history and contents of this treaty, despite the fact that, before it was read, Rudenko tried to dismiss it as irrelevant. Gaus's statement, which Ribbentrop confirmed as correct in answer to a question from Seidl, inevitably embarrassed the Russians; it ran as follows:

'The plane of the Reich Foreign Minister, whom I had to accompany as legal adviser in the intended negotiations, arrived in Moscow at noon on 23 August 1939. On the afternoon of the same day the first conversation between Herr von Ribbentrop and Mr Stalin took place ...

'The Reich Foreign Minister returned very satisfied from this ... conference and indicated that it was as good as certain that it would result in the conclusion of the agreements desired on the part of Germany. The continuation of the conference ... was scheduled for later in the evening. At this second conference I participated ... On the Russian side the negotiations were conducted by Messrs Stalin and Molotov ... An agreement ... was reached quickly and without difficulties.

'Herr von Ribbentrop himself had inserted in the preamble to the agreement which I had drafted a rather far-reaching phrase concerning the formation of friendly German–Soviet relations, to which Mr Stalin objected with the remark that the Soviet government could not suddenly present to the public German–Soviet assurances of friendship after they had been covered with "pails of manure" by the Nazi government for six years. Thereupon this phrase ... was ... changed.

'Besides the Non-Aggression Pact there were negotiations for quite some time on a separate secret document, which according to my recollection was called a "secret agreement" or "secret additional agreement" and the terms of which were aimed at a demarcation of the mutual spheres of interest in the European territories situated between the two countries ... Germany declared herself politically disinterested in Latvia, Estonia and Finland but

* Equally documents showing that the British and French had also tried to get the Russians on their side in 1939 were not allowed to be tabled.

considered Lithuania to be part of her sphere of influence ... A demarcation line was laid down for the Polish territory ... Moreover an agreement was reached in regard to Poland, stating approximately that the two powers would act in mutual agreement in the final settlement of questions concerning this country ... Regarding the Balkan States it was confirmed that Germany had only economic interests there. The Non-Aggression Pact and the secret agreement were signed rather late that evening.'[99]

When this was read Rudenko pointed out angrily to the President that: 'We are not investigating the problems connected with the policy of the Allied nations but are investigating the charges against the major German war criminals.'[100]

The IMT, which had no wish to start a tit-for-tat argument, dealt in detail with the alleged 'raid' by Polish irregulars on the Gleiwitz* radio station engineered by Reinhard Heydrich in August 1939 as justification for German action; meanwhile, in accordance with the treaty, the Soviets waited in the background, ready to pounce. The court also rejected the argument advanced by the German defence that both the German campaign in Norway and Operation 'Barbarossa' were preventive wars, though it was undoubtedly true as far as the Norwegian campaign was concerned.

The fact that in 1939 the Reich was neither militarily nor economically prepared for a long war can be proved. After the overthrow of Poland, for instance, it was known that the German Wehrmacht could have fought for only about another three weeks, had the British and French launched an attack on the Reich.

When war broke out there were considerable deficiencies and shortages both in the German war economy and the German armed forces. When General Karl Bodenschatz was in the witness-box on 8 March 1946 Justice Jackson asked him: 'Göring had more confidence in air power as a weapon of war than most of the other men of his time, did he not?'[101]

Bodenschatz's answer was: 'He was convinced that his Air Force was very good. But I have to repeat ... that at the beginning of the war ... that stage had not been reached by the Air Force ... At that time the Air Force was, as far as leadership, training and material were concerned, not ready for war.'

This answer did not suit Jackson, so he dodged the issue. He wanted it confirmed by some competent German military figure that at least the German Luftwaffe had been ready and waiting for a war of aggression in

---

* See IMT Vol. XXXI, Document 2571–PS. Heydrich had ordered an SD man named Naujoks to occupy the Gleiwitz radio station with five or six other SD men and then get a Polish-speaking German to read a proclamation calling for warlike action against the Germans which would serve as 'proof' of a Polish attack on the Reich. To lend verisimilitude to this Naujoks was provided with a Polish criminal under sentence, unconscious, covered in blood and in civilian clothes, whom Naujoks' commando left behind 'on the spot' as 'proof'. See also 'Heydrich's Legacy' – Senator for Internal Affairs (Berlin), 19 November 1959, Ref: IF–0258–54/56, pp. 10ff.

1939. Since, as he recognized at once, he could not get this confirmation from Bodenschatz by direct questioning, he attempted by roundabout means to extract at least some statement which could be taken to mean what he wanted. He did not achieve his object by this method either, as the record shows:

Mr Justice Jackson: But ever since you first went with Hermann Göring you had been rapidly building up the Air Force, had you not?
Bodenschatz: The building up of the Air Force went relatively fast.
Mr Justice Jackson: And when you first went with Göring ...
Bodenschatz: I came to Hermann Göring in April 1933. At that time there was no Commander-in-Chief of the Air Force but only a Reich Commissariat for Aviation. But even at that time the beginning of the building up of the Air Force – the first beginnings – started. It was only after 1935, however, when freedom from armament restriction was declared, that it was speeded up.
Mr Justice Jackson: And the building up of the Air Force was very largely in bombers, was it not?
Bodenschatz: It was not mainly bombers; it was mixed, both fighters and bombers.[102]

After this reply the US Prosecutor finally realized that his expectations were not to be fulfilled in this way. So he dodged the issue again, asking Bodenschatz: 'Göring also had charge of the Four Year Plan?'

To this the Luftwaffe General replied: 'He was commissioned by the Führer to carry out the Four Year Plan.'

Jackson had reached the end of the road. He made Bodenschatz repeat Göring's various offices, although he knew them already, and finally even went so far as to argue with Bodenschatz about the Nazi expression 'seizure of power', a phrase which he tried to show concealed 'the coming to power of Adolf Hitler'.[103] This too got him nowhere.

Three days later, on 11 March 1946, Field Marshal Milch was in the witness-box and was equally questioned about the level of armament of the German Luftwaffe by Dr Hans Laternser, defence counsel for the General Staff and the High Command of the Armed Forces:

Dr Laternser: What time limits were set for formation of new units of the Luftwaffe?
Milch: The formation of larger units had not yet been ordered although they had been discussed quite a long time before the outbreak of war. It was intended to create a larger Air Force later, but, as far as I can remember, the plans envisaged were scheduled for completion in six or eight years' time.
Dr Laternser: In what year would the plans have been completed?
Milch: I should think about 1944–6 ...

Dr Laternser: Did an organization exist already in 1939 for day- and night-fighter planes?

Milch: No, it did not exist at that time.

Dr Laternser: Did an organization exist for bomb warfare?

Milch: Not to the extent necessary for a war of aggression.

Dr Laternser: What progress had been made at that time in the building of airfields?

Milch: Airfields had been built with runways up to 1,000 metres, but these were only suitable for fighter planes and not for loaded heavier bombers.

Dr Laternser: What was the position of the Luftwaffe Signal Corps network?

Milch: The operational network, that is, the cable network for operations, did not exist at that time; it had to be improvised and built up later on during the war.

Dr Laternser: What was the position of the Aircraft Observer Corps?

Milch: This also had not yet been organized. Reverting to the question of bombers, the most I can add is that originally, in the early years, models of four-engine bombers, which would also have been suitable for night use, were put into production. Although technically perfect, these bombers were abandoned – I believe in 1937. It was thought that the big expense entailed by such heavy bombers should be avoided, since, at that time, nobody was thinking of war ... The question was submitted for decision to the Reich Marshal, who agreed to the discontinuance of these large bombers.

Dr Laternser: When was that?

Milch: ... On 29 April 1937 the Reich Marshal, acting on the recommendation of the Chief of the General Staff, stopped the production of these long-distance bombers. Therefore, in 1939, there were no night bombers which could in any way compare with English machines of the Lancaster type ...

Dr Laternser: What was the position of the Luftwaffe crews?

Milch: We had just sufficient personnel replacements for a comparatively small Luftwaffe at that time. The lack of personnel replacement was the greatest handicap of all in building up the Luftwaffe. The whole question of time limits and so on depended on the training of personnel ... It was possible to build planes more rapidly but it was not possible to expedite the training of the crews. And, as I said ... this was the main consideration when dealing with the question of time limits. Pilots and technical personnel are of no use unless thoroughly trained. It is much worse to have half-trained personnel than no personnel at all.[104]

Such statements did not suit the President, who knew what both the prosecution and the Tribunal were expecting and wanting. He interrupted Dr Laternser, saying: 'I do not want to interrupt your cross-examination but we have been sitting here for nearly twenty minutes now and all I have got from it is that the Luftwaffe was not ready for war in 1939. It seems to me too much is being taken up with detail.'[105]

Dr Laternser, who seems to have anticipated the objection, reacted adroitly, merely putting one more question to the Field Marshal: 'Were there any reserves of aluminium, magnesium and rubber; and did any means exist for producing these materials?'[106]

Milch's answer: 'Not in sufficient quantities',[107] was unwelcome to the court, which had no wish to hear such details confirmed. At an early stage, therefore, the experts foresaw that statements on this subject by Colonel-General Alfred Jodl, who necessarily knew as much as Göring about German military armaments and war economy, would fall on deaf ears.

The Military under Cross-Examination

The true state of German military preparedness was demonstrated most clearly in the cross-examination of Jodl on 4 June 1946.[1] Not only did this call in question the whole basis of the prosecution's case against the military but it also demonstrated how questionable it inevitably was in 1945 and 1946 to pin personal responsibility on certain defendants for military events or punishable crimes and infringements of international law committed under Hitler's leadership and to make these the basis for 'obligatory' verdicts. Alfred Jodl was pronounced guilty on all four Counts; on many occasions, however, he had spoken out courageously against Hitler[2] and he himself had never been prepared to order definite criminal acts.[3] The fact that on occasions he had signed or initialled such orders – thereby giving them the appearance of legality for the mass of the soldiery – was primarily the result of the tragic discrepancy between his concept of the traditional military virtues and the role he played under Adolf Hitler. This did not weigh very heavily, however, in the scales of justice at Nuremberg.

Jodl explicitly emphasized in Nuremberg that the Hague Convention on Land Warfare and the Geneva Convention had lain on his desk 'almost permanently';[4] yet he was made personally responsible by the IMT for crimes with which he could be directly connected only by means of far-fetched arguments and by identifying him with the posts he held. In the Tenth Supplementary Trial, the Krupp Trial, the American court started from the principle that 'guilt must be personal'[5] and that membership of the firm of Krupp was not of itself sufficient for a verdict of guilty. The IMT, however, worked on the opposite assumption. Jodl was condemned as a co-conspirator of Hitler just like Göring, Hess, Ribbentrop, Keitel, Rosenberg, Raeder and von Neurath.

The concept of a 'conspiracy' or 'common plan' was one borrowed from Anglo-Saxon law and was initially firmly opposed by the French.[6] Even before the defendants were confronted with this legal principle, the fact that it led to an accusation very different from one of the commission of actual crime had been obvious at least to continental international lawyers. The French Members of the Tribunal, Donnedieu de Vabres and Robert Falco, were opposed to a collective charge of conspiracy; they demanded a precise definition of crime and were willing to accept only proven personal guilt as a basis for punishment. Although the concept of 'conspiracy' was difficult to define and juridically awkward to deal with, the Tribunal decided to take as its starting point Hitler's secret conference of 5 November 1937.[7] According to notes made subsequently (10 November 1937) by Colonel Friedrich Hossbach, who was present at this conference in the Reich Chancellery, Hitler then unfolded his war plans to Field Marshal von Blomberg, Colonel-General von Fritsch, Admiral Raeder, Colonel-General Göring and Foreign Minister von Neurath. For the Tribunal this was the vital day. Justice Jackson, on the other hand, wanted to carry the start of the conspiracy back to the period immediately following the end of the First World War when Hitler began announcing his extremist demands, threats and prophecies.[8]

In connection with the accusation of 'conspiracy' the IMT ultimately agreed on a statement which seemed to offer a way out of this thorny problem. Hitler, they maintained, could not have conducted 'wars of aggression on his own' and 'the collaboration of statesmen, military leaders, diplomats and businessmen'[9] proved that they were aware of his plans and so had turned themselves into 'participants in the plan he had elaborated'.[10] The Indictment's 'Statement of the Offense' under Count One is as follows:

'All the defendants, with divers other persons, during a period of years preceding 8 May 1945, participated as leaders, organizers, instigators or accomplices in the formulation or execution of a common plan or conspiracy to commit, or which involved the commission of, Crimes against Peace, War Crimes and Crimes against Humanity, as defined in the Charter of this Tribunal, and, in accordance with the provisions of the Charter, are individually responsible for their own acts and for all acts committed by any persons in the execution of such plan or conspiracy. The common plan or conspiracy embraced the commission of Crimes against Peace, in that the defendants planned, prepared, initiated and waged wars of aggression, which were also wars in violation of international agreements, treaties or assurances. In the development and course of the common plan or conspiracy it came to embrace the commission of War Crimes, in that it contemplated, and the defendants determined upon and carried out, ruthless wars against countries and populations, in violation of the rules and customs of war, including as typical and systematic means by which the wars were prosecuted, murder, ill-treatment, deportation for slave labor and for other purposes of civilian populations of occupied territories, murder and ill-treatment of prisoners of war and of persons on the high seas, the taking and killing of hostages, the plunder of public and private property, the indiscriminate destruction of cities, towns and villages, and devastation not justified by military necessity. The common plan or conspiracy contemplated and came to embrace as typical and systematic means, and the defendants determined upon and committed, Crimes against Humanity, both within Germany and within occupied territories, including murder, extermination, enslavement, deportation and other inhumane acts committed against civilian populations before and during the war, and persecutions on political, racial or religious grounds, in execution of the plan for preparing and prosecuting aggressive or illegal wars, many of such acts and persecutions being violations of the domestic laws of the countries where perpetrated.'[11]

The examination of Jodl on 4 June 1946, eagerly awaited particularly by critics of the trial, proved to be a good illustration of the value attached to statements by the defendants on the state of German armaments in 1939 and the attribution of guilt under Counts One and Two. The record is as follows:

Dr Exner: ... Now I shall turn to the alleged Crimes against Peace. First of all we have to make it clear what posts you held during this critical period. Tell us ... what posts you held from 1933.

Jodl: From 1932 to 1935 I was in the division which was later called the Operations Division of the Army. From the middle of 1935 until October 1938 I was Chief of the Department for National Defense in the Wehrmachtsamt, which was later called the OKW ... From October 1938 until shortly before the Polish campaign I was artillery commander at Vienna and at Brünn, in Moravia; and ... on 27 August 1939 I took over the office and the tasks of Chief of the General Staff.

Dr Exner: ... Did you concern yourself with war plans in the years 1932–1935 when you were in the so-called Truppenamt?

Jodl: At that time there were no preparations in the Operations Division, except for combat directives for the improvised Grenzschutz Ost (frontier guard East). This was a militia-like organization and preparations were made to evacuate the whole German border in case of enemy occupation. That was all.

Dr Exner: Had you anything to do with the proclamation of general conscription?

Jodl: No, I had nothing to do with that ...

Dr Exner: What were your duties as chief of the Department for National Defense from June 1935 to October 1938?

Jodl: In this position I had to work out the operational strategic directives according to the instructions of my chiefs, Keitel and Blomberg. I had to study and to clarify the problem of the leadership of the Wehrmacht; to prepare studies and exercises for the big Wehrmacht maneuvers in 1937. I had to supervise the Wehrmacht Academy; I had to work out drafts for laws in connection with the general conscription order and with the unified preparation for mobilization in the civilian sector, that is, of state and people. The so-called Secretariat of the Reich Defense Committee came under me.

Dr Exner: ... What were you at the time? What was your military rank?

Jodl: I acquired that position while I was a lieutenant colonel; and in 1936 – I believe – I became a colonel.[12]

On the previous day Exner had had to try to protect his client against certain definite charges:

Dr Exner: The Prosecution has asserted that you enjoyed the good graces of the Führer and that the Führer lavished his favor on you. How much of that is true?

Jodl: I need not waste many words on that. What I said is the ... truth ... What the Prosecution said is imagination ... If the Prosecution mean that as a so-called political soldier I was promoted especially quickly, they are mistaken. I became a general in my fiftieth year. That is quite normal. In July 1940, when I was appointed General of Artillery, it is true I skipped the grade of lieutenant general, but that was only an accident. A much younger general in the Air Force, Jeschonnek, Chief of the General Staff of the Luftwaffe, was to be promoted to Air Chief Marshal. Then Schmundt said to the Führer: 'Jodl could perhaps do that too.' Thereupon, shortly before the Reichstag session, the Führer decided to promote me also – to General of Artillery.[13]

Exner's next questions (his personal attachment to Jodl was obvious both to the prosecution and the court) were designed to enable the defence to reduce Counts One and Two *ad absurdum*. The record continues:

Dr Exner: Did you not receive exceptional decorations from Hitler?

Jodl: To my surprise ... on 30 January 1943, I received from the Führer the Golden Party Badge.* That was the only decoration I received from the Führer.

Dr Exner: In the entire five and a half years of war?

Jodl: Yes.

Dr Exner: Did you receive a gift or donation from Hitler or from the Party?

Jodl: Not a single cent. If I am to conceal nothing I must mention the fact that at headquarters we received a package of coffee from the Führer each Christmas.

Dr Exner: Did you acquire any property in the territories occupied by us, or receive any as a gift or as a token of remembrance?

Jodl: Nothing at all. When in the Indictment the sentence is found to the effect that the defendants enriched themselves from the occupied terri-

---

*From August 1942 to the end of January 1943 Hitler ostentatiously avoided Jodl, even refusing to shake hands with him. In the witness-box Jodl stated: 'Hitler never came to the mess during the remainder of the war (after August 1943). The report on the situation was no longer given in my maproom but in the Führer's quarters. At every report on the situation from that day on an SS officer took part. Eight stenographers were ordered to be there and from then on they took down every word. The Führer refused to shake hands with me any more. He did not greet me any more, or rarely. This situation lasted until 30 January 1943. He told me, through Field Marshal Keitel, that he could no longer work with me and that I would be replaced by General Paulus as soon as Paulus had taken Stalingrad' (IMT Vol. XV, pp. 300–301).

tories, as far as I am concerned I have only one word for that, and I must be frank – it is libel against a decent German officer.[14]

To return to the cross-examination of 4 June 1946, it continued as follows:

Dr Exner: Did you take any part in the Reich Defense Law?

Jodl: No, that law originated before I entered my office in the Wehrmachtsamt.

Dr Exner: But the Prosecution is accusing you of participation in it ... What can you tell us about that?

Jodl: ... It [Document 2261–PS, US–24] is ... a Reich law of which I had to transmit a copy to one of the other offices. I need not say more than that.

Dr Exner: You yourself did not participate in the drawing up of the law itself?

Jodl: No ...

Dr Exner: Were you a member of the Reich Defense Committee?

Jodl: I was that automatically from the moment I took over the direction of the National Defense Department ...

Dr Exner: What was the purpose of this Committee? ...

Jodl: ... With this Committee a unified mobilization, not of the Army, but the mobilization of the State and people, corresponding to military mobilization, was prepared. These plans were laid down ...

Dr Exner: Did the Reich Defense Committee concern itself with armament?

Jodl: No, it did not concern itself with armament at all.

Dr Exner: Did the Reich Defense Committee concern itself with political plans or intentions?

Jodl: It had nothing to do in any way with political problems.

Dr Exner: But how about war?

Jodl: It was concerned only with mobilization ...

Dr Exner: In this committee you concerned yourself with mobilization books. Is that correct?

Jodl: Yes. I believe I have already explained that. In these books the details of all the chief Reich authorities were set down and indexed according to degrees of tension.

Dr Exner: What do you mean by chief Reich authorities?

Jodl: I mean all the ministries.

Dr Exner: You mean the civil authorities?

Jodl: Yes, the civil authorities. The preparations made by them had to be brought into line with the preparations by the military.

Dr Exner: What were the preparations in the demilitarized zone?

Jodl: The preparations in the demilitarized zone were connected solely with evacuation, that is the surrendering of the areas west of the Rhine in case of a French occupation.

Dr Exner: ... You are accused of having decreed the utmost secrecy concerning all these preparations, which, according to your description, were of a purely defensive nature. Why all this secrecy?

Jodl: Keeping measures of this kind secret is taken for granted all over the world. For us in Germany it was especially important, as for years the civil authorities had no longer been accustomed to concern themselves with military matters, and it seemed to me of particular importance that in foreign countries no misunderstanding should arise by, let us say, the capture of an order of this nature – a very characteristic misunderstanding such as occurred in these proceedings in connection with the 'Freimachung' of the Rhine.*

Dr Exner: And why did you decree secrecy? So that foreign countries would not be disquieted?

Jodl: At that time we were even weaker than during the period when we had an army of only 100,000 men. This army of 100,000 men had been broken up into hundreds of small groups. It was the time of our very greatest impotence, and at that period we had to be extremely careful to avoid any and all tension with foreign countries.

Dr Exner: What were the military plans of those days?

Jodl: ... There were the combat directives for the Grenzschutz Ost. I had also worked out instructions for the commander in East Prussia in case he were cut off from the Reich through a sudden attack by Poland.

Dr Exner: Did you know of any German intentions of attack at that time?

Jodl: There was no thought or talk of that whatsoever ...

Dr Exner: Were you concerned with armament in the Truppenamt, and later in the Department for National Defense?

Jodl: I personally had nothing at all to do with armament in the real sense. That was a matter for the various branches of the Wehrmacht – the Army, the Navy, the Air Force – and it was dealt with and handled by their organizational staffs. The Commanders-in-Chief discussed these matters with the Führer direct. But I hope, and I will not deny, that my work in the General Staff contributed to the reconstruction of the German Wehrmacht.

Dr Exner: Your diary, 1780–P S,[15] does not contain a word about armament ... What were your thoughts ... on the question of armament? ...

Jodl: At that time I was of the same opinion as my superiors, and it was characteristic that on the day before the statement was made that thirty-six divisions were to be formed, Blomberg as well as Fritsch suggested to the Führer that only twenty-four divisions should be formed. They feared a thinning down of the entire army. Perhaps they also feared too stormy a foreign policy, based on forces existing only on paper.

Dr Exner: ... What were the deadlines in connection with armament in 1935?

* Here Jodl is alluding to the argument between Jackson and Göring. See pp. 117ff above.

Jodl: Various stages were provided for. The first deadline set was 1942–3. Most of the West Wall was to be completed by 1945. The Navy's plan of construction ran on to 1944–5.

Dr Exner: At that time what did you consider the objective of the armament?

Jodl: Since it was not possible to achieve general disarmament, the objective was to establish military parity between Germany and the neighbouring countries.

Dr Exner: In this connection I should like to refer to a document which has already been submitted – the two-year report of General George Marshall ... I have a part of it here before me ... Some sentences seem to hit the nail right on the head ... 'The world does not seriously consider the wishes of the weak. Weakness is too great a temptation to the strong, particularly to the brutal who scheme for wealth and power.' Then on the next page there is another sentence: 'Above all we must, I think, correct the tragic misunderstanding that a security policy is a war policy.' Can you tell us ... what the ratio of our military strength to that of foreign countries was at that time?

Jodl: In 1935, when we set up thirty-six divisions, France, Poland and Czechoslovakia possessed ninety divisions for times of peace and 190 divisions for war. We had hardly any heavy artillery and tank construction was in its earliest stages ...

Dr Exner: I should like to quote from an expert, George Marshall again ... 'The only effective defense a nation can now maintain is the power of attack ...' Now, however, the Prosecution asserts that you should have known that such a tremendous rearmament as the German rearmament could serve only for aggressive war. Will you comment on this?

Jodl: I believe this can only be explained as an expression of military ignorance. Up to the year 1939 we were, of course, in a position to destroy Poland alone. But we were never, either in 1938 or 1939, actually in a position to withstand a concentrated attack by these states together, and if we did not collapse already in the year 1939 that was due only to the fact that during the Polish campaign, the approximately 110 French and British divisions in the West were held completely inactive against twenty-three German divisions.[16]

Dr Exner: But ... when did intensive rearmament actually begin?

Jodl: Real rearmament was only begun after the war had already started. We entered into this world war with some seventy-five divisions. Sixty per cent of our total able-bodied population had not been trained. The peacetime army amounted to perhaps 400,000 men as against 800,000 men in 1914. Our supplies of ammunition and bombs ... were ridiculously low.

Dr Exner: In this connection I should like to read a diary entry of yours ... You said: '... Field Marshal reports on state of war potential of Wehrmacht, indicating chief bottleneck is inadequate stocks of ammunition for Army – ten to fifteen days of combat equals six weeks' supply.'

Jodl: That is right, we had ammunition for ten to fifteen days of combat.[17]

In spite of all this the IMT's judgement on Jodl says: '... in the strict military sense Jodl was the actual planner of the war ...'[18] As regards crimes against peace it is even more incomprehensible, saying: '... responsible in large measure for the strategy and conduct of operations.'[19]

One thing is certain: in 1939 Germany was not prepared for a long war and certainly not for a war of aggression even against a comparatively small power. But in 1939 neither the German public nor the Allied secret services[20] knew how bad the state of German armament was.[21] Admittedly Hitler had demanded in 1936 that the Wehrmacht and the economy be ready and prepared for war by 1940;[22] but, viewed in the light of German industrial capacity, the arms programme had started sluggishly. By September 1939 in no branch of the German economy had production reached a level commensurate with war preparations.[23]

Even in May 1940 the arms industry accounted for less than 15 per cent of total industrial production; by 1941 the figure was 19 per cent, by 1942 26 per cent, by 1943 38 per cent and finally in 1944 it reached 50 per cent.[24] According to Speer[25] the index for explosives production rose from 103 for 1941 to 131 for 1942, 191 for 1943 and 226 for 1944; the index for munitions production, including bombs, on the other hand, went from 102 for 1941 to 106 for 1942, 247 for 1943 and 306 for 1944. By May 1940 fewer than forty tanks were being turned out per month; by 1944, on the other hand, the figure was 2,000 per month. In 1939 German aircraft production, including civil aircraft, trainers and transport aircraft, was not even 1,000 a month, whereas in 1944, after prolonged bombing and much damage, the figure for fighters alone over a similar period was 4,000. As things were Hitler's loudly proclaimed allocation of 90 milliard marks for armaments on 1 September 1939[26] was calculated only to impress the non-experts. The military in official positions knew that stocks of raw materials were adequate for at most twelve weeks of war and that 25 per cent of the necessary zinc, 50 per cent of lead, 65 per cent of mineral oil, 70 per cent of copper, 80 per cent of rubber, 90 per cent of tin, 95 per cent of nickel and 99 per cent of bauxite had to be imported from abroad.[27]

Hitler, of course, knew this too; he also knew, however, that since 23 August 1939 with the conclusion of the Russo-German Non-Aggression Pact the Reich's strategic and war economy situation had changed materially.[28] He stepped up production of synthetic rubber[29] and synthetic fuels;[30] he relied on the Soviet Union's neutrality and economic support to enable him, after the overthrow of Poland, to have all his forces available for a campaign in the West with no threat to his rear; he counted on raw material deliveries from south-east Europe and Scandinavia.

Immediately after the Polish campaign, however, Hitler was in a difficult situation. He and the General Staff knew how long they could go on fighting with the expenditure demanded by a 'blitzkrieg'. They could calculate that, although stocks of raw materials were adequate for about three months, the war would have had to end in a fortnight, had the French and British attacked in the West.[31] Ammunition stocks had been almost exhausted during the Polish campaign and the forces manning the West Wall were totally inadequate. Under these conditions continuation of offensive war was little better than an adventure – from which Hitler did not shrink.

Hitler knew that, except in the matter of German armaments, time was on his side rather than against him and he was ready to take the risk. It is difficult to say whether, at the time, he overestimated his power position and underestimated that of his enemies. The General Staff, who had had experience of Hitler's faith in his star and readiness to take risks, was sceptical – he had achieved nothing so far. He did not have the 3·2 million men whom he had demanded should be ready for war by 1939.[32] Only four annual intakes, men born in 1914, 1915, 1916 and 1917, had been trained. But, contrary to the advice of his surprised military advisers,[33] Hitler, who was better informed than the General Staff on many matters of detail, believed that his offensive would not raise additional problems but would lead to a quick victory over France. France, Britain's most important continental ally, was to be overwhelmed in a 'blitzkrieg' and, under the impact of this, Britain could be persuaded to bring the war to an end.

After his successful solution of the 'Sudeten crisis' Hitler was more convinced than ever that at heart the people of the Great German Reich were behind him for better or worse.[34] At the time of the crisis he had overridden the views of the Army High Command and had hectored its Commander-in-Chief, telling him that decisions in that situation were not military but political and only he could take them; this the more susceptible among the officers had pushed out of their minds. During the second half of September 1938 certain influential officers, among whom was Field Marshal Erwin von Witzleben, had planned a rising against Hitler, but in view of his successes in Berchtesgaden, Godesberg and Munich it never took place.

On 12 December 1939 Grand Admiral Erich Raeder drew Hitler's attention to the dangers threatening the Reich and the German war economy if the British occupied Norway, as Winston Churchill, then First Lord of the Admiralty, had recommended in a memorandum dated 19 September. To the consternation of the generals[35] Hitler immediately by-passed the Commander-in-Chief of the Army, the chief of the General Staff and the Army Operations Division on all matters of deployment and command of land forces; on 13 December 1939 Hitler ordered that 'a very small staff should examine methods of occupying Norway' and, contrary to established practice, Jodl passed this to the Luftwaffe General Staff officer in the OKW Operations Staff.[36]

To turn now to Field Marshal Wilhelm Keitel: until 1945 he had been

Hitler's representative of the German Wehrmacht; from February 1938 he had carried the pretentious title of 'Chief of the High Command of the German Armed Forces' (Chef des Oberkommandos der Wehrmacht) but underneath Hitler he had never had any real command authority commensurate with his position; he had never been more than a military 'secretary', totally devoted to the Führer.* He had come to Nuremberg determined to shield his staff and subordinates from the fate which he himself faced.

In his final message to OKW on 15 May 1945 he had said: 'It is hard for me to say farewell for ever to this comradely circle. As a prisoner of war I face sentence as a war criminal; my sole desire now is to shield my previous subordinates from a similar fate. My military career is at an end; my life is drawing to its close.'[37]

Keitel's attitude was dignified; he tried to shield his former subordinates; he never tried to defend himself at the expense of other officers and he never deliberately distorted facts in order to produce a picture of heroism. On 21 May 1946, after the Russians had tried to use against him certain derogatory remarks made about him by Grand Admiral Raeder while interned in Moscow and intended for his personal memoirs,[38] Keitel wrote to Dr Nelte, his defence counsel: 'I am too ashamed of myself to be able to tell you this by word of mouth.'[39] Dr Lehmann, Head of the Wehrmacht Legal Service, said of Keitel that, though brave enough to take on a lion with his bare fists, in face of Adolf Hitler he was 'helpless as a child'.[40] Keitel himself talked of the soldier's duty to obey and, on his relationship to politics, noted, perhaps as a draft of his 'Final Plea':

'As already explained, we [he and Jodl] looked upon our duties in this way: as assistants to the Führer for the operational tasks planned and ordered by him we had nothing to do with the political motives or background. That was no concern of ours. I neither can, nor do I wish to, defend the game of "high politics", the methods of diplomatic camouflage or the numerous infringements of assurances given. Moreover it would not be right were I to say that we had no knowledge of all these things. The truth is that we were not officially concerned with these matters and the Führer had told us categorically that political affairs were no concern of ours. As far as operational orders (the so-called directives) were concerned or the instructions issued for their implementation, they were orders by the Supreme Commander. I do not dispute that, whether they carried my signature or not, I had knowledge of all these orders, that Hitler had discussed them with me and Colonel-General Jodl, that I passed them on to the armed services concerned and supervised their implementation. Colonel-General Jodl and I were not always in agreement with the Supreme Commander's operational decisions but we invariably carried them out. We

* Only once had he refused to obey Hitler – on 22 April 1945 in Berlin, when Hitler ordered him to fly to Berchtesgaden that night. In Jodl's presence Keitel declared: 'In seven years I have never refused to execute an order from you, but this is one order I shall never carry out' (*The Memoirs of Field Marshal Keitel*, p. 202).

never discussed with the Führer the question of aggressive or defensive war. According to our concept that was not our job. I accept responsibility for this point of view and this method of working.'[41]

On 5 April 1945 Rudenko, the Soviet Prosecutor, who was very well informed on Keitel's relationship to Hitler, opened his examination – and the IMT's judgement on Keitel follows the line of Rudenko's cross-examination with disconcerting exactitude.[42] Rudenko began with the psychologically adroit question what was Keitel's judgement, as a German Field Marshal and Chief of the High Command of the German Armed Forces,[43] of the military capabilities of his former Supreme Commander, Adolf Hitler.[44] Keitel, it should be remembered, had joined the Army as a cadet in 1901, had become a regular officer and been promoted in the usual way;[45] after some six years as regimental adjutant he had been given command of a battery on the outbreak of the First World War; in March 1915 he had been posted as General Staff officer in the Great General Staff and, after holding various other important military posts, had taken over the Wehrmacht Office in the Reich War Ministry in 1935.[46] Nevertheless he did not disown Hitler – or his own previous estimate of him. In Nuremberg he took no account of his own personal prestige and so did not fulfil Rudenko's expectations, as the following extracts from the record show:

Gen. Rudenko: Should we not conclude that you, with your thorough military training and great experience, could have had an opportunity of influencing Hitler very considerably in solving questions of a strategic and military nature, as well as other matters pertaining to the Armed Forces?
Keitel: No. I have to declare in that respect that, to a degree which is almost incomprehensible to the layman and the professional officer, Hitler had studied general staff publications, military literature, essays on tactics, operations and strategy and that he had a knowledge in the military fields which can only be called amazing. May I give an example of that which can be confirmed by the other officers of the Wehrmacht. Hitler was so well informed concerning organization, armament, leadership and equipment of all armies, and what is more remarkable, of all navies of the globe, that it was impossible to prove any error on his part; and I have to add that also during the war, while I was at his headquarters and in his close proximity, Hitler studied at night all the big general staff books by Moltke, Schlieffen and Clausewitz and from them acquired his knowledge by himself. Therefore we had the impression: Only a genius can do that.
Gen. Rudenko: You will not deny that by reason of your military training and experience you were Hitler's adviser in a number of important matters?
Keitel: I belonged to his closest military entourage and I heard a lot from him; but I pointed out ... to the question of my counsel that even in the simple everyday questions concerning organization and equipment of the Wehrmacht, I must admit openly that I was the pupil and not the master.[47]

Rudenko, who then tried to convict Keitel of participation in the 'Common Plan', made him describe the part he played under Hitler. In doing so Keitel not only took everyone by surprise with remarks about Hitler which had hardly anything to do with the facts, but he dumbfounded the court by his truly astounding naïveté in matters political. What he knew about or of Hitler was horrifyingly little – and most of it wrong. He thought, for instance, that, despite numerous statements by Hitler to the contrary, Hitler had told him that he had been an officer in 1918.[48] Despite his exalted military position he had clearly never read Hitler's *Mein Kampf.*

The Field Marshal's description of his relationship to Hitler had been promising – from the prosecution's point of view – but the Soviet Prosecutor could do nothing with the answers he now began to receive. The record shows:

Gen. Rudenko: From what date do you consider that your cooperation with Hitler began?
Keitel: Exactly from ... 4 February 1938.
Gen. Rudenko: That means that you were working with Hitler during the entire period of preparation for and realization of aggressive warfare?
Keitel: Yes. I have already given all the necessary explanations as to how ... events followed in quick succession, often in a very surprising manner ...
Gen. Rudenko: Who, besides you, among the military collaborators of the OKH and the OKW, signed decrees together with Hitler and the other Reich Ministers?
Keitel: In the ministerial sector of the Reich government there was the method of the signatures of the Führer and Reich Chancellor and the Ministers immediately involved, and finally of the Chief of the Reich Chancellery. This did not hold good for the military sector, for according to the traditions of the German Army and the Wehrmacht the signatures were given by the principal experts who had worked on the matter, by the Chief of Staff, or by whoever had given or at least drafted the order, and an initial was added on the margin.[49]
Gen. Rudenko: Yesterday you said that you signed such decrees ...
Keitel: Yes, yesterday I mentioned individual decrees and also gave the reasons why I signed them ...
Gen. Rudenko: What organization exercised the function of the War Ministry from February 1938 on?
Keitel: Until the last days of January or the first days of February it was the former Reich Minister for War, von Blomberg. Beginning with 4 February there was neither a Minister for War nor a War Ministry.
Gen. Rudenko: That is precisely why I asked you what government organization had replaced the War Ministry and exercised its function ...
Keitel: I myself with the Wehrmachtsamt, the former staff of the War Ministry, whose chief I was, carried on the work and distributed it ...

that is, I transferred all command functions to the commanders-in-chief of the branches of the Wehrmacht. But this was . . . an order of Hitler's.

Gen. Rudenko: From the diagram you have submitted to this Tribunal it would appear that the OKW was the central, coordinating and supreme military authority of the Reich and that it was directly under Hitler's control. Would this conclusion be correct?

Keitel: Yes, that was the military staff of Hitler.[50]

Though devotedly loyal to Hitler, Keitel had been tormented by scruples; behind Hitler's back he had given Frau Canaris financial support after her husband's arrest and he had persuaded Himmler to treat leniently the families of officers executed in connection with 20 July 1944. Nevertheless, like Dönitz,[51] Raeder[52] and Jodl,[53] he had to take responsibility for passing on Hitler's orders, with which the IMT identified the defendants. The fact that they were obeying the principle of military subordination to the political authority and that, as disciplined soldiers, they kept their personal, moral, legal and military scruples to themselves was a factor telling against them in Nuremberg. Rudenko's cross-examination of Keitel illustrates this with particular clarity. The record continues:

Gen. Rudenko: Who, in the OKW, directly supervised the drafting of military and strategic plans . . . plans for the attacks on Austria, Czechoslovakia, Poland, Belgium, Holland, France, Norway, Yugoslavia and the Soviet Union?

Keitel: . . . the operational and strategic planning, after an order had been given by Hitler, was prepared and then submitted to Hitler by the commanders-in-chief of the branches of the Wehrmacht; that is to say, for the Army by the High Command of the Army and the General Staff of the Army, and then further decisions were made with respect to it.

Gen. Rudenko: With regard to Yugoslavia I should like to ask you the following question: Do you admit that a directive issued under your signature, for the preliminary partition of Yugoslavia, is *per se* a document of great political and international importance, providing for the actual abolition of Yugoslavia as a sovereign state?

Keitel: I did nothing more or less than write down a decree by the Führer and forward it to those offices which were interested and concerned. I did not have any personal or political influence whatsoever in these questions.

Gen. Rudenko: Under your own signature?

Keitel: As to the signatures which I have given, I made a complete explanation yesterday as to how they came about and what their significance is.

Gen. Rudenko: Yes, we did talk about it . . . I should now like to determine with greater precision your own position in the question of Yugoslavia. Do you agree that you, with the direct participation of the OKW, organized acts of provocation in order to find a reason for aggression against

Yugoslavia and a justification for this aggression in the eyes of the world?
Keitel: This morning, in response to questions of the counsel of other defendants, I answered clearly that I did not participate in any preparation of an incident and that Hitler did not wish either that any military officers should ever participate in the discussion, preparation, deliberation or the execution of incidents. I use 'incident' here in the sense of provocation ...
Gen. Rudenko: By whom and for what was the order issued to occupy Ostrau in Moravia and Witkovitz by German troops on 14 March 1939, in the afternoon, while President Hacha was still on the way to Berlin for negotiations with Hitler?
Keitel: The order was eventually released and decided by the Führer. There had been preparations to occupy by a *coup de main* that area where the well-known big and modern steel works were located near Mährisch-Ostrau ... before the date of the march into Czechoslovakia as originally set. As a justification for that decision, Hitler had told me that it was done in order to prevent the Poles from making a surprise attack from the north, and thereby perhaps taking possession of the most modern rolling mill in the world ...
Gen. Rudenko: Yes, but during the same time, President Hacha was on the way to Berlin to negotiate with Hitler.
Keitel: Yes, that is correct.
Gen. Rudenko: This is treachery!
Keitel: I do not believe that I need to add my judgement to the facts. It is true that the occupation was carried out on that evening. I have given the reasons and President Hacha learned about it only after he arrived in Berlin ...
Gen. Rudenko: I have a few more questions to ask you in connection with the aggression against the Soviet Union ... You explained your position with regard to the attack on the Soviet Union. But you informed the Tribunal that the orders for preparing Plan Barbarossa were given at the beginning of December 1940. Is that right?
Keitel: Yes.
Gen. Rudenko: Do you definitely remember and confirm this?
Keitel: I do not know of, or do not remember, any specific order by the High Command of the Wehrmacht which called for the drawing up of this plan called Barbarossa any earlier than that. I explained yesterday, however, that some order had been issued, probably in September, concerning transport and railway facilities and similar matters ...
Gen. Rudenko: In September?
Keitel: It may have been in September or October but I cannot commit myself as to the exact time.
Gen. Rudenko: I wish to know the exact time.
Keitel: More accurate information may probably be obtained at a later stage from General Jodl, who ought to know it better.
Gen. Rudenko: ... I should like you to recollect the following briefly: Did

you first learn of Hitler's schemes to attack the Soviet Union in the summer of 1940? ...

Keitel: ... having been absent from Berchtesgaden for about two weeks, partly on leave and partly on duty in Berlin, I returned to headquarters at Berchtesgaden; and then on one of the subsequent days, probably during the middle of August, I heard for the first time ideas of that kind from Hitler ...

Gen. Rudenko: ... You informed the Tribunal that you were opposed to the war with the Soviet Union. Is that correct?

Keitel: Yes.

Gen. Rudenko: You also stated that you went to Hitler with the suggestion that he should change his plans with regard to the Soviet Union. Is that correct?

Keitel: Yes, not only to change them, but to drop this plan and not to wage war against the Soviet Union. That was the content of my memorandum.

Gen. Rudenko: ... I would now like to ask you about a conference ... which was held three weeks after Germany had attacked the Soviet Union, the conference of 16 July 1941. Do you remember that conference, which dealt with the tasks for the conduct of the war against the Soviet Union?

Keitel: No, at the moment I do not know what you mean ...

Gen. Rudenko: And you tell the Tribunal under oath that you did not know of the Hitlerite plans to seize and colonize the territories of the Soviet Union?

Keitel: That has not been expressed in that form. It is true that I believed that the Baltic provinces should be made dependents of the Reich, and that the Ukraine should come into a closer connection from the point of view of food supply or economy, but concrete plans for conquest are not known to me and, if they were ever touched upon, I never considered them to be serious problems ...

Gen. Rudenko: Do you know that before the beginning of the war against the Soviet Union the Defendant Göring issued a so-called Green Folder containing directives on the economic matters in the territories of the USSR intended for occupation?

Keitel: Yes, that is known to me.

Gen. Rudenko: Do you affirm that in your directive of 16 June 1941 you instructed all the German troops to obey these directives implicitly?

Keitel: Yes, there is a directive which makes known to all units of the Army the organizations which are assigned for important tasks and what their responsibilities are and that all the military commands of the Army must act in compliance therewith. That I passed on; it was not my order, I passed it on.

Gen. Rudenko: Was it your own order or were you merely obeying the Führer's instructions?

Keitel: I merely passed on the orders received from the Führer ...

Gen. Rudenko: You did not disagree with this will of the Führer's?

Keitel: I did not raise any objection, since this did not concern a duty of OKW. I followed the order and passed it on.

Gen. Rudenko: Do you admit that this order gave you instructions for the immediate and complete economic exploitation of the occupied regions of the Soviet Union in the interest of German war economy?

Keitel: I did not give such an order . . . since I had nothing to do with that. I only passed on the contents of the Green Folder . . . to the High Command of the Army for appropriate action.

Gen. Rudenko: Do you admit that the directives contained in Göring's Green Folder were aimed at the plunder of the material wealth of the Soviet Union and all her citizens?

Keitel: No. In my opinion nothing was said about destruction in the Green Folder. Instead of destruction one ought to say, to make good use of surplus, especially in the field of the food supply and the utilization of raw materials for the entire war economy of Germany, but not the destruction of them . . .

Gen. Rudenko: You do not consider that plunder?

Keitel: The quibble about words, whether booty, or exploitation of reserves found during the war, or looting, or the like, is a matter of concepts which I believe need not be defined here. Everyone uses his own expressions in this respect.[54]

What the expressions used by Keitel actually meant was to be seen from Himmler's reports to the Führer. These produced simply the factual statistical data which interested Hitler. On 29 December 1942, for instance, in his 'Report No. 51' headed 'To the Führer on anti-bandit operations'[55] Himmler reported for the period August–November 1942 inclusive, in southern Russia, the Ukraine and Bialystok alone: 3,442 cattle, 2,869 pigs, 2,930 sheep, 486 horses, 65 calves, 80 tons of grain, $2\frac{1}{2}$ tons of linseed and a quantity of tools and machinery captured; 159 localities and villages, 1,978 isolated farms, 113 landed estates, 30 sawmills and forestry buildings and 35 industrial installations burnt down and destroyed.[56]

The record for 5 April 1946 continues:

Gen. Rudenko: . . . I have one . . . question . . . with regard to the attack on the Soviet Union: Do you agree that the methods of warfare adopted by the German Army in the East stood in striking contrast with the simplest concept of military honor of an army and the exigencies of war?

Keitel: No, I cannot admit that in this form. I would rather say, the fact that the brutalizing . . . of the war against the Soviet Union and what occurred in the East is not to be attributed to instigation by the German Army . . .[57]

About an hour later Rudenko asked Keitel whether he remembered a document dated 13 May 1941: 'Do you remember that in that document, drawn up before the war, instructions were given that suspect elements should immediately be brought before an officer and that he would decide whether they were to be shot? ... Did you sign the document?

Keitel's answer was: 'Yes, I have never denied that ...'

The record then continues:

Gen. Rudenko: ... Did you consider that an officer had a right to shoot people without trial or investigation?

Keitel: In the German Army there have always been courts martial for our own soldiers as well as for our enemies, which could always be set up, consisting of one officer and one or two soldiers, all three of whom would act as judges. That is what we call a court martial (*Standgericht*); the only requisite is always that an officer must preside at this court ...

Gen. Rudenko: ... Please reply to this question. Did not this document do away with judicial proceedings in the case of so-called suspects, at the same time leaving to an officer of the German Army the right to shoot them? ...

Keitel: That was an order which was given me by Hitler. He had given me that order and I put my name under it ...

Gen. Rudenko: You, a Field Marshal, signed that decree. You considered that the decree was irregular; you understood what the consequences of that decree were likely to be. Then why did you sign it?

Keitel: I cannot say any more than that I put my name to it and I thereby, personally, assumed in my position a degree of responsibility.

Gen. Rudenko: And one more question. This decree was dated 13 May 1941, almost a month before the outbreak of war. So you had planned the murder of human beings beforehand?

Keitel: That I do not understand. It is correct that this order was issued about four weeks before the beginning of the campaign Barbarossa, and another four weeks earlier it had been communicated to the generals in a statement by Hitler. They knew that weeks before ...

Gen. Rudenko: Defendant Keitel, I am asking you about the directive concerning the so-called communist insurrectionary movement in the occupied territories ... It is an order of 16 September 1941 ... It states: 'In order to nip in the bud any conspiracy, the strongest measures should be taken at the first sign of trouble in order to maintain the authority of the occupying power and to prevent the conspiracy from spreading.' And then it goes on: 'One must bear in mind that in the countries affected human life has absolutely no value and that a deterrent effect can be achieved only through the application of extraordinarily harsh measures.' ... Do you remember this statement, the basic statement of the order, that 'human life has absolutely no value'?

Keitel: Yes.

Gen. Rudenko: You signed the order containing this statement?

Keitel: Yes.[58]

To Rudenko's question whether he, Keitel, knew how 'this decree was actually applied', Keitel replied: 'I wish to point out ... that the higher commanders have the right to suspend this order as soon as their area is pacified and they were allowed to suspend this order as soon as they considered their area to be pacified. That is an individual subjective question for the discretion of the commanders.'[59]

On 20 December 1942 Himmler had reported to the Führer that in connection with anti-bandit operations in southern Russia, the Ukraine and Bialystok the following had been executed by the regular police (Ordnungspolizei) and the Security Police (Sicherheitspolizei) during the previous four months: 1,337 'bandits' during operations, 737 immediately on capture, 7,328 after prolonged exhaustive interrogation, 14,257 'bandit auxiliaries and suspects' and in addition 363,211 Jews – a total of 386,870 people.[60]

Using data from the S S Central Security Department (Reichssicherheitshauptamt), in March 1943[61] Himmler's 'Inspector of Statistics' listed 633,300 Jews as having been 'evacuated' from Russian territory 'including the former Baltic states' between the 'start of the eastern campaign'[62] and 1 January 1943; in addition by that date 170,642 Jews from Reich territory (including the Protectorate of Bohemia and Moravia and the district of Bialystok) and 1,449,692 'from the eastern provinces'[63] had been transported 'to the Russian east'.[64]

The expressions 'from Reich territory' and 'from the eastern provinces' may be obscure to the uninitiated, but their use was deliberate, as Himmler himself confirmed. On 9 April 1943, for instance, he wrote to the Head of the Security Police and S D (Sicherdienst): 'I regard this report as potential material for later use and excellent for camouflage purposes. At present it should neither be published nor distributed.'[65] The report also includes this: 'Between 1937 and early 1945 the number of Jews in Europe should have been reduced by an estimated 4 million, partly through emigration, partly through the surplus of deaths over births among Jews of central and western Europe and partly through evacuation primarily to the more heavily populated eastern territories, which for this purpose may be considered separately. In this connection it should not be overlooked that the number of deaths of Soviet Russian Jews in the occupied eastern territories is only a partial figure, whereas those in the remainder of European Russia and at the front have not been included at all.'[66]

The report also gave global figures estimated by the S S: 'The total number of Jews in the world in 1937 is estimated at about 17 million, of which over 10 million are distributed over Europe. There they are congregated, or rather were congregated, mainly in the German-occupied ex-Polish and Russian territories from the Baltic and the Gulf of Finland to the Black Sea and the Sea of Azov; in central and western Europe they are to be found in the trading centres, in the Rhine district and on the Mediterranean coasts.'

Undoubtedly Keitel was not aware of these figures in 1943. As a result of the 'Instructions on Special Matters attached to Directive No. 21 (Operation Barbarossa)' issued by O K W in March 1941,[67] however, he did at least know that Himmler had been charged by Hitler with certain 'special tasks' in 'the operations zone of the army' in order to 'prepare the political and administrative organization', and that these tasks stemmed from 'the final struggle between two opposing political ideologies'. Neither in 1943 nor in 1946 could Keitel cite in his defence the fact that 'within the framework of these tasks the Reichsführer-SS will act independently and on his own responsibility'.[68]

Hitler's *Mein Kampf*, his manuscript notes[69] and numerous speeches throughout his career prove that from the outset he was convinced that the 'lebensraum' which he considered 'essential' would not produce the desired results unless the Jews were simultaneously exterminated in the Reich and in the conquered territories. The war policy he pursued as Supreme Commander and its resulting directives were closely connected with the decisive declarations he made during the war,[70] which he regarded as integral parts of his ideology. In 1925 in *Mein Kampf* he had bemoaned the fact that 'twelve or fifteen thousand of these Hebrew corrupters of the people had not been gassed'[71] at the start of the First World War or during it; so in his own war he took the necessary precautions. As early as 30 January 1939, seven months before the start of the Polish campaign, he had stated publicly: 'If international financial Jewry inside and outside Europe succeeds in plunging the peoples into a world war once more, the result would be not ... the victory of Jewry but the annihilation of the Jewish race in Europe.'[72]

As the Polish campaign began, with 'a stroke of the pen' he initiated an annihilation campaign to do away with the sick and also badly wounded soldiers[73] as 'useless mouths'. In the East, under the umbrella of the victorious German Army, thirty million Jews and Slavs were to die, the territory was to be depopulated and new living space created for Germans.[74]

Viewed from this angle, the following extract from the I M T record of 6 April 1946 appears in a special light:

Gen. Rudenko: ... you consider this order to have been entirely correct?
Keitel: I have already explained in detail ... my fundamental standpoint with regard to all orders concerning the treatment of the population. I signed the order and by doing so I assumed responsibility within the scope of my official jurisdiction.
The President: The Tribunal considers that you are not answering the question. The question was perfectly capable of an answer 'yes' or 'no' and an explanation afterwards. It is not an answer to the question to say that you have already explained to your counsel.
Gen. Rudenko: I ask you once more, do you consider this order, this particular order – and I emphasize, in which it is stated that 'human life has absolutely no value' – do you consider this order correct?

Keitel: It does not contain these words; but I knew from years of experience that in the Southeastern territories and in certain parts of the Soviet territory, human life was not respected to the same degree.

Gen. Rudenko: You say that these words do not exist in the order?

Keitel: To my knowledge those exact words do not appear, but it says that human life has very little value in these territories. I remember something like that ...

Gen. Rudenko: Mr President, I shall at once present this order to the defendant ... Defendant Keitel, have you familiarized yourself with the document?

Keitel: The text in the German language says that 'in the countries affected human life frequently has no value ...'

Gen. Rudenko: And further?

Keitel: Yes. '... and a deterrent effect can be obtained only by extreme harshness. To atone for the life of a German soldier ...'

Gen. Rudenko: Quite clear. And in this same order, in this same Subparagraph 'b', it is stated that: 'To atone for the life of one German soldier, 50 to 100 communists must, as a rule, be sentenced to death. The method of execution should strengthen the measure of deterrent.' Is that correct?

Keitel: The German text is slightly different. It says: 'In such cases in general, the death penalty for 50 to 100 communists may be considered adequate' ...

Gen. Rudenko: For one German soldier?

Keitel: Yes ...

Gen. Rudenko: ... I ask you whether, when signing this order, you thereby expressed your personal opinion on these cruel measures? In other words were you in agreement with Hitler?

Keitel: I signed the order but the figures contained in it are alterations made personally by Hitler himself.

Gen. Rudenko: And what figures did you present to Hitler?

Keitel: The figures in the original were five to ten.

Gen. Rudenko: In other words the divergence between you and Hitler consisted merely in the figures and not in the spirit of the document?

Keitel: The idea was that the only way of deterring them was to demand several sacrifices for the life of one soldier ...

Gen. Rudenko: You ...

The President: That was not an answer to the question. The question was whether the difference between you and Hitler on this document was a question of figures. That admits of the answer 'yes' or 'no'. Was the only difference between you and Hitler a question of figures?

Keitel: Then I must say that with reference to the underlying principle there was a difference of opinion, the final results of which I no longer feel myself in a position to justify since I added my signature on behalf of my department. There was a fundamental difference of opinion on the entire question.

Gen. Rudenko: All right. Let us continue. I would like to remind you of one more order. It is the order dated 16 December 1942, referring to the so-called 'Fight against Partisans' ... It was presented to you yesterday by your defense counsel.

Keitel: I do not remember that at the moment.

Gen. Rudenko: I shall interrogate you, Defendant Keitel, only on one question in connection with this order ... I would draw your attention to the following sentence: 'The troops are therefore authorized and ordered in this struggle to take any measures without restriction even against women and children, if that is necessary to achieve success.' Have you found this passage?

Keitel: Yes.

Gen. Rudenko: Have you found the order calling for the application of any kind of measures you like without restriction, also against women and children?

Keitel: 'To employ without restriction any means, even against women and children, if that is necessary'. I have found that.

Gen. Rudenko: ... I ask you, Defendant Keitel, Field Marshal of the former German Army, do you consider that this order is a just one, that measures may be employed at will against women and children?

Keitel: Measures, insofar as it means that women and children were also to be removed from territories where there was partisan warfare, never atrocities or the murder of women or children. Never!

Gen. Rudenko: To remove – a German term – means to kill?

Keitel: No. I do not think that it would ever have been necessary to tell German soldiers that they could not and must not kill women and children.

Gen. Rudenko: ... Do you consider this order a just one in regard to measures against women and children or do you consider it unjust? Answer 'yes' or 'no'. Is it just or unjust? Explain the matter later.

Keitel: I considered these measures to be right and as such I admit them; but not measures to kill. That was a crime.

Gen. Rudenko: 'Any kind of measures' includes murder.

Keitel: Yes, but not of women and children.

Gen. Rudenko: Yes, but it says here 'Any kind of measures against women and children'.

Keitel: No, it does not say 'any measures'. It says '... and not to shrink from taking measures against women and children' ... No German soldier or German officer ever thought of killing women and children.[75]

Keitel did not at this point refer to another order which he had initialled; it had been dictated by Hitler ten days after the Stauffenberg assassination attempt and signed by Hitler personally with his name and christian name; it included: 'Accomplices, particularly women, who have not taken a direct part in the fighting, should be put to work. Children should be spared.'[76]

Keitel clearly ignored this document since it was not available to his defence counsel in 1946. He accordingly based his case – unsuccessfully – on the German soldier's concept of legality. In his view a German soldier would never have thought of killing women and children.

Rudenko, who undoubtedly had no wish to hear such evidence, continued to attack Keitel in his own carefully prepared way:

Gen. Rudenko: And in reality ... ?
Keitel: I cannot say in every individual case, since I do not know and I could not be everywhere and since I received no reports about it.
Gen. Rudenko: But there were millions of such cases.
Keitel: I have no knowledge of that and I do not believe that it happened in millions of cases.
Gen. Rudenko: You do not believe it?
Keitel: No.[77]

And so it went on. The noose was round Keitel's neck. Nevertheless, under the law convening the IMT for the purpose of condemning the accused, there was no need for the prolonged questioning and problematical interpretation of documents which it seemed to think necessary in order to condemn Keitel. The IMT need not have punished the Field Marshal, for instance, simply because he had been present when Hitler announced decisions held to be criminal at Nuremberg. On 13 May 1941, for instance, six weeks before the opening of the Russian campaign, Keitel had signed a politically motivated decree by Hitler 'concerning the exercise of juris-diction in the Barbarossa area'; it included the following: 'There is no compulsion to pursue a case against members of the Wehrmacht or auxiliaries for action against hostile civilians even if the act concerned is a military crime or misdemeanour.' The purpose of the decree is clear; the reason given for it is appalling: 'In arriving at a judgement of such acts in any trial it should be remembered that the collapse of 1918, the subse-quent suffering of the German people and the struggle against National-Socialism with the numerous casualties suffered by the Movement are overwhelmingly due to bolshevist influence and that no German has forgotten this fact.'[78]

9

Karl Dönitz

On 8 May 1946, exactly a year after the German surrender, Grand Admiral Karl Dönitz, who had been Commander-in-Chief of the German Navy from 1943 and Head of State in succession to Hitler from 1 May 1945,[1] was summoned to the witness-box by his defence counsel. His counsel was Flottenrichter (Naval Judge Advocate) Otto Kranzbühler, who wore the uniform of a German naval officer with Captain's stripes; until the end of September 1945 he had been working as Head of the Legal Section of the German Mine Clearance organization set up by the British in Glückstadt on the Elbe.[2] His arrival in Nuremberg had been the occasion of quite a scene; as he got out of his car in front of the Palace of Justice the Soviet sentries had presented arms and this had not been without its consequences – he had not been allowed to speak to the Grand Admiral for days. He was likeable, clever and intelligent, unusually expert in his subject and polished in argument; he soon had his admirers among the Allied officers and others attending the trial. He was on terms of some intimacy with Dönitz, who had asked for him as defence counsel.[3]

Kranzbühler, who deliberately and on principle addressed Dönitz as 'Grand Admiral', started by throwing the cat among the pigeons. He requested that he be allowed to send his assistant, Commander Meckel, to London to examine certain entries in the war diaries of Naval Headquarters and Commander-in-Chief U-boats which were held in the British Admiralty as captured material. The prosecution, who had no wish to create a precedent, did not agree, but Kranzbühler countered by saying that he was in the position of a lawyer being asked to defend a businessman without being allowed to examine his books. Kranzbühler's arguments won the day. His assistant was allowed to fly to London and find what his principal wanted. As a result Kranzbühler was able to disprove the prosecution's allegations that Dönitz – who was also accused of 'Crimes against Peace' – had ordered the killing of shipwrecked persons.[4] Dönitz had issued an order forbidding U-boat commanders to surface in order to rescue people in the water and this was interpreted as a camouflaged order deliberately to let them drown but, in face of Kranzbühler's arguments, this did not hold water. Kranzbühler was also able to show that after the sinking of the British transport *Laconia* not only had Dönitz ordered a German U-boat to surface in order to rescue survivors but also, against Hitler's will, had broken off a major naval operation and ordered other U-boats to rescue survivors despite the risk of Allied attack. During their rescue operations the German submarines were 'attacked by American aircraft, one U-boat was damaged and lifeboats in tow were sunk. Nevertheless 800 (out of 811) British and 450 (out of 1,850) Italians were rescued and transferred to a French cruiser which was summoned by radio.'[5] Dönitz (like Keitel and Jodl) was accused of having passed on to the Navy Hitler's Commando Order of October 1942 and so of being responsible for the shooting by the SD of the crew of an Allied torpedo boat; this Dönitz countered with the statement that he had not been informed of the incident and that the Admiral responsible was subordinate to the Army not to him. He was nevertheless held responsible by the IMT because, as Commander-in-Chief of the Navy, he allowed the order to remain in force.[6] Kranzbühler was able to show by numerous documents that the German U-boat commanders did obey Dönitz's orders to observe the general rules of war at sea. He was ready with no fewer than 550 pieces of evidence on the laws of naval warfare.[7] On 10 May 1946, for instance, he opened with: 'I should like to read to the Tribunal from an English document to show that the boats were really acting according to these orders' (order of 3 September 1939 prescribing strict attention to the rules of naval warfare) and he then went on in English: 'Thus the Germans started with the Prize-Ordinance, which was at any rate a clear, reasonable and not inhumane document. German submarine commanders, with some exceptions, behaved in accordance with its provisions during the first month of the war. Indeed, in one case, a submarine had ordered the crew of a trawler to take their boat, as the ship was to be sunk. But when the commander saw the state of the boat, he said: "Thirteen men in that boat. You English are no good, sending a ship to sea with a boat like that." And the skipper was told to reembark his crew on the trawler and make for home at full speed with a bottle of German gin and the submarine commander's compliments.'[8]

The IMT eventually accepted Kranzbühler's well-chosen evidence to the contrary. On 11 May 1946, after his Admiral's cross-examination, he took up the prosecution's charges, starting by repeating their statement that: 'On 30 September 1939 the first sinking of a neutral ship by a submarine took place without a warning signal having been given. On that occasion some people lost their lives. The ship was the Danish steamer *Vendia*.'[9]

He then quoted from the log of the submarine U-3 which had sunk the Danish ship. This, an official record by a German naval officer, showed what actually happened: 'The steamer turns away gradually and increases speed. The boat comes up only very slowly. Obvious attempt to escape. The steamer is clearly recognizable as the Danish steamer *Vendia*. Boat reduces speed and uncovers her machine-gun. Several warning shots are fired across the steamer's bow. Thereupon the steamer stops very slowly; nothing more happens for a while. Then some more shots are fired. The *Vendia* lies into the wind. For ten minutes nothing is visible on deck to remove suspicion of possible intended resistance ... I suddenly see bow waves and screw movements. The steamer swings sharply round towards the boat. The officer on watch and the first mate agree with my view that this is an attempt at ramming. For this reason I turn in the same angle as the steamer. A torpedo is fired thirty seconds later ... point of impact, extreme rear of stern. The stern is torn off and goes down. The front part remains afloat. By risking the loss of our own crew and boat ... six men of the Danish crew are rescued, among them the captain and helmsman. No further survivors are to be seen. In the meantime the Danish steamer *Swawa* approaches and is stopped. She is requested to send her papers across ... The six persons rescued are transferred to the steamer for repatriation ... After the crew of the steamer had been handed over, it was learned that the engineer artificer of the steamer had told the stoker Blank that the captain had intended to ram the submarine.'[10]

The Danish captain was not taking the law into his own hands when trying to ram U-3, for on 1 October 1939 the British Admiralty had encouraged merchant ships to attack German U-boats with the following circular: 'Within the last few days some German U-boats have been attacked by British merchant marine vessels. In this connection the German radio announces that the German U-boats have so far observed the rules of international law in warning the merchant marine vessels before attacking them. Now, however, Germany intends to retaliate by considering every British merchant marine vessel as a warship ... Be prepared to meet it.'[11]

On the same day, 1 October 1939, the British Admiralty published a report that 'German submarines are pursuing a new strategy'; British merchant vessels were called upon to 'ram every German submarine'.[12]

On 8 May 1946 Kranzbühler had already established the more important details by expert questioning of Dönitz and had put the record straight, showing how things actually happened. The I M T record on this subject is more than illuminating:

Flottenrichter Kranzbühler: What were the orders which you received at the beginning of the war ... for the conduct of U-boat warfare?
Dönitz: War against merchantmen according to the Prize Regulations, that is to say, according to the London Pact.
Flottenrichter Kranzbühler: What ships, according to that order, could you attack without previous warning?
Dönitz: ... I could attack without warning all ships which were guarded either by naval vessels or which were under air cover. Furthermore, I was permitted to exercise armed force against any ship which, when stopped, sent radio messages, or resisted the order to stop, or did not obey the order to stop.
Flottenrichter Kranzbühler: Now, there is no doubt that, a few weeks after the beginning of the war, the war against merchantmen was intensified.

Did you know whether such an intensification was planned, and if you do, why it was planned?

Dönitz: I knew that the Naval Operations Staff intended, according to events, according to the development of the enemy's tactics, to retaliate blow for blow, as it says or said in the order, by intensified action.

Flottenrichter Kranzbühler: What were the measures of the enemy and, on the other hand, what were your own experiences with the measures taken by the enemy which led to an intensification of action?

Dönitz: Right at the beginning of the war it was our experience that all merchantmen not only took advantage of their radio installations when an attempt was made to stop them, but that they immediately sent messages as soon as they saw any U-boat on the horizon. It was absolutely clear, therefore, that all merchantmen were cooperating in the military intelligence service. Furthermore, only a few days after the beginning of the war, we found out that merchantmen were armed and made use of their weapons.

Flottenrichter Kranzbühler: What orders on the part of Germany resulted from these experiences?

Dönitz: They first brought about the order that merchantmen which sent radio messages on being stopped could be attacked without warning. They also brought about the order that merchantmen whose armament had been recognized beyond doubt, that is, whose armament one knew from British publications, could be attacked without warning...

Flottenrichter Kranzbühler: Was there a second order* soon after that, according to which all enemy merchantmen could be attacked, and why was that order issued?

Dönitz: I believe that the Naval Operations Staff decided on this order on the basis of the British publication which said that now the arming of merchantmen was completed. In addition there was a broadcast by the British Admiralty on 1 October to the effect that the merchantmen had been directed to ram German U-boats and furthermore – as stated at the beginning – it was clear beyond doubt that every merchantman was part of the intelligence service of the enemy, and its radio messages at sight of a U-boat determined the use of surface or air forces.

Flottenrichter Kranzbühler: Did you have reports about that from U-boats, according to which U-boats were actually endangered by these tactics of enemy merchantmen and were attacked by enemy surface or air forces?

Dönitz: Yes. I had received quite a number of reports in this connection, and since the German measures were always taken about four weeks after it had been recognized that the enemy employed these tactics, I had very serious losses in the meantime – in the period when I still had to keep to the one-sided and, for me, dangerous obligations.

Flottenrichter Kranzbühler: By these obligations, are you referring to the

---

* Kranzbühler referred to a 'second order' having already cited the order of 4 October 1939 which Dönitz had quoted as the basis for the instructions that enemy merchantmen were to be attacked without warning by German U-boats.

obligation to wage war against merchantmen according to the Prize Regulations during a period when the enemy's merchant ships had abandoned their peaceful character?
Dönitz: Yes ...
Flottenrichter Kranzbühler: Was this intensification of the war against merchantmen by the order to fire on armed merchantmen, and later the order to attack all enemy merchantmen, based on the free judgement of the Naval Operations Staff, or was it a forced development?
Dönitz: This development ... was entirely forced. If the merchantmen are armed and make use of their arms, and if they send messages which summon protection, they force the U-boat to submerge and attack without warning. That same forced development, in the areas which we patrolled, was also the case with the British submarines, and applied in exactly the same way to American and Russian submarines.[13]

Not until 17 October, after Hitler had learnt of the British order that merchantmen were to fight U-boats by every possible means including ramming and depth charges,[14] was the following order issued:
'At 1500 hours the following order was issued to Commander of Submarines: "Submarines are permitted immediate and full use of armed force against all merchant vessels recognizable with certainty as being of enemy nationality, as in every case attempts to ram or other forms of active resistance may be expected. Exceptions to be made as hitherto in the case of enemy passenger boats".'[15]
From the beginning of the war many British merchant ships were nothing but armed U-boat decoys; their crews were not entirely civilian but in many cases included definite combatants under international law. On 11 May 1946, for instance, Kranzbühler submitted to the court an extract from confidential British Admiralty orders prescribing among other things that, in addition to the marines acting as gun-layers and gun crews on merchant ships, five to six men of the crew might be used 'to complete the gun crew' (for instance, 'to bring ammunition from the magazine').[16] Lieutenant-Commander Günther Hessler, Dönitz's son-in-law, who had torpedoed the merchant ships *Kalchas* and *Alfred Jones*, told the court on 14 May that they were equipped with guns, anti-aircraft guns and depth charges and had shot at his U-boat and tried to sink it using deception tactics. He concluded: 'It was clear to me, naturally, after such an experience that I could no longer concern myself with crews or survivors without endangering my own ship.'[17]
Besides all this Otto Kranzbühler had managed to get Admiral Chester W. Nimitz, commanding the US fleet in the Pacific, to complete a questionnaire which he had drafted comprising twenty questions on American submarine warfare in the Pacific; it was signed on oath and in it Nimitz confirmed that, from the very beginning of the war against Japan, US submarines had neither given warning nor rescued survivors if commanders

had reason to fear for the safety of their own ships or anticipated further operations.[18]

Kranzbühler was accordingly able to prove that from the outset American submarines in the Pacific had been violating the London Naval Agreement of 1930 and were acting contrary to international law in that they had immediately used the methods adopted by German U-boats as a result of their experiences with the British. He was well aware that he might embarrass others as well as the IMT, since *tu quoque* arguments – counter-charge arguments – were not permitted in Nuremberg; illegal actions by Germans could not be set off against similar actions by the victors. Kranzbühler, therefore, put the matter diplomatically with adroit legal argument; he said:

'I in no way wish to prove or even to maintain that the American Admiralty in its U-boat warfare against Japan broke international law. On the contrary, I am of the opinion that it acted strictly in accordance with international law. In the United States' sea war against Japan, the same question arises as in Germany's sea war against England, namely the ... interpretation of the London Submarine Agreement of 1930 ... My point is that, because of the order to merchant vessels to offer resistance, the London Agreement is no longer applicable to ... merchantmen, further that it was not applicable in declared operational zones in which a general warn-ing had been given to all vessels, thus making an individual warning un-necessary before the attack. Through the interrogatory to Admiral Nimitz I want to establish that the American Admiralty in practice interpreted the London Agreement in exactly the same way as the German Admiralty, and thus prove that the German conduct of sea warfare was perfectly legal.'[19]

This had its effect. Francis Biddle, the American Member of the Tribunal, having no wish to see the USA lose face,[20] considered Kranz-bühler's arguments masterly; he was more or less forced to support Dönitz and his counsel.

The evidence proved that the Allied navies had taken far less account of maritime and international law than had the German U-boat com-manders. The facts weighed so heavily in Dönitz's favour that, in its judge-ment upon him, the IMT stated: 'In the actual circumstances of this case, the Tribunal is not prepared to hold Dönitz guilty for his conduct of submarine warfare against British armed merchant ships.'[21]

On these charges against Dönitz the IMT was compelled, despite all their preparations and objections – and in large measure because of United States infringements of neutrality[22] – to give judgement in Dönitz's favour as follows:

'The Tribunal is of the opinion that the evidence does not establish with the certainty required that Dönitz deliberately ordered the killing of shipwrecked survivors. The orders were undoubtedly ambiguous and deserve the strongest censure. The evidence further shows that the rescue provisions were not carried out and that the defendant ordered that they should not be carried out. The argument of the Defense is that the security of the submarine is, as the first rule of the sea, paramount to rescue, and that the development of aircraft made rescue impossible. This may be so but the Protocol is explicit. If the commander cannot rescue, then under its terms he cannot sink a merchant vessel and should allow it to pass harmless before his periscope. These orders, then, prove Dönitz is guilty of a violation of the Protocol.

'In view of all the facts proved and in particular of an order of the British Admiralty announced on 8 May 1940, according to which all vessels should be sunk at night in the Skagerrak, and the answers to interrogatories by Admiral Nimitz stating that unrestricted submarine warfare was carried on in the Pacific Ocean by the United States from the first day that Nation entered the war,[23] the sentence of Dönitz is not assessed on the ground of his breaches of the international law of submarine warfare.'[24]

Dönitz knew that, with Kranzbühler, he was in the best possible hands.[25] He was convinced that, as a serving officer, he had never done anything wrong. He took no account of Article 8 of the Charter under which 'superior orders, even to a soldier'[26] were inadmissible as a plea in mitigation and referred quite bluntly to orders from above.[27] To the charge that he had participated in a position of authority in wars of aggression he replied quite frankly that during the war he had not thought about the question. His line of argument is well illustrated by the following extract from the record for 8 May 1946:

Flottenrichter Kranzbühler: ... Admiral, in connection with the orders which you issued to the U-boats before the war or in connection with the orders which you issued before the beginning of the Norway action – did you ever have any considerations as to whether it would lead to aggressive war?

Dönitz: I received military orders as a soldier and my purpose naturally was to carry out these military tasks. Whether the leadership of the State was thereby politically waging an aggressive war or not, or whether they were protective measures, was not for me to decide; it was none of my business.[28]

On the first day of his cross-examination Kranzbühler had drawn from the President the remark that the court did not wish to hear Dönitz's 'view on the question of law' (whether the war was one of aggression or not) and that he should 'state the facts – what he did'.[29]

Nevertheless Kranzbühler was successful. The IMT acquitted Dönitz under Count One on the grounds that: 'Although Dönitz built and trained the German U-boat arm, the evidence does not show that he was privy to the conspiracy to wage aggressive wars or that he prepared and initiated such wars. He was a line officer performing strictly tactical duties. He was not present at the important conferences when plans for aggressive wars were announced, and there is no evidence that he was informed about the decisions reached there.'[30]

The judgement continued, however: 'Dönitz did ... wage aggressive war within the meaning of that word as used by the Charter. Submarine warfare, which began immediately upon the outbreak of war, was fully coordinated with the other branches of the Wehrmacht. It is clear that his U-boats, few in number at the time, were fully prepared to wage war.'[31]

Under Counts Three and Four Karl Dönitz was convicted: 'Dönitz, in a conference of 11 December 1944, said: " 12,000 concentration camp prisoners will be employed in the shipyards as additional labor." At this time Dönitz had no jurisdiction over shipyard construction, and claims that this was merely a suggestion at the meeting that the responsible officials do something about the construction of ships, that he took no steps to get these workers since it was not a matter for his jurisdiction and that he does not know whether they were ever procured. He admits he knew of concentration camps. A man in his position must necessarily have known that citizens of occupied countries in large numbers were confined in the concentration camps.'[32]

On 10 May 1946 Dönitz was questioned on this subject by Sir David Maxwell-Fyfe. The record is as follows:

Sir David Maxwell-Fyfe: I want you to come to the next point ... It is a memorandum about more labor for shipbuilding ... If you would look at the first sentence: 'Furthermore, I propose reinforcing the shipyard working party by prisoners from the concentration camps ...' ... If you will look at the end of the document ... you will see Item 2 of the summing-up reads: '12,000 concentration camp prisoners will be employed in the shipyards as additional labor. Security service agrees to this' ... So we may take it that you were familiar with the fact of the existence of concentration camps?
Dönitz: I have never denied it.
Sir David Maxwell-Fyfe: And I think you went further ... when asked about this on 28 September. At that time you said: 'I generally knew that we had concentration camps. That is clear. Question: From whom did you learn that? Answer: The whole German people knew that.' Don't you remember saying that?
Dönitz: Yes. The German people knew that concentration camps existed; but they did not know anything about the conditions and methods therein.
Sir David Maxwell-Fyfe: It must have been rather a surprise for you when the Defendant von Ribbentrop said he only heard of two: Oranienburg and Dachau ... ?
Dönitz: No, it was not at all surprising because I myself only knew of Dachau and Oranienburg.
Sir David Maxwell-Fyfe: But you say here you knew there were concentration camps. Where did you think you were going to get your labor from? What camps?

Dönitz: From these camps.[33]

Sir David Maxwell-Fyfe: Did you think that all your labor was going to be German or that it was going to be partly foreign labor?

Dönitz: I did not think about that at all ... At the end of the war I was given the task of organizing large-scale transports in the Baltic Sea. Gradually the necessity arose to move the hundreds of thousands of poverty-stricken refugees out of the coastal areas of East and West Prussia where they were exposed to starvation, epidemics and bombardment, and to bring them to Germany. For this reason I made inquiries about merchant shipping, which was not actually under my jurisdiction; and in doing so I learned that out of eight ships ordered in Denmark, seven had been destroyed by saboteurs in the final stage of construction. I called a meeting of all the departments connected with those ships and asked them: "How can I help you so that we get shipping space and have damaged ships repaired more quickly?" I received suggestions from various quarters outside the Navy, including a suggestion that repair work, *et cetera*, might be speeded up by employing prisoners from the concentration camps. By way of justification it was pointed out, in view of the excellent food conditions, such employment would be very popular.[34] Since I knew nothing about the methods and conditions in the concentration camps, I included these proposals in my collection as a matter of course, especially as there was no question of making conditions worse for them, since they would be given better food when working ...

Sir David Maxwell-Fyfe: I am sure we are grateful for your explanation. But I just want you to tell me, after you had proposed that you should get 12,000 people from concentration camps, did you get them?

Dönitz: I do not know. I did not do anything more about that. After the meeting I had a memorandum prepared and submitted to the Führer ...

Sir David Maxwell-Fyfe: The answer is that you do not know whether you got them or not, assuming that you did get them.

Dönitz: I did not get them at all. I had nothing to do with shipyards and consequently I do not know how those responsible for the work in the shipyards received their additional workers ...

Sir David Maxwell-Fyfe: But you held a position of some responsibility; if you get 12,000 people from concentration camps into the shipbuilding industry, they would have to work alongside people who weren't in concentration camps, would they not?

Dönitz: Certainly, yes.

Sir David Maxwell-Fyfe: Are you telling this Tribunal that when you ask for and you may have got 12,000 people out of concentration camps, who work alongside people not in concentration camps, that the conditions inside the concentration camps remain a secret to the other people and to all the rulers of Germany?

Dönitz: First of all, I do not know whether they came. Secondly, if they did come, I can very well imagine that they had orders not to talk; and thirdly, I do not even know what camps they came from and whether they were not people who had already been put into other camps on account of the work they accomplished. At any rate, I did not worry about the execution or methods, *et cetera*, because it was none of my business; I acted on behalf of the competent non-naval departments which required work-men in order to carry out repairs more quickly, so that something could be done about repairs for the merchant navy. That was my duty . . . I would do exactly the same thing again today . . .[35]

The defendants concerned with such problems were in fact extremely inadequately informed. Besides Sauckel, defendants from Himmler's empire and those who had to work with SS agencies, Albert Speer was necessarily the best informed on this subject; yet even he, when asked by Dr Flächsner, his defence counsel, on 19 June 1946 whether he had known that concentration camp inmates had certain advantages when employed in factories, replied: 'Yes. My co-workers called my attention to this fact and I also heard it when I inspected the industries.'[36] On 21 June, under cross-examination by the American Francis Biddle, he said: 'Foreign workers were employed without consideration for any agreement.'

The record then continues:

The Tribunal (*Mr Biddle*): . . . You said the concentration camps had a bad reputation . . . Is that right?
Speer: Yes.
The Tribunal (*Mr Biddle*): What did you mean by that phrase 'bad reputa-tion'? What sort of reputation, for what?
Speer: That is hard to define . . . It was known in Germany that a stay in a concentration camp was an unpleasant matter. I also knew that but I did not know any details.
The Tribunal (*Mr Biddle*): Well, even if you did not know any details, is not 'unpleasant' putting it a little mildly? Was not the reputation that violence and physical punishment were used in the camps? Was not that the reputa-tion that you meant? Is it not fair to say that really?
Speer: No, that is going a little too far, on the basis of what we knew. I assumed that there was ill-treatment in individual cases, but I did not assume that it was the rule. I did not know that . . . I must say that during the time in which I was a Minister, strange though it sounds, I became less disturbed about the fate of concentration camp inmates than I had been before, because while I was in office I heard only good and calming reports about the concentration camps from official sources. It was said that the food was being improved and so on and so forth.[37]

When Flächsner had asked him on 19 June: 'What were the working hours of the factory workers who came from concentration camps?' Speer replied: 'They were exactly the same as for all the other workers in the industry, for the workers from concentration camps were on the whole only a part of the workers employed and these workers were not called upon to do any more work than the other workers in the factory.'[38]

The IMT held that an important charge against Dönitz was that on 20 February 1945, when Hitler was proposing to denounce the Geneva Convention, he was supposed to have declared in Jodl's presence: 'It would be better to carry out the measures considered necessary without warning and at all costs to save face with the outer world.'[39] The prosecution was convinced that by 'measures' Dönitz meant, not that the Convention should be denounced, but that it should simply be broken, an interpretation disputed by Dönitz in the witness-box. He had said that by the phrase 'measures' he had meant disciplinary measures to prevent German soldiers surrendering. On this question the IMT eventually decided in favour of the prosecution and against Dönitz, saying in its judgement: 'The Tribunal does not believe this explanation.' The judgement continues however: 'The Geneva Convention was not, however, denounced by Germany. The Defense has introduced several affidavits to prove that British naval prisoners of war in camps under Dönitz's jurisdiction were treated strictly according to the Convention, and the Tribunal takes this fact into consideration, regarding it as a mitigating circumstance.'[40]

This part of Dönitz's defence was also evidently held by the court to be of doubtful validity from another point of view, since the judgement on Dönitz also includes this: 'The Defense explanation is that Hitler wanted to break the Convention for two reasons: to take away from German troops the protection of the Convention, thus preventing them from continuing to surrender in large groups to the British and Americans and also to permit reprisals against Allied prisoners of war because of Allied bombing raids.'

The idea of denouncing the Geneva Convention, initially accepted by Hitler, had been put forward early in February 1945 by Goebbels, Bormann and Ley; in this phase of the war, however, the civilians were not so influential and it was rejected in face of resistance from the military.[41]

Crime by Order

Alfred Jodl's fate was sealed by the orders and directives from Hitler which he passed on through military channels and authenticated by his signature or initials. (Though he became personally acquainted with Hitler only after the start of the Polish campaign, he was Head of the OKW Operations Staff from 1939.) On 4 June 1946, four months before being sentenced, he explained the problem from the witness-box in answer to questions from his defence counsel, Franz Exner:

'One must differentiate as follows: The decrees which the Führer himself signed, if they were of an operational nature, bear my initial at the end, on the lower right; and that means that I at least assisted in the formulation of that order. Then there were orders which also came from the Führer, though they were not signed by him personally, but were signed "by order, Jodl"; but they always had at the beginning the sentence "The Führer has decreed", or that sentence was found ... in the course of the order. There would be a preamble, usually giving reasons for the order, and then it would read: "The Führer has therefore decreed" ... Then there were other orders, which bear my initial on the first page, in the upper right-hand corner. Those were orders issued by other departments. My initial "J" on the first page was merely an office notation to show that the order had been submitted to me. But it did not mean that I had read it for if, on perusing the first page, I saw that the decree dealt with a matter not connected with my sphere of work, then I initialed it and put it aside ... I had to save time.'[1]

Professional soldiers in the West would undoubtedly have judged this statement by Jodl in the light of their own professional standards and practices, but the members of the IMT, none of whom were regular soldiers, did not understand. They were equally unimpressed by the evidence of Percy E. Schramm, the Göttingen high-school teacher, who testified that during 1944 alone some 60,000 teleprinter messages and well over 60,000 other documents transmitted by courier or originating from sections of the OKW Operations Staff passed across Jodl's desk.[2]

In this connection a particularly serious charge against Jodl was that his signature proved that, before the start of the Russian campaign, he had had a hand in drafting the order prescribing the execution without trial of Soviet commissars.

The IMT's judgement includes the following: 'A plan to eliminate

Soviet commissars was in the directive for "Case Barbarossa". The decision whether they should be killed without trial was to be made by an officer. A draft contains Jodl's handwriting suggesting this should be handled as retaliation, and he testified this was his attempt to get around it.'[3]

By 'plan to eliminate Soviet commissars' the IMT meant the so-called 'Commissar Order' of 6 June 1941 which was based on statements made by Hitler on 30 March 1941. He had then said that the forthcoming campaign against the Soviet Union was not to be looked at from the traditional angle but should be regarded as a clash between two opposing ideologies; the result must be the destruction of bolshevism. Bolshevism, Hitler had told the Commanders-in-Chief and Chiefs of Staff of formations concentrated for the invasion of the Soviet Union, was a sociological crime and communism an immense danger for the future; consequently traditional notions of 'military comradeship' were a thing of the past; brutal force was required, courts martial had no role to play in this campaign;[4] political functionaries or political commissars attached to the troops were not to be regarded as soldiers or prisoners of war.[5] What this implied became known to the world at large at latest in Nuremberg. If, for certain reasons, functionaries or commissars could not be handed over to the SD for liquidation, they were to be 'shot by the troops'.[6]

The text of this document of 6 June 1941 is given in Appendix 1. It is one of the vital sources for the planned treatment of political commissars during the Russian campaign. On 3 June 1946 Franz Exner began his cross-examination on the subject as follows:

'... Let us turn to the crimes against the laws of war and humanity which have been charged against you ... I should like to clarify your participation in the commissar decree. A draft by the High Command of the Army on the treatment of Soviet commissars was submitted to you, and you put a notation in the margin of this draft on the grounds of which the Prosecution has accused you ... Perhaps you can tell us first of all: What connection did you have with this matter, that is, with the treatment of commissars?'[7]

The record continues with Jodl's answer and subsequent exchanges:

Jodl: I did not participate in preparing this draft. I was not concerned with prisoners of war nor with questions of martial law at that time. But the draft was submitted to me before it was transmitted to Field Marshal Keitel.

Dr Exner: All right. Now you added: 'We must count on retaliation against German fliers. It is best, therefore, to brand the entire action as retaliation.' What did you mean by this statement?

Jodl: The intention of the Führer which was set forth in this draft was rejected unanimously by all soldiers. Very heated discussions took place about this also with the Commander-in-Chief of the Army. This resistance ended with the characteristic sentence by the Führer: 'I cannot demand that my generals should understand my orders, but I do demand that they follow them.' Now, in this case, by my notation I wanted to indicate to Field Marshal Keitel a new way by which one might possibly still circumvent this order which had been demanded.

Dr Exner: The Prosecution ... have made this order the subject of such a serious charge against the German military authorities because it was drafted before the beginning of the war. These notes are dated 12 May 1941* and there you say: 'It is best to brand the entire action as retaliation.' What did you mean by that?

Jodl: It is correct that, because of his ideological opposition to bolshevism, the Führer counted upon the possible authorization of the commissar decree as a certainty. He was confirmed in this belief and gave his reasons by saying: 'I have carried on the war against communism for twenty years. I know communism but you do not know it.' I must add that we as well were, of course, to a certain extent under the influence of what had been written in the literature of the entire world about bolshevism since 1917. We also had had some experiences, for example, the Räte Republic in Munich. Despite that, I was of the opinion that first of all we should wait and see whether the commissars would actually act as the Führer expected them to act; and if his suspicions were confirmed, we could then make use of reprisals. That was what I meant by my notation in the margin.

Dr Exner: That is to say, you wanted to wait until the beginning of the war; then you wanted to wait until you had had experiences in this war; and then you wanted to propose measures which, if necessary, could be considered as reprisals against the methods of fighting used by the enemy. Was that what you meant when you said: 'It is best, therefore, to brand the entire action as retaliation'? What do you mean by the words 'Man zieht auf'? These words were translated by the Prosecution as ...[8]

After this attempt by Exner to put the best possible answers into Jodl's mouth the following argument began:

Mr G. D. Roberts (Leading Counsel for the United Kingdom): My Lord, in the examination of my learned friend, Dr Exner, he has for several minutes now been asking the defendant very long leading questions ... In my submission, that is not evidence at all by the witness; it is a speech by Dr Exner, and I would ask him not to make another one now.

Dr Exner: I still think that it is necessary in the presentation of evidence to determine what the defendant thought when he wrote those words.

The President: You have heard me say on several occasions that when Counsel ask leading questions, which put the answer into the mouth of the witness, it carries very little weight with the Tribunal. It is perfectly obvious that, if you wanted to ask what the witness meant by his note, he

* Exner is referring to an office minute dated 12 May 1941 signed by General Walter Warlimont commenting upon an OKH draft of the commissar Order dated 6 May 1941 signed by General Müller. Nuremberg Documents PS-884 and PS-1663.

could have answered; and that is the proper way to put the question, and not to suggest the answer to him[9] . . .

Dr Exner: Now, there is another very large volume of documents, of which some are being used as very incriminating evidence against you; they are not orders but summarized notes . . .

Jodl: These summarized notes were an arrangement used on higher staff levels for the convenience of people who had not time to study enormous files. The summarized notes contained, in a short condensed form, a description of some matter or other, frequently the views taken by other departments and sometimes even a proposal. The important point, however, is that it was not an order; it was not a draft of an order, but it formed the basis for an order.

Dr Exner: Perhaps the situation will best be clarified if you can explain this to the Tribunal in connection with the draft notes concerning the commissars, which were touched on yesterday . . .

Jodl: This document is a typical example. First of all it contains the draft by another department of the Army High Command, not verbatim, but in a brief condensed form. Then secondly . . . the views of another department – that of Reichsleiter Rosenberg's – are set forth. Then . . . it contains a proposal of my own staff. The whole matter, therefore, is far from being an order; it is to become one. And on a summarized draft like that, I naturally made very many, I might say, cursory marginal notes to serve as a guide for the further treatment and discussion or disposal of the whole question. Therefore one cannot apply to this the same criteria as would be applied to the well-considered words contained in an actual order.[10]

Chronologically the first document marking the genesis of the Commissar Order originates from General Eugen Müller,[11] 'General Officer specially employed' under the Commander-in-Chief of the Army, Walter von Brauchitsch. On 6 May 1941 he sent a memorandum addressed to 'Chief of OKW, personal for General Warlimont or his representative in office'. It stemmed from an instruction by Hitler to von Brauchitsch and enclosed a 'Draft of a decree by C.-in-C. Army . . . and draft of instructions to ensure uniform execution of the order already issued on 31 March 1941', asking that this not only be noted but also checked.

The wording of the final draft had been decided in detail by Hitler himself but the order is not signed by him or anyone else. When Jodl was informed of this wording, when his personal involvement began and how far it went cannot be definitively established from documents even today. So far it cannot even be proved that Jodl was informed at all about the final version of the order. The last confirmed draft (in the form of an office minute) is dated 22 May 1941 and, surprisingly, is initialled by Lossberg.* The fact that the preamble to a rough draft of the Commissar Order coincided with some twenty manuscript lines written on

* A Colonel of the OKW Operations Staff.

the draft by Jodl[12] was held up against him in Nuremberg, although his suggestion represented a cautious attempt to give unit officers a loophole, something immediately recognized and suppressed by the author of the 1941 preamble but not by the IMT. Hitler drew a red pencil through Jodl's proposal about 'retaliation' which logically presupposed that 'bolshevist methods' would be those continuously forecast by Hitler from 1920[13] to 1939 and so described by him from 1941 onwards. He also erased Jodl's reference – crossed out but probably intentionally left legible – to the innate good nature of the Russian people. Jodl's case was not helped by the initial 'J' beneath a minute marked 'draft' of 18 August 1941[14] written by Lieutenant-Colonel von Tippelskirch, head of the Supply Group in Section L of OKW,[15] answering in the affirmative a question from an Army Group 'whether political assistants attached to companies (Politruks) were to be treated as political commissars under the "Instructions on the Treatment of Political Commissars".'[16] In 1951, however, Adolf Heusinger, the Bundeswehr General, explicitly and in writing described Jodl as a man who checked everything conscientiously and 'a decent honourable character through and through'.[17]

From available documents it must be regarded as certain that Jodl had doubts on the score of morality and international law during the preparation of the order, and also that he at least attempted to mitigate its effects when Hitler was not to be persuaded to forgo its implementation. It is equally clear that it was Jodl who finally persuaded Hitler on 5 May 1942 in effect to cancel the order. On 26 September 1941 he had written in manuscript on a secret memorandum from OKH dated 23 September: 'The Führer is averse to any alteration in the orders already issued for dealing with political commissars.' On the same day a circular was despatched to OKH reading: 'After renewed representations the Führer has refused any alteration in the orders for the treatment of political commissars.' The phrase 'after renewed representations' indicates that Jodl himself had made representations to the Führer. This tragic chapter was closed by Hitler's order of 5 May 1942 prescribing that the lives of Soviet functionaries, Commissars and Politruks should 'temporarily and as an experiment'[18] be spared in order to increase 'the tendency to desert or capitulate'[19] of Soviet Russian troops.

In place of the Commissar Order, however, in October 1942 came a similar order from Hitler – the so-called Commando Order. Looked at through the spectacles of the Western prosecutors and judges this inevitably constituted at least as serious a crime as the Commissar Order, since it laid down that British commandos were henceforth to be 'ruthlessly shot down by German troops'. Its text is given in Appendix 2.

On 4 June 1946 Exner began his cross-examination on this point also with the statement: 'Now we turn to the very delicate topic of the Commando Order ... I should like to hear from you something about the factors that led to this order ... The first order is addressed to the troops; the second is an explanatory order addressed to the commanders-in-chief. The first order threatens enemy soldiers with death if they engage in bandit-like warfare; and it refers to the Wehrmacht communiqué in this connection. Can you explain the connection between the Commando Order and the Wehrmacht communiqué of 7 October 1942?'[20]

Jodl, who undoubtedly realized even more clearly than before that he was in a tight corner at this moment, initially reacted with caution: '... Very much depends on this order; not my person, my own person does not matter in this Trial, but the honor of German soldiers and German officers, whom I represent here, is in question. The Commando Order is inseparably linked with the announcement in the Wehrmacht communiqué of 7 October 1942, for this ... heralded the actual Commando Order.

Dr Exner: And who was responsible for this announcement in the Wehrmacht communiqué? Who wrote it?

Jodl: This Wehrmacht communiqué of 7 October 1942 – it was really a supplement to the communiqué – emanated in the main from me. It deals with the denial of a report by the British Ministry of War ...

Dr Exner: ... Perhaps you can tell us briefly the contents of this Wehrmacht communiqué of 7 October 1942 ...

Jodl: This communiqué is in direct connection with the Commando Order. Only the last paragraph of this Wehrmacht communiqué is important. It was written by the Führer himself ... It is the sentence which reads: '... in future all terror and sabotage troops of the British and their accomplices who do not act like soldiers but like bandits will be treated as such by the German troops and will be ruthlessly eliminated in battle wherever they appear.' This sentence was written word for word by the Führer himself.

Dr Exner: And then you were instructed to issue a detailed order to that effect ... Please state once more which part of the Wehrmacht communiqué you wrote and which part was added by the Führer.

Jodl: The entire first part of this Wehrmacht communiqué has nothing whatever to do with Commando troops but is concerned with the well-known affair of the shackling of German prisoners of war on the beach of Dieppe ...

The President: You mean that I was correct in saying that in the main it emanated from you?

Jodl: Yes, absolutely. The first part of this Wehrmacht communiqué was formulated by me and contains an authentic refutation of a statement by the British Ministry of War broadcast by the British radio. This statement of the British Ministry of War was false ... Initially this affair had nothing to do with Commandos and reprisals. That was only introduced into the Wehrmacht communiqué through the supplement by the Führer, which begins with the sentence: 'The High Command of the Wehrmacht is therefore compelled to decree the following.'[21]

On Hitler's orders Jodl had to draft the daily Wehrmacht communiqué and so in this case he was faced with being more intimately concerned with this order and its background than was Keitel. His reference to a false report from the British War Office and to his hope that, after publication of the Wehrmacht communiqué, London would 'approach us . . . as it had done on several previous occasions'[22] was certainly not a *post hoc* defensive argument. After all, a year before issue of the Commando Order, a New York newspaper had published the results of some remarkable research into the credibility of the war communiqués issuing from various sources and had credited the German Wehrmacht communiqué with the flattering figure of 100 per cent.[23]

In 1942 Jodl had been able to proceed on the assumption that his hopes would be realized, but he needed no convincing now that he had failed. The record continues:

Dr Exner: And it was considered necessary to make this announcement known in the Wehrmacht communiqué in an executive order. Did the Führer demand from you drafts for an executive order?
Jodl: When the Führer had written this last supplementary sentence, he turned to Field Marshal Keitel and to me and demanded an executive order to follow this general announcement in the Wehrmacht communiqué. And he added: 'But I do not want any military courts.'
Dr Exner: Did you make a draft?
Jodl: I had very many doubts which a careful study of the Hague rules of warfare could not dispel. Neither Field Marshal Keitel nor I prepared such a draft; but members of my staff, on their own initiative, asked for drafts and for the views of various departments. Thus the document . . . came into being . . . My wish was an entirely different one. It was my intention to avoid an order altogether and I rather expected that as a result of the announcement in the Wehrmacht communiqué . . . the British Ministry of War would approach us again, either directly or via Geneva, as it had done on several previous occasions. And I hoped that in this way the whole matter would be shifted to the sphere of the Foreign Office. However that did not happen. The British War Ministry remained silent. In the meantime ten days had passed and nothing had been done. Then on 17 October General Schmundt, the Chief Adjutant of the Führer, came to me and said that the Führer was demanding an executive order. I gave him the following answer word for word: 'Give him my best regards but I will not issue an order like that.' Schmundt laughed and said: 'Well, I cannot tell him that,' and my reply was: 'Very well then, tell the Führer that I do not see how a decree like that could be justified under international law.' And with that he left. I hoped now that I would be asked to come to the Führer, so that at last, after many months, I should again be able to speak to him personally . . . I wanted an opportunity either of telling him my misgivings or else being thrown out altogether . . . but neither occurred. A few minutes

later Schmundt called me on the telephone and informed me that the Führer was going to draw up the order himself. On 18 October Schmundt again came in person and brought with him these two orders of the Führer – the order to the troops and an explanation for the commanders.[24]

Ever since the Caucasus operation Hitler had ostentatiously treated Jodl like an NCO – the rank-conscious commander addressing a subordinate, something that Hitler, the 'socialist', had always stressed that he would not tolerate. During the phase, therefore, in which the Commando Order originated, Jodl had not the slightest chance of reducing the severity of Hitler's orders. At this point he was facing not only the ill-will of his Führer but also court-martial proceedings with which Hitler had threatened him. Every day eight stenographers, supervised by an SS officer, took down every word he said during the briefing conferences.

The IMT record of 4 June 1946 continues:

Dr Exner: ... You mentioned that your staff worked out something ... In this document you wrote two remarks ... The first remark on that page is 'No' ... On the same page a little further down it says in your own hand-writing 'That will not do either' and your initial 'J' for Jodl ...

Jodl: As I have already said, the members of my staff ... on their own initiative asked for proposals, firstly from the foreign intelligence depart-ment, Canaris, because he had a group of experts on international law, and secondly from the Wehrmacht legal department, since, after all, we were concerned with a legal problem. On page 106 ... there is the proposal which the foreign division of the intelligence department made: 'Members of terrorist and sabotage troops who are found ... without uniform or in German uniform will be treated as bandits ... or if they fall into German hands outside battle operations, they are to be taken at once to an officer for interrogation. Thereafter they are to be dealt with by summary court martial.'

That was quite impossible, for if one came across a soldier in civilian clothing ... no one could know just who he was. He might be a spy or an escaped prisoner of war or an enemy airman who had saved his life by jump-ing from his plane and now hoped to escape in civilian clothing. That had to be determined by an experienced interrogating officer and not by a summary court martial ... For that reason I wrote 'No'. In paragraph 'b' it was suggested that if such sabotage groups were captured wearing uniforms, a report should be made to the Armed Forces Operations Staff, which should then decide what should be done. But in that case the Armed Forces Operations Staff would have assumed the function of a military court and that it could never be ...

Dr Exner: And so you rejected this proposal. You said that you also had grave misgivings about the Führer Order. Will you tell the court now what misgivings you had?

Jodl: First of all I had a number of doubts as to its legality. Secondly the order was ambiguous ... It was not sufficiently clear for practical application. Particularly in this case I considered military courts absolutely necessary ...

Dr Exner: Therefore you wanted to initiate some legal procedure ... What did you mean by unclear and ambiguous?

Jodl: The theory was that soldiers, who by their actions put themselves outside the laws of war, cannot claim to be treated in accordance with the laws of war. This is a basic principle definitely recognized in international law, for instance in the case of a spy or a *franc-tireur*. The aim of this order was to intimidate British Commando troops ... But the order of the Führer went further and said that all Commando troops were to be massacred. This was the point on which I had grave misgivings.

Dr Exner: What legal doubts did you have?

Jodl: Just this doubt – that on the basis of this order, soldiers also would be massacred ... I was afraid that not only enemy soldiers who, to use the Führer's expression, really behaved like bandits, but also decent enemy soldiers, would be wiped out. In addition, at the very end of the document ... it was ordered that soldiers were to be shot after they had been captured and had been interrogated. What was totally unclear to me was the general legal position, namely whether a soldier who had acted like a bandit would upon capture enjoy the legal status of a prisoner of war, or whether on account of his earlier behavior he had already placed himself outside this legal status ... I mean the Geneva Convention.[25]

Jodl was referring here to the agreement of 27 July 1929 on treatment of prisoners of war. This includes:

'Prisoners of war are in the power of the hostile Government but not of the individuals of the formation which captured them. They shall at all times be humanely treated and protected particularly against acts of violence, from insults and from public curiosity. Measures of reprisal against them are forbidden ... Prisoners of war are entitled to respect for their persons and honour ... [they] retain their full civil capacity ... Prisoners of war shall be subject to the laws, regulations and orders in force in the armed forces of the detaining power ... [when] undergoing disciplinary punishment [they] shall not be subjected to treatment less favourable than that prescribed as regards the same punishment for similar ranks in the armed forces of the detaining power. All forms of corporal punishment ... all forms of cruelty whatsoever are prohibited.'[26]

After Jodl's last reply (above) Exner, who clearly thought that he must give Jodl every possible assistance in this delicate situation, asked: 'Could you understand the idea that enemy soldiers who had acted in an unsoldierly manner should not be treated as soldiers?'

Jodl, however, had already tried to restrict application of the Commissar Order, which was also contrary to international law, to measures of retaliation, and in this case he needed no help. He replied: 'I could quite understand that and so could others, for the Führer had received very bitter reports. We had captured all the orders of the Canadian brigade which had landed at Dieppe ... These orders said that ... German prisoners were to have their hands shackled. But after some time ... I received authentic reports and testimony of witnesses, with photographs, which definitely convinced me that numerous men of the Todt Organization ... unarmed, old people ... had been shackled with a loop round their necks and the end of the rope fastened around their bent-back legs in such a way that they had strangled themselves. I may add that I kept these photographs from the Führer ...[27] I concealed them from the German people and the Propaganda Ministry ... Some time later a Commando troop made an attack on the island of Sercq. Again we received official reports that German prisoners had been shackled ... Finally we captured the so-called British order for close combat. That was the last straw for the Führer ... These close combat instructions showed by pictures how men could be shackled in such a way that they would strangle themselves through the shackling, and it was stated exactly within what time death would occur.

Dr Exner: Therefore the reasons which Hitler gave for his order ... were actually based on reliably reported facts ...

Jodl: ... In it the Führer first makes the general statement that for some time our opponents in their conduct of the war have been using methods which violate the international Geneva Convention ... I do not wish to go into individual cases. There was an outrageous incident with a British U-boat in the Aegean Sea. There was the order in North Africa that German prisoners of war should not be given water before they were interrogated. There were a large number of such reports ... I only want to point out ... that generally speaking the reasons given by the Führer for this order did not spring from a diseased imagination but were based on actual proof in his and our possession. For it is certainly very different whether I, in my own mind, had to admit there was some justification for this order or whether I considered the whole order an open scandal. That is a vital point for my own conduct ...[28]

Citing witnesses' statements and documents in his support, Jodl testified that British commandos were frequently composed of convicts and criminals who took no account of the traditional standards and rules of soldierly behaviour, of the Geneva Convention or the Hague Convention on Land Warfare. This the prosecution in Nuremberg tried to suppress. Frau Jodl, for instance, who was acting as secretary to Professor Exner, was in the document room one day during Jodl's cross-examination; she was passed a document by an American assistant whose parents had been murdered in a concentration camp, with advice to copy it since 'it would no longer be there tomorrow'.[29] It contained details of a commando unit whose men, contrary to international law, wore a 'German Wehrmacht' armband over civilian clothes. Commandos were equipped with special revolvers, worn under the armpit, which fired when the arms were raised ('Hands up') and would kill or might kill those attempting to take the wearer prisoner.

Exner, who could see the sword of Damocles hanging dangerously close to Jodl, finally asked him: 'What was your own part in this Commando Order?'

Jodl's answer was: 'My part* consisted only in distributing this order, or having it distributed, in accordance with express instructions.'[30]

In principle, however, the IMT did not accept compliance with orders from above as a defence – in contrast to the war crimes trials in Leipzig after the First World War. The Germans did not have anything corresponding to the British *Manual of Military Law*[31] but in principle it was accepted in all armies that compliance with orders was admissible as a defence of criminal acts or acts contrary to international law. In 1944, however, whether or not with the trial of the German war criminals specifically in mind, the British and Americans respectively had altered Paragraph 443 of the *Manual of Military Law* and Paragraph 347 of the *Basic Field Manual on Rules of Land Warfare*. Ever since 1914 in the case of the British and 1917 in that of the Americans it had been laid down that members of the armed forces could not be punished by the enemy for infringements of the generally recognized rules of warfare, since their acts did not constitute war crimes so long as they could invoke explicit orders from their commanders or instructions from their government. In 1944, however, British and American soldiers suddenly found themselves confronted with a totally new wording implying that they could not evade personal responsibility in future.[32] The fact that the wording of the new American regulations was vague, unsatisfactory and did not apparently lay down a definite principle[33] did not affect the issue.

In their defence, therefore, the Germans and their allies could not cite the legal military regulations of their former enemies. The defendants and their counsel only discovered that these changes had been made during the Nuremberg trial and they attempted to make use of them. They deliberately overlooked the fact, however, that even the old Paragraphs 443 and 347 had laid down that the enemy was justified in punishing commanders and those in positions of authority responsible for any crime, if they fell into his hands. In May 1944, moreover, referring to Allied bomber crews, Joseph Goebbels had publicly declared: 'There is no international rule of war which lays down that soldiers who have committed common crime can escape punishment by adducing in their defence that they were following the orders of their superiors. This applies particularly when such orders contravene all ethical principles of humanity and the established customs of warfare.'[34]

The fact remains that the defendants were not clear where the line was being drawn in their case. Neither Keitel nor Jodl knew. Even Oswald

* See Appendix 3.

Pohl, the former head of the Economic and Administrative Department of the SS, responsible for administering the concentration camps, did not know. He was tried in the fourth follow-up trial at Nuremberg[35] as being personally responsible, among other things, for the destruction of the Warsaw ghetto and the consequential 'elimination of more than 56,000 Jews'[36] (he was hanged in Landsberg on 7 June 1951). On 22 May 1950 he wrote to an old friend, a doctor: 'As one of the senior SS leaders I had never expected to be left unmolested. No more, however, did I expect a death sentence. It is a sentence of retribution.'[37]

Hitler's unparalleled concentration of authority and his diabolical, mainly ideologically based manipulations of the machine, on which in view of the prevailing power relationships he could always impose his will, were only really first brought to light in front of the IMT. As a result even some of the most conservative military men had been forced to modify their moral standards. A number of oral and written statements[38] had convinced Exner that senior Allied officers were on Jodl's side and so he touched on this problem in cross-examination, asking Jodl on 4 June:

'The Prosecution said once that you also signed this order – one of these two orders, I do not know which one. That is not correct?'[39]

The following argument then ensued:

Jodl: ... I signed only a general decree to have one of the orders kept secret.
Exner: ... Could you have refused to transmit this order?
Jodl: No, if I had refused to transmit an order of the Führer I would have been arrested immediately, and ... with justification. But, as I said, I was not at all sure whether this decree, either in its entirety or in part, actually violated the law; and I still do not know that today. I am convinced that, if one were to convene here a conference of experts on international law, each one of them would probably have a different opinion on the subject.[40]

Study of the Hague Convention on War on Land, which Jodl stated was always on his desk, had not removed the perplexity he had felt ever since 1941 when compelled by Hitler to identify himself with and pass on certain orders. On the contrary the Hague Convention of 18 October 1907 says:

The laws, rights and duties of war apply not only to the army, but also to militia and to corps of volunteers which satisfy the following requirements:
1. That of being commanded by a person responsible for his subordinates;
2. That of having a distinctive mark, fixed and recognizable at a distance;
3. That of carrying arms openly; and
4. That of conducting their operations in accordance with the laws and customs of war.
   In countries where militia or corps of volunteers constitute the army, or form part of it, they are included under the denomination 'army'.
   The population of a territory which has not been occupied who, on the approach of the enemy, spontaneously take up arms to resist the invading

troops, without having had time to organize themselves in accordance with Article 1, shall be regarded as belligerents if they carry their arms openly and if they respect the laws and customs of war.

The armed forces of the belligerent Parties may consist of combatants and non-combatants. In case of capture by the enemy, both have a right to be treated as prisoners of war.

... The State may utilize the labour of prisoners of war, other than officers, according to their rank and capabilities. Such labour shall not be excessive and shall have nothing to do with the operations of war.

Prisoners of war shall be subject to the laws, regulations and orders in force in the army of the State into whose hands they have fallen. Any act of insubordination warrants the adoption ... of such measures of severity as may be necessary.

The right of belligerents to adopt means of injuring the enemy is not unlimited.

Besides the prohibitions provided by special conventions it is especially prohibited:

(a) To employ poison or poisoned arms
(b) To kill or wound treacherously individuals belonging to the hostile nation or army
(c) To kill or wound treacherously an enemy who, having laid down his arms or having no longer means of defence, has surrendered at discretion
(d) To declare that no quarter will be given
(e) To employ arms, projectiles or material of a nature to cause superfluous injury
(f) To make improper use of a flag of truce, of the national flag or the military distinguishing marks and the uniform of the enemy as well as of the distinctive signs of the Geneva Convention.[41]

It is perfectly clear that the instructions given to British commandos contravened the provisions of this Convention quite as much as did the German counter-measures.

Despite his central and influential position as a member of Hitler's immediate entourage Jodl had in fact no prospect of effectively blocking Hitler's instructions or reducing them to a paper exercise. During cross-examination on 4 June 1946 he was forced to admit quite frankly how Hitler treated a Colonel-General whom he found uncongenial. The record shows:

Dr Exner: General ... Could you have made counterproposals?
Jodl: At any other time, probably yes. At that time, however – a time of conflict with the Führer – it was not possible for me to speak to him personally at all. To broach the subject during the general conference on the situation [with other officers present] was quite out of the question. Therefore I intended in the execution of this order [the Commando Order] to adopt a very magnanimous attitude and I was certain that the commanders-in-chief would do the same.[42]

Nevertheless, at the risk of his life Jodl obeyed his uneasy conscience and attempted to influence execution of this order in the field along the lines of his concept of established military tradition. His answer to Exner's question what he had done in this respect was: 'I tried to exert my influence [on 'the practices followed by the troops'] on various occasions. When it was reported to me that a Commando unit had been captured – which according to the Führer decree was not allowed – then I raised no questions or objections. I made no report at all to the Führer on Commando operations which met with only minor success. And finally I often dissuaded him from taking too drastic views ...'[43]

To the next question from his counsel whether 'many units were actually wiped out' Jodl replied: 'Commando operations decreased considerably as a result of the public announcements in the Wehrmacht communiqué. I believe that not more than eight to ten cases occurred in all. For a time, during the months of July and August 1944, increasingly large numbers of terrorists were reported killed in the Wehrmacht communiqué; these, however, were not Commando troops but insurgents who were killed in the fighting in France.'[44]

By the time in question Hitler, who was a sick man and a hypochondriac, was becoming increasingly fanatical, obstinate, headstrong and dogmatic.[45] What it meant for a man like Jodl, particularly when he was being ostentatiously shunned by Hitler, to attempt to dissuade him from decisions already taken was something to which the IMT was unable to attach due weight in 1945/6. So in Nuremberg Jodl became to some extent the scapegoat for the tragic perversion by Hitler not only of the relationship between the Head of State and the military but also of the traditional concept of legality. Hitler, after all, used the law to safeguard his own power and authority; he demoted the judiciary from the status of high authority to that of an organ of government with no control over its own actions and measures; his attitude to the law was based on his ideology leading to the largely illogical conclusion that nothing was legal unless it served the German people and supported his own views, interpreted in the sense of his biological organism concept. All this was something over which the military could have no influence – or alternatively it was adroitly used to motivate the soldiery. Hitler regarded judges as champions of 'the self-preservation of the people'; he demanded from the judiciary that it serve the purposes of the State, not some more lofty concept of legality and justice;[46] faced with the consequences of this, the views held by certain defendants, based on morality and legality, were not considered as mitigating factors in Nuremberg.

As a result of its revolutionary concept of law the IMT refused to recognize or take legal cognizance of Hitler's overriding position of authority, unparalleled in modern times and exploited by him in a manner all his own. Based primarily on the precedent of the *ex parte Quirin* case in the USA in 1942, it held the defendants personally and directly responsible under international law for actions taken on orders.

Despite all the information and documents available to them in Nuremberg the IMT members from democratic countries clearly found the defendants' pleas which rested on obedience to orders to be totally incredible and in any case, under the provisions of the Charter, they could be of no avail. The Soviets, who, under Joseph Stalin's dictatorship, were thoroughly familiar with the methods used by Hitler, were interested only in condemning the accused; they did not care, therefore, what 'justification' was produced by, for instance, Jodl, Keitel, Fritzsche and Ribbentrop for the offences with which they were charged.

The judgement of the IMT includes this passage: 'That international law imposes duties and liabilities upon individuals as well as upon states has long been recognized ... The very essence of the Charter is that individuals have international duties which transcend the national obligations.'[47] The most convincing arguments for this viewpoint were provided to the court by the precedent, already mentioned, of the *ex parte Quirin* case, upon which the Supreme Court of the United States pronounced in 1942. German specialists, not unlike the British commandos, had landed in the United States from submarines in order to carry out acts of sabotage. After capture* they lodged a complaint because they had been brought before an American 'military commission'. Their application for a writ of Habeas Corpus was unsuccessful. The Supreme Court refused issue of a writ on the grounds that Congress had sanctioned court-martial procedure and so the German defendants would have to be judged by military courts.

A sentence from the pronouncement made in the judgement of the *ex parte Quirin* case[48] in the name of the United States Supreme Court in 1942 by the US Justice Stone (by this time deceased) was cited in Nuremberg; it is as follows: 'From the very beginning of its history this Court has applied the law of war as including that part of the law of nations which prescribes for the conduct of war the status, rights and duties of enemy nations as well as of enemy individuals.'[49]

To this the IMT added: 'He went on to give a list of cases tried by the courts, where individual offenders were charged with offenses against the laws of nations and particularly the laws of war. Many other authorities could be cited but enough has been said to show that individuals can be punished for violations of international law.'[50]

On 20 August 1942, some sixty days before issue of the Commando Order, Hitler had commanded the Reich Minister of Justice to depart from

---

* After the first German submarine party had secretly landed on the American coast, a man named Dasch, who had previously lived in the United States and had therefore been selected for this sabotage mission, called an agency of the American Secret Service and announced to the astonished and sceptical officials what his sabotage objectives in the United States were. After his arrest he was sentenced to a relatively short term of imprisonment and quickly pardoned. After the war the American Secret Service found him a post as hotel manager. (Personal information from Dr Kempner, 8 March 1974.)

the existing law if he, the Führer, so wished and if the 'National-Socialist administration of justice', then already under way, so demanded. Hitler's directive stated: 'A stronger administration of justice is required to fulfil the tasks of the Great German Reich. I therefore charge and authorize the Reich Minister of Justice, in accordance with my instructions and directives and in agreement with the Reich Minister and Head of the Reich Chancellery and Head of the Party Chancellery, to set up a National-Socialist administration of justice and to take all necessary measures therefor.'[51] From 1942 onwards the results of the 'Final Solution of the Jewish Question', in effect an order to step up the extermination machinery, the directive to the Reich Minister of Justice to depart from existing law and the Commando Order were that the Wehrmacht and the SS and also civilian authorities and Party agencies were guilty of violations of the law which a court not subordinate to Hitler could not fail to punish.

During this period, when the fortune of war had already deserted him, Hitler was more insistent than ever on imposing a National-Socialist system of law; the degree to which he himself was involved is shown among other things by the fact that he made a personal inspection on the spot to check the speed at which his murder machine was working, something that he had hitherto studiously avoided. Five days before he instructed the Minister of Justice no longer to regard himself as bound by the letter of the old law, he inspected the murder system in a Polish extermination camp, details being given him by Heinrich Himmler and Odilo Globocnik, the senior SS officer who after 1946 maintained that he had been responsible for passing the cyanide capsule to Göring in Nuremberg to enable him to commit suicide. Hitler was tormented by the idea that he had one foot in the grave and would be unable to finish his 'work';[52] in his impatience he criticized the system of murder of persons who in his view were superfluous, saying that it was going too slowly – 'The whole operation must be carried out quicker, much quicker.'[53]

In Nuremberg things came to light which, had it not been for the IMT, might perhaps never have been discovered – the systematically organized murder operations of inconceivable dimensions ordered by Hitler, for instance. From the evidence and documents, however, it could be deduced that these enormities were perpetrated in such secrecy that not even all the major defendants had more than a vague or totally erroneous idea of them, so well were they camouflaged. On 1 September 1939, for instance, Hitler ordered Dr Karl Brandt, the personal physician whom he hardly ever used, and Philip Bouhler, the *Reichsleiter*, to 'make themselves personally responsible . . . for extending to certain named doctors authority to make a critical examination of the state of health of those who, as far as could humanly be judged, were incurable and to grant them euthanasia.'[54]

As a result of this order from Hitler, between September 1939 and summer 1941 over 50,000 people were done to death by so-called euthanasia[55] in Hadamar, Brandenburg, Grafeneck, Hartheim, Sonnenstein and Bornburg – sick people, mentally defectives, Jews, half-Jews, 'Jew-related' persons and foreigners, mostly Poles and Russians; also included, however, were old German 'comrades' who could no longer work and even severely wounded German soldiers who had suffered brain damage or other severe injury at the front and could not be 'repaired'.[56] Viktor Brack, the economist hanged in Landsberg on 2 June 1948, who was head of a department in Bouhler's office from 1936 and, significantly enough, ended as Deputy Reich Leader of the medical profession, said in Nuremberg on 18 October 1946: 'Hitler's ultimate object in introducing the euthanasia programme in Germany was to exterminate people who were being kept in lunatic asylums and similar institutions and were of no further use to the Reich. These people were regarded as useless mouths and Hitler took the view that elimination of these so-called useless mouths should make it possible to release additional doctors, attendants, nurses and other personnel as well as hospital beds and other facilities for use by the Wehrmacht.'[57]

It was difficult for the Nuremberg accused to defend themselves when all this had taken place in Germany and, from the start of his political career, Hitler had threatened and prophesied all that he would do and cause to be done, should he come to power one day. Even today it seems incredible that there should have been anyone among the major defendants without actual knowledge of these and other enormities. The fact remains, however, that so it was.

11

Limits of Responsibility:
The Non-Military Defendants

SPEER

On 19 June 1946 Dr Flächsner opened the cross-examination of Albert Speer, confining his questions to two main subjects, personal responsibility and the political aspects of the case. He began by asking Speer to describe his 'life up until the time you were appointed Minister'.[1] Speer, good-looking, respectful but relaxed, made a definitely agreeable impression on many of those present at the trial. He told a story described by Raginsky, the Russian assistant prosecutor, in cross-examination on 21 June, not without reason – and with a side-swipe at 'Mr Justice Jackson'[2] – as a well-rehearsed account – 'when you told your biography to the Tribunal ... I think you omitted some substantial matters'.[3]

Speer said:

'I was born on 19 March 1905. My grandfather and my father were successful architects. At first I wanted to study mathematics and physics; but then I took up architecture, more because of tradition than inclination. I attended the universities at Munich and Berlin; and in 1929 at the age of 24, I was the first assistant at the technical college in Berlin. At the age of 27, in 1932, I went into business for myself until 1942.

'In 1934 Hitler noticed me for the first time. I became acquainted with him and from that period of time onward I exercised my architect's profession with joy and enthusiasm, for Hitler was quite fanatical on the subject of architecture; and I received many important construction contracts from him ... I ... sketched buildings which would have been among the largest in the world ... Through this predilection which Hitler had for architecture I had a close personal contact with him. I belonged to a circle which consisted of other artists and his personal staff. If Hitler had had any friends at all, I would certainly have been one of his close friends.

'Despite the war this peaceful construction work was carried on until December 1941, and only the winter catastrophe in Russia put an end to it. The German part of the manpower was furnished by me for the reconstruction of the destroyed railroad installations in Russia.'[4]

Speer attempted to counter Raginsky's criticism about his speech being well-rehearsed with the self-assured reply: 'I left out such points as I did not wish to contest, since they are, at any rate, contained here in the documents; I would have a tremendous task if I were to go into all these points in detail.'[5]

Raginsky, however, who wanted to bring Speer's commitment to Nazism to the official notice of the court, then reeled off a list of offices and positions which Speer had held – Hitler's personal architect, Inspector General of Roads, Inspector General of Waterpower and Power Plants, Plenipotentiary for Building, Director of the Todt Organization, Head of the Technological Office of the National-Socialist Party, Leader of the Union of National-Socialist Technicians. When asked whether he had had 'any other leading positions', Speer replied: 'Oh, I had ten or twelve positions. I cannot give you a list of them all now.'[6]

Asked whether he had not been a member of the presidency of the Academy of Culture and a member of the presidency of the Academy of Arts, Speer answered: 'Yes, that also.'

When Flächsner asked him whether he had 'ever participated in the planning and preparation of an aggressive war',[7] Speer replied 'No', pointing out that until 1942 he had been working purely as an architect and that the buildings he constructed were 'completely representative of peacetime building'.[8] They had kept considerable manpower away from military service, he said, and had also used up much money and material, so that in effect his activity had been detrimental to war industry and the war economy.[9]

Two days later Raginsky, who clearly wished to convict Speer at least of complicity and thereby of participation in the crime of the Common Plan and also of deliberate furtherance of war preparations, asked him whether in fact he had not been aware of Hitler's purposes. Raginsky began in a noticeably conciliatory tone, saying: '... will you tell me whether or not your answer was put down correctly. It was the question whether you acknowledged that in his book *Mein Kampf* Hitler stated bluntly his aggressive plans for the countries of the East and West and, in particular, for the Soviet Union. You answered, "Yes, I acknowledge it." Do you remember that?'[10]

Speer answered casually: 'Yes, that is perfectly possible,' after which the following argument ensued:

Mr Counsellor Raginsky: And do you confirm that now?[11]
Speer: No.
Raginsky: You do not confirm that now?
Speer: I shall have to tell you that at that time I was ashamed to say that I had not read the whole of *Mein Kampf*. I thought that would sound rather absurd.
Raginsky: All right, we shall not waste time. You were ashamed to admit that or are you ashamed now? Let us go on to another question.
Speer: Yes, I cheated at that time.

Raginsky: You cheated at that time; maybe you are cheating now?

Speer: No.

Raginsky: ... You worked on the staff of Hess ... you worked with Ley in the Labor Front. You were one of the leaders of the technicians in the Nazi Party ... Yesterday, in court, you said that you were one of Hitler's close friends.* You now want to say that so far as the plans and intentions of Hitler were concerned, you only learned about them from the book *Mein Kampf*?

Speer: ... I was in close contact with Hitler, and I heard his personal views; these views of his did not allow the conclusion that he had any plans of the sort which have appeared in the documents here, and I was particularly relieved in 1939, when the Non-Aggression Pact with Russia was signed. After all, your diplomats too must have read *Mein Kampf*; nevertheless, they signed the Non-Aggression Pact. And they were certainly more intelligent than I am – I mean in political matters.

Raginsky: I will not now examine who read *Mein Kampf* and who did not; that is irrelevant and does not interest the Tribunal. So you contend that you did not know anything about Hitler's plans?

Speer: Yes.[12]

In contrast to Jackson, Raginsky continuously tried to incriminate Speer of active and deliberate preparation for and complicity in war crime. He accused him, for instance, of having taken over the office of Armaments Minister in 1942 and so of being fully implicated. On 21 June Raginsky said: 'And now we shall listen to what you said to the Gauleiter in your speech in Munich' and he then quoted Speer: 'I gave up all my activity, including my actual profession, architecture, to dedicate myself without reservations to the war task. The Führer expects that of all of us.'

Raginsky then asked: 'Is that what you are saying now?' Speer's answers were unequivocal:

Speer: Yes, I believe that was the custom in your State too.

Raginsky: I am not asking you about our State ... I am asking you whether you now affirm before the Tribunal what you then said to the Gauleiter.

Speer: Yes, I only wanted to explain this to you, because apparently you do not appreciate why in time of war one should accept the post of Armaments Minister. If the need arises that is a matter of course, and I cannot understand why you do not appreciate that and why you want to reproach me for it.

Raginsky: I understand you perfectly.

Speer: Good.[13]

The argument ended with the maladroit statement by Raginsky, not

---

* Speer did not trouble to correct Raginsky. In fact he had said: 'If Hitler had had any friends at all, I would certainly have been one of his close friends.'

even answered by Speer: 'When you made your speech before the Gauleiter, you did not, of course, think that you would be held responsible before the International Military Tribunal for the words which you then spoke.'[14]

Raginsky was continually getting the worst of his duel with Speer, who was sometimes assisted by the President, as the following examples from the record clearly show:

Raginsky: Now I shall remind you of another article of yours. You will also be given a copy of it.
Speer: Just a moment. May I ask you to read the whole paragraph? You left out a few sentences in the middle.
Raginsky: Yes, yes, I omitted something, but I shall ask you some questions on that later.
Speer: But it shows for what offenses prison and death sentences were provided. That is surely relevant. I believe you should quote the passage fully, otherwise the context will be lost.
Raginsky: You will give your consents or explanations to the questions afterwards. But meanwhile listen to the questions as I put them to you. If you want to give your explanation with regard to this, you are entitled to do so later.
The President: No, no, General Raginsky, the Tribunal would prefer to have the comments now ...
Raginsky: ... after September 1943 you were responsible not only for war industry but for the whole war economy as well, and those are two different things.
Speer: No, exactly that is the mistake. It says here 'industrial war economy', which means something like production, war economy, or production in trade and industry, with that qualification; and when it says earlier 'the entire war economic production', the person who wrote this also meant production. But the concept ...
Raginsky: You mentioned here already that ... in 1942 you inherited a great and heavy task ... what was the situation with regard to strategic raw materials, and in particular with regard to alloy metals used in the war industry?
The President: General Raginsky, is it necessary for us to go into details? Is it not obvious that a man who was controlling many millions of workers had a large task? What is this directed to?
Raginsky: Mr President, the question is preparatory; it leads to another question, and inasmuch as it is connected ...
The President: Yes, but what is the ultimate object of the cross-examination? You say it is leading to something else. What is it leading to?
Raginsky: The object is to prove that the Defendant Speer participated in the plundering and looting of occupied territories.
The President: Yes, then ask him directly about that ...[15]

Raginsky: ... You spoke of your objection to using foreign workers ... This testimony was presented by your Defense Counsel; I shall read only one paragraph and you will please confirm whether it is correct or not: 'Insofar as he – Speer – repeatedly mentioned to us that utilization of foreign workers would create great difficulties for the Reich with regard to the food supply for these workers ...' Were these the motives for your objection?

Speer: The translation must be incorrect here ... If we brought new workers to Germany, we had first of all to make available to them the basic calories necessary to feed a human being. But the German laborers still working in Germany had to receive these basic calories in any case. Therefore food was saved if I employed German workers in Germany and the additional calories for persons doing heavy work and working long hours could again have been increased ...

Raginsky: Defendant Speer, you have evaded a direct answer to my question.

Speer: I will gladly ...

Raginsky: You are now going into details which are of no interest to me. I asked you whether I understood this particular passage [from the testimony of a witness named Schmelter] correctly or not.

Speer: No, it was falsely translated. I should like to have the original in German.

Raginsky: The original is in your document book and you can read it. I will pass to the next question.

Speer: Yes, but it is necessary to show it to me now. In cross-examination by the Russian prosecutor I do not really need to bring my document book to the stand with me.

The President: You must give him the document if you have got the document.[16]

Speer even refused to answer questions if he thought he was not justified in doing so – something quite unusual for the IMT. Raginsky, for instance, wished to know the names of the people in Hitler's entourage of whom, on his own admission, Speer had been 'highly critical', but he had to be content with the blunt answer: 'No, I will not name them.'[17] Moreover Speer won the subsequent argument:

Raginsky: You will not name these persons because you did not criticize anybody; am I to understand you in that way?

Speer: I did criticize them, but I do not consider it right to name them here.

Raginsky: Well, I will not insist on an answer to this question.[18]

Raginsky realized that he was no match for Speer, who had been treated with conspicuous civility by Jackson. When he, Raginsky, pointed out that a great deal of time was being wasted if Speer did not answer his questions

186 Part Two: The Trial

the President interrupted him magisterially with: 'But, General Raginsky, from the outset of this defendant's evidence . . . he admitted that he knows that prisoners of war and other workers were brought to Germany forcibly, against their will. He has never denied it.'[19]

Speer cut a figure not unlike the monumental buildings planned by the Führer and constructed by him – designed for effect. Of his buildings, the designs for which usually carried the note 'prepared in accordance with the Führer's ideas',[20] he said after his release from Spandau that they had become more and more foreign to what he regarded as his style.[21] The same could not be said of his appearances in Nuremberg, where he made no attempt to evade responsibility, so much so that members of his former staff and others referred to him as the 'Nuremberger' unable to divest himself of his 'hair shirt'.[22] Speer was a success in Nuremberg; he showed obstinacy and arrogance only to the Russians; despite his almost embarrassing vanity he made a good impression on the Western lawyers and observers at the trial and this stood him in good stead at the end. Jackson described him as the best man in the witness-box[23] and his liking for Speer was at times so obvious that observers at the trial suspected some secret agreement between them. And in fact there was, as Jackson's personal papers showed and Speer himself has since admitted.[24] Jackson and Speer carried on a secret correspondence and reached agreements,[25] the effects of which Speer clearly wished had not been so obvious. On 21 June 1946, for instance, he declared: 'First I should like to say, as you have so often mentioned my non-responsibility, that if in general these considerations had been true, on the basis of my statement yesterday, I should consider myself responsible. I refuse to evade responsibility but the conditions were not what they are said to have been here.'[26] Shortly before this a 'discussion' had taken place between the US Prosecutor and Speer, which ran as follows:

Mr Justice Jackson: This policy of driving Germany to destruction after the war was lost had come to weigh on you to such a point that you were a party to several plots, were you not, in an attempt to remove the people who were responsible for the destruction, as you saw it, of your country?
Speer: Yes, but I want to add . . .
Mr Justice Jackson: There were more plots than you have told us about, weren't there?
Speer: During that time it was extremely easy to start a plot. One could accost practically any man in the street and tell him what the situation was and then he would say: 'This is insane'; and if he had any courage, he would place himself at your disposal. Unfortunately I had no organization behind me which I could call upon and give orders to, or designate who should have done this or that. That is why I had to depend on personal conversations to contact all kinds of people. But I do want to say that it was not as dangerous as it looks here because actually the unreasonable people who

were still left only amounted perhaps to a few dozen. The other 80 million were perfectly sensible as soon as they knew what it was all about.[27]

A glaring case of pure rhetoric. Speer must have known that the facts would disprove this statement. He had clearly failed to foresee that his admission that he had unsuccessfully planned to do away with Hitler would lead him straight *ad absurdum*. After all – and significantly – only a few minutes earlier he had told the court:

'On 23 April I flew to Berlin in order to take leave of several of my associates and – I should like to say this quite frankly – after all that had happened, also in order to place myself at Hitler's disposal. Perhaps this will sound strange here, but the conflicting feelings I had about the action I wanted to take against him* and about the way he had handled things, still did not give me any clear grounds or any clear inner conviction as to what my relations should be toward him, so I flew over to see him. I did not know whether he knew of my plans and I did not know whether he would order me to remain in Berlin. Yet I felt that it was my duty not to run away like a coward, but to stand up to him again.'[28]

Jackson's ostentatious support for Speer became quite clear. Speer, after all, was being arraigned as a major war criminal and Jackson was not as a rule known for indulgence in cross-examination, but very soon he was saying: 'Perhaps you had a sense of responsibility for having put 80 million people completely in the hands of the Führer Principle. Did that occur to you, or does it now, as you look back on it?'

Speer's puzzled reply speaks for itself: 'May I have the question repeated because I did not understand its sense.'

The record then continues:

Mr Justice Jackson: You have 80 million sane and sensible people facing destruction; you have a dozen people driving them on to destruction and they are unable to stop it. And I ask you whether you have a feeling of responsibility for having established the Führer Principle, which Göring has so well described for us, in Germany.

Speer: I, personally, when I became Minister in February 1942, placed myself at the disposal of this Führer Principle. But I admit that in my organization I soon saw that the Führer Principle was full of tremendous mistakes, and so tried to weaken its effect. The terrible danger of the authoritarian system, however, became really clear only at the moment when we were approaching the end ...[29]

The record of this same session an hour or so later, extracts from which are given here, fits into this picture so completely that all comment is superfluous. It is as follows:

Mr Justice Jackson: Now if you did not know what these measures were,

---

* Here Speer is referring to his (so far unproved) statement that he had intended to use gas to kill Hitler. See IMT Vol. XVI, p. 493 and pp. 190ff below.

how can you tell us that you approved of them? We always get to this blank wall ...

Speer: When I say that I approved I am only expressing my wish not to dodge my responsibility in this respect. But you must understand that a Minister of Production, particularly in view of the air attacks, had a tremendous task before him and that I could only take care of matters outside my own field if some particularly important matter forced me to do so. Otherwise I was glad if I could finish my own work and, after all, my task was by no means a small one.[30]

Shortly thereafter Speer was even clearer, saying: 'In my opinion a state functionary has two types of responsibility. One is the responsibility for his own sector and for that, of course, he is fully responsible. But above that I think that in decisive matters there is, and must be, among the leaders a common responsibility, for who is to bear responsibility for developments, if not the close associates of the head of State? This common responsibility, however, can only be applied to fundamental matters; it cannot be applied to details connected with other ministries or other responsible departments, for otherwise the entire discipline in the life of the State would be quite confused and no one would ever know who is individually responsible in a particular sphere. This individual responsibility in one's own sphere must, at all events, be kept clear and distinct.'[31]

The record goes on:

Mr Justice Jackson: Well, your point is, I take it, that you as a member of the government and a leader in this period of time acknowledge a responsibility for its large policies, but not for all the details that occurred in their execution. Is that a fair statement of your position?

Speer: Yes indeed.

Mr Justice Jackson: I think that concludes the cross-examination.[32]

As a major war criminal Speer was indicted on all four Counts. Not only did he accept responsibility himself but he resolutely opposed any blame being attached to the German people as a whole. When, for instance, Justice Jackson presented him with an affidavit by a German stating that Russian, French, Italian and other foreign civilians who had been captured and were working in a German firm in Essen had been ill-treated, beaten and robbed by a German employee of the firm, Speer became indignant, saying: ' I consider this affidavit a lie. I would say that among German people such things do not exist and if such individual cases occurred, they were punished. It is not possible to drag the German people in the dirt in such a way.'[33]

When, towards the end of the war, with Hitler seriously ill and semi-senile,[34] there could be no more question of a German victory, Speer prevented the destruction of German potential ordered by Hitler, thus largely preserving a basis for the continued existence of the German people after their catastrophic defeat. Until 19 March 1945 he was responsible for the 'destruction or non-destruction of industry in Germany'[35] but, as he said in cross-examination, this authority was removed from him by a Hitler decree; on 30 March 1945, however, it was restored by another decree which he himself had drafted. Speer was able to prove to the IMT that (sometimes via Martin Bormann) he had been able to prevent destruction in certain cases and had explicitly forbidden it in others.[36] When asked by Raginsky: 'What about ... those who are sitting in the dock? Did not any of them support Hitler in this [scorched earth] policy?', Speer replied: 'As far as I recall, none of those now in the dock was in favor of the scorched earth policy. On the contrary Funk, for example, was one of those who opposed it very strongly.'[37]

Even in Nuremberg these arguments made an impact. Speer had quickly realized that 'repudiation of responsibility' during cross-examination could only make the defendants' situation worse.[38] He had also realized that even *post hoc* delimitation of responsibilities might be a means of saving his life. It was important for him, for instance, that he should not carry the blame for decisions made by Sauckel in connection with the forced-labour programme; even before the IMT's opening session he had taken his precautions, writing to Jackson on the day of the final preparatory sessions. In his memoirs he tells of his first interrogation in Nuremberg:

'A young American officer awaited me. He pleasantly invited me to sit down and then began asking for explanations of various matters. Apparently Sauckel had tried to make a better case for himself by branding me as solely responsible for the importation of foreign workers. The officer proved to be well disposed and of his own accord composed an affidavit which straightened out this matter. This somewhat eased my mind, for I had the feeling that since my departure from Mondorf a good deal had been said about me on the principle of " Incriminate the absent".'[39]

Speer also felt that he should appear as a would-be assassin. He had in fact planned to kill Hitler in 1945, as he somewhat theatrically introduced into his cross-examination. In his memoirs, written twenty-three years later, he says:

'In court I intended merely to mention my plan to assassinate Hitler, chiefly in order to show how dangerous Hitler's destructive intentions had seemed to me ... The judges put their heads together ... I did not want to make any further statements on the matter for fear of seeming to boast about it.'[40]

On this subject the IMT record for 20 June 1946 is so eloquent that it can be given without comment:

Dr Flächsner: Generaloberst Jodl has ... testified before this court that both Hitler and his co-workers saw quite clearly the hopelessness of the military and economic situation. Was no unified action taken by some of Hitler's closer advisers in this hopeless situation to demand termination of the war?

Speer: No. No unified action was taken by the leading men in Hitler's circle. A step like this was quite impossible, for these men considered themselves either as pure specialists or else as people whose job it was to receive orders – or else they resigned themselves to the situation. No one took over the leadership in this situation for the purpose of bringing about at least a discussion with Hitler on the possibility of avoiding further sacrifices. On the other side was an influential group which tried, with all the means at their disposal, to intensify the struggle. That group consisted of Goebbels, Bormann and Ley and, as we have said, Fegelein and Burgdorf ...

Dr Flächsner: Herr Speer, the witness Stahl[41] said in his written interrogatory that about the middle of February 1945 you had demanded from him a supply of the new poison gas in order to assassinate Hitler, Bormann and Goebbels. Why did you intend to do this then?

Speer: I thought there was no other way out. In my despair I wanted to take this step as it had become obvious to me since the beginning of February that Hitler intended to go on with the war at all costs, ruthlessly and without consideration for the German people. It was obvious to me that in the loss of the war he confused his own fate with that of the German people and that in his own end he saw the end of the German people as well. It was also obvious that the war was lost so completely that even unconditional surrender would have to be accepted.

Dr Flächsner: Did you mean to carry out this assassination yourself, and why was your plan not realized?

Speer: I do not wish to testify to the details here. I could only carry it through personally because from 20 July only a limited circle still had access to Hitler. I met with various technical difficulties ...

The President: The Tribunal would like to hear the particulars but will hear them after the adjournment.

[A ten-minute recess was taken at this point.]

Dr Flächsner: Herr Speer, will you tell the Tribunal what circumstances hindered you in your undertaking?

Speer: I am most unwilling to describe the details because there is always something repellent about such matters. I do it only because it is the Tribunal's wish.

Dr Flächsner: Please continue.

Speer: In those days Hitler, after the military situation conference, often had conversations in his shelter with Ley, Goebbels and Bormann ... because they supported and cooperated in his radical course of action. Since 20 July it was no longer possible even for Hitler's closest associates to enter this shelter without their pockets and briefcases being examined by the SS for explosives. As an architect I knew this shelter intimately. It had an air-conditioning plant similar to the one installed in this courtroom.

It would not be difficult to introduce the gas into the ventilator of the air-conditioning plant ... It was then bound to circulate through the entire shelter in a very short time. Thereupon, in the middle of February 1945,

I sent for Stahl ... since I had worked in close cooperation with him during the destructions. I frankly told him of my intention ... I asked him to procure this new poison gas for me from the munitions production. He inquired of one of his associates ... of the armament office of the Army on how to get hold of this poison gas; it turned out that this new poison gas was only effective when made to explode, as the high temperature necessary for the formation of gas would then be reached ... An explosion was not possible, however, as this air-conditioning plant was made of thin sheets of tin which would have been torn to pieces by the explosion. Thereupon I had conferences with ... the chief engineer of the Chancellery, starting in the middle of March 1945. By these discussions I managed to arrange that the anti-gas filter should no longer be switched on continuously. In this way I should have been able to use the ordinary type of gas. When the time came I inspected the ventilating shaft in the garden of the Chancellery ... and there I discovered that on Hitler's personal order this ventilator had recently been surrounded by a chimney four meters high ... Due to this it was no longer possible to carry out my plan.[42]

The Tribunal did not adhere to the Indictment. They acquitted Speer under Counts One and Two, holding that he was not involved in preparation for aggressive war or in the conspiracy (Common Plan) since he was only appointed head of the armament industry late in the day ('Reich Minister for Armaments and Munitions' from 15 February 1942 and 'Reich Minister for Armaments and War Production' from 2 September 1943).[43]

He was pronounced guilty, however, under Counts Three and Four on the grounds that: 'The evidence introduced against Speer under Counts Three and Four relates entirely to his participation in the slave labor program. Speer himself had no direct administrative responsibility for this program. Although he had advocated the appointment of a General Plenipotentiary for the Utilization of Labor ... he did not obtain administrative control over Sauckel[44] ... As Reich Minister for Armaments and Munitions and General Plenipotentiary for Armaments under the Four Year Plan Speer had extensive authority ... His original authority was over the construction and production of arms for the OKH. This was progressively expanded to include naval armaments, civilian production and finally, on 1 August 1944, air armament. As ... member of the Central Planning Board, which had supreme authority for the scheduling of German production and the allocation and development of raw materials, Speer took the position that the Board had authority to instruct Sauckel to provide laborers for the industries under its control ... The practice was developed under which Speer transmitted to Sauckel an estimate of the total number of workers needed. Sauckel obtained the labor and allocated it to the various industries in accordance with instructions supplied by Speer.

'Speer knew when he made his demands on Sauckel that they would be supplied by foreign laborers serving under compulsion ... Sauckel continually informed Speer and his representatives that foreign laborers were being obtained by force ... In some cases Speer demanded laborers from specific foreign countries. Thus at the conference of 10–12 August 1942 Sauckel was instructed to supply Speer with "a further million Russian laborers for the German armament industry up to and including October 1942". At a meeting of the Central Planning Board on 22 April 1943 Speer discussed plans to obtain Russian laborers for use in the coal mines and flatly vetoed the suggestion that this labor deficit should be made up by German labor ... Speer was also directly involved in the utilization of forced labor as Chief of the Todt Organization ... Speer has admitted that he relied on compulsory service ... He also used concentration camp labor in the industries under his control ... Speer was also involved in the use of prisoners of war in armament industries but contends that he used Soviet prisoners of war only in industries covered by the Geneva Convention ...

' In mitigation it must be recognized that Speer ... in the closing stages of the war ... was one of the few men who had the courage to tell Hitler that the war was lost and to take steps to prevent the senseless destruction of production facilities both in occupied territories and in Germany. He carried out his opposition to Hitler's scorched earth program in some of the Western countries and in Germany by deliberately sabotaging it at considerable personal risk.'[45]

RIBBENTROP

'Everyone knows that the verdict is quite untenable,' Joachim von Ribbentrop[46] wrote to his wife Anneliese on 5 October 1946, 'but I happen to have been Adolf Hitler's Foreign Minister[47] and political considerations therefore call for my conviction. Fate willed it that my principal witness, Adolf Hitler, is dead. Were he able to give evidence the whole verdict would collapse. As it is I must bear the fate of the followers of such a mighty and perhaps demoniac personality.'[48]

In the witness-box six months earlier, on 28 March 1946, he had followed Göring in giving detailed explanations and descriptions of his work. He had given a long-winded account of where he was born, whence his parents originated and where he went to school; he told the court that he had studied languages in London as a youngster and had gone to Canada as a railway worker at the age of seventeen; then 'to see the world' he had taken posts in banks and the building trade. When the First World War began, 'with some difficulties' he had returned to Germany since 'every man was needed at home'. After about four years' service at the front, during which he was wounded, his career became orientated towards foreign policy; he was sent to Constantinople and in March 1919 was present at the Versailles Treaty negotiations as aide to General von Seeckt. He said: '... When the Treaty of Versailles came, I read that document in one night and it was my impression that no government in the world could possibly sign such a document. That was my first impression of foreign policy at home.'[49]

He went on to say that his father had had 'a strong interest in foreign politics' and that immediately after the First World War he, Joachim von Ribbentrop, had made 'several contacts with politicians' in England and France as a businessman and had tried 'to help my country' by 'voicing my views against Versailles'.[50]

As if he had been addressing an assembly of National-Socialists, who hardly ever left the Treaty of Versailles out of the argument from 1920 onwards, Ribbentrop told the IMT:

'The stipulations of Versailles were not observed ... either territorially speaking or in other very important points. I may mention that one of the most important questions – territorial questions – at that time was Upper Silesia and particularly Memel ... The events which took place made a deep impression on me personally. Upper Silesia particularly because ... right from the beginning German minorities ... suffered very hard times ... Further, the question of disarmament was ... one of the most important points of Versailles ... It was ... the denial of equal rights which made me decide ... to take a greater part in politics ... It was already a well-known fact ... – after 1930 the NSDAP received over 100 seats in the Reichstag, that here the natural will of the German people broke through.'[51]

Ribbentrop, who was pronounced guilty on all four Counts by the IMT, produced a picture of himself as the ideal Foreign Minister for Hitler's Reich; he often answered the prosecution's questions as if he was interviewing journalists from the *Völkischer Beobachter*. He went on:

'I saw Adolf Hitler for the first time on 13 August 1932 at the Berghof ... I visited Adolf Hitler and had a long discussion with him ... that is to say, Adolf Hitler explained his ideas on the situation in the summer of 1932 to me. I then saw him again in 1933 ... at my house in Dahlem which I placed at their disposal so that I, on my part, should do everything possible to create a national front. Adolf Hitler made a considerable impression on me even then. I noticed particularly his blue eyes in his generally dark appearance, and then, perhaps as outstanding, his detached, I should say reserved – not unapproachable ... – nature and the manner in which he expressed his thoughts. These thoughts and statements always had something final and definite about them, and they appeared to come from his innermost self. I had the impression that I was facing a man who had an unshakable will and who was a very strong personality. I can summarize by saying that I left that meeting with Hitler convinced that this man, if anyone, could save Germany from these great difficulties and that distress which existed at the time. I need not go further into detail about the events of that January. But I would like to tell about one episode which happened in my house in Dahlem ... I heard with what enormous strength and conviction – if you like also brutality and hardness –

he could state his opinion when he believed that obstacles might appear which could lead to the rehabilitation and rescue of his people.'[52]

Even in Nuremberg there had been no noticeable change in Ribbentrop's ideas. On 11 December 1945, for instance, the defendants were shown German news films, lasting some hours, recording scenes of triumph during the war, parades, demonstrations, scenes from Party rallies, speeches by Hitler and even Roland Freisler literally foaming at the mouth in the People's Court (the latter no doubt selected to show the defendants that their treatment was different). Afterwards Ribbentrop said to Dr Gilbert, the prison psychologist: 'You know, even with all I know, if Hitler should come to me in this cell now and say "Do this", I would still do it. Isn't it amazing?'[53]

Dr Horn, Ribbentrop's defence counsel, was obviously afraid that his client might start to sing Hitler's praises in this of all places. He tried to stop Ribbentrop's flow of words, though with an argument which carried no weight with the IMT; his question was: 'Did you believe in the possibility of a revision of the Versailles Treaty by means of mutual understanding?'[54]

Ribbentrop: I must say that the numerous business trips which in the years 1920 to 1932 took me abroad proved to me how endlessly difficult it was or would have to be under the system which then existed to bring about a revision of the Versailles Treaty by means of negotiations ... During those years I established many contacts with men of the business world, of public life, of art and science, particularly in universities in England and France. I learned thereby to understand the attitude of the English and the French ... Even shortly after Versailles it was my conviction that a change of that treaty could be carried out only through an understanding with France and Britain ... It was clear ... that only by means of an understanding with the Western Powers, with England and France, would a revision of Versailles be possible ... I had the distinct feeling that only through such an understanding could a permanent peace in Europe really be preserved ... I should like to add ... that right from the beginning, from the first day in which I saw ... the Versailles Treaty, I, as a German, felt it to be my duty to oppose it and to try to do everything so that a better treaty could take its place. It was precisely Hitler's opposition to Versailles that first brought me together with him and the National-Socialist Party.[55]

The prosecutors and members of the Tribunal, who were pressed for time, had listened in silent impatience to Ribbentrop until 5.0 p.m., when the court normally adjourned unless otherwise announced beforehand. When proceedings reopened at 10.0 a.m. next day the President announced that henceforth the IMT would not permit a defendant, as it had done in Göring's case, to recount from his own point of view 'the whole history of the Nazi regime from its inception to the defeat of Germany without any interruption', also that the court had decided that it was not permissible to give or submit evidence based on 'the injustice of the Versailles Treaty or whether it was made under duress'.[56]

Ribbentrop, who was badly and feebly advised, almost invariably missed the point. Again and again the argument ended with victory for the prosecution. Initially Ribbentrop had been unwilling to give evidence before an 'enemy court'[57] but when eventually he did so he cut a piteous figure. He, the Reich Foreign Minister from 1938 to 1945, was forced for instance, to admit ignorance of important League of Nations declarations. His cross-examination by Sir David Maxwell-Fyfe, the British Deputy Chief Prosecutor, on 1 April 1946 speaks for itself:

Sir David Maxwell-Fyfe: Witness, when you began to advise Hitler on matters of foreign policy in 1933, were you familiar with the League of Nations declaration of 1927?

Ribbentrop: I do not know which declaration you mean.

Sir David Maxwell-Fyfe: Don't you remember the League of Nations declaration of 1927?

Ribbentrop: The League of Nations has made many declarations. Please tell me which one you mean.

Sir David Maxwell-Fyfe: It made a rather important one about aggressive war in 1927, didn't it?

Ribbentrop: I do not know this declaration in detail, but it is clear that the League of Nations, like everyone, was against an aggressive war, and at that time Germany was a member of the League of Nations.

Sir David Maxwell-Fyfe: Germany was a member, and the preamble of the declaration was: 'Being convinced that a war of aggression would never serve as a means of settling international disputes, and is in consequence an international crime ...' Were you familiar with that when you ...

Ribbentrop: Not in detail, no.

Sir David Maxwell-Fyfe: It was rather an important matter to be familiar with if you were going to advise Hitler, who was then Chancellor, on foreign policy, wasn't it?

Ribbentrop: This declaration was certainly important and corresponded entirely with my attitude at that time. But subsequent events have proved that the League of Nations was not in a position to save Germany from chaos.[58]

The end of Ribbentrop's cross-examination by Rudenko on 2 April 1946 was flabbergasting, as the record shows:

Gen. Rudenko: ... Do you consider the seizure of Czechoslovakia as an act of aggression by Germany?

Von Ribbentrop: No, it was no aggression in that sense ...

Gen. Rudenko: Do you consider the attack on Poland as an act of aggression by Germany?

Von Ribbentrop: No, I must again say 'no' ...

Gen. Rudenko: Do you consider the attack on Denmark as an act of aggression by Germany?

Von Ribbentrop: No, the 'invasion' of Denmark ... was, according to the Führer's words and explanations, a purely preventive measure adopted against imminent landings of British fighting forces ...

Gen. Rudenko: ... Do you consider the attack on Belgium, Holland and Luxembourg as an act of aggression on the part of Germany?

Von Ribbentrop: That is the same question. I must again say 'No' ...

Gen. Rudenko: Do you consider the attack on Greece as an act of aggression on the part of Germany?

Von Ribbentrop: No ...

Gen. Rudenko: Witness Ribbentrop ... do you or do you not consider the attack on the Soviet Union as an act of aggression on the part of Germany?

Von Ribbentrop: It was no aggression in the literal sense of the word.[59]

To the very end Ribbentrop acknowledged that he had at all times been a faithful and devoted paladin of Hitler; he admitted that he had invariably said 'yes' when that was what the Führer wanted of him; in his defence he was continually stating that he had not thought up this or that for himself but had been given the idea and had it explained by Hitler. The prosecution's view of him is shown by the following extract from his cross-examination on 2 April by John Harlan Amen, United States Associate Trial Counsel:

Col. Amen: ... You speak English pretty well ...

Von Ribbentrop: I spoke it well in the past and I think I speak it passably well today.

Col. Amen: Almost as well as you speak German?

Von Ribbentrop: No, I would not say that, but in the past I spoke it nearly as well as German, although I have naturally forgotten a great deal in the course of the years and now it is more difficult for me.

Col. Amen: Do you know what is meant by a 'yes man' in English?

Von Ribbentrop: A 'yes man' – *per se*. A man who says 'yes' even when he himself – it is somewhat difficult to define. In any case I do not know what you mean by it in English. In German I should define him as a man who obeys orders and is obedient and loyal.

Col. Amen: And as a matter of fact you were a 'yes man' for Hitler, isn't that correct?

Von Ribbentrop: I was always loyal to Hitler, carried through his orders, differed frequently in opinion from him, repeatedly tendered my resignation, but when Hitler gave an order, I always carried out his instructions in accordance with the principles of our authoritarian state.[60]

Ribbentrop's case was lost even before Sir David Maxwell-Fyfe caught him out lying on a relatively trivial question, as the record shows; it needs no comment:

Sir David Maxwell-Fyfe: ... Now I want you to tell us a word about your connection with the SS. You are not suggesting, are you, at this stage that you were merely an honorary member of the SS? It has been suggested by your counsel, and I am sure it must have been on some misunderstanding of information, that you were merely an honorary member of the SS. That is not the case, is it?

Von Ribbentrop: That is no misunderstanding. This is exactly how it was: I received the SS uniform from Adolf Hitler. I did not serve in the SS, but as ambassador and later as Foreign Minister it was customary to have a rank of some sort and I had received the rank of SS Führer.

Sir David Maxwell-Fyfe: I put it to you that that is entirely untrue, that you joined the SS by application before you became ambassador-at-large in May 1933, isn't that right?

Von Ribbentrop: I know that. At any rate I always belonged to the SS.

Sir David Maxwell-Fyfe: You said just now it was honorary, because Hitler wanted you to have a uniform. I am putting it to you; you applied to join the SS in May 1933, in the ordinary way. Did you?

Von Ribbentrop: Of course one had to make an application ... I occasionally went around in a grey greatcoat and thereupon Hitler said I must wear a uniform. I do not remember when that was. It must have been 1933. As ambassador I received a higher rank, as Foreign Minister I received a still higher one.

Sir David Maxwell-Fyfe: And in May 1933, after you made application, you joined the SS in the not too high rank of Standartenführer, didn't you?

Von Ribbentrop: Yes, that could be.

Sir David Maxwell-Fyfe: And you became an Oberführer only on 20 April 1935, a Brigadeführer on 18 June 1935, and Gruppenführer on 13 September 1936 – that was after you became an ambassador – and Obergruppenführer on 20 April 1940.[61] Before you were made an ambassador you had been in the SS for three years and you had received promotion in the ordinary way, when you did your work with the SS, isn't that so?

Von Ribbentrop: Without ever taking any steps or doing anything myself in the SS, yes, that is correct.

Sir David Maxwell-Fyfe: Just look. It is document ... GB–294. The correspondence is 744 (b) ... That is your application with all the particulars. I just want to ask you one or two things about it. You asked to join, did you not, the 'Totenkopf', the Death's-Head Division of the SS?

Von Ribbentrop: No, that cannot be true.

Sir David Maxwell-Fyfe: Don't you remember getting a special Death's-Head ring and dagger from Himmler for your services? Don't you?

Von Ribbentrop: No, I do not remember. I never belonged to a Death's-Head Division ...

Sir David Maxwell-Fyfe: It says here 'Death's-Head Division'.

Von Ribbentrop: No, that is not so. If it says so here, it is not true. But I

think that I at one time received a so-called dagger, like all SS Führer.
That is correct.
Sir David Maxwell-Fyfe: And the ring too. Here is a letter dated the
5 November 1935, to the Personnel Office of the Reichsführer-SS: 'In
reply to your question I have to inform you that Brigadeführer von
Ribbentrop's ring size is 17 ...' Do you remember getting that?
Von Ribbentrop: ... I do not remember precisely. No doubt it is true.[62]

Ribbentrop was not unlike Fritz Sauckel and Ernst Kaltenbrunner (to
cite only these two), who believed that the accusations against them were
unjust and resulted from errors in translation, document forgeries and
perjured evidence. He tried to lay the blame on others rather than himself.
For instance he complained in writing to his defence counsel about the
behaviour of certain prosecution witnesses – State Secretary Ernst von
Weizsäcker, Erich Kordt,[63] Paul Otto Schmidt, Hitler's interpreter, and
Ambassador Friedrich Wilhelm Gaus.[64] He accused Weizsäcker and Kordt
of speaking before the IMT on matters and problems on which he had
never spoken to them;[65] he reproached Schmidt and Gaus for showing
incredible ingratitude to him.[66] He referred to Sir Nevile Henderson's
Failure of a Mission, which criticized him severely, as a 'propaganda
book';[67] he dismissed the diary of Count Ciano, the Italian Foreign
Minister, which was tabled as a 'document' against him, as a 'forgery'.[68]

Despite – or perhaps because of – his 'eloquence', which degenerated
into mere verbiage, the Ribbentrop seen in Nuremberg was so insipid and
colourless that even Rudenko clearly tried to give him a helping hand,
though he had the least reason to wish to assist this particular defendant of
all people. On 2 April, just before Ribbentrop was due to return to the dock,
Rudenko asked him: '... Your appointment to this post coincided with the
initial period when Hitler had launched on a series of acts involving a foreign
policy which in the end led to the World War. The question arises: Why
did Hitler appoint you his Minister of Foreign Affairs just before embarking
on a wide program of aggression? Don't you consider that he thought you
the most suitable man for the purpose, a man with whom he could never
have any differences of opinion?'[69]

Ribbentrop's answer was staggering even for those who were not well-
drilled Marxist-Leninist communists: 'I cannot tell you anything about
Adolf Hitler's thoughts. He did not tell me about them. He knew that I was
his faithful assistant, that I shared his view that we must have a strong
Germany and that I had to get these things done through diplomatic
and peaceful channels. I cannot say any more. What ideas he may have
had, I do not know.'[70]

Rudenko's final question was: '... How can you explain the fact that
even now, when the entire panorama of the bloody crimes of the Hitler
regime has been unfolded before your eyes, when you fully realize the
complete crash of that Hitlerite policy ... that you are still defending this

regime ... that you are still praising Hitler ... ?'

At this point, however, Rudenko was interrupted by the President with the comment: 'I do not think it is a proper question to put to the witness.' The conclusion of Rudenko's cross-examination also marked the end of the case against Ribbentrop. Dr Horn, his feeble defence counsel, did not even attempt to make a few points in his client's favour. The record concludes:

Gen. Rudenko: I thought that this was only one question which summarizes everything. Will you please answer, Defendant Ribbentrop.

The President: I told you, General Rudenko, that the Tribunal does not think it a proper question to put.

Gen. Rudenko: I have no further questions.

The President: Dr Horn, do you want to re-examine?

Dr Horn: I have no further questions to put to the defendant, Mr President.

The President: Then the defendant can return to his seat.[71]

After the IMT had pronounced sentence Ribbentrop declared: 'The defence had no fair chance to defend German foreign policy. Our prepared application for the submission of evidence was not allowed ... Half of the 300 documents which the defence had prepared were not admitted without good cause being shown. Witnesses and affidavits were only admitted after the prosecution had been heard; most of them were rejected. For instance, statements by some policeman or private individual who had served on a government commission were admitted as official evidence, but correspondence between Hitler and Chamberlain, reports by ambassadors and diplomatic minutes etc. were rejected. Only the prosecution, not the defence, had access to German and foreign archives. The prosecution only searched for incriminating documents and their use was biased; it knowingly concealed exonerating documents and withheld them from the defence. In cross-examination tricks and so-called "surprise documents" were used; there was no fair chance to give a considered reply.'[72]

The IMT convicted Ribbentrop of having urged Hitler in 1938 to take political steps to prevent England and France intervening in a European war; this was regarded as particularly serious since, in the view of the prosecution and the Tribunal, Ribbentrop started from the premiss that 'a change in the status quo ... in the German sense could only be carried out by force'.[73] Twenty-three years later, however, Anneliese von Ribbentrop was able to show that the documents concerned are susceptible of quite a different interpretation. With equal authenticity they can be taken to indicate that in his reports to Constantin von Neurath, the Reich Foreign Minister, while he was Ambassador in London from December 1936 to December 1937, Ribbentrop was not urging Hitler to take warlike steps but, on the contrary, was trying to warn him not to attempt to change the status quo by war.[74]

On this subject the IMT came down unanimously against Ribbentrop.

He also had to pay the penalty for the fact that on his appointment as Reich Foreign Minister in 1938 Hitler had said to him that the problems of Austria, the Sudetenland, Memel and Danzig would have to be solved by 'some sort of showdown' or 'military settlement'.* Also chalked up against him under 'Crimes against Peace' was his participation in high-level diplomatic activity in preparation for wars clearly characterized by the IMT as wars of aggression – against Czechoslovakia, Poland, Norway, Denmark, Holland, Belgium and Greece – and 'the political exploitation of Soviet territories' agreed between him and Alfred Rosenberg.[75]

Under 'War Crimes and Crimes against Humanity' the IMT condemned him for:

Participation (which, referring to a statement by Göring, he denied) in a meeting of 6 June 1944 at which it was agreed that crews of Allied aircraft engaged in low-flying attacks should be lynched if they were shot down or force-landed;

Deliberate and systematic concealment of the murder of the French General Mesny in January 1945 during the drive from the prisoner of war camp at Königstein to Colditz near Dresden, designedly camouflaged by the Gestapo as reaction to an attempted escape;

War crimes and crimes against humanity committed by Foreign Office representatives primarily in Denmark and Vichy France;

The 'ruthless occupation policy' pursued by the Italians in Yugoslavia and Greece (based on Ribbentrop's advice);

His personal involvement (which he consistently denied to the end) in the 'Final Solution of the Jewish Question'.[76]

The final paragraph of the judgement summarizes the question:

'Von Ribbentrop's defense to the charges made against him is that Hitler made all the important decisions and that he was such a great admirer and faithful follower of Hitler that he never questioned Hitler's repeated assertions that he wanted peace or the truth of the reasons that Hitler gave in explaining aggressive actions. The Tribunal does not consider this explanation to be true. Von Ribbentrop participated in all of the Nazi aggressions from the occupation of Austria to the invasion of the Soviet Union. Although he was personally concerned with the diplomatic rather than the military aspect of these actions, his diplomatic efforts were so closely connected with war that he could not have remained unaware of the aggressive nature of Hitler's actions. In the administration of territories over which Germany acquired control by illegal invasion von Ribbentrop also assisted in carrying out criminal policies, particularly those involving extermination of the Jews. There is abundant evidence, moreover, that von

* In his *Memoirs*, written in Nuremberg (p. 193), Ribbentrop denied that Hitler had used these words which clearly presaged war.

Ribbentrop was in complete sympathy with all the main tenets of the National-Socialist creed and that his collaboration with Hitler and with other defendants in the commission of Crimes against Peace, War Crimes and Crimes against Humanity was whole-hearted. It was because Hitler's policy and plans coincided with his own ideas that von Ribbentrop served him so willingly to the end.'[77]

Ribbentrop denied the charges made against him; he dismissed them even when writing his memoirs at the very end, noting that 'the defendants are not responsible for the atrocities. Those who committed them or were responsible for them are dead.'[78] As regards the 'Final Solution of the Jewish Question' he maintained that it was 'a term which I heard mentioned for the first time here in Nuremberg', which manifestly was not true. Equally untrue was his statement that his participation in the 'Final Solution' was 'free invention' by the IMT.[79]

It was proved that Reinhard Heydrich had informed him on 24 June 1940 that a solution of the Jewish problem could 'no longer' be arrived at 'by emigration', so that 'a final territorial solution' was necessary. Heydrich's letter said: 'The overall problem – the existence of $3\frac{1}{4}$ million Jews in territories now under German sovereignty – can no longer be solved by emigration. A territorial solution therefore becomes necessary. I request you to participate in the forthcoming discussions dealing with the final solution of the Jewish question.'[80]

On the murder of General Mesny, Ribbentrop noted after he had been convicted: 'The court refers to the killing of a French general by way of reprisal for the killing of a German general in similar circumstances. The court knew very well that I had made representations against this plan with Hitler and that the Legal Department of the Foreign Office had been called in on my behalf.'[81] It is true that Ribbentrop did bring in the Legal Department of his ministry but for reasons other than those he gave in Nuremberg. Document 4051–PS, the record of a telephone conversation of 12 January 1945, shows quite clearly why he did so: 'The instruction of the Reich Foreign Minister is to discuss the matter with Counsellor Albrecht [Head of the Legal Department of the Foreign Office] in order to establish precisely what rights the protecting power has in this matter, so as to bring the project into line with them.'

Ribbentrop was not telling the truth, as the prosecution was able to prove on 1 and 9 August 1946. On 1 August they tabled a report signed by Kaltenbrunner – intended for submission on behalf of Ribbentrop – dated 30 December 1944 and addressed to Heinrich Himmler, giving the Reichsführer-SS details of the murder plan. This document shows Ribbentrop's involvement so clearly that his statements to the IMT could only be described as transparent efforts to protect himself:

'The discussions about the matter in question with the Chief of Prisoners of War Organization and the Foreign Office have taken place as ordered and have led to the following proposals:

'1. In the course of a transfer of five persons in three cars with army identifications, the escape is staged while the last car suffers a puncture.

'2. Carbon dioxide is released by the driver into the closed back of the car. The apparatus can be installed with the simplest means and can be removed again immediately. After considerable difficulties a suitable vehicle has now become available.

'3. Other possibilities, such as poisoning of food or drink, have been considered but have been discarded as too unsafe.

'Provision for the completion of subsequent work in accordance with plans, such as report, post-mortem examination, documentation and burial, has been made. Convoy leader and drivers are to be supplied by the RSHA [Reichssicherheitshauptamt-SS Central Security Department] and will appear in army uniform and with pay books delivered to them.

'Concerning the notice for the press, contact has been established with Geheimrat Wagner of the Foreign Office. Wagner reports that the Reich Foreign Minister wishes to speak with the Reichsführer about this matter. In the opinion of the Reich Foreign Minister, this action must be co-ordinated in every respect.

'In the meantime, it has been learned that the name of the man in question has been mentioned in the course of various long-distance calls between the Führer's headquarters and the Chief of the Prisoners of War Organization; therefore the Chief of the Prisoners of War Organization now proposes the use of another man with the same qualifications. I agree with this and propose that the choice be left to the Chief of the Prisoners of War Organization.'[82]

STREICHER

With Julius Streicher, who was cross-examined in April 1946, matters followed the same pattern as for Ribbentrop. All his efforts to argue his way out and shift the blame on to other authorities were of no avail. His statements that he had known nothing of and had never wanted the mass murders of Jews, that his inflammatory tirades in *Der Stürmer* were produced as a method of creating a home for Jewry outside the Reich, were mere obvious and transparent evasions. The hopelessness of his position before the IMT was demonstrated by the fact that he thought he could present the anti-Jewish hate campaigns which he had written or published, with their calls to killing, murder, extermination and annihilation, as emotionally coloured efforts of authorship without a concrete logical purpose. The following extract from his cross-examination on 29 April is so illuminating that addition or explanation is unnecessary.

Griffith-Jones had tabled one of his publications dated 24 January 1944, quoting the following passage from it: 'Whoever does what a Jew does is a scoundrel, a criminal, and he who repeats and wishes to copy him deserves the same fate – annihilation, death,'[83] and he then asked Streicher: 'Are you still advocating a national Jewish home?'

Streicher's disarming reply was: 'Yes, that has nothing to do with the big political plan. If you take every statement by a writer, every statement from a daily newspaper, as an example, and want to prove a political aim by it, then you miss the point. You have to distinguish between a newspaper article and a great political aim.'[84]

Griffith-Jones, who knew what to make of that, remained unperturbed, saying: 'Very well, let us just turn now to the next page, 2 March 1944, where it says: "Eternal night must come over the born criminal race of Jews so that eternal day may bless awakening non-Jewish mankind."'

Descending to Streicher's level, he then asked sarcastically: 'Were they going to have eternal night in their national Jewish state? Is that what you wanted?'[85]

The record then continues:

Streicher: That is an anti-semitic play of words. Again it has nothing to do with the great political aim.
Lt-Col. Griffith-Jones: It may be an anti-semitic play of words, but the only meaning it can have is murder. Is that not true?
Streicher: No.
Lt-Col. Griffith-Jones: Will you turn to the next page, 25 May 1944 ... I quote the second paragraph:
'How can we overcome this danger and restore humanity to health? Just as the individual human being is able to defend himself against contagious diseases only if he proclaims war against the cause of the disease, the germ, so the world can be restored to health only when the most terrible germ of all times, the Jew, has been removed. It is of no avail to battle against the outward symptoms of the world disease without rendering the morbific agents innocuous. The disease will break out again sooner or later. The cause and the carrier of the disease, the germ, will see to that. But if the nations are to be restored to health and are to remain healthy in the future, then the germ of the Jewish world plague must be destroyed, root and branch.' ... Are you saying there when you say 'must be destroyed root and branch' – did you mean to say 'ought to be given a Jewish national state'?
Streicher: Yes, it is a far cry from such a statement in an article to the act, or to the will, to commit mass murder.
Lt-Col. Griffith-Jones: Turn over to 10 August: 'When it loses this struggle, Judaism will be ruined, then the Jew will be extinguished. Then will Judaism be annihilated down to the last man.' Are we to read from these words: Provide the Jews with a Jewish national state?
Streicher: That is a vision of the future. I would like to call it an expression of a prophetic vision. But it is not incitement to kill 5 million Jews. That is an opinion, a matter of belief, of conviction.

Lt-Col. Griffith-Jones: It is the prophetic vision of what you wanted, is it not – of what you have been advocating now for the last four years – the beginning of the war? Isn't that what it is?

Streicher: Mr Prosecutor, I cannot tell you today what I may have been thinking years ago at a certain moment when writing an article. But I still admit that when I saw lying before me on the table declarations from the Jewish front, many declarations saying: 'The German nation has to be destroyed; bomb the cities, do not spare women, children or old men' – if one has declarations like these in front of one, it is possible that things will come from one's pen such as I have often written.

Lt-Col. Griffith-Jones: You know, do you not, now, even if you do not believe the full figures, that millions of Jews have been murdered since the beginning of the war? Do you know that? You have heard the evidence, have you not?

Streicher: I believe it ...

Lt-Col. Griffith-Jones: I only wanted to know whether you had heard that evidence. You can answer 'yes' or 'no' and I presume it will be 'yes'.

Streicher: Yes, I have to say, evidence for me is only the testament of the Führer. There he states that the mass executions took place upon his orders. That I believe. Now I believe it.[86]

Ultimately the IMT did not condemn Streicher either as having participated in the conspiracy against peace or as having been one of Hitler's advisers.[87] They did, however, convict him of having 'infected the German mind with the virus of anti-semitism' by speeches and articles over a period of twenty-five years and of having 'incited the German people to active persecution'. The judgement concludes: 'Streicher's incitement to murder and extermination ... clearly constitutes persecution on political and racial grounds in connection with War Crimes, as defined by the Charter, and constitutes a Crime against Humanity.'[88]

Even under German criminal law Streicher would certainly have been condemned in 1945 for conscious and deliberate co-operation with other persons and groups responsible for the elimination of Jews.

Admittedly the IMT's judgements reflect the uncertainty of the basis upon which, in many respects, the court worked. The fact, for instance, that it is not possible to deduce with any certainty what were the characteristics which branded a war as one of aggression shows clearly the sort of problems with which the IMT had to wrestle. Dr Otto Kranzbühler, in his book on Nuremberg,[89] quotes from the IMT's judgement that 'renunciation of war as an instrument of national policy necessarily involves the proposition that such a war is illegal in international law' and comments aptly: 'If that is the definition, it applies equally to a defensive war.' The connection established in Nuremberg between the individual and international law and the resulting direct responsibility of each defendant under international law inevitably led the court to place an interpretation on certain relationships which was obscure not only to the defendants and their counsel, particularly seeing that the precedents which were cited concerning the duty of individuals were in general based on the laws of war, not on international law. A further relevant point was that the existence of Hitler's totalitarian dictatorship with all its consequences was not allowed to be taken into account as a mitigating factor.

Nevertheless, despite all the IMT's deficiencies and taking into account that Nuremberg was intended to constitute a revolutionary step forward – with fundamental consequences for the future – the accused were given a fair trial. The following extracts from the IMT's judgements on Frick, Kaltenbrunner, Sauckel, Seyss-Inquart, Frank and Rosenberg consequently need only brief comment.

FRICK

In the IMT's judgement Wilhelm Frick[90] was described as a 'Nazi administrative specialist and bureaucrat'; he was held responsible for abolishing 'with ruthless efficiency' all opposition parties by means of laws which he drafted and signed, for suppressing the trade unions and the churches, for incorporating local governments into the central Reich authority and for 'bringing the German Nation under the complete control of the NSDAP – matters which, in the opinion of Ribbentrop and Hess in Nuremberg, were no concern of the IMT. These statements, together with the additional charge raised against Frick of having 'prepared the way for the Gestapo and their concentration camps',[91] wherein not only Germans and Jews from all over the world but also nationals of the victor powers and other countries were done to death, also appeared in National-Socialist eulogies of Frick. Only the facts were presented somewhat differently, as the following comparison shows:

Nazi appreciation of Frick in a publication marked 'For use only within the Ordnungspolizei'	*Extract from the judgement of the IMT*
In 1934 Frick created the foundation for the German unified State. A year later the local government ordinance valid for the whole of Reich territory came into force. The law governing civil servants of 26 January 1937, also drawn up by Frick, further serves the unity of the Reich. The ... Nuremberg Laws ... the Reich Citizenship Law and the Law for the Protec-	Always rabidly anti-Semitic, Frick drafted, signed and administered many laws designed to eliminate Jews from German life and economy. His work formed the basis of the Nuremberg Decrees and he was active in enforcing them. Responsible for prohibiting Jews from following various professions and for confiscating their property, he signed a final decree

tion of German Blood and German Honour are also the work of Frick. In many other fields within the competence of the Reich Ministry of the Interior, in those of health, sport, the Labour Service, social welfare etc. Frick has done revolutionary, statesmanlike work. The war has brought the Reich Minister of the Interior, who is also Minister for Civil Defence, new large-scale responsibilities. As Plenipotentiary appointed by the Führer for Reich Administration he is responsible for centralized direction of the entire German administrative system. In his hands – with the cooperation of all other relevant government and Party agencies – lies the administrative and organizational solution of all problems raised by the war (maintenance of soldiers' families, welfare of persons injured by enemy action etc.). As Plenipotentiary for Reich Administration he is a member of the Ministerial Council for the Defence of the Reich, which, under the chairmanship of Reich Marshal Göring, deals with legislative matters of importance for the defence of the Reich.

Dr Frick was also responsible for the internal political and administrative arrangements for territories returned to the Reich – Austria, the Sudetenland, Memel, Danzig and West Prussia, the Warthegau and territories south-east of Austria etc. In general officials for the administration of occupied territories were seconded from the administrative organizations under his central direction – to the in 1943, after the mass destruction of Jews in the East, which placed them 'outside the law' and handed them over to the Gestapo. These laws paved the way for the 'final solution' and were extended by Frick to the incorporated territories and to certain of the occupied territories ... As the Supreme Reich Authority in Bohemia and Moravia Frick bears general responsibility for the acts of oppression in that territory after 23 August 1943, such as terrorism of the population, slave labor and the deportation of Jews to the concentration camps for extermination. It is true that Frick's duties as Reich Protector were considerably more limited than those of his predecessor and that he had no legislative and limited personal executive authority in the Protectorate. Nevertheless Frick knew full well what the Nazi policies of occupation were in Europe, particularly with respect to Jews at that time, and by accepting the office of Reich Protector he assumed responsibility for carrying out those policies in Bohemia and Moravia. German citizenship in the occupied territories as well as in the Reich came under his jurisdiction while he was Minister of the Interior. Having created a racial register of persons of German extraction, Frick conferred German citizenship on certain groups of citizens of foreign countries. He is responsible for Germanization in Austria, Sudetenland, Memel, Danzig, Eastern territories (West Prussia and Posen) and Eupen, Malmédy and

Government General, to Norway, to Holland, to Occupied France and to conquered Russian territories.

Frick's great services during the war were recognized by the award to him by the Führer of the War Service Cross, First and Second Class.

Dr Frick has always maintained specially close and cordial relations with the police ... At an early stage he intervened with reforms in Thuringia, nationalizing the local police and building them into a powerful, reliable instrument in the hands of central authority. In this matter Frick emerged victorious from the bitter political struggle against the central government. Then in 1936, under his direction, unification of the entire German police force under the Reichsführer SS and Chief of the German Police, Heinrich Himmler, was carried through.

As a professional civil servant, as a politician of stature and finally as a statesman, Frick has given his people faithful and lasting service in difficult times. He will go down to history as a man who, by his work in reorganizing the Reich, has opened a new chapter in the development of our people.

Moresnet. He forced on the citizens of these territories German law, German courts, German education, German police security and compulsory military service.

During the war nursing homes, hospitals and asylums in which euthanasia was practiced, as described elsewhere in this Judgement, came under Frick's jurisdiction. He had knowledge that insane, sick and aged people, 'useless eaters', were being systematically put to death. Complaints of these murders reached him, but he did nothing to stop them. A report of the Czechoslovak War Crimes Commission estimated that 275,000 mentally deficient and aged people, for whose welfare he was responsible, fell victim to it.[92]

Rudenko's final address on 29 July 1946 was illuminating.[93] He described Frick in terms similar to those of the judgement. He did not, however, accuse Frick of the murder of Jews, although the main mass murders had taken place in the East. He merely said that Frick 'took part in the issue of numerous laws, ordinances and acts, the purpose of which ... was discrimination against Jews etc.'. Sir Hartley Shawcross, in his address (tabling a letter written to Frick in July 1940 by Bishop Wurm giving full details), accused Frick of having known all about the euthanasia programme, with all its consequences.[94]

KALTENBRUNNER

Ernst Kaltenbrunner was indicted under Counts One, Three and Four but acquitted under Count One.[95] The judgement on him says: 'As leader of the SS in Austria Kaltenbrunner was active in the Nazi intrigue against the Schuschnigg Government. On the night of 11 March 1938, after Göring had ordered Austrian National-Socialists to seize control of the Austrian Government, 500 Austrian SS men under Kaltenbrunner's command surrounded the Federal Chancellery while Seyss-Inquart was negotiating with President Miklas. But there is no evidence connecting Kaltenbrunner with plans to wage aggressive war on any other front. The Anschluss ... is not charged as an aggressive war and the evidence ... does not ... show his direct participation in any plan to wage such a war.'

The War Crimes and Crimes against Humanity, however, of which Kaltenbrunner was accused and proved guilty, were so monstrous that, during his absence owing to a brain haemorrhage,[96] even some of his hard-boiled fellow defendants turned against him in disgust, and Dr Kauffmann, his defence counsel, refused to shake hands with him when he reappeared in the courtroom on 10 December 1945 after recovery.

Before the IMT Kaltenbrunner, Reinhard Heydrich's successor, was confronted with proof of crime actually committed, not merely authorized by his signature. Nevertheless, despite the wealth of documentary and oral evidence, he apparently thought that he could lie his way out. Even when documents carried his own signature, he attempted to dismiss them by denying their authenticity. Under the overwhelming weight of evidence he did admit that agencies under his command had committed most serious crimes, but even these he tried to present as the continuance of a process which had already started before he had had anything to do with it in any position of authority. Jackson's oft-quoted remark in his final address that 'it would be as true to say that there had been no war as to pronounce these men innocent'[97] fitted Kaltenbrunner's case precisely. Rudenko quoted Himmler's opinion of him as 'the most deserving successor to that hangman Heydrich executed by Czech patriots'.[98] Rudenko concluded the case for the prosecution with: 'Successor to a hangman and himself a hangman, Kaltenbrunner carried out the most revolting function in the common criminal plan of the Hitlerite clique.'[99] In his closing address Rudenko cited the written evidence of a witness, an ex-inmate of Mauthausen concentration camp, who had watched Kaltenbrunner having 'three methods of execution' demonstrated to him during a visit to the camp – 'hanging, shooting and gassing'.

The IMT's judgement continues:

'... Kaltenbrunner took charge of an organization which included the main offices of the Gestapo, the SD and the Criminal Police. As Chief of the RSHA Kaltenbrunner had authority to order protective custody in ... concentration camps ... Kaltenbrunner was aware of conditions in concentration camps ... Kaltenbrunner himself ordered the execution of prisoners in those camps and his office was used to transmit to the camps execution orders which originated in Himmler's office. At the end of the war Kaltenbrunner participated in the arrangements for the evacuation of inmates of concentration camps and the liquidation of many of them, to prevent them being liberated by the Allied armies.

'During the period in which Kaltenbrunner was Head of the RSHA, it was engaged in a widespread program of War Crimes and Crimes against Humanity. These crimes included the mistreatment and murder of prisoners of war. Einsatz Kommandos operating under the control of the Gestapo were engaged in the screening of Soviet prisoners of war. Jews, commissars and others ... were reported to the RSHA, which had them transferred to a concentration camp and murdered. An RSHA order issued during Kaltenbrunner's regime established the "Bullet Decree", under which certain escaped prisoners of war who were recaptured were taken to Mauthausen and shot. The order for the execution of commando troops was extended by the Gestapo to include parachutists while Kaltenbrunner was Chief of the RSHA. An order signed by Kaltenbrunner instructed the police not to interfere with attacks on baled-out Allied fliers* ...

'During the period in which Kaltenbrunner was head of the RSHA, the Gestapo and SD in occupied territories continued the murder and ill-treatment of the population, using methods which included torture and confinement in concentration camps, usually under orders to which Kaltenbrunner's name was signed ...

'Kaltenbrunner established a series of labor reformatory camps ... When the SS embarked on a slave labor program of its own, the Gestapo was used to obtain the needed workers by sending laborers to concentration camps.

'The RSHA played a leading role in the "final solution" of the Jewish question by the extermination of the Jews. A special section under the Amt IV of the RSHA was established to supervise this program ... Kaltenbrunner had been informed of the activity of these Einsatzgruppen ...

'The murder of ... Jews in concentration camps ... was also under the supervision of the RSHA when Kaltenbrunner was head of that organization, and special missions of the RSHA scoured the occupied territories and the various Axis satellites arranging for the deportation of Jews to these extermination institutions. Kaltenbrunner was informed ... A letter which he wrote on 30 June 1944 described the shipment to Vienna of 12,000 Jews for that purpose and directed that all who could not work would have to be kept in readiness for "special action", which meant murder.†

'Kaltenbrunner has claimed ... that the criminal program had started

* What is meant is lynch law by the civil population.

† This was one of the signatures stoutly denied by Kaltenbrunner in front of the IMT.

before his assumption of office; that he seldom knew what was going on; and that when he was informed he did what he could to stop them . . . But he exercised control over the activities of the R S H A, was aware of the crimes it was committing, and was an active participant in many of them.'

SAUCKEL

Fritz Sauckel had joined the Nazi Party in 1923; he had been appointed Gauleiter of Thuringia in 1927 and Head of the Thuringian State Ministry in 1933; he was Hitler's General Plenipotentiary for the Employment of Labour and held the formal rank of Obergruppenführer in both the S A and S S. He was acquitted of the charge of Crimes against Peace. The I M T's judgement on him begins:

'The evidence has not satisfied the Tribunal that Sauckel was sufficiently connected with the common plan to wage aggressive war or sufficiently involved in the planning or waging of the aggressive wars to allow the Tribunal to convict him on Counts One or Two.'

Sauckel was found guilty, however, under Counts Three and Four – War Crimes and Crimes against Humanity. He had been a working man and a merchant seaman and both in cross-examination and in his final plea he tried to present himself as a christian socialist who, as a former worker, had always urged humane treatment in the enforcement of the gigantic forced-labour programme. He had to pay the penalty, however, for the fact that, under his administration and authority, more than 5 million people had been deported to Germany from abroad for forced labour, 'many of them under terrible conditions of cruelty and suffering'. The judgement says that he used: '. . . so-called "voluntary" recruiting by a whole batch of male and female agents just as was done in the olden times for "shang-haiing". That real voluntary recruiting was the exception rather than the rule is shown by Sauckel's statement on 1 March 1944 that "out of five million foreign workers who arrived in Germany not even 200,000 came voluntarily". Although he now claims that the statement is not true, the circumstances under which it was made, as well as the evidence presented before the Tribunal, leave no doubt that it was substantially accurate.'[100]

In his closing address on 27 July 1946 Sir Hartley Shawcross had quoted from documents which showed Sauckel personally as 'the greatest slaver since the Pharaohs' (Sir Hartley's words). In one of them Sauckel was recorded as saying: 'Should we not succeed in obtaining the necessary labor on a voluntary basis, we must immediately institute conscription of forced labor ... a gigantic number of new foreign workers ... men and women ... an indisputable necessity.'[101]

Owing to his background this old Party functionary was treated somewhat condescendingly by most of the defendants. In Nuremberg he adopted the attitude of the hero in *Don Quixote* or 'The Sad-faced Knight'. He simply took refuge in the totally unrealistic story that, despite all the evidence piled up against him, he was being misunderstood and condemned in his innocence.

The court's finding was:

'On 21 March 1942 Hitler appointed Sauckel Plenipotentiary General for the Utilization of Labor with authority to put under uniform control "the utilization of all available manpower, including that of workers recruited from abroad and of prisoners of war". Sauckel was instructed to operate within the fabric of the Four Year Plan, and on 27 March 1942 Göring issued a decree as Commissioner for the Four Year Plan transferring his manpower sections to Sauckel. On 30 September 1942 Hitler gave Sauckel authority to appoint Commissioners in the various occupied territories and "to take all necessary measures for the enforcement" of the decree of 21 March 1942.

'Under the authority . . . obtained by these decrees, Sauckel set up a program for the mobilization of the labor resources available to the Reich. One of the important parts . . . was the systematic exploitation, by force, of the labor resources of the occupied territories. Shortly after Sauckel had taken office, he had the governing authorities in the various occupied territories issue decrees establishing compulsory labor service in Germany. Under the authority of these decrees Sauckel's Commissioners, backed up by the police authorities of the occupied territories, obtained and sent to Germany the laborers which were necessary to fill the quotas given them by Sauckel . . . The manner in which the . . . slave laborers were collected and transported to Germany and what happened to them after they arrived has . . . been described. Sauckel argues that he is not responsible for these excesses in the administration of the program. He says that the total number of workers to be obtained was set by the demands from agriculture and from industry; that obtaining the workers was the responsibility of the occupation authorities, transporting them to Germany that of the German railways and taking care of them in Germany that of the Ministries of Labor and Agriculture, the German Labor Front and the various industries involved . . .

'There is no doubt, however, that Sauckel had overall responsibility for the slave labor program. At the time of the events in question he did not fail to assert control over the fields which he now claims were the sole responsibility of others. His regulations provided that his commissioners should have authority for obtaining labor, and he was constantly in the field supervising the steps which were being taken. He was aware of ruthless methods being taken to obtain laborers and vigorously supported them on the ground that they were necessary to fill the quotas. Sauckel's regulations also provided that he had responsibility for transporting the laborers to Germany, allocating them to employers and taking care of them . . . He was informed of the bad conditions that existed.'

The court's judgement did allow Sauckel this, however:

'It does not appear that he advocated brutality for its own sake or was an advocate of any program such as Himmler's plan for extermination through work. His attitude was thus expressed in a regulation: "All the men must be fed, sheltered and treated in such a way as to exploit them to the highest possible extent at the lowest conceivable degree of expenditure".'[102]

SEYSS-INQUART

Arthur Seyss-Inquart, an attorney born in Moravia in 1892, who was given very high marks for intelligence by the American prison psychologist in Nuremberg, had had only a relatively short political career as official National-Socialist[103] when the IMT condemned him to death.[104] In his closing address Jackson described him as 'the champion of the Austrian Fifth Column' and as having taken over the government of Austria in 1938 in order to 'make a present' of his country to Hitler.[105] Nevertheless he became a member of the Nazi Party only after the Austrian Anschluss. In 1939 Hitler appointed him Reichsstatthalter (Governor) of the Ostmark, as Austria was called, Reich Minister without Portfolio and Deputy to Hans Frank in the 'Government General' of Poland. In 1940 he was made Reich Commissar for the Occupied Eastern Territories and Reichsstatthalter for the occupied Netherlands. From March 1938 he was a general in the SS.

From the very beginning of the war, therefore, he had been entrusted by Hitler with the administration of occupied territories; he was allotted offices and functions, the legacies and consequences of which inevitably weighed heavily against him in Nuremberg. The IMT's judgement states:

'As Reich Governor of Austria, Seyss-Inquart instituted a program of confiscating Jewish property. Under his regime Jews were forced to emigrate, were sent to concentration camps ... At the end of his regime he cooperated with the Security Police and SD in the deportation of Jews from Austria to the East. While he was Governor of Austria political opponents ... were sent to concentration camps by the Gestapo, mistreated and often killed ... In November 1939, while on an inspection tour through the General Government, Seyss-Inquart stated that Poland was to be so administered as to exploit its economic resources for the benefit of Germany. Seyss-Inquart also ... was informed of the beginning of the AB action which involved the murder of many Polish intellectuals. As Reich Commissioner for the Occupied Netherlands, Seyss-Inquart was ruthless in applying terrorism to suppress all opposition to the German occupation, a program which he described as "annihilating" his opponents. In collaboration with the local Higher SS and Police Leaders he was involved in the shooting of hostages for offenses against the occupation authorities and sending to concentration camps all suspected opponents of occupation policies ... Many of the Dutch police were forced to participate in these programs by threats of reprisal against their families. Dutch courts were also forced to participate in this program ... when they indicated their reluctance to give sentences of imprisonment because so many prisoners were in fact killed, greater emphasis was placed on the use of summary police courts.'[106]

The IMT also charged Seyss-Inquart with compelling Dutch financial institutions to support the measures he ordered for the pillage of public and private property and thus give them an air of legality.[107]

Seyss-Inquart, the lawyer who liked to dress in military-style leather attire and was a collector of clocks,[108] ruled the Netherlands without regard for the Hague Convention, which he regarded as obsolete. His administration was exploitationist and he had large numbers of Dutchmen deported to Germany for forced labour. The judgement continues:

'In 1942 Seyss-Inquart formally decreed compulsory labor service and utilized the services of the Security Police and SD to prevent evasion of his order. During the occupation over 500,000 people were sent from the Netherlands to the Reich as laborers and only a very small proportion were ... volunteers. One of Seyss-Inquart's first steps as Reich Commissioner of the Netherlands was to put into effect ... laws imposing economic discriminations against the Jews ... requiring their registration ... compelling them to reside in ghettos and to wear the Star of David, sporadic arrests and detention in concentration camps and finally, at the suggestion of Heydrich, the mass deportation of almost 120,000 of Holland's 140,000 Jews to Auschwitz and the "final solution".'

His statement that he did not know what happened to inmates of Auschwitz gained no credence from the IMT (he was acquitted only under Count One), the court pronouncing: 'In the light of the evidence and on account of his official position it is impossible to believe this claim.'

The court, however, did give some weight to certain of his defensive arguments, saying:

'Seyss-Inquart contends that he was not responsible for many of the crimes committed in the occupation of the Netherlands because they were either ordered from the Reich, committed by the Army, over which he had no control, or by the German Higher SS and Police Leader, who, he claims, reported directly to Himmler. It is true that some of the excesses were the responsibility of the Army, and that the Higher SS and Police Leader, although he was at the disposal of Seyss-Inquart, could always report directly to Himmler. It is also true that in certain cases Seyss-Inquart opposed the extreme measures used by these other agencies, as when he was largely successful in preventing the Army from carrying out a scorched earth policy, and urged the Higher SS and Police Leaders to reduce the number of hostages to be shot.'

This was not enough to save his life, however, for the judges concluded: 'The fact remains that Seyss-Inquart was a knowing and voluntary participant in War Crimes and Crimes against Humanity which were committed in the occupation of the Netherlands.'[109]

FRANK

The judgement on Hans Frank,[110] Hitler's Governor-General in Poland, showed up the absurdity of the idea current in Nuremberg that a display of penitence and confession of guilt in front of the IMT would generally result in a lenient sentence. Frank was an old Nazi and a day-dreamer; on the one hand he was a broken man, a devoted disciple of Hitler but unsure of himself and unstable; on the other hand he had an almost pathetic need to assert himself and to boast of his relationship to Hitler – which from 1942 onwards had not been particularly good; during his last days in Nuremberg he made a great show of being a believing Catholic. In front of the IMT he staged a display of penitence, of humble confession, adroitly phrased and liberally larded with legal terminology. At the outset of the trial he had referred with contrition to his 'terrible guilt'[111] and at the end, in his final plea on 31 August 1946, he declaimed:

'I beg of our people not to continue in this direction, be it even a single step; because Hitler's road was the way without God, the way of turning from Christ ... the way of disaster and the way of death. His path became more and more that of a frightful adventurer without conscience or honesty, as I know today at the end of this Trial ... Over the graves of millions of dead ... this state trial was conducted, lasting for many months as a central legal epilogue, and the spirits passed accusingly through this room. I am grateful that I was given the opportunity to prepare a defense and a justification against the accusations raised against me ... I am thinking of all the victims of the violence and horror of the dreadful events of war. Millions had to perish unquestioned and unheard.'

On only one point in this final plea did he diverge from the line he had taken in the witness-box:

'I assumed responsibility on the witness stand for all those things for which I must answer. I have also acknowledged that degree of guilt which attached to me as a champion of Adolf Hitler, his movement and his Reich ... There is still one statement of mine which I must rectify. On the witness stand I said that a thousand years would not suffice to erase the guilt brought upon our people because of Hitler's conduct in this war. Every possible guilt incurred by our nation has already been completely wiped out today, not only by the conduct of our war-time enemies towards our nation and its soldiers, which has been carefully kept out of this Trial, but also by the most tremendous mass crimes of the most frightful sort which – as I have now learned – have been and still are being committed against Germans by Russians, Poles and Czechs, especially in East Prussia, Silesia, Pomerania and Sudetenland.'[112]

The main theme of Frank's defence was that he had not really been responsible for the crimes with which he was charged but, in Poland, had merely given instructions for the essential pacification measures. He ascribed the crimes, somewhat generously described by the IMT as 'excesses', to the activities of the police, who were not under his control; he maintained that he had not been informed of what went on in concentration camps; though he had energetically supported Sauckel's forced-labour programme, in Nuremberg he stated that he had had no great influence over it; he shifted all blame for the extermination of the Jews entirely on to the shoulders of his rival Himmler – who stood higher in Hitler's esteem – and the SS and police under his, Himmler's, command. To the very end he was convinced of the rightness of his views, self-contradictory though they were, and of the attitudes he had adopted. In his final notes, written in Nuremberg, he says:

'Unfortunately the military administration set up in the areas of Poland occupied by German troops after the conclusion of operations at the end of September was only of short duration ... With effect from 26 October 1939 the area of Poland allotted to Germany was divided into two main parts ... The larger part was incorporated into the German Reich; the smaller became the autonomous Government General with Cracow as capital and was placed under me as Governor General. The military administration was not ... allowed to expand or set up any effective administrative infrastructure ... These few weeks of military administration illustrated the vast difficulties resulting from the over-lapping and competing powers which Hitler had given to various Reich agencies in respect of occupied territories. The main result was to allow the typical activities of Himmler and his agencies to take over; they were directly dependent on Hitler and exercised power and authority entirely independently of all other agencies ... Simultaneously with the formation of the Government General and my appointment as Governor General Hitler had signed a secret decree placing Krüger, the SS and Police Leader for the Government General, together with all SS and police forces in the area under Himmler's direct and exclusive command; this decree was concealed from me to the very end and I only discovered it during the course of the proceedings in Nuremberg. This was sheer deceit on the part of Hitler, who outwardly had appointed me as his representative but secretly had handed the area over to the crazy tyranny of Himmler and his minions. All my complaints to Hitler over their activities, against which I was in effect powerless and which I frequently tried to counter by the most desperate measures, were met with silence ... People say that I destroyed the Warsaw ghetto. It has been proved that this frightful event took place on a direct and personal order from Himmler, without my knowledge and without my being informed either beforehand or subsequently ... No reference has been made* to the fact that in regard to the SS and police I referred to them as my mortal enemies. It has been totally forgotten under what inconceivable pressure anyone had to work at this stage of the Hitler regime if he wanted to do so objectively and justly and to have any effect at all ... Another matter which has been quietly ignored is that I was

* Here Frank is referring to the extracts from his war diaries selected by the IMT.

most cruelly compelled by Hitler to continue as Governor General although I offered my resignation fourteen times ... Hitler knew what he was doing to me ... The post in Cracow was his revenge on me ... He knew what went on in Treblinka and other places. And he knew the load of crime with which he was besmirching me and my name.'[113]

In his defence Frank maintained that, as a result of Hitler's secret decree referred to above, Obergruppenführer Krüger with all SS and police units was answerable not to him but to Himmler, thus making his powers illusory.[114]

Though it was a well-known fact, he did not divulge that in the summer of 1941 he himself had given Krüger certain special tasks which did not necessitate Himmler's permission. On 19 June 1941 Himmler wrote a 'Top Secret' letter to Krüger: 'As you have informed me the Governor General has commissioned you to ensure that the harvest is collected, also to supervise of the employment of non-German labour in the Government General and the recruitment of non-German labour from the Government General for the Reich.'[115]

Himmler was always jealous of his prerogatives, as Frank undoubtedly knew. In this letter, from which neither extracts nor notes were to be made, he laid down in detail for Krüger what forces and resources were to be used to bring in the harvest and what labour was to be recruited for the Reich. Documents show clearly that these 'guidelines' and 'directives' as Himmler called them, though radical, were less severe than the threats issued by Frank in 1940. Initially Himmler attempted only to lay down 'policy' but from the outset Frank thought only in terms of brutal force.

In Nuremberg Frank, the former Governor General of Poland, attempted to talk his way out of the truth. He had managed to convince himself that he had always been an 'isolated, impotent man', 'without influence on events' and forced to have recourse to the 'most frightful, sophisticated and desperate measures' to 'deceive' and to 'curb' the SS. Nor was this all. Turning the facts upside down, he finally maintained that he had been responsible for saving thousands of lives.[116] It was typical of him, therefore, that in Nuremberg he should write:

'But apart from all this it is not for me to haggle or negotiate over my "guilt" with a conclave of the victors. Moreover I feel myself generally guilty as a participant in Hitler's overall enterprise; I therefore owe it to my overburdened conscience, and consequently to God and mankind, to take upon myself the blame for all that happened in Poland because, though entangled in Hitler's overall system, I was frequently at fault both in word and deed.'[117]

In his closing address Shawcross quoted from certain statements by Frank in January, May and December 1940 which have already been referred to and are repeated here. They leave no doubt of the truth:

January: 'Cheap labor must be removed from the Government General by hundreds of thousands. This will hamper the native biological propagation.'

May: '... taking advantage of the focusing of world interest on the Western Front by liquidations of thousands of Poles, first the leading representatives of the Polish intelligentsia.'

December: 'The Poles must feel that they have only one duty: to work and to behave. We must carry out all measures ruthlessly. Rely on me.'[118]

The IMT's judgement did not disregard Frank's arguments put forward either before the trial or in cross-examination; in fact they were explicitly emphasized:

'It may ... well be true that some of the crimes committed in the Government General were committed without the knowledge of Frank, and even occasionally despite his opposition. It may also be true that some of the criminal policies put into effect in the Government General did not originate with Frank but were carried out pursuant to orders from Germany. But it is also true that Frank was a willing and knowing participant in the use of terrorism in Poland; in the economic exploitation of Poland in a way which led to the death by starvation of a large number of people; in the deportation to Germany as slave laborers of over a million Poles.'[119]

The judgement also pronounces:

'The evidence establishes that ... occupation policy was based on the complete destruction of Poland as a national entity and a ruthless exploitation of its human and economic resources for the German war effort. All opposition was crushed with the utmost harshness. A reign of terror was instituted, backed by summary police courts which ordered such actions as the public shootings of groups of twenty to 200 Poles and the widespread shootings of hostages. The concentration camp was introduced in the Government General by the establishment of the notorious Treblinka and Maidanek camps. As early as 6 February 1940 Frank gave an indication of the extent of this reign of terror by his cynical comment to a newspaper reporter on von Neurath's poster announcing the execution of Czech students: "If I wished to order that one should hang up posters about every seven Poles shot, there would not be enough forests in Poland with which to make paper for these posters." '

ROSENBERG

Alfred Rosenberg,[120] the zealot, the eccentric, fanatical, obsessive anti-semite and anti-bolshevist, had opted for Hitler in 1919. For a long time he believed himself to be the philosopher of the Nazi 'movement' but in fact, as far as Hitler was concerned, he was dead before the Allies ever crossed the Reich frontiers. He was born in Esthonia, a Balt who in 1919 spoke Russian better than German;[121] early in his political career he was accused of being a French spy[122] and later of being of Jewish origin,[123] something totally impossible for a National-Socialist. Most people regarded his case as hopeless before he ever reached Nuremberg.

Under Count One, 'Crimes against Peace', Rosenberg's 'catalogue of crime' consisted primarily of his commitment to Hitler's plan for Norway and its implementation, the 'Guidelines for establishment of an administration in the Occupied Eastern Territories' drafted by Rosenberg and his activities as Minister for the Occupied Eastern Territories. Documents and evidence were so convincing that the IMT's judgement dismissed Rosenberg's defence in a couple of lines. The deciding factor, however, for pronouncement of the death sentence on Rosenberg was his 'War Crimes and Crimes against Humanity'. The judgement – with only brief comment – set them out as follows:

'Rosenberg is responsible for a system of organized plunder of both public and private property throughout the invaded countries of Europe. Acting under Hitler's orders of January 1940 to set up the "Hohe Schule" he organized and directed the "Einsatzstab Rosenberg", which plundered museums and libraries, confiscated art treasures and collections and pillaged private houses. His own reports show the extent of the confiscations. In "Action-M" [Möbel – furniture] instituted in December 1941 at Rosenberg's suggestion, 69,619 Jewish homes were plundered in the West, 38,000 of them in Paris alone, and it took 26,984 railroad cars to transport the confiscated furnishings to Germany. As of 14 July 1944 more than 21,903 art objects, including famous paintings and museum pieces, had been seized by the Einsatzstab in the West.'[124]

On 17 October 1944 Rosenberg had himself reported in a letter to Lammers, Head of the Reich Chancellery, that 1,418,000 railway wagons and 427,000 tons of shipping space would be required to move the 'goods seized'.[125] In his closing address on 27 July 1946 Sir Hartley Shawcross quoted from a report by Commissar-General Wilhelm Kube (another stock-taking by Rosenberg): 'We have liquidated in the last ten weeks about 55,000 Jews in White Ruthenia. In the territory Minsk Land Jewry has been eliminated ... In the preeminently Polish territory Lida 16,000 Jews, in Slonim 8,000 Jews and so forth have been liquidated.'[126]

Even Kube, who according to Shawcross was an executive of Rosenberg, was not always in agreement with Rosenberg's measures, as the following minute by Himmler dated 15 November 1941 clearly shows:

'I had a discussion today, lasting from about 3.0 p.m. to 7.0 p.m., with Reichsleiter Rosenberg. We first discussed the question of confiscations and provision of the necessary requirements in SS and police. I complained of the narrow-mindedness of Reich Commissar Lohse regarding provision of the troops' requirements for workshops and handling of goods; I also criticized Commissar Kube's ludicrous complaints about alleged theft and removal of pictures and *objets d'art*. I stated that I did not propose to reply to such letters and complaints in future. Rosenberg was most sympathetic over this and thought that such matters would sort themselves out.

He agreed that the SS and others should be given the management of such agricultural and other concerns as they required for supply purposes.'[127]

The IMT's judgement continues:

'With his appointment as Reich Minister for Occupied Eastern Territories on 17 July 1941, Rosenberg became the supreme authority for those areas. He helped to form the policies of Germanization, exploitation, forced labor, extermination of Jews and opponents of Nazi rule and he set up the administration which carried them out. He took part in the conference of 16 July 1941, in which Hitler stated that they were faced with the task of "cutting up the giant cake according to our needs in order to be able: first, to dominate it; second, to administer it; and third, to exploit it", and indicated that ruthless action was contemplated. Rosenberg accepted his appointment on the following day.

'Rosenberg had knowledge of the brutal treatment and terror to which the Eastern people were subjected. He directed that the Hague Rules of Land Warfare were not applicable in the Occupied Eastern Territories. He had knowledge and took an active part in stripping the Eastern Territories of raw materials and foodstuffs which were all sent to Germany ... His directives provided for the segregation of Jews, ultimately in ghettos. His subordinates engaged in mass killings of Jews and his civil administrators in the East considered that cleansing the Eastern Occupied Territories of Jews was necessary. In December 1941 he made the suggestion to Hitler that in a case of shooting 100 hostages Jews only be used ... He gave his civil administrators quotas of laborers to be sent to the Reich, which had to be met by whatever means necessary. His signature of approval appears on the order of 14 June 1944 for the "Heu Aktion", the apprehension of 40,000 to 50,000 youths, aged ten to fourteen, for shipment to the Reich ...'[128]

Closing Addresses and Final Pleas

On the afternoon of 26 July 1946 Mr Justice Jackson made the first of the prosecution's closing addresses. His statements gave yet another indication of the point of view from which the Tribunal would take its decisions on the fate of the defendants and the framework within which it would do so.

Some of the twenty-one defendants may have been disappointed, for in accordance with the Charter Jackson, as Prosecutor, made no demand for any specific degree of punishment nor did he say anything to exonerate them. On the contrary: he laid emphasis on the crimes committed by Dönitz, Keitel, Jodl, Speer, Raeder, von Papen, von Neurath, Sauckel, Kaltenbrunner, Rosenberg and Frick and once again showed his contempt for them. He began:

'An advocate can be confronted with few more formidable tasks than to select his closing arguments where there is great disparity between his appropriate time and his available material. In eight months – a short time as state trials go – we have introduced evidence which embraces as vast and varied a panorama of events as has ever been compressed within the framework of a litigation. It is impossible in summation to do more than outline with bold strokes the vitals of this trial's mad and melancholy record, which will live as the historical text of the twentieth century's shame and depravity ... These two-score years ... will be recorded in the book of years as one of the most bloody in all annals. Two World Wars have left a legacy of dead which number more than all the armies engaged in any way [probably a misprint for 'war'] that made ancient or medieval history. No half-century ever witnessed slaughter on such a scale, such cruelties and inhumanities, such wholesale deportations of peoples into slavery, such annihilations of minorities. The terror of Torquemada pales before the Nazi Inquisition. These deeds are the overshadowing historical facts by which generations to come will remember this decade.'[1]

The defendants had heard this often enough during the months of the trial, though sometimes expressed differently. They first began to prick up their ears, however, and realize how it applied to them personally when Jackson continued:

'If we cannot eliminate the causes and prevent the repetition of these barbaric events, it is not an irresponsible prophecy to say that this twentieth century may yet succeed in bringing the doom of civilization.

Goaded by these facts we were moved to redress the blight on the record of our era. The defendants complain that our pace is too fast. In drawing the Charter of this Tribunal, we thought we were recording an accomplished advance in international law. But they say we have outrun our times, that we have anticipated an advance that should be, but has not yet been made. The Agreement of London, whether it originates or merely records, at all events marks a transition in international law which roughly corresponds to that in the evolution of local law when men ceased to punish crime by "hue and cry", and began to let reason and inquiry govern punishment. The society of nations has emerged from the primitive "hue and cry", the law of "catch and kill". It seeks to apply sanctions to enforce international law but to guide their application by evidence, law and reason instead of outcry. The defendants denounce the law under which their accounting is asked. Their dislike for the law which condemns them is not original. It has been remarked before that "No thief e'er felt the halter draw with good opinion of the law".'[2]

The noose loomed even more clearly when Jackson posed the rhetorical questions:

'Where shall we look for those who mobilized the economy for total war if we overlook Schacht and Speer and Funk? Who was the master of the great slaving enterprise if it was not Sauckel? Where shall we find the hand that ran the concentration camps if it was not the hand of Kaltenbrunner?'

At this point in his final address Jackson made full use of scorn and sarcasm:

'To escape the implications of their positions and the inference of guilt from their activities, the defendants are almost unanimous in one defense. The refrain is heard time and again: These men were without authority, without knowledge, without influence, without importance. Funk summed up the general self-abasement of the dock in his plaintive lament that: "I always, so to speak, came up to the door, but I was not permitted to enter." In the testimony of each defendant, at some point there was reached the familiar blank wall: nobody knew anything about what was going on. Time after time we have heard the chorus from the dock: "I only heard about these things here for the first time."

'These men saw no evil, spoke none and none was uttered in their presence. This claim might sound very plausible if made by one defendant. But when we put all their stories together, the impression which emerges of the Third Reich ... is ludicrous. If we combine only the stories of the front bench, this is the ridiculous composite picture of Hitler's Government which emerges. It was composed of:

'A Number 2 man who knew nothing of the excesses of the Gestapo which he created and never suspected the Jewish extermination program although he was the signer of over a score of decrees which instituted the persecutions of that race;

'A Number 3 man who was merely an innocent middleman transmitting Hitler's orders without even reading them, like a postman or delivery boy;

'A Foreign Minister who knew little of foreign affairs and nothing of foreign policy;

'A Field Marshal who issued orders to the Armed Forces but had no idea of the results they would have in practice;

'A security chief who was of the impression that the policing functions of his Gestapo and SD were somewhat of the order of directing traffic;

'A Party philosopher who was interested in historical research but had no idea of the violence which his philosophy was inciting in the twentieth century;

'A Governor-General of Poland who reigned but did not rule;

'A Gauleiter of Franconia whose occupation was to pour forth filthy writings about the Jews but who had no idea that anybody would read them;

'A Minister of the Interior who knew not even what went on in the interior of his own office, much less the interior of his own department, and nothing at all about the interior of Germany;

'A Reichsbank President who was totally ignorant of what went in and out of the vaults of his bank;

'And a plenipotentiary for the war economy who secretly marshaled the entire economy for armament, but had no idea it had anything to do with war.

'This may seem like a fantastic exaggeration, but this is what you would actually be obliged to conclude if you were to acquit these defendants. They do protest too much. They deny knowing what was common knowledge. They deny knowing plans and programs that were as public as *Mein Kampf* and the Party program. They deny even knowing the contents of documents they received and acted upon.'[3]

From the viewpoint of the individual defendants they could extract nothing in their favour from Jackson's closing address, as is shown by the following passages from his comments on Schacht (whom the IMT acquitted):

'Let us illustrate the inconsistencies of their positions by the record of one defendant – who, if pressed, would himself concede that he is the most intelligent, honorable and innocent man in the dock. That is Schacht. And this is the effect of his own testimony – but let us not forget that I recite it not against him alone, but because most of its self-contradictions are found in the testimony of several defendants ... When we ask why he remained a member of the criminal regime, he tells us that by sticking on he expected to moderate its program. Like a Brahmin among untouchables, he could not bear to mingle with the Nazis socially, but never could he afford to separate from them politically ... Having armed Hitler to black-mail a continent, his answer now is to blame England and France for yielding. Schacht always fought for his position in a regime he now affects to despise. He sometimes disagreed with his Nazi confederates about what was expedient in reaching their goal, but he never dissented from the goal itself. When he did break with them in the twilight of the regime, it was over tactics, not principles.'[4]

After speaking for over three and a half hours Jackson concluded his address as follows:

'It is against such a background that these defendants now ask the Tribunal to say that they are not guilty of planning, executing or conspiring to commit this long list of crimes and wrongs. They stand before the record of this Trial as bloodstained Gloucester stood by the body of his slain king. He begged of the widow, as they beg of you: "Say I slew them not." And the Queen replied: "Then say they were not slain. But dead they are . . ." If you were to say of these men that they are not guilty, it would be as true to say that there has been no war, there are no slain, there has been no crime.'[5]

Sir Hartley Shawcross, the British Chief Prosecutor, proposed, as Jackson had already indicated, to set out in his address 'the legality of this trial' of the vanquished by the victors; in the first few minutes of his address, however, he had already emphasized: 'That these defendants participated in and are morally guilty of crimes so frightful that the imagination staggers and reels back at their very contemplation is not in doubt.'

It is not necessary to quote this outstanding address in detail; it rested on the overriding conviction that the 'guilt of the defendants' must be regarded as proved in the light of the 'salient and outstanding features of the evidence'. Some embarrassment was caused later when Sir Hartley quoted an anti-German passage which he wrongly attributed to Goethe. He led up to the conclusion of his address as follows: 'The state and the law are made for men, that through them they may achieve a fuller life, a higher purpose and a greater dignity. Ultimately the rights of man, made as all men are made in the image of God, are fundamental . . . And so, after this ordeal to which mankind has been submitted, mankind itself – struggling now to re-establish in all the countries of the world the common simple things – liberty, love, understanding – comes to this court and cries: "These are our laws – let them prevail." '

And then came his lapse of memory: 'Then shall those other words of Goethe be translated into fact, not only, as we must hope, of the German people but of the whole community of man: "Thus ought the German people to behave – giving and receiving from the world, their hearts open to every fruitful source of wonder, great through understanding and love, through mediation and the spirit – thus ought they to be; that is their destiny."

'You will remember when you come to give your decision the story of Gräbe,* but not in vengeance – in a determination that these things shall not

* Hermann G. Gräbe, a German construction engineer, had given evidence about the murder of Jews in Dubno, Ukraine, on 5 October 1942 (IMT Vol. XIX, p. 507).

occur again. "The father" – do you remember – "pointed to the sky and seemed to say something to his boy.""[6]

The words used by Jackson at the start of his address to paint a picture of horror recurred again and again – slaughter, annihilation of minorities, slavery on a gigantic scale. Again and again concrete proof was referred to until eventually on 30 July 1946 Rudenko, the last Prosecutor, made his demand: 'I appeal to the Tribunal to sentence all the defendants without exception to . . . death.'[7]

This was not the end of the prosecution, however. Witnesses were then heard on behalf of the groups and organizations. They too attempted to evade, conceal or deny their actual knowledge of crime. Two extracts from the cross-examinations will suffice as examples. On 1 August 1946 Karl Hein Hoffmann, a lawyer and a member of the Gestapo from 1937, was in the witness-box:

Dr Merkel: Did you or your office know anything about the true conditions existing in the concentration camps?[8]
Hoffmann: No . . .
Dr Merkel: Were the concentration camps under the Gestapo?
Hoffmann: No. Concentration camps were under the inspector of concentration camps at Oranienburg and, as far as I know, this inspectorate was under the SS Economic and Administrative Main Office . . .
Dr Merkel: Did you know about the annihilation of Jews at Auschwitz?
Hoffmann: No. I only heard about these things after the surrender.
Dr Merkel: Did you know that Eichmann's activity was directly connected with the biological extermination of the Jews at Auschwitz?
Hoffmann: As long as I was in office and before the surrender, I heard nothing about problems of that kind.
Dr Merkel: When did you first receive reliable knowledge about these things?
Hoffmann: After the surrender.[9]

At this point Francis Biddle, the American Member of the Tribunal, started to cross-examine:

The Tribunal (Mr Biddle): . . . you spoke of a decree under which the Gestapo were permitted to use third-degree methods in Denmark, right?
Hoffmann: Yes, indeed.
The Tribunal (Mr Biddle): Was that decree in writing?
Hoffmann: That was a written decree by the Chief of the Security Police and SD . . .
The Tribunal (Mr Biddle): Who signed it?
Hoffmann: As far as I recall, the first decree was signed by Heydrich and the second one by Müller on behalf of someone, but I cannot say for certain on whose behalf.
The Tribunal (Mr Biddle): What was the date of the first decree?
Hoffmann: I believe it was 1937.

14. *(top left)* Fritz Sauckel in his cell.
(top right) Alfred Rosenberg in his cell.
(below left) Julius Streicher in the dock during a recess of the court.
(below right) Ernst Kaltenbrunner during a session of the IMT.

15. Wilhelm Keitel leaves the courtroom and goes to his cell.

16. Alfred Jodl in the courtroom.

17. Otto Kranzbühler, Dönitz's defence counsel and a leading light of the defence.

18. *(above)* Gustav Gilbert, the American prison psychologist, talking to the defendants. (From right to left): Schacht, Fritzsche, Funk, von Neurath, Speer.

19. *(below)* Gilbert in front of the dock in which are (left to right) in front Göring, Hess, von Ribbentrop, behind Dönitz (in dark glasses) and von Schirach. All are studiously ignoring him. Those condemned to death were told of their sentences by Gilbert even before they had been officially informed that their pleas had been turned down by the Control Council.

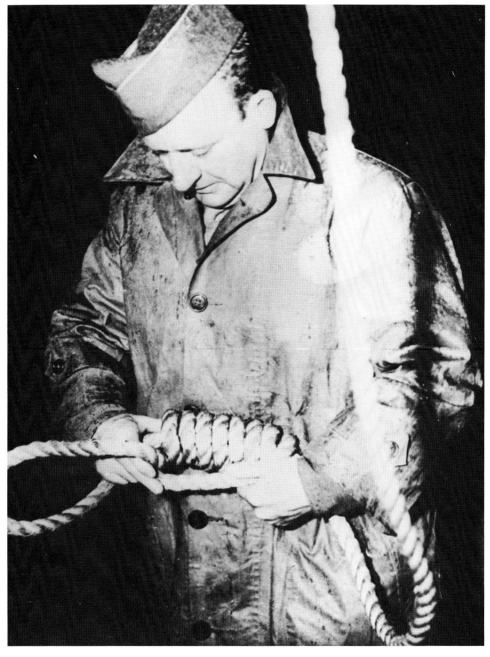

20. John C. Woods, the American hangman in Nuremberg, who had a remarkable escape in 1950. Numerous Germans and foreigners complained to Jackson about him. He is shown preparing for an execution.

The Tribunal (Mr Biddle): What month?

Hoffmann: That I cannot tell you any more.

The Tribunal (Mr Biddle): What was the date of the second decree?

Hoffmann: 1942.

The Tribunal (Mr Biddle): Did you see both decrees yourself?

Hoffmann: Yes.

The Tribunal (Mr Biddle): What was in the first decree?

Hoffmann: The contents of the first decree provided that for the purpose of uncovering organizations hostile to the Reich, if no other means were available, the person involved could receive a certain number of blows with a stick. After a specified number a physician had to be called in. This order could only be used for extracting a confession for conviction in individual cases. Approval for this had to be obtained in every case from the Chief of the Security Police and SD.

The Tribunal (Mr Biddle): Wait a minute. Was the decree limited to any particular territory or did it cover all the occupied territories?

Hoffmann: The decree of 1937 applied to the Reich territory, but I believe it then applied automatically to the activities of the Sipo in those regions where it was stationed . . .

The Tribunal (Mr Biddle): Were there any other methods of third degree which were allowed as well as beating in this first decree?

Hoffmann: No. According to the second decree the only measures approved were those which were milder than blows with a stick – standing at interrogations or fatiguing exercises . . .

The Tribunal (Mr Biddle): You remembered one of them – standing up, for instance. What was the provision of the decree with respect to standing up during interrogations?

Hoffmann: I personally never attended such an interrogation.

The Tribunal (Mr Biddle): I did not ask you that. I said, what was the provision with respect to standing up?

Hoffmann: It only said that the person involved could be required not to sit down during the interrogation but had to stand.

The Tribunal (Mr Biddle): And how long were the interrogations? How long were they actually?

Hoffmann: The decree did not mention that but . . .

The Tribunal (Mr Biddle): I did not ask you that. I said, how long were the interrogations?

Hoffmann: Well, under certain circumstances they naturally lasted very long. It was only in that way that standing up was a severe measure.

The Tribunal (Mr Biddle): Was the number of strokes that could be used mentioned in the decree? Did it say how many times a man could be struck with a stick?

Hoffmann: As far as I recall, this measure could be applied only once to the same individual; that is, it could not be repeated. And the number of blows, in my opinion, was specified in the decree.

The Tribunal (Mr Biddle): And then the doctor was called?
Hoffmann: No, I believe it was this way. If a fairly large number of blows was provided for in advance, then the physician had to be present immediately.
The Tribunal (Mr Biddle): And what was the number of blows that was to be permitted? Do you remember that?
Hoffmann: As far as I recall, twenty ...
The Tribunal (Mr Biddle): And both decrees covered all of the German Reich including the occupied territories, is that true?
Hoffmann: Yes.
The Tribunal (Mr Biddle): And the decrees were effective in France as well as in Denmark, isn't that true?
Hoffmann: Yes, later. In the second decree the power of approval of the Chief of the Security Police was delegated to the commanders. That was in 1942.
The Tribunal (Mr Biddle): So that after that the commanders could order beatings without going to the head of the Security Police?
Hoffmann: Yes, after 1942.[10]

Rolf Heinz Hoeppner, former SS-Gruppenführer in the Reichssicherheitshauptamt (Central Security Department), fared similarly. He was first examined by Dr Gawlik, the defence counsel. The record is as follows:

Dr Gawlik: Now I come to a short discussion of the individual war crimes with which the SD is charged. First the Einsatzgruppen ... Were the Einsatzgruppen and Einsatzkommandos which were used in the East a part of the SD?
Hoeppner: No; these Einsatzgruppen and Einsatzkommandos were establishments of an entirely original type.
Dr Gawlik: Was the organization of the domestic SD used for the activities of the Einsatzgruppen and Einsatzkommandos? ...
Hoeppner: That question, in the way it has been put, must be answered by 'no'. It is not true that any of the units of that organization were transferred to the Einsatzgruppen. If individual members of the SD entered the Einsatzgruppen or Einsatzkommandos, then it is comparable to military induction ...
Dr Gawlik: Did the members of the SD and its subordinate offices obtain any knowledge about mass shootings and other crimes – war crimes or crimes against humanity – through the reports from the East, or by reports from the Einsatzgruppen?
Hoeppner: Such reports from Einsatzgruppen were never forwarded to the subordinate offices in the Reich, so that the members of these offices could not have any knowledge of these incidents either.
Dr Gawlik: Was the SD responsible for the establishment, arrangement, guarding and administration of concentration camps?
Hoeppner: No.

Dr Gawlik: Could you give me any reason for that answer?

Hoeppner: There are no reasons for it. The Security Service never had anything to do with these matters because it lacked jurisdiction there.

Dr Gawlik: Did the SD establish any concentration camps?

Hoeppner: No.

Dr Gawlik: Did the SD organize any concentration camps?

Hoeppner: No.

Dr Gawlik: Was the organization of the SD used for the guarding of concentration camps?

Hoeppner: No.

Dr Gawlik: Did the SD have authority for the commitment and treatment of concentration camp inmates?

Hoeppner: No.[11]

When asked by the President on 27 August 1946 what the SD did in concentration camps, Dr Gawlik told the court:

'The SD, as a Party organization, had nothing to do with concentration camps ... One must differentiate between two facts: assignment to concentration camps by means of a protective custody order; the protective custody order was always issued by the Gestapo [a State institution]. The SD was not competent for that. And, secondly, the administration of concentration camps: concentration camps were under the jurisdiction of the SS Economic and Administrative Main Office, Obergruppenführer Pohl. This was an independent organization ... alongside the RSHA. Thus, if the Gestapo issued a protective custody order, then the detainee came under the jurisdiction of the SS Economic and Administrative Main Office. The Economic and Administrative Main Office was directly under Himmler, just as was the RSHA.'[12]

Under cross-examination by Hartley Murray, one of the US Assistant Trial Counsel, however, Hoeppner, though still adroitly evasive, was forced to come out in his true colours:

Major Murray: I would like to have shown to you a series of fifty-five weekly reports of the activities of the Einsatzgruppen, and, incidentally, the Einsatzgruppen are known as the Einsatzgruppen of the Security Police and the SD.

Hoeppner: No, no; there were no Einsatzgruppen of the Security Police and the Security Service, but rather there were only the Einsatzgruppen A, B, C and D in the East ...

Major Murray: Before submitting that document to you [Document 3876–PS] ... I call your attention to the title page ... signed by Heydrich which reads as follows: 'I herewith enclose the ninth summary report concerning the activity of the Einsatzgruppen of the Security Police and the SD in the USSR. This report will be sent continuously in the future. Signed, Heydrich.' Aren't you mistaken in saying that these were not known as Einsatzgruppen of the Security Police and SD?

Hoeppner: No. These Einsatzgruppen figured as Einsatzgruppen A, B, C and D. They were commanded by a deputy of the Chief of the Security Police and the SD with the army groups in question or with an army. The designation 'Einsatzgruppen of the Security Police and the SD' is ... wrong.

Major Murray: Either Heydrich is wrong again ... and all the documents are wrong?

Hoeppner: No, I do not want to say that the document is false but I merely maintain that the expression is not correct ...

Major Murray: This ... is a report of your chief, Heydrich, and I won't enlarge on that point. Turn now to page ... 32 ... It is a very short passage. I will read it to you: 'In White Ruthenia the purge of Jews is under way. The number of Jews in the part up to now handed over to the civil administration amounts to 139,000.'

Hoeppner: Yes.

Major Murray (continuing): 'In the meantime' – in the last sentence – 'in the meantime 33,210 Jews were shot by the Einsatzgruppen of the Security Police and the SD.'

It doesn't say anything there about Groups A, B, C or D, does it?

Hoeppner: No, it says Security Police and SD ...[13]

Twenty-one years later, in his standard work on the SS, *The Order of the Death's-Head*, Heinz Höhne set out the composition of the Einsatz-gruppen – 9 per cent Gestapo men, 3·5 per cent SD men, 4·1 per cent from the Criminal Police, 13·4 per cent from the Ordnungspolizei (Regular Police), 8·8 per cent foreign auxiliary police personnel and 34 per cent from the Waffen-SS; he continues: 'The remainder consisted of technical personnel and clerks. The strength of an Einsatzgruppe varied between 990 men in Einsatzgruppe A and 500 men in Einsatzgruppe D. Each Einsatzgruppe was divided into two sections – a number of Einsatz-kommandos or Sonderkommandos of about 70–120 men each attached to an Army and sub-commandos of about 20–30 men.[14]

Through all the frightful details and connected explanations the hearings pursued their laborious way until 30 August 1946, the day preceding that on which the principal defendants began their final pleas, preceded by a last challenge from Rudenko: 'May the judgement of the Nations – severe but just – fall upon these Fascist hangmen.'[15] He had already explained what he meant by that on 30 July – the death sentence for all the defendants.

An unparalleled number of journalists, correspondents and foreign press men had arrived in Nuremberg for the final pleas. Not only did they want to hear what the sentences were likely to be but they also wanted to see how the defendants would react to this phase of the trial and what its effect upon them had been.

The meeting point for correspondents, reporters and all those not officially connected with the trial was a former school near the Palace of Justice. Here, if they had special passes, they could have meals – not without their attraction in 1946 – exchange information and discuss the Nuremberg 'news' on the spot. Many knew each other well, so that they seemed like a large family – and felt themselves to be so.

Reports on the IMT were allowed to contain only what the Allies wanted. Anyone who was not prepared to comply with their instructions did not get a seat either in the Palace of Justice or in the old Nuremberg school. A woman on the staff of the British Press Officer of Rhineland-Westphalia reported: 'When the Nuremberg Trial was being prepared, the British Press Officer of Rhineland-Westphalia looked for a German reporter. The agency's German secretariat suggested Margret Boveri and she came from Berlin to discuss the matter. She turned down the job, however, giving roughly the following reasons: "You wish me to report in a certain definite sense and that I will not do. Naturally you will say that I wrote for newspapers under the Third Reich (*Das Reich* among others). At that time, however, any intelligent man knew that one could not write freely and readers were accustomed to read between the lines. Today people believe in the freedom of the press on the English model. My reporting, therefore, must be free from restrictions and you cannot guarantee me that." My chief was impressed and Margret Boveri was sent back to Berlin in an official car.'[16]

In addition to the swarm of journalists from all sovereign countries relatives of the defendants had arrived, though naturally, in contrast to the reporters, their motives were neither sheer curiosity nor a thirst for information. There were Emmy and Edda Göring, Frau Sauckel and her four children, Henriette von Schirach, Frau Funk, Frau Frick, Frau von Ribbentrop, Frau Speer, Frau Fritzsche, Frau Schacht, Frau Jodl, Frau Frank with her son and two daughters, Frau Raeder and her son – all waiting to see what would happen.

Frau von Schirach was emotional, excitable and absorbed. Frau Funk, Frau Frick and Frau von Ribbentrop were quiet and reserved. Frau Sauckel, wife of the ex-working-class merchant seaman, sat sadly and modestly in a corner with her children, barely noticed by anyone else present.

The defendants' final pleas, made about one month after the opening of the prosecution's final addresses, constituted more or less another high spot in the trial.

On 31 August 1946, the 216th day of the trial, each of the defendants was called upon to make his final statement.[17] All were ready to do so; all concluded their case – at least for the present – in this way.

As for the hearing of evidence Hermann Göring was called upon first as 'Defendant Number One'. He opened with a statement which, throughout the trial, the IMT had heard from most of the defendants and their defence counsel:

'The Prosecution, in the final speeches, has treated the defendants and

their testimony as completely worthless. The statements made under oath
by the defendants were accepted as absolutely true when they could serve to
support the Indictment, but conversely the statements were characterized
as perjury when they refuted the Indictment. That is very elementary ...
not a convincing basis for demonstration of proof.'[18]

After this introduction, which was no news to anyone, he proceeded
somewhat self-importantly:

'The Prosecution uses the fact that I was the second man of the State
as proof that I must have known everything that happened. But it does not
present any documentary or other convincing proof in cases where I have
denied under oath that I knew about certain things, much less desired
them.'

This was not true, but his next line of defence was:

'Therefore it is only an allegation and a conjecture when the Prosecution
says: "Who should have known that if not Göring, who was the successor
of the Führer?"'

After this transparent admission, however, he stated that he 'condemned
these terrible mass murders to the utmost' and did not understand them.
He continued: 'I should like to state clearly once more before the High
Tribunal that I have never decreed the murder of a single individual at any
time and neither did I decree any other atrocities or tolerate them, while I
had the power and the knowledge to prevent them. The ... allegation ...
that I had ordered Heydrich to kill the Jews lacks every proof ...'[19]

Certainly Göring had never directly ordered the 'killing' of Jews. Nevertheless at a meeting on 12 November 1938, at which Heydrich was present,
he had said: 'Gentlemen, the present meeting is of decisive importance. I
have received a letter, written on the Führer's behalf by Bormann, head of
the Deputy Führer's office, according to which the Jewish question must
now be dealt with in a coordinated fashion and brought to a conclusion by
hook or by crook. In addition a telephone call which I received from the
Führer yesterday instructed me to coordinate now the decisive steps.'[20] In
addition to this, as he himself had emphasized on 28 December 1938, for
instance, he had 'merely' urged the Führer to take fundamental decisions
against the Jews with the object of 'legally' excluding them from the
German economy.[21] He did not regard himself as responsible for the
inevitable consequences of these actions, even though he played an
important part in the 'Final Solution of the Jewish Question'. On
25 January 1942, for instance, when launching preparations for the 'Final
Solution', Reinhard Heydrich made specific reference to an instruction
from Göring dated 31 July 1941.[22] The meaning of these words was
explained in front of the IMT. Otto Ohlendorf,[23] commander of an
Einsatzgruppe, was asked by Colonel Amen, for instance, what instructions
had been given to the Einsatzgruppen for the treatment of Jews and communist functionaries and he replied: 'An instruction was issued ... to
liquidate Jews ... and also Soviet political commissars.'[24] To eliminate any

possible doubt Amen then asked: 'When you use the word "liquidate", do you mean "kill"?' to which Ohlendorf replied unequivocally: 'By that I mean "kill".'[25]

When, for instance, Kesselring, Karl Bodenschatz[26] and Erhard Milch,[27] all of whom had tried to exonerate Göring, said that they had known nothing of the SD, the murders of Jews, the concentration camps and the crimes committed there, their statements sounded credible. The same was not true of Göring, however, and this was primarily the result of Jackson's efforts to let documents speak for themselves during this trial. It was therefore more or less inevitable that Göring should end with the statement that he still stood by what he had done and with a demand to the IMT not to condemn the German people:

'If we, the leaders as individuals, are called to account and condemned – very well; but you cannot punish the German people at the same time. The German people placed their trust in the Führer and under his authoritarian government they had no influence on events. Without knowledge of the grave crimes which have become known today, the people, loyal, self-sacrificing and courageous, fought and suffered through the life-and-death struggle which had broken out against their will. The German people are free of guilt.

'I did not want a war nor did I bring it about. I did everything to prevent it by negotiations. After it had broken out I did everything to assure victory ... I stand up for the things that I have done but I deny most emphatically that my actions were dictated by the desire to subjugate foreign peoples by wars, to murder them, to rob them, or to enslave them, or to commit atrocities or crimes.

'The only motive which guided me was my ardent love for my people, its happiness, its freedom and its life. And for this I call on the Almighty and my German people to witness.'[28]

Immediately after Göring Rudolf Hess was called. With ludicrous self-importance he started by saying that the four prophecies which he had made both orally and in writing while in England had been fulfilled: (1) False statements on oath before the court; (2) Affidavits containing untrue statements; (3) Surprises for the defendants from some German witnesses; (4) 'Shameless utterances (by some of the defendants) about the Führer', incriminating 'their own people' and each other.[29] However trite these prophecies may sound, Hess knew some of his 'comrades', as he usually called his fellow defendants, from the period before May 1941 better than they thought. On several occasions during the trial they had made crude accusations against each other, from which the more intelligent and more articulate generally profited. This continued even after judgement had been pronounced; Göring, for instance, accused Speer of having shuffled off on to Sauckel, whose intellectual equipment was very moderate, considerable blame which he should have taken upon himself.[30]

Göring was not the only one to know of a statement by Speer referred to by Jackson during cross-examination of Milch on 11 March 1946. It shed a different light on Speer's activities. The record speaks for itself:

'The question of slackers is another point to be dealt with. Ley has ascertained that the number of people reporting sick decreased to one-fourth or one-fifth where there are factory doctors and the workers are examined by them. S S and police could go ahead with the job and put those known as slackers into undertakings run by concentration camps. There is no other choice. Let it happen a few times and the news will go round.'[31]

Speer was also the originator of the proposal to use deception to get the French to release names of craftsmen held in prisoner-of-war camps so that they could be used as labour in the German arms industry. On 3 November 1942 he had recommended:

'Under the pretext of industry we could deceive the French into believing that we would release all prisoners of war who are rollers and smelters if they give us the names[32] ... The French firms know exactly which prisoners of war are smelters. Unofficially you [Field Marshal Milch] should create the impression that they would be released. They give us the names and then we get them out. Have a try.'

A little later in this cross-examination Jackson read out a statement by Milch from the minutes of the 53rd Session of the Central Planning Board on 16 February 1944:

'The armament industry employs foreign workers in large numbers – according to the latest figures 40 per cent. The latest allocations ... are mostly foreigners and we had to give up many German workers in the recruitment drive. Particularly the aircraft industry, which is a young industry, employs a great many young men who should be called up. This will, however, be very difficult, as those working for experimental stations cannot be touched. In mass production the foreign workers preponderate and in some instances represent 95 per cent and even more; 88 per cent of the workers engaged in the production of our newest engines are Russian prisoners of war and the 12 per cent are German men and women. On the Ju-52s, which are now regarded as transport planes only and the monthly production of which is from fifty to sixty machines, only six to eight German workers are engaged; the rest are Ukrainian women who have lowered the record of production of skilled workers.'[33]

But to return to Hess and his final plea – even in those days he was not taken entirely seriously by the majority of the defendants or their defence counsel and he made the longest speech of all. This is probably why the mysterious allusions, produced in a ludicrously theatrical manner in his pleas, interested no one. After speaking for a quarter of an hour he said:

'Obviously it would have been of the utmost importance if I had stated under oath what I have to say about the happenings during my own imprisonment in England. However it was impossible for me to persuade my counsel to declare himself willing to put the proper questions to me. It was likewise impossible for me to get another counsel to agree to put these questions to me. But it is of the utmost importance that what I am saying be said under oath. Therefore I now declare once more (Hess then rose): I swear by God the Almighty and Omniscient that I shall speak the pure truth, that I shall leave out nothing and add nothing. I ask the High Tribunal, therefore, to consider everything that I shall say from now on as under oath. (Hess sat down again.) Concerning my oath, I should also like to say that I am not a church-goer; I have no spiritual relationship with the Church but I am a deeply religious person. I am convinced that my belief in God is stronger than that of most other people. I ask the High Tribunal to give all the more weight to everything which I declare under oath expressly calling God as my witness. (Turning to Göring.) Please do not interrupt me. In the spring of 1942 . . .'

The President: I must draw the attention of the Defendant Hess to the fact that he has already spoken for twenty minutes, and the Tribunal has indicated to the defendants that it cannot allow them to continue to make statements of great length at this stage of the proceedings. We have to hear all the defendants. The Tribunal, therefore, hopes that the Defendant Hess will conclude his speech.[34]

Up to this point the other defendants had regarded Hess as a joke. Suddenly, however, he surprised them with the following peroration:

'The statements which my counsel made in my name before the High Tribunal I permitted to be made for the sake of the future judgement of my people and of history. That is the only thing which matters to me. I do not defend myself against accusers to whom I deny the right to bring charges against me and my fellow-countrymen. I will not discuss accusations which concern things which are purely German matters and therefore of no concern to foreigners.* I raise no protest against statements which are aimed at attacking my honor, the honor of the German people. I consider such slanderous attacks by the enemy as a proof of honor.

'I was permitted to work for many years of my life under the greatest son whom my people has brought forth in its thousand-year history. Even if I could, I would not want to erase this period of time from my existence. I am happy to know that I have done my duty to my people, my duty as a German, as a National-Socialist, as a loyal follower of my Führer. I do not regret anything.

'If I were to begin all over again, I would act just as I have acted, even if I knew that in the end I should meet a fiery death at the stake. No matter what human beings may do, I shall some day stand before the judgement seat of the Eternal. I shall answer to Him and I know that He will judge me innocent.'[35]

Apart from Speer's final plea, the meanderings of Hess and the statements by Papen, Schacht and Fritzsche, who were counting on acquittal or

* This objection was a futile one since internal German matters were largely excluded from the trial.

lenient sentences, all the final pleas took the same line. The defendants raised objection to the court, they referred to orders from above, they accused people who were dead and maintained that they had learnt here for the first time, before the court, of the terrible crimes committed in German-occupied countries and in the Reich up to the end of the war. Some of them did admit that they had made themselves guilty; these admissions, however, did not invalidate their earlier statements that they felt themselves 'not guilty in the sense of the Indictment'.

Keitel's 'confession' was the one which hit the nail on the head and expressed most clearly what almost all the defendants were trying to say in their own way. He concluded his plea as follows:

'Now at the end of this trial I want to present equally frankly the avowal and confession I have to make today. In the course of the trial my Defense Counsel submitted two fundamental questions to me, the first one already some months ago. It was this: "In the case of victory would you have refused to participate in any part of the success?" I answered: "No, I should certainly have been proud of it." The second question was: "How would you act if you were in the same position again?" My answer: "Then I would rather choose death than to let myself be drawn into the net of such pernicious methods."

'From these two answers the High Tribunal may see my view-point. I believed but I erred, and I was not in a position to prevent what ought to have been prevented. That is my guilt.

'It is tragic to have to realize that the best I had to give as a soldier, obedience and loyalty, was exploited for purposes which could not be recognized at the time, and that I did not see that there is a limit set even for a soldier's performance of his duty. That is my fate.

'From the clear recognition of the causes, the pernicious methods, and the terrible consequences of this war, may there arise the hope for a new future in the community of nations for the German people.'[36]

Now all the defendants were preoccupied simply with the stark question: what would the IMT's judgement bring each of them, although they had undoubtedly known for some time that the Tribunal would not await this particular day before beginning to formulate its judgements. Sixteen years later Francis Biddle, the US Member of the Tribunal, admitted: 'At this time [when the final pleas ended on 31 August 1946] almost all the evidence had been submitted; while proceedings continued my assistants had summarized it and classified it not only under the names of the defendants but by specific subjects such as "The Common Conspiracy", "Economic Planning and Mobilization for Aggressive War", "Slave Labor Program" and "War Crimes". There were also summaries of evidence against the six organizations which had been declared as criminal. We met to consider the judgement for the first time on 27 June (five days before the start of the prosecution's final addresses and the defendants' final pleas, which lasted twenty days) and we deliberated until 26 September in twenty-one sessions in all. At the first meeting in June we began by discussing proofs of guilt.'[37]

As early as 23 May 1946 the word had gone round the courtroom that, at the very latest, the court would begin to formulate its findings as soon as the prosecution and the defence had begun their closing addresses. The Prosecutors, who more than anyone were under instructions to save time, were impatient; they had even met on 5 April 1946 to find ways and means of accelerating the proceedings, but, despite their pressure, the court was determined to finish the proceedings in an orderly manner. Shawcross, Jackson, Rudenko and de Ribes were agreed at that time that the Tribunal had no further need of proof to formulate its judgement. Although the judges never publicly stated that they were prepared to formulate their findings ahead of time, they had in fact long since done so. Viktor Freiherr von der Lippe, for instance, one of the defence assistants in Nuremberg, noted in his diary on 12 July 1946: 'From a court source ... the rumour went round today that, irrespective of the final pleas, the Tribunal was so far advanced with its findings that, as things stood, death sentences must be reckoned with except for Schacht, Papen and Fritzsche.'[38] The hangman had even been designated before the defendants had made their final pleas. He was John C. Woods, who had executed 347 criminals by hanging in the United States over a period of fifteen years; in August he was given a secret assignment telling him that he would shortly have to go to Nuremberg where he would have to execute the German war criminals.[39]

Dr Pflücker, who was now keeping a particularly close watch on the defendants, noted: 'Yesterday the defendants said farewell to their relatives. Hess was the only one who wished to see no one; he even refused a proposed meeting with Speer. Moreover he is more relaxed than usual. Göring saw a member of his former staff, whose indignation he took as an indication of the popular mood. He is firmly convinced that people still revere him just as they did in the days of glitter and glory ... Work was being done last night on a wooden fence and he asked with a bitter chuckle whether the gallows were already being built, adding that it was not very considerate to parade the preparations for their execution before the criminals so soon. He talks of the possibility of his execution having to be postponed since he will be required as a witness in later trials. He repeats his old theory that many of those who have appeared as witnesses will be following in his footsteps – "These boiling fowls will be allowed to cackle once more, lay an egg for the Americans and then they too will go into the big pot ..."'[40]

In a talk which he had with Gilbert, Göring learnt what the American psychologist thought of him. He reminded him of a visual test, asking: 'Do you remember the card with the red spot?' and, without waiting for Göring's reply, went on: 'Well, morbid neurotics frequently draw back at sight of this card and say there is blood on it. You drew back but you did not call it blood. You tried to flick it away with your fingers. You did the same throughout the trial. When proof of your guilt became intolerable to you, you took off your headphones in the courtroom. You did just the same during the war when you tried to make yourself unconscious of atrocities by drugs ... You are a moral coward.'[41]

Wilhelm Keitel had been irritated by the 'red spot'; Frank had pushed it away saying 'Horrible, disgusting ... like Stalin.'[42]

The opinions of such observers and the broadcasting of them, however, carried little weight; moreover they differed sharply from each other, as a comparison between the prison doctor's entries in his diary and the notes by the prison psychologist shows. Dr Pflücker, for instance, described Albert Speer as an intelligent, humorous, convivial person, always ready to help; Miale and Selzer, on the other hand, when evaluating Gilbert's material, came to the conclusion that Speer was unimaginative, lacked spontaneity and was tentative and indecisive in his ideas.[43] They credited him with 'a degree of obstinacy frequently to be found in small children, persons with damage to the central nervous system and advanced schizophrenics'[44] and concluded that his admission of guilt before the IMT had been 'largely verbiage'.[45]

As far as Ribbentrop was concerned the Americans Miale and Selzer, using their peculiarly dilettante methods of 'research', simply wrote him off as a 'skunk' because, during one of Gilbert's Rorschach tests, he had described blotches on a test card as skunks. Pflücker, however, noted that he was 'very depressed but calmer than during the trial. His wife's visit raised his spirits.'[46]

Pflücker's notes continue: 'Raeder is calm. He is worried solely about the fate of his wife, who is living in the Russian zone and whom the Russians have repeatedly promised to allow to visit him. His daughter and his son, however, have been able to visit him from the British zone. He was relieved to hear that the conditions under which his wife was living had improved.

'Von Neurath is calm as always. He remains the old-school diplomat who retains his poise without effort. Von Papen too, despite his vivacity, is outwardly calmer; he is friendly and cheerful as always.

'Seyss-Inquart has long since accepted his fate and is now calmly awaiting the court's sentence. "If one was in the front row in the good days," he says, "one cannot try to sneak away in the bad." I do not know how he behaved before the court but I am sure that at heart he has changed totally. His return to the Church was a deeply felt need and there were no outside reasons for it. For this reason he did not try to exonerate himself before the court by incriminating others but took responsibility for what he had done.

'Frank too is cheerful. He showed me a little picture drawn by his daughter showing children on the way to a meal in the Palace of Justice.

'Rosenberg is calm and composed. He has made some pen-and-ink drawings for his daughter showing scenes from his home on the Baltic. He is convinced that he is dying as a martyr for an ideology which will inevitably prevail. Today he asked that Father Gerecke should help his womenfolk with food for their journey. His wife and daughter were too proud to accept the good food offered by the Americans in the Palace of Justice and lived off their ration cards in Nuremberg. The good Father will find it difficult to obtain anything now but I am sure that he has done all he can.

'Speer cracks jokes as always.

'Schacht says that he is pleased that it is over at last. He tells me that his little daughter has had to have an operation.

'Streicher is bright; he makes fun of the last-minute christians and weaklings who previously played the strong man. He asks whether I shall be present at the execution.

'Kaltenbrunner talks sadly of his wife and children.

'Funk is very poorly physically and had to have local treatment yesterday. He laments that he always had bad luck at the decisive moments. I remember how tongue-tied he was when he took over the office which landed him in the dock. Göring once said in Mondorf: "What do you expect out of Funk? He was a cipher; if he didn't do what we wanted, then away with the cabbage-head."

'Frick is cheerful and is glad that at last the decision is near.

'Schirach too is in good form.'[47]

Alfred Jodl looked thin, sad and worn but he continued to radiate dignity and serenity; on 28 August, three days before he made his final plea, he had written a letter to his wife which is more revealing than the report of the doctor, who could see no more than the calm and serenity of his 'patient'; like most of the soldiers (including those of the Allies) he was hoping for a lenient sentence; he wrote:

'If I had to say now what sentence I am really counting on, I should have to admit quite frankly that I am expecting anything under the sun. I find it quite impossible to fix my thoughts on anything. Perhaps it will be worse than we hoped in our brighter moments or perhaps it will be better than we feared in our gloomier ones. My little bag is all ready whatever happens. I have only to pick it up. And should death stand at my cell door, I shall not be surprised. Death will find here no broken penitent victim but a proud man who can look him coldly in the eye. He will find no willing submissiveness and certainly no penitence or contrition, for I cannot rid myself of the conviction that I have not merited this fate. But I do not want to write you a farewell letter now; it is not yet time for that; moreover – and this is a change which has come over me in recent weeks – in my heart of hearts I do not believe that this will be my sentence and I do not want to believe it for your sake. Since, however, one can never know what cruel trick fate may play, whether we shall be separated for a long time or a short one, whether one of us may not suddenly be called, I would like to send you this simple rhyme from Kayssler's "Dein Weg" of which I am so fond:

"So geht ein Tür zu Gott hinein
Die Tür is klein
Hat sie Raum für Dich und mich?
Kaum
Jedes geh getrost für sich
Drüben dann, wie hier an Land
gehen wir wieder Hand in Hand."

"There is a door leading to God
The door is narrow
Is there room for Thee and me?
Barely
Let each go forward confident in
    himself
Over there as here on earth
We walk hand in hand once more."

'But we will hope fervently, my darling, that we shall do so here on earth . . .'[48]

13

The Judgement

Some time before the members of the Tribunal had made up their minds on the sentences, the thirty-two American journalists present had made up theirs. On a blackboard in the foreign press room industrious pollsters had chalked up the correspondents' forecasts in columns headed 'Guilty', 'Not Guilty', 'Death Sentence' and 'Prison'. The pressmen were unanimous on the death sentence only for Göring, Ribbentrop and Kaltenbrunner; as regards the rest, bets on the death sentence were: Keitel and Sauckel 29, Hans Frank 27, Seyss-Inquart 26, Rosenberg 24, Hess 17, Raeder 15, Dönitz and Streicher 14, Jodl 13, Frick 12, Speer 11, von Schirach 9, von Papen 6, Schacht 4, von Neurath 3 and Fritzsche 1.[1]

Jackson, who was hoping that the SA, the Reich Cabinet, the General Staff and the High Command of the Armed Forces would also be condemned as definitely criminal organizations, had also made his 'calculation'. In a secret meeting with his closest associates he had even proposed that, since the defendants had so continuously incriminated each other during their period under arrest, they should themselves vote on the guilt or innocence of each of them. It may be regarded as fairly certain that, had this happened, none of them would have escaped the gallows. The Tribunal,[2] however, worked on other hypotheses. The last stage now having been reached, most of the defendants awaited the judgements with calm and composure, some of them even cheerfully. The trial had revealed details and events against which no argument could carry weight, yet it seems that, when the trial ended, none of the defendants was really clear as to what sentence awaited him in Room 600 of the Palace of Justice.

After the reading of the judgement, awaited with impatience by the numerous press correspondents, the defendants were led back to their cells, each handcuffed to a US soldier. Pflücker, the German prison doctor, noted:

'Hess has his usual colic but of course wants to attend the proceedings. When I twitted him, saying that he must not fail to listen to everything today, he replied with a chuckle: "I shan't listen."'

'Neurath, who is suffering from high blood pressure, was given a quick heart check and found to be in good shape. He shows no trace of agitation. We talked about how well his heart had stood up to imprisonment and were both of the opinion that one is saved many of the agitations of the outside world when in prison.

'Frank asks whether I am staying to the end and says jokingly that I shall undoubtedly take his pulse on the very last day.

'Keitel is calm and composed. He knows what is coming, he says – "Having once got into this position, the only deliverance for me is death."

'With Seyss-Inquart I talk about acceptance of the anticipated sentence without hatred. He says: "Of all things no hatred. There are already enough obstacles to reconstruction."

'Papen is very cool and collected and is glad that the decision is near.

'Speer cracks jokes.

'Schacht,* whose lively mind invariably found the course of the proceedings too slow, says after his check-up: "I am very well as always, but I've put on weight."

'Göring had to send for me in the evening owing to an attack of tachycardia. He was highly indignant over the first part of the judgement.'[3]

This had brought the long period of uncertainty to an abrupt end and demolished the hopes still being secretly harboured by some defendants. Each in his own way now tried to come to terms with his fate. Everyone could now see that those condemned to death were only allowed out of their cells handcuffed; at night they had to sleep on their plank beds with arms outside the bedclothes and faces towards the light. What was going on behind the façade carefully cultivated by some of them could now only be judged by the chaplains, the relatives of the condemned men, the American prison psychologist and the German prison doctor. It is upon their accounts that the following description relies.

Gilbert, the prison psychologist, had carried out a number of tests which placed Schacht, Seyss-Inquart, Göring and Dönitz in the category of genius; Schacht and Seyss-Inquart possessed an IQ such as is vouchsafed to only 1 per cent of mankind. In the light of facts scientifically proved since then[4] there can be little doubt that Adolf Hitler would have passed such tests with a similarly high rating. Schacht, rated as a genius by Gilbert with 143 points, said of Hitler:

'He read an enormous amount and acquired a wide knowledge. He juggled with that knowledge in a masterly manner in all debates, discussions and speeches. He was undoubtedly a man of genius in certain respects. He had sudden ideas of which nobody else had thought and which were at times useful in solving great difficulties, sometimes with astounding simplicity, sometimes, however, with equally astounding brutality. He was a mass psychologist of really diabolical genius ... I believe that originally he was not filled only with evil desires; originally, no doubt, he believed he

* The Russian members of the Tribunal held the view that the IMT should not have acquitted von Papen, Schacht and Fritzsche; they also considered that Hess was not adequately punished. They had demanded the death sentence for him. They also wished to see recorded in the protocol their minority view concerning the judgement on the Reich Cabinet, the General Staff and the High Command of the Armed Forces, all of which they held to be criminal organizations.

was aiming at good, but gradually he himself fell victim to the same spell which he exercised over the masses ... He was a man of unbending energy and of a will-power which overcame all obstacles ... Only those two characteristics – mass psychology and his energy and will-power – explain that Hitler was able to rally up to 40 per cent, and later almost 50 per cent, of the German people behind him.'[5]

Göring, who scored 138 points, said of Hitler:

'After a certain time, when I had acquired more insight into the Führer's personality, I gave him my hand and said: "I unite my fate with yours for better or for worse ... in good times and in bad, even unto death."[6] ... With the dynamic personality of the Führer, unsolicited advice was not in order and one had to be on very good terms with him. That is to say one had to have great influence, as I had ... as I had beyond doubt for many years ... Suggestions and advice were curtly brushed aside whenever he had once made his decisions or if ... the would-be adviser had not that influence or that influential position[7] ... Foreign policy above all was the Führer's very own realm ... Foreign policy on the one hand and the leadership of the Armed Forces on the other hand enlisted the Führer's greatest interest and were his main activity ... He busied himself exceptionally with these details[8] ... In certain cases he would ask for data to be submitted to him without the experts knowing the exact reason. In other cases he would explain to his advisers what he intended to do and get from them the data or their opinion. Final decisions he took himself[9] ... In my opinion the Führer did not know about details in the concentration camps, about atrocities ... As far as I know him I do not believe he was informed.'[10]

Dönitz, who scored 138 points, had said:

'A powerful personality ... with extraordinary intelligence and energy, with a truly universal education, a nature radiating force and an enormous power of suggestion. I deliberately went to his headquarters only rarely because I felt that was the best way to retain my own will-power and ... because after a few days' stay in the headquarters I felt that I must remove myself from his power of suggestion[11] ... In principle there was no question of a general consultation with the Führer.'[12]

Hans Frank (130 points) had said:

'In his heart he was always opposed to lawyers ... He did not want to admit formal responsibility and that, unfortunately, applied to his policy too ... Every lawyer was to him a disturbing element.'[13]

Wilhelm Keitel (129 points):

'To a degree which is almost incomprehensible ... Hitler had studied general staff publications, military literature, essays on tactics, operations and strategy and ... he had a knowledge in the military fields which can only be called amazing ... Hitler was so well informed concerning organization, armament, leadership and equipment of all armies and ... all navies of the globe that it was impossible to prove any error on his part ... Hitler studied at night all the big general staff books by Moltke, Schlieffen and Clausewitz ... Therefore we had the impression: Only· a genius can do that ...[14] even in the simple everyday questions concerning organization and equipment of the Wehrmacht ... I was the pupil and not the master ...[15] Concerning ... decision he did not brook any influence ... The final answer always was ... the announcement of his decision ... None of the really important decisions after the year 1938 had ever been formulated as the result of joint counsel ... it was Hitler's way to speak, privately as a rule, to each ... department chief ... In these assemblies, which the documents here speak of as conferences, there was never any deliberation.'[16]

Joachim von Ribbentrop (129 points):

'His thoughts and statements always had something final and definite about them, and they appeared to come from his innermost self. I had the impression that I was facing a man who knew what he wanted and who had an unshakable will and who was a very strong personality.'[17]

Albert Speer (128 points):

'Hitler's dictatorship ... was the first dictatorship ... which made complete use of all technical means in a perfect manner for the domination of its own nation ... It was thereby possible to subject them [80 million people] to the will of one man.'[18]

Alfred Jodl (127 points):

'Hitler was a leader to an exceptional degree. His knowledge and his intellect, his rhetoric and his will power triumphed in the end in every spiritual conflict over everyone. He combined to an unusual extent logic and clarity of thought, scepticism and excess of imagination, which very frequently foresaw what would happen but also very often went astray. I really marveled at him when, in the winter of 1941–2, by his faith and his energy he established the wavering Eastern Front ...[19] The modesty in his mode of life was impressive ...[20] I became convinced – at least during the years 1933 to 1938 – that he was not a charlatan but a man of gigantic personality who, however, in the end assumed infernal power. But at that time he definitely was an outstanding personality ...[21] My influence on the Führer was unfortunately not in the least as great as it might, or perhaps even ought to have been in view of the position I held. The reason lay in the powerful personality of the despot who never suffered advisers gladly.'[22]

Konstantin von Neurath (125 points):

'I had already learned from personal experience that Hitler could not stand contradiction of any kind and that he was not amenable to any kind of petition if it was made before a fairly large group, because he would always develop the complex that he was facing some sort of opposition ... It was different when one confronted him alone. Then, at least during the early years, he was accessible, thoroughly amenable to reasonable arguments and much could be achieved in the way of moderating or weakening radical measures.'[23]

Walter Funk (124 points):

'I immediately received the impression of an exceptional personality ...
He grasped all problems with lightning speed and knew how to present
them very impressively, with great fluency and highly expressive
gestures.'[24]

Finally Julius Streicher (106 points – 'of mere average intelligence'):

'Adolf Hitler was a little eccentric in every respect,' and 'The Führer
could not be influenced.'[26]

Göring still regarded himself as the representative of the Führer, for
whom he was sacrificing his life. Hitler, he stressed yet again, could never
have been allowed to be brought before a foreign court. Hess, who now
took his meals lying on the floor, prophesied his early release and acted
as if the whole affair was nothing to do with him. Keitel, who had asked
for his first sleeping pill on the previous evening, repeated in general
terms what he had said in his final plea. Hitler, the prototype of evil,
whom almost all of them now accused unreservedly, had 'broken his
heart', as he put it. All he wanted now was to 'keep the Wehrmacht's
escutcheon clean'; he hoped that he would be given a bullet like a soldier
sentenced to death in any army. Frank had made his peace with the
Almighty and so appeared calm and relaxed, though there was a suspicious
glitter in his eye.

Seyss-Inquart was composed;[27] he even tried to console his fellow-
sufferer Sauckel, whom he now addressed as 'My dear Party comrade
Sauckel'. On 13 October he wrote him the following letter:

'You voice harsh criticism of the judgement. That is right if one considers the finding from the viewpoint of balance and justice. You think
that judgement has been given against you because what you said was
wrongly translated and interpreted. That is not my impression. It was
established, as you must note with satisfaction, that you did not work
on the principle of extermination through work, although the Prosecution
went to great pains to charge you with this. It was assumed that you
had exploited to the utmost the forced, or as we would say conscripted,
labourers for the benefit of the German war economy. The court did
not inquire whether this was the most rational thing to do either from
the physical or economic point of view. From the viewpoint of humanity
such exploitation or rather utilization of labour is a crime. You were
not accused of having deliberately engineered the abuses which took
place; it was merely stated that you should have known about them –
a charge of secondary significance. In principle anyone who, in whatever
form, exploits conscripted labour for war purposes, will be condemned.

'The fact that there were orders from the Führer cannot remove
responsibility from us, the men who had the courage and strength to
be in the forefront during our people's life-and-death struggle. Our
enemies have defeated Germany and now they are doing away with her
leaders. Whether that is just or wise is another question but it will not
reduce our achievements on behalf of the German people.

'Your self-sacrifice has in fact a special significance for the German people. Whether you are rightly or wrongly accused of it, this method of employment of labour ranks as a crime. The German people will base their future legislation on this fact and, after your self-sacrifice, others will not be able to evade this moral principle in the long run. Your significance thereby appears in its true light. Your family too will give you your due; no doubt they are now silently drawing strength from this thought.

'For us the thought should be this: the worst charge against us would have been that of failure to do our utmost in our people's life-and-death struggle.

'If we were in the leading ranks in the days of triumph, we have a claim to be in the foremost rank in the days of misfortune. By our attitude we can help to rebuild our people's future.

'I shake your hand, my dear Party comrade Sauckel, whom I have learned to appreciate and love. Germany!

Your

Seyss-Inquart.'[28]

To the very last day, however, Sauckel was unable to accept his sentence, leading Göring to accuse him of having tried to excuse himself too much and play the repentant sinner. In 1952 Dr Pflücker recalled:

'I had to spend some time with Sauckel and go over with him the regulations issued for the treatment of foreign workers. Since he had been a workman himself, he said, he knew that satisfactory output could only be achieved if men were well treated and worked willingly; again and again he had issued instructions in this sense. Admittedly pressure had been employed in recruitment, but responsibility for that lay, not with him, but with the agencies of the Wehrmacht and civil administration in the occupied territories. He was firmly convinced that the judgement upon him was wrong and would have to be altered. He would fight for this to the last moment.

'I have the impression that he actually fails to take an overall view and honestly believes that what he wanted and did was for the best. He shut his eyes to everything that did not fit into his picture. A few photographs from a convalescent home for foreign workers, a few regulations and instructions enabled him to forget the hardships implicit in any forced labour, including removal from home and family separation. He forgot all the horrors of the journey, the increasingly inadequate food and accommodation in impoverished Germany and the high mortality among deportees. Undoubtedly he did not actually want all this but such horrors are the inevitable accompaniment of any forced labour system and will always be so.'[29]

On 5 and 6 October Dr Pflücker noted in his diary:

'During my rounds on 5 October I find all those sentenced in a calm frame of mind. Kaltenbrunner had had his birthday on the previous day.

He says that it feels odd to spend one's birthday with a death sentence in one's pocket.

'Ribbentrop is mainly interested in the question where they will be taken. I am glad that I really know nothing about this.

'Sauckel is still lamenting that too little notice was taken of his instructions for the treatment of foreign workers. The court would have had to acknowledge, he says, that his intentions were only of the best. An error of translation made one of his comments refer to exploitation of labour when he had meant utilization.

'Seyss-Inquart receives Holy Communion. We talk about the occasion early in the Nuremberg period, when the first requests for a priest were made ... and Colonel Andrus commissioned me to discover in conversation whether Seyss-Inquart and von Papen were genuine Catholics[30] or whether they wished to see a priest for other reasons. This was not easy for me since I had long been sure that both were convinced christians. Though Seyss-Inquart had temporarily turned his back on the church, he had never actually left it.

'Frank is cheerful. We talk about Franz Werfel's book *Von der Heiligen von Lourdes*, of which he is very fond.

'Streicher[31] speaks with great affection of his wife, who lived with us for some time and stayed with us during her recent visit. She was a very unaffected cheerful person.

'October 6 is a particularly dull wet day and almost all those condemned discuss the date of their execution. I am glad that I know nothing.

'Keitel asks me to say to the organist, who often plays one or two songs in the evening, not to play *Schlafe mein Kindchen, schlaf ein* too frequently since it carries specially melancholy memories for him. He talks about his time as a junior officer saying that he became regimental adjutant at a very early age.

'Today Funk has a slight feverish reaction to the local treatment of his bladder complaint yesterday. He was brought for treatment handcuffed and accompanied by an officer. He would certainly not have tried to escape even if he had not been handcuffed. During treatment he said that survivors would often think back to their time in the "Hotel Justice Prison". Their next residence would certainly not be better. He is always pleased when, at the end of the treatment, he gets a sleeping pill and a cup of lemonade and can talk for a few minutes to me and the dentist who is generally with us.

'Kaltenbrunner asks me to come into his cell for a moment this evening. Any word he can speak to a German is a comfort to him, he says. He is pleased that the Catholic priest is taking so much trouble about him.[32]

'Göring has asked to be allowed to see his wife once more. He knows that it will be grievous for himself and his wife but is prepared to put up with anything if he can see her once more.

'On 6 October the last employees leave to go back home and the rest of us are allowed out. We can move about freely for the first time. It is a curious feeling to walk down the street and watch the heavy traffic. It is easy to lose one's way. The number of well-dressed people is striking. The damage in Nuremberg makes one inexpressibly sad.'[33]

In theory at least all the condemned now had an opportunity to see their relatives once more and some of them made their preparations to say good-bye for ever. Even before announcement of the verdicts some of the wives had been referred to as 'the widows of Nuremberg' in the newspapers and this had naturally penetrated within the prison walls. Now once more the 'widows' sat opposite their husbands in the defence's conference cells, separated from them by wire-meshed plate glass and watched by American soldiers. Frau Dönitz, Frau von Neurath, Frau Kaltenbrunner, Frau Seyss-Inquart, Frau Streicher and Frau von Ribbentrop availed themselves of the opportunity. Ribbentrop's eldest son, who had won the Knight's Cross in the SS, was transferred to Nuremberg from a prisoner-of-war camp so that he might see his father once more.

Frau Göring arrived with her eight-year-old daughter, who prattled happily that she would see 'Papa another ten times'.[34] After their departure Göring said to the prison doctor: 'I saw my wife for the last time, my dear doctor. It was a very bad moment but my wife wanted it. She was wonderful. She is a really great woman ... she was about to give way only towards the end but then she took a grip of herself again and was quite composed when we said goodbye. She proposed to go from me to Frau Jodl to comfort her.'[35]

Luise Jodl too saw her husband once more. Keitel, who was still hoping for death by firing squad, told Dr Pflücker that he had never thought of suicide;[36] he was reading a letter from his wife, considerably abbreviated by the censor. Sauckel wrote to the Control Council. Streicher was still preoccupied with racial science even at this stage. Funk lamented over his sentence and accused the Russians of having engineered it. Frank was writing and praying; as he himself said, he had made his peace with the Almighty in Nuremberg.[37] Jodl, whom many Allied officers would gladly have saved from hanging, was reading a book by Wilhelm Raabe;* he reckoned on his execution 'about 14 October'.[38] On that day he wrote to his wife: 'If you have friends round you on the evening after my death, that should be like a funeral parade ... and all German soldiers will be marching with you, the dead in front and the living behind.' On 15 October, the day of his execution, he wrote: 'I intend to die just as I have lived. I know that I have had faults, but

---

* After petitions for mercy from his counsel and Luise Jodl many prominent people on the Western side were doubtful whether Jodl should be executed despite the verdict. The idea came to nothing, however, in face of a determined veto from the Soviets, who demanded Jodl's death. The executions, originally set for 10 October, were accordingly postponed to the night 15/16 October.

if there is a God in Heaven as I conceive Him and as He must be, then he will forgive me ... and I can look Him in the eye ...'[39]

Thus they waited for the end without knowing when the last hour would come.

Albert Speer, who had escaped with his life, wrote in his diary on 4 October: 'Ever since sentence was pronounced, our cells have been locked. We can no longer talk to one another or go for a refreshing walk in the prison yard. The loneliness is growing unbearable. So far not one of us has accepted the offer of a daily hour's walk on the ground floor of the cell block ... those condemned to death ... are no longer taken for walks. Now and then one of their cell doors is opened, perhaps for the chaplain or the doctor.'[40]

On 13 October he wrote in a moralizing, self-righteous, supercilious accusing vein: 'A guard goes from cell to cell. He asks whether we want to make use of our right to a daily walk on the ground floor. The yard is still barred to us ... I ask to go. But I shudder at the prospect of seeing the men in death row. The guard holds out the chromium-plated handcuffs. Linked together we have some difficulty in descending the winding staircase. In the silence every step on the iron stairs sounds like a thunderclap. On the ground floor I see eleven soldiers staring attentively into eleven cells. The men inside are eleven of the surviving leaders of the Third Reich. Wilhelm Keitel, chief of the High Command of the Armed Forces, was unpopular and despised; during the Nuremberg trial he grew in understanding and dignity. General Alfred Jodl was Keitel's closest associate. He was typical of the intelligent General Staff officers who were so fascinated by Hitler that they largely cast aside the moral traditions of their class. Hermann Göring, the principal in the trial, grandiloquently took all responsibility, only to employ all his cunning and energy to deny that he bore any specific guilt. He had become a debauched parasite; in prison he regained his old self and displayed an alertness, intelligence and quick-wittedness such as he had not shown since the early days of the Third Reich. Joachim von Ribbentrop, Hitler's Foreign Minister, is said to have abandoned his arrogance for a faith in Christ that sometimes strikes a grotesque note. Julius Streicher ... one of Hitler's oldest companions, was always an outsider in the Party because of his sex-obsessed anti-semitism and his flagrant corruption; during the trial all the other defendants avoided him. Then there is Wilhelm Frick, a taciturn man who, as Minister of the Interior, turned Hitler's grudges into laws. Alfred Rosenberg, the complicated thinker and Party philosopher, was ridiculed by everyone, including Hitler; to the surprise of us all Rosenberg's defense during the trial was able to prove that he had considered the ferocious policy of annihilation in the East a fatal error, although he had remained devoted to Hitler. Then there is Fritz Sauckel, a sailor who rose to be one of Hitler's Gauleiters and who was overtaxed, intellectually and morally, by the wartime assign-

ment to provide Germany with slave laborers from the occupied territories. Arthur Seyss-Inquart, Hitler's Reich Commissioner for the
Netherlands, sat on my right in the dock for nine months – an amiable
Austrian who had tested out as having the highest IQ of us all; during
the trial I had come to like him because he did not seek evasions among
other reasons. And then there is Hans Frank, Governor-General of
Poland, whose own diary revealed his ruthlessly brutal actions; but in
Nuremberg he freely confessed his crimes, abjured them and became
a devout Catholic; his capacity to believe fervently and even fanatically
had not deserted him. Gilbert recently told me that Frank is working
on his memoirs. Last of all is Ernst Kaltenbrunner, the Gestapo chief,
a tall Austrian with sharp features but a curiously mild look in his eyes
who, during the trial, in all seriousness denied the authenticity of documents he had signed.

'As the rules prescribe, most of them are lying on their backs, hands
on the blanket, heads turned towards the inside of the cell.[41] A ghostly
sight, all of them in their immobility; it looks as though they have already
been laid on their biers. Only Frank is up, sitting at his table and writing
away. He has a damp towel round his neck; he used to tell Dr Pflücker
he did that to keep his mind alert. Seyss-Inquart looks out through the
doorway; he smiles at me each time I pass and each time that smile
gives me the chills. I cannot stand it for long. Back in my cell I decide
not to go back down again.'[42]

Defence counsel were now working feverishly on petitions for clemency
for their clients. Göring, Ribbentrop, Frick and Streicher did not want
petitions to be made, but their defence counsel insisted on availing themselves of the last chance, although they themselves had little faith in it.
Göring's counsel tried to raise once more the argument that the former
Reich Marshal's true intentions were peaceful. Ribbentrop's counsel
referred to his client's weak character as a result of which he inevitably
carried no weight with Hitler. Dr Servatius handed in a petition on behalf
of Sauckel who, in his opinion, had been too severely punished, as had
Speer. Dr Flächsner, on the other hand, simply repeated Speer's contention that the punishment awarded him was just.

Keitel wrote to his defence counsel, Dr Nelte, on 1 October: 'I have
not been surprised by the death sentence but I am most upset by the
method of execution. I request you to afford me once more your ever-
ready help in this situation and to assist me by a petition for clemency,
the object of which is to transform my execution into a soldier's death
by firing squad. I consider it purposeless to ask for more.' He himself
signed the petition on 5 October, adding one of his own addressed to
the Control Council for Germany, the recipient of all petitions: 'I am
happy to offer my life, as demanded by the judgement in expiation, in
the hope that this sacrifice will be of benefit to the German people and
exonerate the German Wehrmacht. I have only one request: that I be

granted death by firing squad ... I hope that the members of the Control Council for Germany, who are old soldiers, will appreciate that my guilt stemmed from a sense of duty held by all armies in the world to be essential, correct and fundamental for a good soldier. Though I failed to recognize the limits which must be set to this military virtue, I do not think that thereby I can have forfeited the possibility of making amends for this error by a death such as is granted to a soldier in all armies of the world if faced with a soldier's death sentence.'[43]

Exner and Jahrreiss fought for Jodl, whose sentence was considered unjust even by some of his co-defendants; they warned the Control Council not to make a martyr of this particular criminal. But it was all in vain. Even their request that, if executed, he too should be granted death by firing squad was unsuccessful. On the day the sentences were announced Jodl had written to his wife: '... Do not fill my stupid old heart with hopes; let it quietly swing itself away,'[44] but she was determined to try everything and he let her go on. Her mother was English and she had worked as secretary in the offices of defence counsel, quite close to her husband, therefore, although she had been unable to see him since before the beginning of September 1946.[45] She now wrote to Field Marshal Montgomery and, with the support of Allied officers and journalists, sent a telegram to Winston Churchill as follows: 'Sir: You have always been proud of being a soldier – you were the mast when in deadly peril England kept the flag flying. May I as the daughter of a British-born mother appeal to you as a soldier to give your voice of support for the life of my husband, Colonel General Jodl who – like yourself – did nothing but fight for his country to the last.'[46]

Churchill's reply on 13 October was terse and impersonal. His telegram read: 'I have received your communication and have passed it to Attlee, the Prime Minister.'[47] Montgomery reacted similarly.[48]

Before the condemned had received official notice that their petitions had been refused by the Control Council, they had already been told as much in confidence by Dr Gilbert, who was interested in their immediate reactions.

The press had already announced ahead of time that the day of execution was to be 16 October and this had penetrated through to the prisoners; they now began to discuss quite openly with Dr Pflücker, the prison doctor, the question of where it would take place. Some suspected that it would be Landsberg am Lech; others, who had noticed many new faces in the passages and electricians reinforcing the lighting in the courtyard, thought that it would be somewhere within the Nuremberg prison compound. They were unable to see the beams and planks delivered by Army lorries on the evening of 15 October disappearing into the gymnasium. Only when 'carpenters' began hammering in the gymnasium[49] were they left in no doubt that their last hour would come in Nuremberg – and in the prison gymnasium.

At 3.30 p.m. the German prison doctor and German prisoner foreman were told that the men condemned to death were to be woken at 11.45 p.m., that they would then be informed that their execution was imminent and that they would be at liberty to choose a last meal – either sausage and potato salad or pancakes and fruit salad. When making his evening round Dr Pflücker was to act as if this was no different from any other night in prison. He was even to hand out the usual sleeping pills, although it had been decided that the executions should start shortly after midnight, as is customary in the USA. In course of time Pflücker had got to know his patients very well and so he knew what he could or must anticipate from each of them; he was also anxious not to lose the confidence of the Americans, however; he himself dealt with Göring's sleeping pills.

All the condemned awaited their end with composure. Keitel and Seyss-Inquart asked Dr Pflücker to give their tobacco ration to others who were smokers. Sauckel, who was still a law unto himself, was now writing to the King of England – as if he could do anything for him. Streicher sang the praises of his second wife who, as he kept on saying, had meant a great deal to him. Frick admitted that had long been afraid that it would end like this. Kaltenbrunner accused Himmler, saying that he had demanded deference and loyalty from others but had then slipped away himself. Frank hoped that God would be merciful to him.[50]

About 10.0 p.m. Dr Pflücker visited Göring to give him the sleeping pills for which he had asked but which the doctor had taken the precaution of faking. As the most important of the criminals Göring had been under especially heavy guard since announcement of the sentences; the fact that he contrived to commit suicide immediately after Pflücker's visit at first placed the doctor in a highly precarious situation; his notes are therefore of particular importance. 'Regularly every evening,' he wrote, 'Göring was given a capsule of amycal and one of seconal; both are American drugs; one was in a blue capsule and the other in a red one. The seconal in the red capsule acted more quickly but its effect was not very prolonged. The amycal in the blue capsule acted more slowly but lasted longer. In order not to put Göring into too deep a sleep, that afternoon I emptied the blue capsule and filled it with sodium bicarbonate. I explained my idea and the reasons to Dr Hoch, the dentist, and he helped me to do this. At the time I had no idea how important that would be to me. Göring took his pills and asked whether there was any point in getting undressed. I replied that a night was very short sometimes but that I could not tell him anything definite. "But there is certainly something in the wind," Göring said, "one sees all sorts of strange people in the passage and there are more lights burning than usual." He thanked me warmly for taking such good care of him both in Mondorf and in Nuremberg. He took leave of me with a smile and a handshake.'[51]

Fifty minutes later, some two and a quarter hours before the time set for the executions, Pflücker was alerted and summoned to Göring; in the opinion of Gerecke, the evangelical chaplain who was with him, he seemed to have suffered a heart attack. When the doctor entered the cell – before which an American officer was posted in addition to the usual guard – Göring was lying on his bed propped on his elbows; the chaplain was kneeling beside him whispering texts from the Bible.

Pflücker records: 'I called out to him: "Have you had a heart attack?" His face turned blue ... he sank back. A quick rattle in the throat and it was over. I whipped back the blanket to listen to his heart since I could still feel a trace of pulse.'[52] But it was already too late. There was no corneal reflex; the heart was no longer audible; the pupils did not react. Göring was dead.

Colonel Andrus ordered the chaplain to go to the other men due for execution and tell them of Göring's suicide. There then assembled at once in his office the Control Council representatives who had come to Nuremberg for the executions, the chaplains, the doctors together with Wilhelm Hoegner and the Nuremberg Public Prosecutor, the two German witnesses for the executions. Dr Pflücker already suspected suicide by cyanide and he had no wish to come under suspicion of having helped Göring obtain the poison; he accordingly asked that Dr Martin, the American doctor, should go into Göring's cell and look for glass splinters in the dead man's mouth.

Dr Martin found splinters of a cyanide capsule and this, of course, at once raised the question whence and from whom Göring had obtained the poison and where he had hidden it all this time. Four hours later, after the executions, the Russians openly accused the Americans of having passed the poison to Göring.

On 28 November 1975 Robert M. W. Kempner, who had had much to do with Göring and his family in Nuremberg and had talked to Frau Göring shortly before her death in 1974, reported: 'An official American Commission of Inquiry met on the very night of the suicide; it consisted of a Colonel, a Lieutenant-Colonel and a Major. They were to establish the detailed circumstances of the suicide and in particular examine whether any of the prison personnel were involved. All persons who had had to do with Göring in prison were examined under oath. In its report the "Board of Proceedings" came to the conclusion that no member of the prison personnel had passed the poison capsule to Göring.'[53]

Under Göring's left hand Dr Pflücker found a manuscript letter and an empty metal capsule which had been unscrewed.[54] His opinion was that Göring had brought the capsule with him to Nuremberg and had kept it hidden under the edge of the water-closet; the fact that the defendants never had to move cells supported this theory. Moreover in the letter found by Pflücker Göring said that he had had the poison 'ever since commitment to prison'.[55] The letter was addressed to the Commandant and ran:

'On commitment to Mondorf I had three capsules. The first I left in my clothes so that it might be found during a search. The second I put under the clothes-horse when I undressed and hid it on my person again when I dressed. I hid this one so well, both in Mondorf and here in the cell, that it could not be found despite the frequent and very thorough searches. During the court sittings I had it on me in my jackboots. The third capsule is still in my small toilet case, in the round box containing face-cream ... None of those responsible for searches is to blame since it was almost impossible to find the capsule.'

Talking to Dr Kempner, however, Emmy Göring contradicted her husband and maintained that a friend, whose name she would not give, had passed the poison to her husband in Nuremberg. When visiting the prison, so she told Kempner, she used the code 'Have you got the comb?' to make certain that Göring still had the cyanide. According to his wife[56] Göring did not intend to use the poison unless his application to be shot as a soldier was refused and this is very probably true, for the postscript to his letter to the Commandant reads: 'Dr Gilbert tells me that the Control Council has refused to change the method of execution to one of shooting.'

Now that Emmy Göring is dead, the answer to the question whether Hermann Göring or his wife was telling the truth will undoubtedly never be known.[57]

On 7 October 1946 Göring had asked the doctor whether he did not want to come to his execution in order to see how he would die.[58] Dr Pflücker did see but in a way very different from that implied by Göring's remark.

Immediately after the condemned men, now only ten in number, had been woken the death sentences were read to them once more in accordance with Control Council instructions in the presence of two German witnesses, Hoegner, the Minister-President of Bavaria, and Leistner, the Public Prosecutor. The two Germans, Colonel Andrus, an interpreter and an American officer went round the cells. Most of them listened in silence; Colonel-General Jodl stood proudly against the cell wall, legs astraddle; Streicher said in a harsh sullen voice that he knew his sentence already; Sauckel was in despair, cursed and said that he had great respect for American officers and soldiers but none for American justice.

The sentences having been read, the condemned were offered their last meal. But hardly any of them touched it. American soldiers then handcuffed them. There was to be no chance of anyone committing suicide like Hermann Göring. Colonel Andrus then conducted the witnesses for the executions to the gymnasium where three gallows stood side by side on wooden scaffolding, draped in black curtains. Thirteen steps led up to the square platform in which was a trapdoor underneath an iron hook from which hung a rope, apparently new.

Towards 1.0 a.m. the execution witnesses were taken to the journalists' quarters and Colonel Andrus together with Gerecke, the evangelical chaplain, and Father O'Connor, the Catholic priest, appeared on the cell floor. For the last time Dr Pflücker went round his patients whom he had treated and cared for for months. The execution witnesses were now summoned back to the gymnasium where were waiting foreign journalists, American officers and soldiers, one American, one Russian, one British and one French general from the Control Council and the two German witnesses. The US military had ignored a request from Whitney Harris, Jackson's personal representative, who had come from the US specially to be present at the executions. When Harris nevertheless presented himself at the door of the gymnasium, it was slammed in his face by soldiers. This was the pay-off for Jackson's attitude to the military, whom he had not allowed on to the prosecution bench when the judgements were being read.

The curtain now rose on the final scene. The door to the gymnasium had been locked by an American soldier. Shortly after 1.0 a.m. it was opened again and Colonel Andrus, accompanied by the Catholic and evangelical chaplains, led Joachim von Ribbentrop, handcuffed to two soldiers, to the gallows; he was pale and an obvious physical wreck. At the foot of the gallows his hands were tied with a black cord. Once more he had to give his full name. Then he was led up the thirteen steps accompanied by the interpreter and the American who had asked him his name as he entered the gymnasium.

Now, with his life at an end, Ribbentrop was allowed to say once more what he thought was important. Asked through the interpreter 'Have you anything to say?', Hitler's last Foreign Minister replied: 'God guard Germany! God have mercy on my soul! My final wish is that Germany should recover her unity and that, for the sake of world peace, there should be understanding between East and West.' The evangelical chaplain then assured him that they would see each other again one day and stood aside to make room for two men – the hangman's assistant who tied Ribbentrop's legs together, and the man who was so happy to act as executioner in Nuremberg.

He was the US Master-Sergeant John C. Woods, thick-set and muscular, with a coarse red face which not only the sensitive found repellent. He drew a black hood over Ribbentrop's head and tied it beneath his chin. Then round the neck of the criminal, who had had to wait 'an infinity of time' for death, he placed the twisted rope. He stepped back and actuated the mechanism opening the trapdoor. Joachim von Ribbentrop fell like a stone. Nevertheless he took ten minutes to die, as the officiating doctors, two Americans and one Russian, discovered on examining him.

Wilhelm Keitel, the next candidate for death, entered the gymnasium; he had put on his uniform trousers with the broad red general's stripes. Though unsuccessful in his repeated requests for 'a bullet', he died proudly and with dignity. His last words were: 'I call upon the Almighty to have mercy on the German people. Over two million German soldiers have gone to their death for their Fatherland before me. I am following my sons. Everything for Germany.' He did not know that only one of his sons had been killed. The other, Major Ernst Wilhelm Keitel, had been severely wounded and taken prisoner by the Russians. He was not released until 1955.[59]

Then came the others, taking turns on two of the gallows. First Ernst Kaltenbrunner, who said: 'I have served my people and my Fatherland with all my heart. I have done my duty according to the laws of my country. I regret that, at this grave time, my people are not being led exclusively by military men. I regret that crimes have been committed. I had no part in them. Good luck to Germany.'

The next was Alfred Rosenberg, followed by Hans Frank, who said in a whisper: 'I am grateful for the good treatment accorded me during imprisonment. I pray the Lord God to receive me with mercy.' Then came Wilhelm Frick, who merely called out, 'Long live eternal Germany.' He was followed by Streicher, who had refused to dress and appeared in his underclothes; he was literally dragged into the gymnasium by the soldiers shouting 'Heil Hitler'; his last words were: 'Festival of Purim 1946 – and now to God (short pause) The Bolshevists will hang you too (another short pause) I am with God, Father' and with the hood over his head 'Adele, my beloved Adele'.

The final trio consisted of Fritz Sauckel (in a great state of agitation), Alfred Jodl (proud and calm) and Arthur Seyss-Inquart (calm and solemn). Their last words were : Sauckel: 'I die in innocence. The judgement is wrong. God protect Germany and make Germany great once more. Long live Germany. God protect my family'; Jodl: 'I salute you, my Germany'; Seyss-Inquart: 'I hope that this execution is the last act in the tragedy of the Second World War, that lessons will be drawn from this world war and that peace and understanding between peoples will be the result. I have faith in Germany.'

The witnesses were allowed to smoke and talk between executions, but at one moment, when Wilhelm Hoegner had a cigarette in his hand as the next candidate for death appeared at the door, he was called sharply to order by an American – 'Out with that cigarette, you German!'

By 2.45 a.m. all was over. The executions had lasted precisely 103 minutes.

Woods, the hangman from San Antonio, who had a remarkable escape in 1950 when testing an electric chair,[60] was pleased. Four days after the executions the American soldiers' magazine *Stars and Stripes* carried an interview with him, at which he said: 'I hanged these ten Nazis in Nuremberg and I am proud of it; I did a good job. Everything went A1. I have ... never been at an execution which went better. I am only sorry that that fellow Göring escaped me; I'd have been at my best for him. No, I wasn't nervous. I haven't got any nerves. You can't afford nerves in my job. But this Nuremberg job was just what I wanted. I wanted this job so terribly that I stayed here a bit longer, though I could have gone home earlier. But I'll say one thing about these Nazis. They died like brave men. Only one of them showed signs of weakness. As Frick climbed the thirteen steps to the gallows, one of his legs seemed to fail and the guard had to hold him up. They were all haughty. One could see how they hated us. The old Jew-baiter Streicher looked at me as he said: "One day the Bolshevists will hang you." I looked him back straight in the eye. They couldn't ruffle me. There's not much to say about the executions themselves. They went off ... like all other routine executions. Ten men in 103 minutes. That's quick work. Only one of them moved after he fell. He groaned for a bit but not for long. Another, I think it was Sauckel, started to shout "Heil Hitler" after I had put the hood over his head. I stopped that – with the rope. I used a new rope and a new hood for each man. I put the noose round myself and attached each rope myself to make sure nothing went wrong. The ropes and the hoods were burnt with the bodies so that there was nothing left for the souvenir-hunters[61] ... What do I think of the gallows job? Someone has to do it after all ... But I'm glad the Nuremberg affair is over. It was a strain. I had never seen any of the condemned men before they came through the door of the execution chamber ... they gave their names as they came to the scaffold ... It is difficult to remember exactly what each one did or said. To hang ten people one after the other it has to go fairly quick, you know. And what I had in my hand was a rope, not a notebook.'[62]

The 'job' had certainly not gone off 'A1', as the hangman maintained.* Streicher groaned for a long time after his execution. Jodl took eighteen minutes and Keitel as much as twenty-four minutes to die. Some of the victims' faces were scratched and bleeding. Frick had severe wounds on his face and neck. Possibly the trapdoors were too small or the ropes had not been correctly positioned. The hangman's story, which is only a story, is that the faces were smeared with blood because 'they had bitten their tongues at the moment they fell'.[63] As far as the Allies were concerned all this was a closely guarded secret. When a German journalist named Helmut Kamphausen managed to persuade an American-licensed newspaper in Berlin to publish photographs of the blood-smeared faces and wounded heads, he was promptly arrested.[64] The victors only released 'touched-up' pictures of the eleven bodies lying in a row on the gymnasium floor – with Göring at one end.

That night the bodies were photographed – both naked and clothed – by a US Army photographer; they were in wooden packing cases. Göring's right eye was open, staring glassily at nothing; all the others still had the rope round their necks. Each carried a long narrow identification plate on the chest showing the initial of the christian name and the surname in full.

* The American hangmen who executed criminals in Landsberg during the next five years did an even worse 'job' than Woods. After their official execution some of their victims had to be suffocated with cotton wool pushed into their noses and mouths by US soldiers standing underneath the gallows.

The bodies, still in their packing cases, were then taken to Munich on two U S Army lorries. There, in the Heilmannstrasse, they were cremated and the ashes scattered into the Conwentz brook. Journalists who attempted to follow the lorries were stopped on the way and forcibly prevented from continuing their 'pursuit'. Meanwhile the gymnasium had been cleaned by the survivors, Dönitz, Raeder, Speer, Funk, von Schirach, Hess and von Neurath. On 18 July 1947, nine months after the execution of their former comrades, they were taken to serve their sentences in the 600 cells of Spandau prison.

So this great trial ended as everyone knew that it would. It had cost $4,435,719, the equivalent in the devasted Germany of 1946 of R M88,704,380 at the official rate of exchange and up to R M434,000,000 on the black market.[65]

Part Three

Nuremberg in History

Nuremberg in History

The International Military Tribunal's legality, its basis in law, its competence under international law and its rules of procedure have been matters of frequent dispute not solely occasioned by post-1945 national and international developments in East and West. Anglo-American procedures presented the German defence counsel with a situation foreign to them; their ideas and expectations of the initial period led them, on 19 November 1945, to raise objection to 'the legal elements of this Trial under the Charter of the Tribunal'.[1] They got nowhere; Article 3 of the Charter quite clearly laid down that neither the prosecution nor the defendants nor their counsel could challenge the court;[2] any hope, therefore, that an objection to its competence would be accepted, inevitably proved illusory. Only two days later the defence was told that the Tribunal refused even to consider their motion.[3]

Objections to the 'international' competence of American tribunals raised by the German defence counsel during the twelve follow-up trials in Nuremberg were rejected as invalid both by the Tribunals themselves and by the US Supreme Court.[4]

The 'Motion adopted by all Defense Counsel' and signed by Dr Stahmer began as follows:

'Two frightful world wars ... caused the tortured peoples to realize that a true order among the States is not possible as long as such State, by virtue of its sovereignty, has the right to wage war at any time and for any purpose ... Public opinion in the world ... [makes] a distinction ... between just and unjust wars and it is asked that the community of States call to account the State which wages an unjust war and deny it, should it be victorious, the fruits of its outrage. More than that, it is demanded that not only should the guilty State be condemned and its liability be established, but that furthermore those men who are responsible for unleashing the unjust war be tried and sentenced by an International Tribunal ... This thought is at the basis of the first three counts of the Indictment which have been put forward in this Trial, to wit, the Indictment for Crimes against Peace. Humanity insists that this idea should in the future ... be valid international law. However, today it is not as yet valid international law. Neither in the statute of the League of Nations ... nor in the Kellogg-Briand Pact nor in any other of the treaties which were concluded after 1918 ... has this idea been realized. But above all the practice of the League of Nations has ... been quite unambiguous in that regard. On several occasions the League had to decide upon the lawfulness or unlawfulness of action by force of one member against another member, but it always condemned such action by force merely as a violation of international law by the State, and never thought of bringing up for trial the statesmen, generals and industrialists of the State which recurred to force. And when the new organization for world peace was set up last summer in San Francisco, no new legal maxim was created under which an international tribunal would inflict punishment upon those who unleashed an unjust war.[5] The present Trial can, therefore, as far as Crimes against Peace shall be avenged, not invoke existing international law; it is rather a proceeding pursuant to a new penal law ... enacted only after the crime. This is repugnant to a principle of jurisprudence sacred to the civilized world, the partial violation of which by Hitler's Germany has been vehemently discountenanced outside and inside the Reich. This principle is to the effect that only he can be punished who offended against a law in existence at the time of the commission of the act imposing a penalty. This maxim is one of the great fundamental principles of the political systems of the Signatories of the Charter for this Tribunal themselves, to wit, of England since the Middle Ages, of the United States since their creation, of France since its great revolution, and the Soviet Union. And recently when the Control Council for Germany enacted a law to ensure the return to a just administration of penal law in Germany, it decreed in the first place the restoration of the maxim "No punishment without a penal law in force at the time of the commission of the act". This maxim derives from the recognition of the fact that any defendant must needs consider himself unjustly treated if he is punished under an *ex post facto* law.

'The Defense of all defendants would be neglectful of their duty if they acquiesced silently in a deviation from existing international law and in disregard of a commonly recognized principle of modern penal jurisprudence and if they suppressed doubts which are openly expressed today outside Germany ... Wherever the Indictment charges acts which were not punishable at the time the Tribunal would have to confine itself to a thorough examination and findings as to what acts were committed ... The States of the international legal community would then create a new law under which those who in the future would be guilty of starting an unjust war would be threatened with punishment by an international tribunal. The Defense are also of the opinion that other principles of a penal character contained in the Charter are in contradiction with the maxim "*Nulla Poena Sine Lege*".

'Finally the Defense consider it their duty to point out at this juncture another peculiarity of this Trial which departs from the commonly recognized principles of modern jurisprudence. The Judges have been appointed exclusively by States which were the one party in this war. This one party to the proceeding is all in one: creator of the statute of the

Tribunal and of the rules of law, prosecutor and judge. It used to be until now the common legal conception that this should not be so; just as the United States of America, as the champion for the institution of international arbitration and jurisdiction, always demanded that neutrals and representatives of all parties should be called to the Bench. This principle has been realized in an exemplary manner in the case of the Permanent Court of International Justice at The Hague.'

In conclusion the Motion asked that 'an opinion be submitted by internationally recognized authorities on international law on the legal elements of this Trial'.[6]

The competence of Anglo-American courts to create law was something fundamentally foreign to continental legal thinking and so this expression of criticism was a matter of duty for the defence; their main argument was that the IMT could not 'be based on existing international law' since the criminal laws which it cited had been made after commission of the crimes. In the light of the provisions of the Charter, however, it was obvious that such arguments could do the defendants no good. Not until November 1950, some two years after the General Declaration of Human Rights by the General Assembly of the United Nations and four years after judgement had been passed on the Germans accused as major war criminals, did the United Nations agree that retrospective application of criminal law was a violation of human rights. Until the Convention for Protection of Human Rights and Basic Freedoms of 1950,[7] the first guarantee of protection for certain human rights, there were only declarations which carried moral weight but no legal validity. Even afterwards, however, the Nuremberg prosecutors defended the IMT. In 1966, for instance, Robert M. W. Kempner stated: 'The notion of aggressive war as a criminal act was a new one (in 1945), even though wars of aggression had been outlawed in the Kellogg-Briand Pact.' And he went on: 'The prosecution and the court took the view that wars of aggression, as systematically planned by Hitler, were the worst war crimes there could be, far more punishable than ill-treatment of groups of prisoners of war, which had always been regarded as punishable. To this extent Nuremberg was intended to serve as a precedent – as is customary under Anglo-Saxon law.'[8]

This new concept, war of aggression, formed one of the main counts in the Indictment of 'Herman Wilhelm Göring et al.' – to use the court's terminology. Yet one of the signatory powers sitting in judgement on the defeated Germans in Nuremberg, the Soviet Union, had – like the defendants – prepared, and from mid-September 1939 waged, a war of aggression (against Poland). Moreover on 14 December 1939, primarily at the instigation of Great Britain and France, the Soviet Union had been expelled from the League of Nations for attacking Finland; finally, on 8 August 1945, the day the London Charter was signed, the Soviet Union had declared war on Japan despite the non-aggression pact of 13 April 1941. All this was ignored in Nuremberg.

No retribution was exacted from the Russians for the fact, which was never in doubt in Nuremberg, that they had waged definite wars of aggression against Poland, against Finland and against Japan. So accomplices were sitting in judgement on their erstwhile fellow-conspirators, something inconceivable under any modern legal system except those of the Nazis and the Soviet Union. On 5 October 1946, barely a week after the IMT had pronounced judgement, the court's silence on the Russo-German agreement of 23 August 1939 was criticized as follows in the London *Economist*:

'Such silence unfortunately shows that the Nuremberg Tribunal is only within certain limits an independent judiciary. In ordinary criminal law it would certainly be a remarkable case if a judge, summing up on a charge of murder, were to avoid evidence on the part played by an accomplice in the murder because the evidence revealed that the judge himself had been that accomplice. That nobody thinks such reticence extraordinary in the case of Nuremberg merely demonstrates how far we still really are from anything that can be called a "reign of law" in international affairs. Both Britain and France are on record as having concurred in the expulsion of the Soviet Union from the League of Nations for its unprovoked attack on Finland in 1939; this verdict still stands and is not modified by anything that has happened since.'

The weakness of the IMT's arguments concerning aggressive war is highlighted by its judgement on Hess. This says among other things:

'As deputy to the Führer Hess was ... responsible for all Party matters with authority to make decisions in Hitler's name on all questions of Party leadership. As Reich Minister without Portfolio he had the authority to approve all legislation suggested by the different Reich Ministers before it could be enacted as law. In these positions Hess was an active supporter of preparations for war. His signature appears on the law of 16 March 1935 establishing compulsory military service. Throughout the years he supported Hitler's policy of vigorous rearmament in many speeches. He told the people that they must sacrifice for armaments, repeating the phrase "Guns instead of butter". It is true that between 1933 and 1937 Hess made speeches in which he expressed a desire for peace and advocated international economic cooperation. But nothing that they contained can alter the fact that of all the defendants none knew better than Hess how determined Hitler was to realize his ambitions, how fanatical and violent a man he was and how little likely he was to refrain from resort to force, if this was the only way in which he could achieve his aims.

'Hess was an informed and willing participant in German aggression against Austria, Czechoslovakia and Poland. He was in touch with the illegal Nazi Party in Austria throughout the entire period between the murder of Dollfuss and the Anschluss, and gave instructions to it during that period. Hess was in Vienna on 12 March 1938 when the German troops moved in; and on 13 March 1938 he signed the law for the reunion of Austria within the German Reich. A law of 10 June 1939 provided for his participation in the administration of Austria. On 24 July 1938 he made a speech in commemoration of the unsuccessful putsch by Austrian National-Socialists which had been attempted four years before, praising the steps leading up to the Anschluss and defending the occupation of Austria by Germany ...

'These specific steps which this defendant took in support of Hitler's plans for aggressive action do not indicate the full extent of his responsibility. Until his flight to England [on 10 May 1941] Hess was Hitler's ... personal confidant. Their relationship was such that Hess must have been informed of Hitler's aggressive plans when they came into existence. And he took action to carry out these plans whenever action was necessary.

'With him on his flight to England Hess carried certain peace proposals which he alleged Hitler was prepared to accept. It is significant to note that this flight took place only ten days after the date on which Hitler fixed 22 June 1941 as the time for attacking the Soviet Union. In conversations carried on after his arrival in England Hess ... supported all Germany's aggressive actions up to that time and attempted to justify Germany's action in connection with Austria, Czechoslovakia, Poland, Norway, Denmark, Belgium and the Netherlands. He blamed England and France for the war.'[9]

Rudolf Hess is now the sole surviving 'Nuremberger' who has had to serve his sentence without remission* despite all the efforts even of some of the former Nuremberg prosecutors.[11] Hitler, on the other hand, does not seem to have considered him sufficiently important to be included in the secret conferences of 23 May, 22 August, 5 and 23 November 1937 when he revealed his political and military intentions and plans to the Commanders-in-Chief of the three services and Joachim von Ribbentrop, conferences to which the IMT ascribed first-rate importance under the Count of 'Crimes against Peace'.

In 1970 Telford Taylor, who had compiled the American list of Germans to be brought to trial in 1945, had acted as prosecutor in the case against the German General Staff at the main trial and had then been Chief Prosecutor for war crimes in the subsequent 'minor trials' in Nuremberg,[12] said in his book *Nuremberg and Vietnam*:

'The Tribunal in its judgement acknowledged the Charter as "binding upon the Tribunal" and deduced that "it is not therefore strictly necessary to consider whether and to what extent aggressive war was a crime before the execution of the London Agreement." Not content to rest on the Charter alone, however, the Tribunal included a long passage in support of the conclusion that Kellogg–Briand and other recent treaties and international resolutions had made aggressive war "not merely illegal but criminal". The Tokyo and later Nuremberg Tribunals reached the same

* According to Eugene K. Bird, former American Commandant of Spandau prison, Hess's funeral ceremony has been laid down in detail for years.[10]

result. Having thus confirmed the legitimacy of the charge of "Crimes against Peace", the Nuremberg courts had little difficulty in deciding that Germany's wars against Poland, Denmark, Norway, Belgium, the Netherlands, Luxemburg, Yugoslavia, Greece, the Soviet Union and the United States were aggressive wars. The Tokyo tribunal came to the same conclusion with respect to Japan's wars against China, the British Commonwealth, France, the Netherlands, the Soviet Union and the United States. At Nuremberg the court's task was greatly aided by the circumstances that voluminous German military and diplomatic records had fallen into Allied hands at the end of the war, that Germans are meticulous record-makers and that Hitler and some of his subordinates had revealed their aggressive intentions very explicitly in the documents. There remained, however, the far more difficult question of which, if any, of the individual defendants could be held guilty of the "Crime against Peace".* By what standards should this sort of criminal liability be determined? It takes a number to plan and many to wage war, but knowledge of its aggressive or defensive character may be confined to a small group and even among members of the inner circle there may be disagreement. In Nazi Germany those close to Hitler and present at the meetings where he revealed his plans might legitimately be held to share his guilt and at the first Nuremberg trial most defendants convicted on the aggressive war charges were of that description.'[13]

As Taylor admits, the Nuremberg IMT did not find this point much of a stumbling block. It regarded the London Charter and its provisions as binding, although definition of 'aggressive war' had inevitably created difficulties during the drafting in London. A remark during the discussion by a representative of the Russian delegation is illuminating; 'When people speak about "aggression", they know what that means, but when they come to define it, they come up against difficulties which it has not been possible to overcome up to the present time.'[14] Nuremberg in no way solved the problem, as was strikingly confirmed in 1950 by the rapporteur of the United National International Law Commission; in 1950 he said: 'Any attempt to define aggression would be a pure waste of time.'[15]

There is still no universally accepted interpretation of the term 'aggression', though a definition has been agreed very recently in the United States. If it existed, the former victors would now be in some difficulty, since, if they followed the Nuremberg judgements, they would have to pronounce themselves guilty in respect of various events since 1945/6. To

---

* In the main trial before the IMT Göring, Hess, von Ribbentrop, Keitel, Rosenberg, Frick, Funk, Dönitz, Raeder, Jodl, Seyss-Inquart and von Neurath were found guilty of Crimes against Peace (see Sir David Maxwell-Fyfe's statement of the prosecution's case, IMT Vol. II, p. 48); in the subsequent 'minor' trials held by the Americans from 1947 to 1949 under the provisions of Control Council Law No. 10 of 20 December 1945 (Control Council Gazette No. 3 of 31 January 1946, pp. 50 ff.) forty-nine of the fifty-two defendants were acquitted on this count.

cite only a few of the acts of aggression and their instigators – there have been the Soviet interventions in Hungary in 1956 and Czechoslovakia in 1968, the British involvement in aggressive war against Egypt in October 1956, interventions by the British in Kuwait and the Americans in Lebanon, the USA's wars in Vietnam, Cambodia and elsewhere, the Israeli–Egyptian conflicts supported by the Americans and Russians. Viewed from the standpoint of the legal principles adopted in Nuremberg, all these must rank with Hitler's wars of aggression against, for instance, Poland, Belgium, Greece and the Soviet Union; some of them would undoubtedly have led to death sentences in Nuremberg.

In 1970 Telford Taylor dismissed the idea of an international court sitting in judgement on war crimes; he wanted the legality or illegality of the American commitment in Vietnam to be established by a purely American court; only to a limited degree did he accept the Nuremberg and Tokyo judgements as a guide, saying: 'There is no longer an international tribunal competent to render judgement,'[16] and a little further on: 'An American court undertaking to pass judgement on the legality of our Vietnam actions would have to review these and numerous other questions of comparable difficulty and complexity with little guidance from the Tokyo and Nuremberg judgements.' His argument that in this case the aggressor could not be established as clearly as in the Second World War, and that the intentions and motives of this aggressive war were different, is a weak one; it is only partially validated by his statements that 'at Nuremberg and Tokyo individuals were on trial' and that 'it was possible to declare the wars to be aggressive because of their proven intentions and declarations'.[17] As regards the Vietnam war, he argued, the question was not whether individuals were guilty of a crime against peace; the problem was that of the American citizens who, basing their case on Nuremberg, refused to serve in the Army in Vietnam or pay their taxes because they were not prepared to support the US government's aims and the government itself could not be indicted as an individual.* In his conclusion he completely ignored Nuremberg, saying: 'In terms of individual guilt of crimes against peace the question of intent might be decisive. But where only the "government" is the focus of inquiry, it might be quite impossible to determine the intent with which a particular decision was taken.'[18]

The IMT's judgement on the Reich government, however, states that it is 'clear that those members of the Reich Cabinet who have been guilty of crimes should be brought to trial'[19] – as in fact happened. The Reich Cabinet as such was acquitted by the IMT of being a criminal organization,

* Some of these Americans took the view that US intervention in Vietnam was not aimed at protecting the country from aggression in accordance with the United Nations Charter and the SEATO Treaty, but was merely an alibi for transformation of Vietnam into a military base against communism in South-East Asia and acquisition of the country's considerable mineral resources.

but its membership was not confined to the major war criminals who were condemned to death – Göring, Ribbentrop, Rosenberg, Frank and Frick. Decisions were taken in the USA comparable to those held punishable in Nuremberg and Tokyo; those who took or approved those decisions should have been brought before a court convened under the 1945 London Charter.

Since Nuremberg every President of the United States has embarked on military action abroad without the agreement of Congress – Truman in Korea, Eisenhower in Lebanon, Kennedy in Cuba, Johnson in Vietnam and the Dominican Republic, Nixon in Cambodia. Yet even Adolf Hitler was on no war criminals list in his lifetime and his headquarters was never bombed by the Allies, even though they knew precisely where it was.[20]

Jackson, the US Chief Prosecutor, said in Nuremberg that the law then being applied for the first time against German ministers, officers and senior officials should thenceforth 'condemn aggression by any other nation';[21] had this been implemented, the post-Nuremberg crimes committed all over the world in the form of wars of aggression should also have been brought to court as war crimes.

The IMT's charge of 'Crimes against Humanity' was a new one in law. The argument, put forward in all seriousness, that it was comparable to Hitler's doctrine of actions contrary to sound popular sentiment, is an irresponsible one in the light of the crimes committed under this Count. Criticism which draws comparisons and weighs these crimes against those committed by the former Allies both before and after Nuremberg does nothing to clarify the situation and in any case is usually made with inadequate knowledge of the facts.

A reader raised the question, for instance, in *The Times* of 28 May 1951:

'As for crimes against humanity, the most the Tribunal could bring against Raeder was that he was the indirect cause of the deaths of two British Commandos by reason of his passing on the "Commando Order" issued by his political superior, in doing which he was observing that principle of the subordination of the military power to the political that is virtually sacrosanct in our own country. I naturally do not wish to justify the killing of these two Commandos, but it would be useful if Sir Hartley Shawcross could say why Raeder's complicity – apparently only technical – in their execution was considered deserving of life imprisonment,* while the destruction of scores of thousands of Japanese men, women and children by atom bomb is to be regarded as entirely meritorious. If he cannot, the British service officer is bound to remain uncertain why Raeder received his fearful sentence or how he himself is to avoid a similar ghastly fate in another war.'

The shooting of the British commandos, who were in uniform, was not in fact charged under 'Crimes against Humanity' but under 'War Crimes'. Raeder had retired from active service at his own request in January 1943.

* Raeder was released in 1955.

He was nevertheless convicted of having been 'the indirect cause of the deaths of two British commandos' in Bordeaux on 10 December 1942, and also of having conducted unrestricted submarine warfare, sinking unarmed merchant ships and neutral ships and 'machine-gunning of survivors'.[22]

The IMT made transparent efforts to abide by the decisions of the London Conference; accordingly it interpreted the provisions of the Briand–Kellogg Pact[23] (signed in August 1928 by Germany among other countries) as 'extending' to charges against individuals and justifying the charge of Crimes against Peace.[24] These efforts exposed the fact that the IMT was 'creatively' interpreting the provisions of international law to the prejudice of the defendants and was also deliberately applying criminal law retrospectively. In addition, however, they exposed a certain hesitancy on the part of the Tribunal, obviously stemming from realization that, as far as war crimes were concerned, classic international law was being overridden and a new law applied[25] as contained in certain provisions of the London Charter[26] and Control Council Law No. 10. The most serious aspect was the court's refusal to allow the defence to use the argument of superior orders or to submit that the actions concerned were official and not taken in an individual capacity. Inevitably many Allied officers were opposed to this decision. Field Marshal Montgomery, for instance, stated on 26 July 1946: 'It is the duty of the soldier unquestioningly to obey all orders which the Army, that is the Nation, gives him.'[27]

One of the points made against the defendants was their failure to offer resistance to Hitler and his regime. The right and duty of resistance has long been a matter of debate in philosophical treatises; frequently – at the time of the French Revolution, for instance – it has been held to be legitimate. It has definitely not been universally accepted as an axiom and as indisputably legal and certainly was not in the German Reich as ruled by Hitler between 1933 and 1945. This of course was well known to the Americans in Nuremberg but they brushed it aside. Consequently they have not infrequently been reproached since Nuremberg for having lent support to a dangerous tendency. The Fulda Bishops Conference, for instance, thought that there should have been a court of appeal against the provisions of the London Charter and in October 1948 the German Cardinal Joseph Frings asked General Clay, the US High Commissioner, to obtain a decision invalidating the view of this matter taken in Nuremberg, at least for the future. In his letter written on behalf of the Conference, he said: 'A complex question of conscience may arise if a man is expected to make his own judgement or conform to supra-national norms when in doing so he runs contrary to the orders of his legal superiors. No country has so far had the courage to settle this question as far as its own citizens are concerned, still less to attach a threat of punishment to its decision.'[28]

There is a wide discrepancy between the principle, regarded as self-evident in all countries, of the citizen's duty to carry out orders and the

IMT's principle that the individual is subject to international law, thereby making him directly responsible under that law*; international law was therefore given precedence over the sovereignty of the State with inevitable disastrous consequences. In 1945/6, however, this was accepted neither by the prosecution nor the IMT Tribunal.

Despite the IMT's claim to be 'itself a contribution to international law',[30] the fact remains that the London Conference was not designed to produce a code of international law – like the Hague Agreement, for instance; the Charter merely demonstrated the signatories' intention to condemn certain Germans with the greatest possible certainty. This was undoubtedly a contributory factor to the IMT's defects and shortcomings from a formal legal point of view. The prosecution and the court, however, took a different view. In 1966, for instance, Robert M. W. Kempner stated: 'One of the myths is to the effect that in Nuremberg the defendants were sentenced for deeds which were not punishable at the time they were done. The overwhelming majority of the defendants, however, were sentenced for crimes which are punishable under the laws of any civilized state. Mass murder of Jews, Catholic priests, gypsies, prisoners of war, so-called useless mouths, baled-out enemy airmen, "racially undesirables" etc. is still murder and a crime against the eternal immutable law "Thou shalt not kill". This is not altered by the fact that in Nuremberg a new terminology for these crimes was used, such as Crimes against Humanity, genocide etc.'[31]

During the reading of the judgement on 30 September 1946 Nikitchenko quoted from Annex 2 to the Fourth Hague Agreement of 18 October 1907, citing Articles 49, 52, 53, 55 and 56 dealing with military authority in occupied enemy territories. These the IMT claimed as a basis in law, although the defence not unreasonably rejected them as obsolete in view of the numerous changes in the laws and customs of war which had arisen since 1907.[32] Articles 23h and 43, on the other hand, which dealt with the rights of the defeated, were ignored.

The Hague Agreement laid down that the occupying power should exercise legal authority 'respecting, unless absolutely prevented, the laws in force in the country'[33] and that 'the rights and requirements of nationals of the enemy Power' should neither be abrogated nor suspended.[34] The IMT, however, followed the London Charter, pronouncing that: 'The making of the charter was the exercise of the sovereign legislative power by the countries to which the German Reich had unconditionally surrendered; and the undoubted right of these countries to legislate for the occupied territories has been recognized by the civilized world.'[35]

Kempner subsequently expanded on this: 'It was in accordance with

---

* The IMT's judgement includes the following: 'That international law imposes duties and liabilities upon individuals as well as upon states has long been recognized ... The very essence of the Charter is that individuals have international duties which transcend national obligations.'[29]

the tradition of our legal history that the "victors" should be the executors of justice in the occupied country after the war. It would never have occurred to anyone that, during the German occupation of Holland or Belgium, it should have been left to the Dutch or Belgian courts instead of the German courts martial to pass judgement on similar crimes. The idea would never have entered anyone's head that, in the event of the invasion of Germany by Power X, crimes committed by that power's functionaries should have been left to the invading power's courts after he had been successfully driven out.'[36]

The IMT prosecutors and members of the Tribunal later spread the story that in the prostrate Germany of 1945 there was no possibility of bringing before German courts the persons named as major war criminals. This cannot be totally dismissed, but it is an entirely separate issue with no bearing on the statements made by the Allies from 1941 onwards demanding punishment of war criminals by the victor powers. Twenty years after the IMT had pronounced sentence Kempner explained: 'The question has often been raised why the Nazi criminals were not left to German justice. In fact during the immediate post-war period there was no properly functioning German legal system. Even the telephone lines and means of transport essential to an effective criminal proceeding did not exist. In numerous cases it was suggested to the German judicial authorities of the time that certain of the accused be brought before German courts – the notorious anti-semite Julius Streicher, for instance. Neither judicial nor political circles in the new Germany, however, wished to be burdened with such trials.'[37]

In 1945 there was no independent authority in a position to set up a genuinely international court composed of Allied, German and neutral judges; not only did this mean that the defendants were in a hopeless position but it also showed up the weakness of the system of international law, of which even its experts and creators had been dimly aware. The occasional quarrels between the victor powers buoyed up some of the defendants with false hopes that some decisive international development would come to their rescue; the results of these disagreements, however, were almost invariably unfavourable from their point of view; they died away to nothing and left the defendants still facing a cold blast. It was of no help to them, for instance, when one day the Palace of Justice was suddenly surrounded by French tanks, the French delegation having been told that the Americans proposed to arrest and 'abduct' to the United States a member of the House of Hohenzollern after interrogation by one of Jackson's staff. The defendants and their counsel were soon compelled to recognize that the French action had nothing to do with their case and was merely a French attempt to demonstrate to the three major partners, by whom they felt 'not fully accepted', both their presence and their ability to insist on their rights, by force if necessary.

The IMT maintained that the authority of international law, which had remained relatively unimpaired until the bolshevist revolution in Russia, had been flouted by most of the major defendants while in the service of Hitler; after the end of the Second World War, therefore, the defeated could expect no protection from it. They even found used against them the theory, accepted as a guiding principle both in Great Britain and the USA since the end of the nineteenth century, that not only the individual subject but also the highest political authority was subject to the 'might of the law' and that the law could limit the use of power. One of the most important legal problems raised by the Nuremberg Trial was the question whether the principle of the independent authority of international law was recognized or whether the victors should be accorded the right arbitrarily to modify that law in order to be able to punish as they wished the leaders of their defeated enemy according to their own ideas. This question the Allies answered in the way they had been preparing to do since 1941. They wanted neither an international nor a German court on the lines of that set up after the First World War.* They accordingly created the basis of law necessary to achieve their aims. Numerous striking pronouncements show that many reputable non-German international lawyers were opposed to this procedure. Even before the IMT had pronounced judgement, for instance, H. A. Smith, the British international lawyer, who thought that the IMT would take over from the Permanent Court of International Justice at The Hague, wrote that in the United Nations Charter and 'in many other solemn documents our government together with those of all other civilized countries has re-affirmed its loyalty to the supreme authority of international law. The Charter of the International Court, which is attached to the United Nations Charter, may be regarded as an accepted exposition of the principles of this law. It is here laid down that the Court shall reach its decisions on the basis of international conventions, international usage and "the principles of law generally recognized by civilized nations".[38] The phraseology used here corresponds to that in the Charter of the Permanent Court of International Justice, the successor to which is the new tribunal, and it must carry the same weight as was attributed to it in 1920.† The question we must ask ourselves is whether the Nuremberg Courts conform to this recognized rule.'[39] That they did not needs no further proof at this point.

There was no need for an International Tribunal to demonstrate that, so long as they were in Hitler's service, the accused were in no position to accept the independent authority of the law or of international law in the Anglo-American sense. Everyone knew that the law could be set aside at any time by Hitler's 'Führer orders'‡ and had been turned into an

* See pp. 20ff above.

† It was then laid down, as in all European criminal codes, that no one should be punished for an act which was not a breach of law when it took place.

‡ As an example, a decision of the Reichstag on 26 April 1942 (*Reichsgesetzblatt* I, p. 247) stated: 'There can be no doubt that, at the present stage of the war, the Führer

instrument of political power. As a result there was literally a world of difference between the outlook of the defendants and that of the court, except for the Soviet Union representatives, who basically thought like the Nazis. National-Socialist courts took their decisions as subordinate agencies of Hitler's leadership hierarchy and so acted as tools of the political authority, whose will they had to impose; the inevitable result, therefore, was a concept of law regarded as punishable – and not only in Nuremberg. In principle, therefore, the IMT could tolerate no classification or comparison of guilt* since, despite all the justified objections by the champions of continental international law, it regarded the basis of its case and of its judgement as legitimate.

Initially the defence laid much emphasis on the principle that no one should be punished for an action which was not a breach of the law at the time it was taken, but in the circumstances no other interpretation than that of the IMT was possible. Traditional concepts of legality had already lost all meaning and validity when Stalin and Hitler started to label certain actions as 'legally' punishable crimes simply because they were not in accordance with their own ideas. On 20 August 1942, for instance, Hitler said:

'The law is not an end in itself. Its function is to maintain public order ... All means used to this end are justifiable ... It must adapt itself to this end. The legislator cannot possibly catalogue or prescribe for every conceivable crime. It is the duty of the judge to pass sentence on the merits of the case. The Body Judicial must be recruited from the best elements of the nation. The judge must possess a keen sensitivity which permits him to grasp the intentions of the legislature ... It is essential that a judge have the clearest possible picture of the intentions of the legislature and the goal which this latter pursues ... The fact that the Executive intervenes ... in the application of the law must not ... be regarded as a violation of the judicial prerogative ... It is rather an attempt to coordinate the desires of the legislature and the duties of the Body Judicial, both of whom have the same object in view. The idea that the judge is there to give absolutely

---

must have the right which he requires to do anything serving or contributing to the attainment of victory. The Führer must therefore, without being bound by the existing rules of law, be in a position at any time to use any methods which seem suitable to him to compel any German to fulfil his duties and, in the event of a breach of these duties, to award the necessary punishment without regard to so-called well-established rights.'

* The *tu quoque* principle (a similar standard for similar findings) was disallowed by the IMT except in the case of the charge against Dönitz of violating international rules of submarine warfare. The IMT accepted that the Americans had waged unrestricted submarine warfare in the Pacific (see pp. 157ff above). The principle was also indirectly accepted in so far as German air warfare was concerned. Since German cities had been destroyed by Allied bombing, some of them (Dresden for instance) when an Allied victory was imminent or at least completely certain, the prosecution did not mention the German bombing of Rotterdam, Coventry or London.

irrevocable judgement, even if the world should come to an end as a result, is nonsense. The judge's primary duty, on the contrary, is to secure law and order for the community. The officers of the law must be the best-paid officials of the State, a corps d'élite whose whole education teaches them not to take cover behind the legislature but to have the courage to act on their own responsibility ... No Body Judicial conscious of its responsibilities and willing to assume them, will condone a shameful act. But should the government act shamefully, the law is in no position to prevent it ... If the government of a State is composed of indifferent individuals, then the Body Judicial can do nothing to correct the mistakes of the legislators. When the reins are in the hands of an honest and capable legislator, then the law can support him wholeheartedly in his task of strengthening the bonds of the national community and of thus laying the ideal foundation on which a healthy and dignified constitution can be built. The task of the judge is a mighty one ... He must be as ready to accept responsibility as the legislator himself; he must cooperate with him in the closest possible manner so that together they may protect society from destructive elements ... by such means as the times ... dictate ... The legislature will then find itself relieved of the necessity of for ever having to promulgate new laws ... There must be the closest collaboration between the State incarnate and the Body Judicial ... In my opinion it is vital that no judge ... be appointed who has not had previous administrative experience in the Party. A judge must have profound personal experience of the matters in which he will be called upon to pass judgement.'[40]

Hitler felt himself in no way bound by law; he declared that the law was in no position to prevent crime on the part of political rulers, as he proved conclusively over the years. After his death over 10,000 of his henchmen[41] had to pay for this by court sentences. Over 250 paid with their lives.[42] None of them could have cited international law in defence of his rights and none of them would have remained unscathed had they ignored the domestic laws in force or the Führer's orders. Keitel and Jodl would not have been the only officers to be brought before a firing squad had they really tried to make international law the rule governing their actions. Keitel's comment that, if he had to live his life under Hitler all over again, he would prefer death to obedience to certain of Hitler's directives, was the result of having his eyes opened for him by the IMT.

The Nuremberg Trial was conducted according to the rules of Anglo-American legal procedure with two parties contesting the case. The rules of the court were very different from those governing continental legal procedure. The court was not 'bound by technical rules of evidence';[43] it did not have to 'require proof of facts of common knowledge' but was to 'take judicial notice of them'.[44] This inevitably restricted the rights of the defendants. They were not allowed, for instance, to refer to the 'imposition and injustice of Versailles',[45] so that the defendants' reasoning and thinking behind some of their actions could not be explained by reference to facts. Moreover the court was able to study beforehand the cases presented by the defence, to abridge them, as happened in certain cases, and to demand to know the nature of the evidence to be presented by the defence in order to decide on its 'relevancy'.[46] The result was a sort of prior censorship by the prosecution. The problem was well illustrated by the court's consternation when Otto Kranzbühler, Dönitz's defence counsel, said blandly: 'I ask the Tribunal just to imagine what would have happened if, before the presentation of their case by the Prosecution, I had said that I should like to speak about the relevancy of the documents of the Prosecution.'[47]

The production of evidence and examination of the defendants were entirely in the hands of the prosecutors and defence counsel; the judges confined themselves to the purely formal conduct of proceedings. A German court follows the 'investigation principle' but this was superseded by the Anglo-American 'proceedings principle' under which the Bench, while having the sole prerogative of decision, was under no obligation to contribute to clarification of the facts of the case by intervening in the hearing of evidence. Obviously, in 1945/6, such procedure was not the best method of establishing the truth and arriving at a just finding and sentence. Moreover the prosecutors, in disregard of continental rules of procedure, refused to submit evidence from documents confiscated by the Allies when it might have exonerated the defendants.

This trial was largely based on documents, and their number, evaluation and presentation raised a considerable problem. They were all in the custody of the Allies, who selected them and sometimes arbitrarily altered them before issue (by the Americans).[48] Important evidence suddenly 'disappeared' when the defence required it. The weight of paper was enormous; IMT documents included: 17,000 pages of shorthand record* from 403 open sessions; thousands of pages of 'prosecution document books',† 'rebuttal books',‡ 'defence document books',§ 'briefs',¶ 'motions'‖ and finally the judgements together with the dissenting or supporting opinions of individual judges. In addition there were many thousands of affidavits – 38,000 signed by 155,000 people on behalf of

---

* The records for all thirteen Nuremberg trials combined ran to 150,000 pages.

† In all the trials combined these ran to 185,000 pages in each of the four languages (English, Russian, French and German).

‡ Rebuttal books were compiled and used by the prosecution to contest the defence's evidence.

§ Individual defence counsel compiled defence document books for each defendant, for the organizations under trial and for certain ranges of subject.

¶ These were primarily: prosecution briefs, opening speeches, statements and arguments by the prosecution and the defence, pleas in mitigation, general legal presentations and special exposés incriminating or exonerating the defendants.

‖ The so-called 'motions' by the prosecution and the defence dealing with particular matters concerning the conduct of business.

the political leaders, 136,213 on behalf of the SS, 10,000 on behalf of the SA, 7,000 on behalf of the SD, 3,000 on behalf of the General Staff and OKW and 2,000 on behalf of the Gestapo.[49] More than 35,000 defence witnesses, of whom some 25,000 were ex-SS members, had reported to the IMT secretariat by the beginning of January 1946.[50] So a mountain of paper had to be dealt with. It was therefore entirely understandable that there were misunderstandings, breakdowns and on occasions inaccuracies and errors, although the Allied authorities, despite the pressure of time, did an outstanding job.

The Nuremberg court called itself '*International* Military Tribunal' although the occupants of the Bench were drawn only from the four victor Powers; moreover none of them could be counted as a regular soldier. In 1945/6, therefore, the Germans, the peoples of the former Axis Powers, the Japanese and many others inevitably regarded it as an inter-allied victors' tribunal, from which justice was not to be expected. The Russians attempted to cover this more than ostensible 'flaw' in their appearance in Nuremberg by investing their judges with high military ranks. The result was ludicrous – Nikitchenko, their Member of the Tribunal, appeared as a Major-General and Volchkov, his Alternate, as a Lieutenant-Colonel. The more self-assured Americans did not even try; there were no genuine regular officers even among the judges for the twelve 'follow-up' trials which, different though their composition was, all took place under American aegis; all were selected by the United States War Ministry, nominated by the American Military Governor and given military rank for the period of their service in Nuremberg. The only genuine officers with the IMT were: the General Secretaries Mitchell (Brigadier-General) and Ray (Colonel), the Soviet Secretary Poltorak (Major), the Marshals Mays (Colonel) and Gifford (Lieutenant-Colonel), the Chief of Interpreters Dostert (Colonel) and Steer (Naval Commander), the head of the Administrative Section Bailey (Major), the head of 'Witness Notification and Procurement' Sullivan (Captain), the head of the 'Applications and Motions Section' Neave (Lieutenant-Colonel), the head of the 'Defendants' Information Center' Schrader (Lieutenant-Commander), the 'Editor of the Record' Egbert (Lieutenant-Colonel) and the 'Director of Printing' Roth (Captain).[51] Of the American Prosecution Counsel one of the two 'Executive Trial Counsel', two of the four 'Associate Trial Counsel' and fourteen of the sixteen 'Assistant Trial Counsel' had military rank ranging from Lieutenant to General. Of the British only the four 'Junior Counsel' were officers (two Majors, one Lieutenant-Colonel, one Colonel). Of the Russians the Chief Prosecutor was a General, the Deputy Chief Prosecutor a Colonel and of the seven Assistant Prosecutors one was a Captain, one a Lieutenant-Colonel and one a Colonel. No one in the French prosecuting team was an officer.[52]

None of the actual Members of the Military Tribunal was a regular soldier. The German officers arraigned as major war criminals and their defence counsel initially thought this an advantage, but they were soon disillusioned, primarily because the IMT would not accept superior orders as a defence. Otto Kranzbühler, defence counsel for Grand Admiral Dönitz, wrote: 'In the matter of military orders the Nuremberg courts were more or less prisoners of their own theories.'

In his 'reflections', which also covered the United States follow-up trials, Kranzbühler continued: 'In certain cases they [the courts] laid down that a military order was binding only when it was legally valid and that it was not legally valid if it prescribed something forbidden. This leaves out of account the overriding consideration that, according to peacetime standards, the typical warlike actions – killing of human beings and destruction of property, for instance – are forbidden. The problem, therefore, is: to what extent does the waging of war render such actions permissible and to what extent may the subordinate cite the views of his superior on this subject as a defence? The American courts largely relied on the assumption that war as a whole was a crime and that the waging of war was therefore no defence. The basic attitude seems to be to explain why the standards by which the obligation to obey orders was judged in Nuremberg were unacceptable to any army in the world.'[53] It was therefore not surprising that most of the criticism of the IMT on this point came from officers, primarily in the USA, Great Britain and France; they were mainly worried about the future of their profession.[54]

Under international law as set out in the Hague Convention of 1907 the State is responsible for the general correctness of behaviour of its armed forces; individuals may only be punished by the detaining Power if they have infringed the rules generally accepted at least until the Second World War.* This led the German military defendants, their defence counsel and others to ask whether a soldier should be punished for obeying a criminal order if he was unable to offer resistance to it. Only under severe pressure from the USA were the British prepared to try one of the senior German military commanders (Erich von Manstein). The French simply refused to do so. Neither during the trial nor afterwards was there general agreement on the success of Jackson's efforts not to let the punishment of German officers seem to be 'directed against the military profession'.†[55]

How short-sighted and unrealistic the IMT's judgements were in this respect is clear if one considers the roles – and not merely mechanical roles – in subsequent events played by members of the armed forces of the countries providing the judges and prosecutors at Nuremberg in 1945/6 – at Hiroshima and Nagasaki, in Korea and Indo-China, in Hungary and

---

* I: Infringements of the recognized rules of warfare by members of the armed forces. II: Illegitimate hostilities, using weapons, by persons not members of the armed forces. III: Espionage and treason. IV: Looting. Points III and IV above were not relevant in Nuremberg.

† See pp. 277ff below.

Czechoslovakia and in Vietnam, to mention only a few instances. In 1946 German officers were awarded the most severe sentences including 'death by hanging', held to be ignominious by soldiers the world over, and years of imprisonment; their successors, on the other hand, provided they belonged to the former victor countries, received very different treatment.[56]

In August 1945, when Hitler's Reich had already been non-existent for some months and the war crimes trial was about to open, the decision to drop atomic bombs on Hiroshima and Nagasaki was taken by one solitary man, Harry S. Truman, President of the United States. He was never worried by scruples and he never had to justify his decision before a court of law.[57] His argument that the atomic bomb had brought the war to an end and so, by making the invasion of Japan unnecessary, had saved $1\frac{1}{2}$ million casualties in killed and wounded[58] would not have told entirely in his favour before the Nuremberg prosecution, particularly seeing that the Russians did not yet possess the bomb and at least suspected that Hiroshima and Nagasaki were intended as warnings to them.

The crew (six officers, four sergeants, one corporal) of the aircraft which dropped the bomb on Hiroshima on 6 August 1945 were treated and regarded by everybody as heroes. Interviewed in 1975 Colonel Paul Tibbets, the crew commander,[59] said: 'I have never regretted it or been ashamed; I thought at the time that I was doing my patriotic duty in carrying out the orders given me.'[60] For Tibbets the fact that, as a result of these orders, 85,000 people in Hiroshima were killed instantaneously and a further 120,000 were never found was no concern of his, nor did he have to answer for the fact that his methods had been treacherous and underhand. His answers to journalists at the same interview make this quite clear:

Question: General, in Hiroshima it is said that you had overflown Hiroshima in your bomber and only made your run when you could be sure that the 'All Clear' signal had been given in the city and people would no longer be in their shelters but on the streets. Is that correct?
Answer: We had to reckon that the Japanese would try to engage us in aerial combat and shoot us down. So we had to play one or two tricks. My tactics were to send a single aircraft into the target zone on each of the three days before D Day. The idea was that the Japanese should assume that it was only a reconnaissance aircraft and should also think so when we arrived with the bomb.
Question: You were, so to speak, putting on a show for Hiroshima?
Answer: We wanted to deceive the Japanese. When we arrived with the bomb, we wanted them to think: 'Oh, it's only another reconnaissance plane.'
Question: Early on the morning of the day on which you dropped the bomb did you carry out this deception manoeuvre once more?
Answer: We despatched an aircraft to check the weather. There was an

alert in Hiroshima when this aircraft arrived. Then it turned away and the 'All Clear' signal was given in the town. And then we arrived.[61]

Probably the most publicized incident is that of the American massacre of civilians at My Lai in Vietnam. The junior officer immediately responsible was Lieutenant William L. Calley. Initially he was sentenced by court martial to life imprisonment and discharged from the Army with ignominy, but this was soon commuted to twenty years' and finally ten years' imprisonment and in October 1974 he was released. Even while under arrest President Nixon had granted him the privilege of house arrest. The US Army protested against his release, but this was no more than an attempt to find a scapegoat for the numerous massacres in Vietnam. Calley was soon a free man again, feted as a 'hero' by the public and able to make considerable capital out of his murderous activities.[62] None of his superiors, neither General Westmoreland, commanding in Vietnam, nor Melvin Laird, the Defence Minister, nor President Johnson were ever indicted for this crime or for the bombings of the civilian population in Vietnam, though they had issued the orders.

An article in *Times Herald* of 8 August 1953 clearly indicated that the only reason why there have been no trials comparable to the IMT since 1945 has been the absence of clear-cut victory. It said: 'The American Army had prepared at least sixty trials for enemy war crimes ... But not a word is heard about them now ... The reasons are clear. In Korea we have not won a military victory giving us the right to deal with our enemies as we wish without worrying about how we should have to tailor the "law".'

In mid-November 1945 a Select Committee of the US Senate published a report on the machinations and murder plans of the CIA, the American Secret Service. It gave full details of the plans and methods to be used for the 'elimination' of Fidel Castro, Patrice Lumumba, Rafael Trujillo, General Rene Schneider and Ngo Dinh Diem;[63] The order for the murder of Lumumba was given personally by President Eisenhower.[64] Here, fifteen years after Nuremberg, were the United States authorities providing weapons, money, poison and other things for the murder of foreign statesmen and soldiers whom they found tiresome – a situation far worse than that disclosed in Kaltenbrunner's report to Himmler of 30 December 1944 about the plan to murder General Mesny.*

To the IMT, sitting in Nuremberg, the 'outside world' was miles away. Even while the trial was being prepared, the victor powers were committing crimes which logically should have been brought before a 'Nuremberg tribunal' (during the proceedings Jackson 'proclaimed' that the law as applied in Nuremberg should in future apply to nationals of the victor powers). After the German surrender, for instance, the British assisted the Soviets in a crime resulting in the deaths of thousands of Cossacks near Lienz, Austria. The fact that neither the Nuremberg defendants nor

* See pp. 201ff above.

their counsel were informed is unimportant, since, as a matter of principle, comparisons of guilt were not permitted in front of the IMT. How far the British, Russian and French delegations to the IMT were in the know cannot be established; the American prosecutors knew nothing.[65] Considerable publicity has recently been given to these horrors by Count Nicolai Tolstoy's book *Victims of Yalta* and the debate to which it has given rise. There is no need to go into the details here.

On the surface all this is no different from the horrors and atrocities for which the IMT sentenced the defendants in Nuremberg. None of the British officers or officials responsible, however, were ever brought before either a national or international court. Instead they completed a normal, and in many cases successful, career.

As far as the Russians were concerned, during the Nuremberg Trial they had sworn that they accepted international law as a legal basis and they joined the Western Allies in emphasizing this over and over again. After the trial, however, their glaring violations of international law in connection with their westward territorial expansion showed how little stock they really took of it. Though shortly after Nuremberg they were already accusing the Americans, British and French of being 'imperialists', it was they and their 'satellites' who took possession of German territories. In 1945 they simply annexed East Prussia, Silesia and other German eastern territories and in addition they robbed the German inhabitants of those districts of their property, a further violation of the universally recognized provisions of international law. Under Article 55 of the Hague Convention on Land Warfare, adduced by the IMT as one of the bases of its case, the 'occupying power' has the right to act as 'administrator and beneficiary of public properties, forests and agricultural concerns'; under Article 46, however, it is not entitled to confiscate the private property of the inhabitants. The Hague Convention may be considered obsolete in some respects, but the Russians were also violating the provisions of the Kellogg Pact.[66] After Nuremberg they violated not only the Nuremberg Charter but also both the letter and spirit of international law, the laws of war and the right of self-determination as set out in the Atlantic Charter, the 1949 Geneva Convention, numerous UNO declarations and the Vienna Treaty of 1969. The German civil population, of whom over 2 million lost their lives, was driven from their homes under horrifying conditions and never allowed to return. Russian, Polish and Czechoslovak nationals were settled in the annexed German territories, all of which is contrary to international law under the provisions of Articles 8 and 22 of the 1949 Geneva Convention.[67]

Punishment of a defeated enemy by the victors is an idea that has constantly reappeared ever since 321 BC, when the Roman legions were surrounded and disarmed by the Samnites at the Caudine Forks pass and publicly humiliated by passing with bowed head beneath a yoke formed of three spears. Nothing comparable occurred when the Thirty Years War ended in 1648 although the devastation, killing and looting had been unparalleled; future peace-breakers were merely warned of the consequences. But this does not provide adequate grounds for the criticism that until Nuremberg no one had ever thought of punishing war criminals. The trials before the Reich Court in Leipzig after the First World War prove the opposite.

The case of Napoleon Bonaparte, who had much in common with Hitler, provided the best indication of what would inevitably happen one day – punishment of the peace-breaker who had lost the war. Napoleon should have been taken to court and made to answer for what he had done, as proposed by General von Gneisenau, Blücher's Chief of Staff. The British, who were not in the firing line at the time, were against this. Nevertheless Wellington, Clancarty, Cathcart and Stewart joined with Austria, Portugal, Spain, Prussia, France, Russia and Sweden in signing the declaration of 13 March 1815, clearly directed against Napoleon; among other things it said that the former Emperor had proved to be an incorrigible enemy of public order and could henceforth claim protection from no treaty or law. 'Napoleon Bonaparte,' it went on, 'has placed himself without the pale of civil and social relations ... and ... as an enemy and disturber of the tranquillity of the world ... has rendered himself liable to public vengeance.'[68]

Banishment on the Napoleonic model was a sentence which Hermann Göring 'feared'[69] might be meted out to him and his co-defendants at Nuremberg. Before 1941 few legal experts would have dared prophesy that Göring and the other defendants would be indicted as individual criminals, as eventually happened. Until the Allies started preparing to punish Germans, the law, largely held to be self-evident by the IMT, was not regarded as an overriding principle by either side.

The IMT was not an international court of justice but a victors' tribunal. It followed the American tradition of putting an enemy in the dock and imposing sanctions on him as a punishment for having gone to war. During the Mexican war of 1845–8, for instance, the American General Winfield Scott arranged for military commissions to punish violations of the laws of war by American troops against the Mexican population and by Mexican civilians against the American troops. During the War of Independence of 1776–83 an American Captain, Nathan Hale, was brought before a British court martial and a British Major, John André, before a 'Board of General Officers' convened by George Washington; both were sentenced to death for espionage and executed.[70] In Nuremberg, however, punishment for war crime was meted out only to Germans.

The missionary faith in the trial's educational effect, with which almost everyone in Nuremberg was inspired, came from America. Ever since the War of Independence Americans had tended to regard any war against the USA as a crime; criminal proceedings and other sanctions were regarded as providing moral justification for political measures. Criticism of Nuremberg was therefore aimed primarily at the USA, which, after all, had been providing Great Britain with warships as early as 1940,[71] although Hitler did not declare war on the USA until December 1941, after Pearl Harbor.

The man who exerted the greatest personal influence on the drafting of the London Charter[72] and was the most insistent upon it as the legal basis for Nuremberg was Robert H. Jackson, the US Chief Prosecutor. Though he was the target of much criticism and numerous attacks were made on him while the trial was in progress, he obviously did not wish to answer them himself at the time. In 1947, however, when the major war criminals sentenced to death had long since been executed, he arranged for his son, W. E. Jackson, who had been a member of the US delegation at Nuremberg, to take up the cudgels in public on his behalf – not the happiest of solutions, as the results showed. W. E. Jackson wrote: 'Ever since the Nuremberg trials of major Nazi criminals ended ... there has been a crescendo of debate concerning the legality of the proceedings. Violent attacks have been made by one fanatical circle. Some people are satisfied with labelling Judge Jackson an "extremely corrupt politician" and a "mountebank in judge's robes" who is "ready to sell at a price all principles of legal procedure". Others, for whom the scapegoat theory is gospel, maintain that the trial was a gigantic Jewish conspiracy, the voice being Jackson's voice but the real string-pullers Rosenman and Baruch[73] ... The sharpest attack has come from the professional soldiers who contend that it was unjust to condemn Generals and Admirals for defending their country.'[74]

At the start of the trial, it will be remembered, Robert Jackson himself had admitted that it might not be a shining example of 'finished crafts-manship' and had gone on to emphasize the difficulties facing the organizers and the prosecution. He had then, in tones of emotional optimism, appealed to history as a sort of supreme court for the future which, with the methods available to it, would balance the arguments of the prosecution and the judges against those of the defence and the defendants, setting them against the facts, and then setting the trial itself in its correct historical perspective.* History, however, cannot yet give a final verdict.

If, for instance, history starts from the premiss that Nuremberg was an instrument of Allied foreign policy – which is easily demonstrable – then its purely legal aspect and claim to legality inevitably appear as dis-tortions. If history accepts that the IMT represented a revolutionary development in international law – which it was – it must also accept that objection to the *ex post facto* application of the Nuremberg principles, though hallowed by tradition, is an obsolete one and that this historic event cannot be judged from the viewpoint of conventional law. If it accepts the IMT's claims and its legal basis as valid in international law in the sense postulated by the IMT in 1945/6, it cannot avoid recognizing the

* Jackson's opening address – see pp. 85ff above.

sentences on, for instance, Dönitz* and Jodl as justified. If, however, history judges these sentences in the light of the crimes committed, both under international and criminal law, by the former Allies between 1939 and 1945 and even more later (in Korea and Vietnam for instance), it cannot do other than characterize those sentences as an illegal act (of vengeance). Finally, if history accepts occasional utterances by both the prosecutors and members of the Tribunal, it must inevitably accuse the IMT of misusing the legal process for the furtherance of political power. Douglas, one of the nine US Supreme Court judges, said of the Tokyo Tribunal: 'It did not sit as a judicial tribunal. It was solely an instrument of political power.'[76] It is difficult to place any other interpretation on the remark made by Robert Jackson on 24 November 1945 that the Nuremberg IMT must prove to Germany and the world that the Hitler government was as wicked and criminal as the Americans had represented it to be.[77]

A further point affecting the IMT and the view taken of it is that neither the USA nor any of the other three countries under whose aegis the IMT took place wanted to take responsibility for the twelve US follow-up trials in Nuremberg which dealt with 175 defendants and ostensibly sat as international courts. In 1948 some of the German defence counsel, in order to ensure fair conduct of these trials, sent a telegram to the US President requesting cancellation of certain restrictions imposed by the American Military Governor for the American Occupation Zone; the answer from the US Ministry of War was that, in view of the international character of the Nuremberg proceedings, the United States had no jurisdiction in the matter.[78] The Americans refused to take responsibility although they were in sole charge of the trials.

In the summer of 1949 the Bishop of Chichester asked the British government for clarification. The reply given by Henderson, the Under-Secretary of State, was: 'His Majesty's Government has no responsibility for proceedings taken subsequent to the conclusion of the International Trial in Nuremberg.'[79] Numerous remarks and statements by prominent personalities in the victor countries, some of them with no direct responsibility for events in Nuremberg, betray a sense of disquiet, of guilt and self-criticism. The US Senator Robert Taft, for instance, said: 'In these trials we have accepted the Soviet Russian view that a trial is directed towards a certain purpose; in other words we have been pursuing the aims of government policy, not justice. By dressing up politics in the form of legal procedure we have discredited the idea of justice in Europe for many years to come. All the sentences pronounced in Nuremberg were permeated by the spirit of vengeance.'[80] During a debate in November 1950 on the

---

* With reference to the sentence on Dönitz Telford Taylor wrote in 1970: 'Inferentially though not explicitly the judgement of Nuremberg was repudiated by a later Nuremberg court that acquitted on the same charge commanders of much higher rank than Dönitz on the ground that they were not at the "policy level". Although this pronouncement made nonsense of the Dönitz judgement it has not been explicitly retracted.'[75]

legal principles adopted in Nuremberg the Legal Committee of the UN General Assembly stated: 'Germans were sentenced and executed on the basis of principles, the legal validity of which is now contested.'[81]

The main impression left by events in Nuremberg on Charles F. Wennerstrum, a member of the Supreme Court of Iowa who acted as President for 'Case VII' in the follow-up trials, was one of disillusionment. He said: 'Had I known seven months ago what I know today, I would never have come here [to Nuremberg]. The high ideals proclaimed as guiding principles when these courts were set up have not been realized. The prosecution has failed to retain its objectivity uninfluenced by desire for vengeance or personal ambition to obtain verdicts of guilty. The whole atmosphere here is an unhealthy one. Many of the lawyers, secretaries, interrogators and investigators employed here have only become Americans in recent years. Their personal past is rooted in the hatreds and prejudices of Europe.'[82]

In 1967 Lord Shawcross, the British Chief Prosecutor at the IMT, wrote: 'The point now is what effect this trial will have on the future course of history. In this I must confess to great disillusionment. During the trial we had close friendly relations with our Russian colleagues despite the fact that we raised violent objection to their inclusion of the Katyn massacre in the Indictment. We thought that we were on terms of confidence with the Russians and would keep them as friends. But when the trial was over and they went back to Russia, we lost all contact with them. All attempts to gain touch with them again failed. This communist veto on normal human relationships is a sad fact. Even sadder were the cynical violations of international law as created in Nuremberg which we have had to witness meanwhile – Korea, Hungary, Kashmir, Algeria, Congo, Vietnam. Our Nuremberg hope that we had made some contribution to transition to a peaceful world under the rule of law has not been fulfilled.'[83]

During the actual trial Sir Norman Birkett, the British Alternate Member of the Tribunal, had made a statement not unlike that of Robert Taft. In a private letter written in April 1946 he lamented that 'the trial is only in form a judicial process and its main importance is political'.[84]

Sixteen years later Francis Biddle, the American Member of the Tribunal, openly admitted: 'We were an international Bench and looked at our legal and political obligations from different angles. Diplomatic horse-trading was combined with the duties of the judge. It necessarily played some part in certain decisions since an agreed judgement would not have been possible otherwise ... In our deliberations we could not leave out of account the effect of our decisions on public opinion.'[85]

In 1947, after sentence had been pronounced on the Germans convicted as major war criminals, Judge Donnedieu de Vabres, the French Member of the Tribunal, expressed himself most diplomatically, saying that the sentences were 'an expression of human, and therefore relative and fallible justice'; they could not be characterized as sentences of revenge, although they 'probably coincided neither with the judgement of history nor with that of God'.[86]

Telford Taylor's comments reflect particularly clearly the change of view that has taken place on Nuremberg and the subsequent 'minor' trials. He totally rejects any idea that their purpose was vengeance through a process of law and champions the entirely inaccurate notion that the IMT was never intended to provide a historical analysis of what happened under the Hitler Reich. In April 1949 he wrote: 'Nuremberg's influence on world politics is of a high order, both now and in the long term.'[87]

On 11 October 1950 the *Chicago Daily News* reported: 'Telford Taylor proposed yesterday ... creation of a UNO tribunal to punish all war crimes committed in Korea – by Koreans, the UN Allies and even the Russians. The Prosecutor said in an interview ... that trials must not be run on the lines of those at Nuremberg when only the defeated Germans were in the dock. "If international law is to have meaning," he said, "we must bring both sides to court or alternatively admit that extenuating circumstances are valid for both sides and let everyone go their own way."'

In 1949 Taylor wrote: 'It is undoubtedly a dim but growing awareness that we have deeply committed ourselves to the Nuremberg principles by undertaking to judge men under them and punish men for their violation that explains the comment one so often hears today that "Nuremberg has established a dangerous precedent".'[88] By 1970 he was resigned, saying: 'Somehow we failed ourselves to learn the lessons we undertook to teach at Nuremberg and that failure is today's American tragedy.'[89]

Nevertheless the view was, and still is, held that in principle it is not right to criticize the IMT. The World War generation in the United States, for instance, looks upon the IMT almost as an immutable law of nature and is still sensitive to any criticism of it as a tribunal of victors that perhaps created a new global or historical law of morality,[90] but otherwise merely giving rise to embarrassment and justified criticism. The view generally held in America – though an untenable one for the historian – that the prosecution was correct in presenting the Nazi tyranny as a 'conspiracy' from its inception, still raises passions among the 'old Nuremberg hands' – those who were actually there.

In course of time the arguments of people who feel that they must defend Nuremberg against all criticism have become out of date; they were never very good anyway. A typical example is a comment by Sir David Maxwell-Fyfe, the British Deputy Chief Prosecutor, that 'there have been no more skilled apologists in the past than German professors and historians'.[91] In the same vein Gerhard Gründler, the German journalist who edited the Social Democrat newspaper *Vorwärts* until 1976 and was co-author of the book *Das Gericht der Sieger*, published in 1967, recommended his readers to 'adjust their standards' if they thought that Nuremberg had merely applied the law of vengeance.[92] Realistic criticism of the IMT is not synonymous with apology for and defence of the past nor is it tantamount to saying that the law of vengeance alone was applied in Nuremberg.

The Germans above all people were largely ignorant of the horrors to which an end had to be put by force at the price of enormous sacrifices. The fact that they became known to the world through the medium of the IMT has clouded the German people's judgement of the Nuremberg Trial. Very many Germans considered the revelations at the trial to be extravagant exaggerations produced as an excuse for application of the law of vengeance. For German listeners this negative attitude was reinforced by the intolerable day-to-day presentation of the trial over the radio by Gaston Oulman, the radio commentator convicted as an impostor shortly afterwards. It was not surprising, therefore, that the criticism of those who were asking themselves whether victory was to be the basis of future law fell on willing ears. Even during the trial a question-mark hung over it in that Russians were acting as prosecutors and judges when they had been on the same side as the defendants for a time, had waged aggressive wars on Finland and Japan and had committed fearful crimes in East Prussia, Silesia, Pomerania and Mecklenburg in 1944/5. The subsequent policy of the victors did nothing to erase these impressions.

Nuremberg did not succeed in producing what the victors clearly intended – an exemplary definition of punishable guilt for crimes stemming from the Nazi ideology and its system of domination. Inevitably conflicting analyses were the result.[93] A contributory factor was the IMT's didactic prescription of standards of behaviour basically unattainable by future mankind.

In most of the treatises dealing with Nuremberg the effect of the trial on major political developments is judged by the fact that the London Charter and to some extent also the IMT's judgements are reflected not only in the United Nations Charter and the Convention for the Protection of Human Rights and Basic Freedoms but also in numerous laws and constitutions. In the light of the facts, however, this is not an invariably accurate statement, as a number of examples show. Here there is no need to do more than compare such statements with the constitutions of the two halves of the nation on whose political and military leaders the IMT sat in judgement. Article 5, for instance, of the German Democratic Republic's constitution of 7 October 1949 lays down: 'The generally recognized rules of international law are binding on the State executive and on every citizen. Maintenance and preservation of friendly relations with all peoples is the duty of the State executive. No citizen may participate in warlike action designed to oppress a people.'[94] There is no need to point out that in this context 'oppression' can be exercised only by capitalist countries. This being so, the Soviet Russian interventions in Korea, in central Germany (after the popular rising of 17 June 1953 and construction of the Berlin Wall on 13 August 1961), in Vietnam, in Hungary and Czechoslovakia, in Egypt and finally in Rhodesia (arms deliveries in 1976) are justified. In the light of this the 'generally recognized rules of international law' lose some of the authority attributed to them in Nuremberg; moreover Article 5 concludes by describing 'service in defence of the Fatherland and the achievements of the workers' as 'a national duty for the citizens' of East Germany. The treaty between the Soviet Union and the German Democratic Republic of 7 October 1975, reflecting the total Eastern orientation of East German foreign policy, shows that the references to international law are mere lip-service.*

In the Federal Republic crimes against humanity have been punishable under Paragraph 220a of the criminal code since 1954, when the country adhered to the Genocide Agreement. Going further back, under Article 26 of the Basic Law preparations for aggressive war and actions 'likely or intended to disturb the peaceful co-existence of peoples' are forbidden; under Article 25 the individual citizen is obligated to obey the rules of international law which override German domestic law. This leaves open the question whether the criminality of aggressive war as laid down in Nuremberg is regarded as valid under international law. The fact that under Article 25 the general rules of international law are made an integral part of German federal law and that preparation of aggressive war is specifically stated to be punishable in Article 26 is clearly based on the idea (or the fear?) that current international law does not regard aggressive war as punishable – despite Nuremberg.

With its Article 26 the Basic Law, which was drafted under the shadow of Nuremberg, included in its instructions to the German citizen the judgement of the IMT in addition to the rules of international law, which in its view were valid (and shortly after Nuremberg thought to be enforceable). Since preparation for aggressive war (in contrast to officially ordered war crimes and crimes against humanity) is not criminally justiciable by national courts, provisions of this nature are necessarily no more than mere verbiage and flowery phrases. Though punished as a crime in Nuremberg, such a policy cannot normally either be prevented or punished by national courts. The IMT decided that members of a government who, in that capacity, themselves created a law of the land bringing them into conflict with international law should not in future be able to cite in their defence a law for which they themselves were responsible.[95] Moreover in the Nuremberg follow-up trials, which dealt with persons who were not members of the government, it was laid down that they too must obey current international law as a matter of priority[96] despite the fact that up to that time not only continental European but also Anglo-American international lawyers had held the opposite view.

Before Nuremberg the definition produced by Oppenheim, senior legal

---

* Since the conclusion of the treaty, if ever the USSR is attacked East Germany, Bulgaria, Rumania and Hungary are bound to provide the Russians with military assistance. In the revised East German constitution of 7 October 1974 it was laid down that East Germany shall 'for ever and irrevocably be allied to the USSR', a clause which, in view of the relative strengths of the two countries, could have unpredictable consequences.

adviser to the British Admiralty for years and generally regarded as one of the greatest authorities on international law, was considered authoritative: 'Should some precept of the laws of a country be in indubitable contradiction to some precept of international law, then local courts should apply the former.'[97] Even twenty-five years after its publication this still seemed to international lawyers to be an incontestable principle. The following extract from the judgement in the OKW trial, however, not only shows that the US military court – following the example of the IMT – brushed the question aside but also illustrates the problems inevitably raised thereby for the legislators and citizens of the future. The OKW judgement says: 'International law ... may ... limit the obligations which individuals owe to their states and create for them international obligations which are binding upon them to an extent that they must be carried out even if to do so violates a positive law or directive of State.'[98]

Articles 25 and 26 of the Federal Republic's Basic Law reflect this problem yet once more.

The present and future problem is not what happened in Nuremberg after the end of the Second World War but what happened after that – and what is still to come.

Crimes against peace, aggression, violations of the laws of war and crimes against humanity have not been swept away either by mere humiliation of a defeated enemy as at the Caudine Forks, or by treaties such as those of Osnabrück and Münster where christian piety was the watchword, or by the Holy Alliance between Russia, Austria and Prussia, the terms of which sound more like a sermon than a political agreement,[99] or by the Treaty of Versailles, generally considered to be of unparalleled severity. Shame has proved to be no preventive. Practice has not followed the christian message of love of one's neighbour and reliance on the mercy of God; the savage sanctions of Versailles after the First World War produced the opposite of what the victors anticipated. Their results – Hitler, the Second World War and Nuremberg – were so patently obvious that the IMT forbade the defendants and their counsel to mention them as justification or motivation.

Nuremberg, the example *par excellence* of the victors sitting in judgement on the vanquished, intended both as a symbol and a light in the darkness, has not succeeded in giving mankind an assurance of peace. Post-Nuremberg judicial confirmation of personal responsibility for crimes against peace, criminal violations of the laws of war and crimes against humanity have been of no practical value. Labelling men 'war criminals' achieved practically nothing; it carries little weight among men of that ilk; the terms 'just war' and 'unjust war' generally do not apply exclusively to the actions of one side only. Comparison on political, religious, moral and humanitarian grounds of the IMT and its judgements with the crimes for which death sentences and long sentences of imprisonment were pronounced in Nuremberg and Tokyo ultimately proves to be mere theorizing without noticeable practical result.

Those who have to answer for crime do not ask why, primarily because it is not in their power to do so.[100] The threat of being subjected to Nuremberg-type punishment does not intimidate them as long as no institution exists capable of bringing them to court and perhaps to the gallows. And even were there such an institution, they would continue to wreak destruction to the very end, as Hitler did in Germany's case since he prophesied Germany's extinction as a result of surrender. The murderer caught in the act, who knows that his life will be ended by guillotine as soon as he is brought to court and convicted, does not generally react very sensibly. The Allied demand for unconditional surrender had a similar effect.

Despite all the criticism made of it in 1945 the Nuremberg Trial was essential and not only for the future of mankind. Before it the great developments in world politics had been personified by the men who became the wartime leaders – Hitler, Mussolini,[101] Stalin, Roosevelt and Churchill. These developments ended in the Second World War and were the subject of the victors' proceedings in Nuremberg. The very different ends which these men met were not unconnected with Nuremberg and its preparation from 1941 onwards.

Hitler committed suicide in 1945. Mussolini had been shot without trial by his political opponents shortly before. The other leading figures of this period of history, though in some cases no less incriminated than Hitler and Mussolini, died in their beds as honoured statesmen. If the problem revolved solely round these men as individuals and round the major war criminals sentenced in Nuremberg in 1946 as violators of international law, then the historian would merely be able to take note with some detachment of the double standards by which these men were judged. But the historian cannot remain detached, not because of the fate of these men but because the authority of international law is still being flouted by statesmen, politicians and military men. Since Nuremberg and Tokyo the historian inevitably feels himself bound to take up the cudgels on behalf of international law in face of the attitude of politicians who are the people least prepared to learn from history.[102]

The victors of 1945 took a revolutionary step and the historian must accept it. Nuremberg having happened, however, it is now the responsibility, not only of the victors of that time but even more of their heirs and of every other nation, to show, by their attitude to international law, what value history is to place on the victors' tribunal.

Appendices

THE COMMISSAR ORDER

OKW Operations Staff/Section L (IV/Qu)   Führer H.Q.   6.6.41
No. 44822/41   TOP SECRET   By Hand of Officer only
Further to the Führer decree of 14 May regarding the exercise of military juris-
diction in the area of 'Barbarossa' (OKW/Ops. St/Sec. L IV/Qu No. 44718/41
Top Secret) the attached document 'General Instructions on the Treatment of
Political Commissars' is forwarded herewith.

It is requested that its distribution be limited to Commanders of Armies and
Air Fleets and that it be further communicated to lower commands by word of
mouth.

> Chef des Oberkommandos der Wehrmacht
> By Order   Signed   Warlimont.

[Nuremberg Document NOKW–1076]

Annexe to OKW/Ops. St/Sec. L IV/Qu No. 44822   TOP SECRET
Instructions on the Treatment of Political Commissars
In the struggle against Bolshevism it must *not* be assumed that the enemy's conduct
will be based on principles of humanity or of international law. In particular hate-
inspired, cruel and inhuman treatment of prisoners can be expected on the part
of *all grades of Political Commissars*, who are the real leaders of resistance.

The troops must be made aware that:

1. To show consideration to these elements during this struggle or to act in accordance with international rules of war is wrong and endangers both our own
   security and the rapid pacification of conquered territory.
2. Political Commissars have initiated barbaric, Asiatic methods of warfare. Consequently they will be dealt with *immediately and with maximum severity*. As
   a matter of principle they will be shot at once whether captured during operations or offering resistance.

The following regulations will apply:

1. Theatre of Operations
   (i) Political Commissars *who oppose our forces* will be treated in accordance
   with the decree on 'The Exercise of Military Law in the area of Barbarossa'.
   This applies to every kind and rank of Commissar, even if only suspected of
   resistance or sabotage or incitement to resist. In this connection see 'General
   Instructions on the Conduct of Troops in Russia'.
   (ii) Political Commissars *serving with enemy forces* are recognizable by their
   distinctive insignia – a red star interwoven with a hammer and sickle on the
   sleeve (details in 'Armed Forces of the USSR' – OKH Gen. StdH OQu Section
   IV, Foreign Armies East (II) No. 100/41 of 15.1.41, annexe 9d). They will
   immediately – on the battlefield – be separated from other prisoners. This is
   essential to prevent them influencing other prisoners in any way. These Commissars will not be recognized as soldiers. The protection afforded to prisoners
   of war by international law will not apply in their case. After being segregated
   they will be liquidated.

(iii) Political Commissars who are neither guilty nor suspected of being guilty of hostile actions will initially be exempt from the above measures. Only as our forces penetrate further into the country will it be possible to decide whether remaining officials should be allowed to stay where they are or whether they should be handed over to the *Sonderkommandos*, who should where possible carry out the investigation themselves. In reaching a verdict of 'guilty or not guilty' greater attention will be paid to the character and bearing of the Commissar in question than to his offence, for which corroborative evidence may not be forthcoming.

(iv) Under (i) and (ii) a short report (on report proforma) on the case will be forwarded:

(a) by divisional units to divisional headquarters (Intelligence Section)

(b) by units directly subordinate to a Corps, Army Group or Armoured Group to the Intelligence Section at Corps etc. headquarters.

(v) None of the above measures must be allowed to interfere with operations. Systematic screening and mopping-up operations by combat units will therefore not take place.

2. In the Communications Zone

Commissars apprehended in the Communications Zone for acting in a suspicious manner will be handed over to the Einsatzgruppen or Einsatzkommandos of the SD.

3. Modification of General or Regimental Courts Martial

General and Regimental Courts Martial will not be responsible for carrying out the measures in Sections 1 and 2.

APPENDIX 2

THE COMMANDO ORDER

The Führer   Führer Headquarters   18.10.1942

No. 003830/42   OKW Operations Staff

TOP SECRET

1. For some time now our enemies have been using methods of warfare which do not conform to the Geneva international agreements. Members of the so-called Commandos who, as has been established, are in some cases recruited from the ranks of ex-criminals in enemy countries, act in a particularly brutal and underhand manner. Captured orders show that they are instructed not only to handcuff prisoners but to kill defenceless prisoners out of hand whenever they think that such prisoners may constitute an encumbrance or other obstacle to the pursuit of their objectives. Finally orders have been found prescribing the killing of prisoners as a matter of principle.

2. Consequently it was announced in an annexe to the Wehrmacht report of 7.10.1942 that in future Germany would adopt the same procedure against these sabotage troops of the British and their hirelings, in other words that they will be ruthlessly shot down in battle by German troops wherever they appear.

3. I therefore order:

In all so-called commando operations in Europe or in Africa from now on the enemy, whether or not ostensibly soldiers in uniform or members of a raiding party, whether with or without arms, whether in battle or in flight, will be killed to the last man by German troops. It is immaterial whether, for the purpose of these operations, they have landed from ships or aircraft or jumped by parachute. Even when, on discovery, these people ostensibly make preparations to give themselves up, no quarter will be given them on principle. A full report on each individual case will be rendered to OKW for inclusion in the Wehrmacht report.

4. Should individual members of such commandos acting as agents, saboteurs, etc. fall into the hands of the Wehrmacht through other channels – the police, for instance, in territories occupied by us – they are to be handed over to the SD forthwith. Retention under military custody – in POW camps etc. – even if only temporarily, is strictly forbidden.

5. This instruction does not apply to the treatment of enemy soldiers captured or surrendering in open fight in the context of normal operations of war (major offensives, major landing operations and major airborne operations). Equally this instruction does not apply to enemy soldiers who fall into our hands after maritime operations or who are trying to save their lives by parachuting after air combat.

6. I shall hold all commanders and officers responsible before court martial for non-compliance with this order if they fail in their duty to inform the troops of this order or act in contravention of this order.

Signature

[This document is quoted from Hubatsch, Walther: *Hitlers Weisungen für die Kriegführung 1935–1945. Dokumente des Oberkommandos der Wehrmacht* (Munich, 1965), pp. 237ff.]

APPENDIX 3
STAGES IN THE GENESIS OF THE COMMANDO ORDER WITH PARTICULAR REFERENCE TO JODL'S PARTICIPATION THEREIN

1. Via the Wehrmacht report of 7 October 1942 Hitler issues a threat that British terrorist parties who act 'like bandits' will be shot down in future.

2. Hitler orders Keitel and Jodl to prepare an executive order for Wehrmacht commanders on these lines. Jodl adopts an attitude of reserve because (according to the testimony of General Christian, Luftwaffe aide to Hitler) he regards the order as contrary to international law. He consequently refuses to deal with the matter himself and commissions Professor Kipp to examine the basis for such an order under international law.

3. Keitel telephones Dr Lehmann, head of the Wehrmacht Legal Section in OKW, to inquire about the legal position. Dr Lehmann regards the order as impossible.

4. Following Hitler's briefing conference on 8 October 1942 Jodl instructs General Warlimont, head of Section L in OKW, to prepare the draft of an order; documentary proof of this, however, could not be produced in Nuremberg. The American court in the 'OKW Trial' stated: 'The defendant's [Warlimont's] statement that he was given detailed instructions concerning the desired content of this order is not confirmed by the wording of this directive.'

5. The Deputy Head of the OKW Operations Staff passes on the instruction to draft an order as required by Hitler.

6. The Wehrmacht Legal Section, on instructions from the OKW Operations

Staff, submits a draft which, if possible, is also to be checked by Heinrich Himmler.

7. On 10 October 1942 Ausland-Abwehr (Military Intelligence) points out that troops should take retaliatory action on their own initiative only if the actions of British terrorist and espionage parties are clearly contrary to international law. Parties not in uniform or in German uniforms should be treated as bandits.

The intermediate stages in the history of the order are irrelevant to the subject and are not set out here. During the period 7–15 October the order was checked, redrafted, marginal notes inserted etc. In all, fourteen documents were produced, on six of which Jodl's initial 'J' appears. None of them are signed with his full name.

8. As a result of the illegal treatment of German prisoners in Dieppe (they were tied in such a way that they inevitably strangled themselves) Ausland-Abwehr shifts its position: sabotage units in uniform are soldiers and have a right to be treated as prisoners of war; reprisals against prisoners of war not permitted.

9. At the briefing conference on 17 October 1942 Keitel or Jodl (it is not clear which) submits to Hitler a draft which he rejects as 'insufficiently clear for the troops'.

10. On 18 October 1942 Hitler dictates an order (letter-heading 'Der Führer') giving reasons for the Commando Order and threatening commanders and officers with court martial if they contravene his instructions. A violent argument between Hitler and Jodl ensues; Major Engel, Army Aide to the Supreme Commander of the Wehrmacht, notes in his diary that Jodl 'resisted special measures against sabotage parties tooth and nail'. Hitler, supported by Keitel, uses strong language about the troops' half-hearted attitude to deterrent measures; he counters Jodl by saying that the Army has boycotted the Commissar Order (according to Engel his words were 'had obeyed it not at all or only hesitantly') and sings the praises of his SS. Jodl declares that 'for the good of our own troops' international agreements should be regarded as valid even in wartime. Jodl passes on Hitler's order.

11. An order signed by Keitel and dated 26 June 1944 restricts the Commando Order as follows: 'Restrictions in para 5 of the basic order dated 18 October 1942 apply to enemy soldiers in uniform in the immediate zone of the bridgehead, in other words in the area of divisions fighting in the front line and reserves up to Corps level inclusive.'

On his own initiative Jodl extends this restriction, adding in manuscript on the order: 'The same procedure is to be followed in the Italian theatre of war.'

12. The IMT's judgement on the matter (IMT Vol. I, p. 228) is as follows: 'Under the provisions of this order Allied "Commando" troops and other military units operating independently lost their lives in Norway, France, Czechoslovakia and Italy. Many of them were killed on the spot and in no case were those who were executed later in concentration camps ever given a trial of any kind.'

The judgement on Jodl (IMT Vol. I, p. 324) states: 'On 18 October 1942 Hitler issued the Commando Order and a day later a supplementary explanation ... The covering memorandum was signed by Jodl. Early drafts of the orders were made by Jodl's staff with his knowledge.'

Glossary

Bannführer	A district leader in the Hitler Youth organization
Brigadeführer	A rank in the SS equivalent to Major-General
Einsatzgruppe	An operational group of the Security Police and SD for special missions in occupied territory
Einsatzkommando	A detachment of the Security Police and SD forming part of an Einsatzgruppe
Gauleiter	The highest ranking Nazi Party official below the central government. Responsible for a Gau (region)
Gruppenführer	A rank in the SS equivalent to Lieutenant-General
Land	One of the fifteen territorial divisions of republican Germany
NSDAP	Nationalsozialistische Deutsche Arbeiter Partei (National-Socialist German Workers Party) – the official title of the Nazi Party
Oberführer	A rank in the SS equivalent to Brigadier
Obergruppenführer	A rank in the SS equivalent to full General
OKH	Oberkommando des Heeres (High Command of the Army)
OKL	Oberkommando der Luftwaffe (High Command of the Air Force)
OKW	Oberkommando der Wehrmacht (High Command of the Armed Forces)
Ordnungspolizei	The regular uniformed police
Reichsleiter	The highest ranking Nazi Party official
RSHA	Reichssicherheitshauptamt. The central Security Department covering both the Security Police and SD
Reichsstatthalter	The Reich Governor of a Land or a Gau
SA	Sturmabteilung – the 'Brownshirts' or Stormtroopers
SD	Sicherheitsdienst. The Security Service of the SS
SS	Schutzstaffel; literally protection or guard detachment. The strong-arm force of the Nazi Party
Standartenführer	A rank in the SS equivalent to Colonel
Todt Organization	A semi-military government agency for construction of strategic highways and military installations
Waffen-SS	The fully militarized combat formations of the SS

Notes

CHAPTER 1: BEFORE THE END OF HOSTILITIES

1. Joe J. Heydecker and Johannes Leeb: *The Nuremberg Trials*, Heinemann, 1962, p. 358.
2. *Waldeckische Landeszeitung*, 8 October 1952.
3. Heydecker and Leeb, op. cit., p. 358.
4. Heydecker and Leeb (p. 358) ask incredulously '... a shrine?' adding: 'More than a decade has passed and the men and events of 1946 have shrunk into an incomprehensible distance.' There is plenty of evidence today to show that they were wrong.
5. On this subject see David Bergamini: *Japan's Imperial Conspiracy. How Emperor Hirohito Led Japan into War against the West*, New York, 1971.
6. Heydecker and Leeb: *Der Nürnberger Prozess*, p. 525 – not in English translation.
7. *International Military Tribunal, Nuremberg*, Nuremberg, 1947 (henceforth referred to as IMT) Vol. I, p. 107.
8. See Keitel's comment on the period immediately after his arrest quoted on p. 16 below and given in *The Memoirs of Field Marshal Keitel*, Wm. Kimber, 1965, p. 234.
9. See introduction to *Instrumentum pacis caesario-gallicum monasteriense* in *Quellen zur Neueren Geschichte*, Berne, 1949, Nos. 12/13, pp. 81ff.
10. Treaty of Osnabrück, 20 October 1648, Article II in *Consolidated Treaty Series* (editor Clive Perry), Oceana Publications Inc., New York, 1969, Vol. 1, pp. 200ff.
11. ibid., Article IV, para. 7.
12. ibid., Article I.
13. ibid., Articles I and XVII, paras. 2 and 4–6. See also K. Zeumer: *Quellensammlung zur Geschichte der deutschen Reichsverfassung*, 2nd edition, Tübingen, 1913, Document 197, pp. 395ff.; F. W. Ghillany: *Diplomatisches Handbuch 1648–1867*, 3 vols., Nordlingen, 1855, Vol. 1, pp. 9ff and *Europäische Chronik von 1492 bis Ende April 1577*, 5 vols., Leipzig, 1865/78, Vol. 1, pp. 148ff.
14. See Note 8 above.
15. See Werner Maser: *Hitler*, Allen Lane, 1973, pp. 11ff.
16. On this subject see Hans-Adolf Jacobsen: *Nationalsozialistische Aussenpolitik 1933–1945*, Frankfurt/Main, 1968, p. 339.
17. See Llewellyn Woodward: *British Foreign Policy in the Second World War*, HMSO, 1971, Vol. 3, p. 202.
18. Signatories of the Washington Pact (sometimes referred to as the '26-Nation Declaration') were: USA, Great Britain, Soviet Union, China, Australia, Belgium, Canada, Costa Rica, Cuba, Czechoslovakia, Dominican Republic, El Salvador, Greece, Guatemala, Haiti, Honduras, India, Luxemburg, Netherlands, New Zealand, Nicaragua, Norway, Panama, Poland, South Africa, Yugoslavia. Between

June 1942 and March 1945 the following additional countries adhered: Mexico (5 June 1942), Philippines (10 June 1942), Ethiopia (28 July 1942), Iraq (16 January 1943), Brazil (8 February 1943), Bolivia (27 April 1943), Iran (10 September 1943), Columbia (22 December 1943), Liberia (26 March 1944), France (26 December 1944), Ecuador (7 February 1945), Peru (11 February 1945), Chile (12 February 1945), Paraguay (12 February 1945), Venezuela (16 February 1945), Uruguay (23 February 1945), Turkey (24 February 1945), Egypt (27 February 1945), Saudi-Arabia (1 March 1945), Lebanon (1 March 1945), Syria (1 March 1945).

19. *Punishment for War Crimes: The Inter-Allied Declaration Signed at St James's Palace, London, 13 January 1942 and Relative Documents*, issued by Inter-Allied Information Committee, London, 1942, pp. 3/4. Quoted from Telford Taylor: 'The Nuremberg Trials. War Crimes and International Law' in *International Conciliation*, April 1949.
20. ibid.
21. Woodward, op. cit., Vol. 3, p. 644.
22. On signature of the Anglo-American-Soviet Protocol of 1 October 1942 the USA granted the Russians 1 billion dollars under the law of Lend-Lease. In May 1942, some six months after Hitler's declaration of war on the USA and nearly a year after his attack on the USSR, the USA promised to open a Second Front and increase their deliveries of material.
23. The communiqué refers, not to the Four powers, but to the 'three Foreign Secretaries' – Cordell Hull for the USA, Anthony Eden for Great Britain and W. M. Molotov for the USSR. The preamble, however, reads: 'The governments of the United States of America, Great Britain, the Soviet Union and China ...' – see *The Times*, 2 November 1943.
24. Admiral Leahy and General Marshall for the USA, General Brooke and Air Chief Marshal Portal for Great Britain, Marshal Voroshilov and Pavlov for the USSR.
25. Quoted from *The Teheran, Yalta and Potsdam Conferences*, Progress Publishers, Moscow, 1969, pp. 51–2.
26. See *The Times*, 7 December 1943.
27. See AFP Basic Document 79.8, pp. 487ff.
28. According to a list handed in by the French in Berlin, up to the end of February 1920 numbers of named war criminals whose extradition was demanded were as follows: by the British 100, by the French 334, by the Belgians 334, by the Italians 29, by the Poles 53 and by the Rumanians 41. The German government had already stated on 25 January 1920 that it was not in a position to comply with the Allied demands for extradition. In this situation the German Crown Prince declared himself ready to place himself at the disposal of the victor powers for trial. This action, hardly in accord with all the other charges made against him, he took despite an explicit order to the contrary from his father Wilhelm II who had fled to Holland in 1918, had been designated as a war criminal but had not been handed over by the Dutch in accordance with international law. The Allies neither accepted nor answered his offer. As a result of the stand by the German government and people (even the German communists refused to agree to extradition of 'war criminals'), in February 1920 the victor powers declared themselves ready to accept as a test case the trial of forty-six war criminals by German courts; they would then decide which of some 800 war criminals named by them should be brought to trial (in addition to the Kaiser and General Ludendorff they included Princes, politicians, Army Commanders, scientists,

officers, officials and even NCOs and private soldiers). The first trials took place in January 1921 and ended with sentences of hard labour for looting in the field. At the end of January 1921 Joseph Wirth, the German Chancellor, publicly refused to hand the accused over forcibly to the victors. On 5 May 1921 Lloyd George, the British Prime Minister, demanded through the German Ambassador that the German government sentence the war criminals forthwith. The trials ended in late 1922, some having concluded with acquittals or quashing of proceedings.

29. See J. L. Chase: 'The Development of the Morgenthau Plan through the Quebec Conference' in *Journal of Politics*, May 1954, Vol. 16, No. 2, pp. 324ff.
30. German News Agency, 1 January 1945.
31. Para. 2 of Yalta Declaration. See Control Council Gazette for Germany, Berlin, 1945–9.
32. IMT Vol. XVI, p. 492.
33 See *Kriegsdokumente über Bündnisgrundlagen, Kriegsziele und Friedenspolitik der Vereinten Nationen* published by Institut für internationales Recht, University of Kiel (henceforth referred to as *Kriegsdokumente*), folio 1 (edited by von Mangold), Hamburg, 1946, pp. 47ff.
34. German News Agency, 30 January 1942.
35. Sir Basil Liddell Hart: *History of the Second World War*, p. 488. On Stalin's efforts to come to some arrangement with Hitler see also Sven Allard: *Stalin und Hitler. Die sowjetrussische Aussenpolitik 1930 bis 1941*, Berne and Munich, 1974. See also review by Andreas Hillgruber in *Frankfurter Allgemeine Zeitung*, 20 February 1975 – 'Welche Rolle spielte Stalin in Hitlers Kalkül?', and Alexander Fischer: *Sowjetische Deutschland-Politik im Zweiten Weltkrieg 1941–1945*, Stuttgart, 1975.
36. See Hildegard Kotze (editor): *Heeresadjutant bei Hitler 1938–1943. Aufzeichnungen des Majors Engel*, Stuttgart, 1974, pp. 116ff.
37. Maser, op. cit., p. 299.
38. See Robert M. W. Kempner: *Eichmann und Komplizen*, pp. 92ff.
39. ibid.
40. Max Domarus: *Hitler. Reden und Proklamationen 1932–1945*, Vol. II/4, pp. 2054ff.
41. Winston Churchill: *The Second World War*, Vol. V, p. 330.
42. See Elliott Roosevelt: *Wie er es Sah*, Zurich, 1947, pp. 235ff; also *Foreign Relations of the United States. Diplomatic Papers. The Conferences at Cairo and Teheran 1943*, pp. 552ff.; Günter Holtmann: *Amerikas Deutschlandpolitik im Zweiten Weltkrieg. Kriegs-und Friedensziele 1941–1945*, pp. 83ff, 115ff.
43. Max M. Laserson: *Russia and the Western World*, p. 204; Gerhard Gründler and Arnim von Manikowski: *Das Gericht der Sieger* (henceforth referred to as Gründler/Manikowski), p. 55.
44. Maser, op. cit., p. 307.
45. ibid., p. 301. On Stalingrad see Manfred Kehrig: *Stalingrad*, Stuttgart, 1976.
46. Maser, op. cit., p. 307.
47. See Albert Speer's statements to the International Military Tribunal, IMT Vol. XVI, p. 492.

CHAPTER 2: AFTER THE END OF HOSTILITIES

1. Letter from Dr Robert M. W. Kempner dated 31 October 1975.
2. *Hansard*, 7 December 1943 (House of Lords, Vol. 130, pp. 126–7); Louise

W. Holborn: *War and Peace, Aims of the United Nations*, World Peace Foundation, Boston, 1943, 1948, Vol. II, pp. 449ff.

3. *Jackson Report, United States Representative to the International Conference on Military Trials*, Department of State Publication 3080 (1949); see also Robert H. Jackson: *The Nürnberg Case*, Knopf, New York, 1947.

4. See Executive Order 9547 dated 2 May 1945: 'Concerning representation of the United States in the preparation and conduct of the case against leaders of the European Axis Powers and their most important representatives and accomplices on grounds of barbarities and war crimes' (10 Federal Register 4961).

5. Jackson, op. cit., pp. 7ff.

6. ibid., pp. 9–10.

7. ibid., p. 10.

8. Roosevelt, Churchill and Stalin had agreed at Yalta on the functions of the Security Counc:., participation as United Nations members of two Soviet republics (in addition to the USSR) and assembly of the first United Nations conference in San Francisco.

9. The American record (PP II, pp. 89, 96) gives the additional sentence: 'If we mean pre-war Germany, I agree with that.'

10. The American record (PP II, pp. 90, 96) adds to Stalin's proposal the words 'Austria is not part of Germany'.

11. The American record (PP II, pp. 90, 96) gives a different version, adding to Stalin's remark the words 'discounting what Germany has lost in 1945'.

12. Quoted from *The Teheran, Yalta and Potsdam Conferences*, Progress Publishers, Moscow, 1969, pp. 161–2.

13. ibid., p. 320.

14. ibid., p. 328.

15. On this subject see Josef Ackermann: 'Die Konferenz von Potsdam' in *Frankfurter Allgemeine Zeitung*, 9 August 1975.

16. In the American record this remark is attributed to Attlee but in the British to Bevin. See also Ackermann, op. cit.

17. *Teheran, Yalta and Potsdam Conferences*, op. cit., pp. 300–301.

18. Ackermann, op. cit.

19. ibid.

20. On this subject see Werner Maser: *Hitler*, pp. 314ff.

21. The basis for delineation of zones was the frontiers 'as they existed on 31 December 1937' (*Control Council Gazette*, Folio 1, pp. 7ff). Inevitably an important factor was the question of German reparations during the occupation period, together with the provisions of the Moscow Declaration of 30 October 1943 and the London Agreement of 8 August 1945 concerning the 'trial of war criminals and other evil-doers of this nature' (see *Control Council Gazette*, No. 3 of 31 January 1946, p. 50).

22. *Control Council Gazette*, Folio 1, pp. 7ff.

23. The governments of the following countries adhered to the London Four-Power Agreement of 8 August 1945: Greece, Yugoslavia, Denmark, the Netherlands, Czechoslovakia, Poland, Belgium, Abyssinia, Australia, Honduras, Norway, Panama, Luxemburg, Haiti, New Zealand, India, Venezuela, Uruguay and Paraguay.

24. IMT Vol. I, p. 8.

25. Article 2 of the Agreement read: 'The constitution, jurisdiction and functions

of the International Military Tribunal shall be those set out in the Charter annexed to this Agreement, which Charter shall form an integral part of this Agreement' (IMT Vol. I, p. 8).

26. The official communiqué issued on 11 February 1945 included: 'It is our inflexible purpose to destroy German militarism and Nazism and to ensure that Germany will never again be able to disturb the peace of the world. We are determined to ... bring all war criminals to just and swift punishment and exact reparations in kind for the destruction wrought by the Germans' (see *Control Council Gazette*, No. 1).

27. The prosecution regarded this point purely pragmatically. In 1967, for instance, Lord Shawcross, the British Chief Prosecutor, stated in a foreword to Gerhard Gründler's and Arnim von Manikowsky's book *Das Gericht der Sieger* (p. 16): 'Leaving out of account for the moment all the arguments and the dispute about the position under international law, about the constitution and competence of the Tribunal and about the novelty of certain rules of procedure, anyone who studies the evidence at Nuremberg can have no doubts on one subject: had those executed in Nuremberg been accused solely of participation in ordinary murder, they would not have escaped being sentenced. These men differed from ordinary murderers only in that they occasioned or approved the murder, not of an individual but of millions.'

28. The Charter also laid down details concerning the composition of the court (one member and one alternate member from each of the signatories) and confirmed its legitimization – Article 3 stated: 'Neither the Tribunal, its members nor their alternates can be challenged by the Prosecution or by the defendants or their counsel' – it prescribed rules of procedure (proceedings and decisions of the court only in the presence of all four members or their alternates), the election of the President, and the voting procedure for decisions (majority vote with a casting vote for the President in case of equality, convictions and sentences by 'affirmative votes of at least three members'). (IMT Vol. I, p. 10).

29. The semicolon at this point in the English and French texts was replaced by a comma. See Protocol rectifying discrepancy in text of Charter (IMT Vol. I, p. 17).

30. IMT Vol. I, p. 11.

31. See Article 7 of Charter, IMT Vol. I, p. 12.

32. ibid., Article 8.

33. IMT Vol. I, p. 13. The Article continued: 'The Committee shall act ... by a majority vote ... If there is an equal division of votes concerning the designation of a defendant to be tried by the Tribunal or the crimes with which he shall be charged, that proposal will be adopted which was made by the party which proposed that the particular defendant be tried or the particular charges preferred against him.'

34. IMT Vol. I, pp. 27ff.

35. ibid., p. 96.

36. ibid., pp. 98ff.

37. Under Article 18 of the Charter the Tribunal was to 'confine the trial to an expeditious hearing' and 'take strict measures to prevent any action which will cause unreasonable delay and rule out irrelevant issues and statements of any kind whatsoever' (IMT Vol. I, p. 14).

38. ibid., p. 12.

39. ibid., p. 16.
40. Basically, for instance, the explicit right of the accused to conduct their own defence under Article 16(d) of the Charter (IMT Vol. I, p. 14) was not accepted.

CHAPTER 3: ON THE ROAD TO NUREMBERG

1. IMT Vol. IX, pp. 143–4.
2. Quoted from Leonard Mosley: *The Reich Marshal*, p. 313.
3. ibid., p. 317.
4. Personal information from Karl Dönitz, May 1969.
5. cf. Mosley, op. cit., p. 321.
6. In the original certain pages of the record of a meeting held on 1 August 1944 (the day on which the Warsaw rising began) are missing, as are about a dozen pages referring to the period 14 August to 9 September 1944. One suspects that they included material incriminating Frank.
7. See Dr Pflücker in *Waldeckische Landeszeitung*, October 1952, Serial 19.
8. Personal information from Karl Dönitz, May 1969.
9. Typewritten memo marked 'Secret'. Ref. No. 1202/44g-R/H in US Document Center, Berlin.
10. Typewritten memo. Two copies. Ref. No. 1750 G.K S . . . in US Document Center, Berlin.
11. See IMT Vol. II, pp. 87ff.
12. On 7 June 1946, for instance, Jodl was accused of having been 'Rosenberg's collaborator'. Jodl explained the problem from his point of view and in this connection demolished the accusation of a conspiracy between political and military leaders for the preparation and conduct of wars of aggression. (IMT Vol. XV, p. 559.)
13. ibid., p. 294.
14. IMT Vol. XII, p. 310. See also p. 389.
15. ibid., p. 389.
16. ibid., p. 312.
17. On this subject see also Schirach: *Ich glaubte an Hitler* (I believed in Hitler), p. 314. Schirach's statements in this book about events between 2 April and 5 June 1945 were proved correct by his son, Klaus von Schirach, in the course of a lawsuit against a German illustrated paper which was bound over by the court not to repeat at least one of its statements. (Letter from Klaus von Schirach, 23 July 1974.)
18. Schirach, op. cit., p. 315.
19. ibid., pp. 315ff.
20. ibid., p. 316.
21. ibid., p. 317.
22. ibid., p. 318.
23. ibid. The statement in Heydecker and Leeb (*The Nuremberg Trials*, pp. 44ff.) that until his arrest Schirach had acted as an interpreter for the Americans is legendary.
24. Personal information from Karl Dönitz, May 1969.
25. IMT Vol. XII, p. 392.
26. Evidence by Julius Streicher, IMT Vol. XII, p. 310; evidence by Adele Streicher, ibid., p. 392.
27. Evidence by Adele Streicher ibid., p. 392.

28. Information from Frau Streicher, 1 August 1974. The imaginative account by Heydecker and Leeb (op. cit., pp. 30ff.) of the discovery of Streicher is not based on fact.
29. Copy of Julius Streicher's manuscript report in the author's possession.
30. See Walter Görlitz: *Keitel. Verbrecher oder Offizier? Erinnerungen Briefe, Dokumente des Chefs des OKW*, p. 381.
31. ibid., pp. 341ff. See also *The Memoirs of Field Marshal Keitel*, edited with an Introduction and Epilogue by Walter Görlitz, translated by David Irving, Wm Kimber, 1965, henceforth referred to as *Keitel Memoirs*. See also *Nazi Conspiracy and Aggression*, Office of United States Chief of Counsel for Prosecution of Axis Criminality, Washington, 1948, Supplement B; Karl Koller: *Der letzte Monat. Die Tagebuchaufzeichnungen des Chefs des Generalstabes der deutschen Luftwaffe v. 14 April bis 27 Mai 1945*; Joachim Schultz: *Die letzten 30 Tage. Aus dem Kriegstagebuch des OKW*; Walter Lüdde-Neurath: *Regierung Dönitz. Die letzten Tage des Dritten Reiches*; also research conducted by Walter Baum in 'Der Zusammenbruch der obersten deutschen militärischen Führung 1945', *Wehrwissenschaftliche Rundschau*, No. 5 of 1960, pp. 237ff.
32. *Keitel Memoirs*, pp. 230ff.
33. Albert Speer: *Inside the Third Reich*, p. 505. Speer states explicitly (ibid., p. 506) that the US Army sergeant responsible for him increased his rations 'so that, as he said, I would have my strength for the trial'.
34. ibid., pp. 504ff.
35. There were some eighty prisoners in Schloss Kransberg. Speer had all his heads of department with him, other members of his Ministry staff, heads of important committees and Hans Kehrl, head of the Raw Materials department in his Ministry. There were well-known industrialists, engineers and designers (Ferdinand Porsche, for instance, the rocket designer, Oberth and Anton Flettner, the rotor designer, Dr Karl Brandt, Hitler's personal physician and others) who were later in the dock at the follow-up trials in Nuremberg. So it was a distinguished company.
36. Speer, op. cit., p. 505.
37. ibid., p. 507.
38. In an interview on German TV Channel 2 on 23 November 1975 Dr Kempner mentioned in particular Dr Otto Meissner, who had served Friedrich Ebert, Paul von Hindenburg and Adolf Hitler as Presidential Secretary.
39. Speer, op. cit., p. 505.

CHAPTER 4: THE PRISON

1. Hanged in Landsberg am Lech on 7 June 1951.
2. Hanged in Landsberg on 28 May 1947.
3. Written report by a witness for the defence dated 10 May 1974.
4. Personal information from Dr Robert M. W. Kempner dated 8 March 1974. After the conclusion of the Nuremberg follow-up trials Kordt made a name for himself as a writer of contemporary history. See also Ribbentrop's last notes in *The Ribbentrop Memoirs*, pp. 180ff.
5. Personal information from Dr Kempner, 8 March 1974.
6. Dönitz, Funk, Hess, Raeder, von Schirach, Speer and von Neurath.
7. Pflücker in *Waldeckische Landeszeitung*, 11 October 1952.

8. Speer: *Inside the Third Reich*, p. 507.
9. Typewritten report, undated (1946), in the author's possession. Minor stylistic corrections have been made to the text.
10. Pflücker in *Waldeckische/Landeszeitung*, 10 October 1952. See also Speer: *The Secret Diaries*, p. 7.
11. This description is based on an account by General von Vormann, who was detained as a defence witness (signed typescript, six pages, dated 1946, in the author's possession). On Vormann see IMT Vol. XV, pp. 551–2.
12. Pflücker in *Waldeckische Landeszeitung*, 13 October 1952.
13. Unpublished report by a British minute-writer at the trial, 1946. In the author's possession.
14. See Schellenberg's affidavit on 12 July 1946, quoted in IMT Vol. XLII, pp. 456ff.
15. Written communication from Lina Heydrich, 4 October 1974.
16. Pflücker in *Waldeckische Landeszeitung*, 10 October 1952.
17. Fritz Sauckel, who came of working-class background, wrote in bad German: '... I request you to be so good as to give me a sleeping pill this evening.'
18. Pflücker in *Waldeckische Landeszeitung*, 29 October 1952.
19. ibid., 10 October 1952.
20. Written communication from Dr Meissner dated 19 September 1975.
21. Written report by a defence witness. Typescript, undated (certainly 1946), in the author's possession.
22. Agreement on treatment of prisoners of war of 27 July 1929.
23. Under the terms of the Geneva Convention of 29 July 1929 prisoners of war were to retain all personal effects and articles of daily use (apart from weapons, horses and military equipment); they were entitled to 'respect for their persons and honour'; they were to retain their personal papers, decorations, badges of rank and valuables. Article 56 states explicitly: 'In no case shall prisoners of war be transferred to penitentiary establishments (prisons, penitentiaries, convict establishments etc.) in order to undergo disciplinary sentences there. Establishments in which disciplinary sentences are undergone shall conform to the requirements of hygiene. Facilities shall be afforded to prisoners ... to keep themselves in a state of cleanliness.' Article 57 states: 'Prisoners of war shall be permitted to read and write, and to send and receive letters.' In addition under Article 58 they were to have opportunity for a daily visit from a doctor and daily medical treatment if necessary. See Command Paper 3794, 1931.
24. These details are based on General Vormann's report already referred to (Note 11 above). Numerous reports by former witnesses tell a similar story.

CHAPTER 5: THE TRIAL OPENS

1. IMT Vol. I, p. 24.
2. ibid., p. 25.
3. ibid., p. 26.
4. ibid., p. 25.
5. Gustave M. Gilbert: *Nuremberg Diary*, p. 4.
6. Personal information from Karl Dönitz, May 1967.
7. Gerhard E. Gründler and Arnim von Manikowsky: *Das Gericht der Sieger*, p. 87.
8. ibid., p. 88.
9. ibid., p. 90.

10. cf. IMT Vol. VII, pp. 250ff.
11. IMT Vol. VII, p. 251.
12. For Göring's remark see Gilbert, op. cit., p. 86.
13. Article 16(d) of the Charter, IMT Vol. I, p. 14.
14. Written communication from Luise Jodl, 6 October 1975.
15. Albert Speer: *Inside the Third Reich*, p. 511.
16. Six (in other words 16 per cent) of the principal defence counsel were said to have been members of the Nazi Party. Suzanne Czapski: *Rechtsanwälte in Nürnberg*, DANA Report, 8 June 1946.
17. Gründler, op. cit., p. 99.
18. IMT Vol. I, p. 96.
19. ibid., p. 14.
20. ibid., p. 15.
21. ibid., pp. 19–20.
22. Speer, op. cit., p. 510.
23. See Francis Biddle: *In Brief Authority*, pp. 373ff.
24. *Welt am Sonntag*, Hamburg, 26 September 1971.
25. IMT Vol. II, pp. 29ff.
26. IMT Vol. I, pp. 27–92, and Vol. II, pp. 30ff. Count One (The Common Plan or Conspiracy) was put forward by Alderman (IMT Vol. II, pp. 31–43). Count Two (Crimes against Peace) was read by Sir David Maxwell-Fyfe (ibid., pp. 43, 44). The French Prosecutor, M. Mounier (ibid., pp. 44–52, 57–9), and Assistant Prosecutor, M. Charles Gerthoffer (ibid., pp. 52–6), read part of Count Three (War Crimes), which was then concluded by the Soviet Assistant Prosecutors, J. A. Ozol (ibid., pp. 59–65) and V. V. Kuchin (ibid., pp. 65–9). Kuchin (pp. 69–72) also read Count Four (Crimes against Humanity). There followed the reading of the so-called Appendix A (Statement of Individual Responsibility for Crimes set out in Counts One, Two, Three and Four), Appendix B (Statement of Criminality of Groups and Organizations) and Appendix C (Charges and Particulars of Violations of International Treaties, Agreements and Assurances caused by the Defendants in the course of Planning, Preparing and Initiating the Wars) (ibid., pp. 72–94).
27. IMT Vol. II, pp. 30–31. Gustav Krupp von Bohlen und Halbach was accused of Crimes against Peace, War Crimes and Crimes against Humanity, also of participation in the Common Plan (see IMT Vol. I, p. 27, Vol. II, pp. 31, 78–9); he was not tried, since a medical committee appointed by the court on 5 November 1945 found that he was suffering from 'senile softening of the brain' and, as a result of his mental state, was not in a position to follow the proceedings or examination of witnesses (IMT Vol. II, p. 21). Instead, by unanimous agreement of the Allies (IMT Vol. II, pp. 10, 14ff., Vol. I, pp. 145ff.), his son Alfried was placed in the dock; he was eventually tried on 31 July 1948 by an American court under 'Case 10' and sentenced with ten other persons (see IMT Vol. II, pp. 15ff.).
28. IMT Vol. I, pp. 155ff.
29. ibid., p. 155.
30. ibid., p. 156.
31. ibid.
32. ibid., p. 157.
33. ibid., p. 163.
34. ibid.

35. Eugene C. Gerhard: *America's Advocate: Robert H. Jackson*, p. 359.
36. Florence R. Miale and Michael Selzer: *The Nuremberg Mind. The Psychology of the Nazi Leaders*, Quadrangle, New York, 1975.
37. Statement by Bird in T V programme 'Augenzeugen berichten', Z D F, 22 August 1976.
38. Gilbert, op. cit.
39. See later in this book.
40. Douglas M. Kelley: *22 Cells in Nuremberg*.
41. Document in possession of the author. Kelley had kept all sorts of 'Nazi memorabilia' (pieces of uniform, whips, instruments of torture etc.) in a secret cupboard in his study. On New Year's Eve he went up to the attic in his house while his family was downstairs. He suddenly appeared on the staircase and announced that he had just swallowed the cyanide capsule found on Hermann Göring. Then he collapsed dead. If Göring's statements in his letter to the Commandant of 11 October 1946 are correct, Kelley would have had two possibilities of acquiring the cyanide from Göring: (1) the capsule which he had hidden in his clothing so that it would be discovered – which it was; (2) the capsule which Göring said he had kept hidden in his tin of ointment.
42. I M T Vol. I I, pp. 95ff.
43. ibid., p. 97.
44. ibid.
45. ibid.
46. ibid., pp. 97–8.

CHAPTER 6: VENGEANCE OR JUSTICE

1. See Werner Maser: *Hitler*, Allen Lane, 1973, p. 299.
2. Personal information from Heinrich Heim (18 August 1971), who was standing next to Hitler when Heinz Lorenz, representing the Reich Press Officer in the Führer's Headquarters, gave Hitler the news that Japanese aircraft had attacked the US fleet in Pearl Harbor.
3. Quoted in a British weekly newsreel in November 1945 and repeated as a 'contemporary document' on German television (Programme 3 'South-west') on 24 November 1975.
4. Personal information from Dr Robert M. W. Kempner, May 1974.
5. At the last elections in 1932 the N S D A P had scored a majority of votes and so was the strongest party in the Reichstag. At the Reichstag elections on 31 July 1932 it became the strongest party with 37·3 per cent of the votes and 230 seats out of 608. From then on its ascent to power was as follows: on 31 August 1932 Hitler, together with Papen, was received by the Reich President; Hitler refused the office of Vice-Chancellor offered him by Hindenburg. On 6 November 1932 a Reichstag election took place; despite a loss of votes (31·1 per cent instead of 37·3 per cent) the N S D A P remained the strongest party in the Reichstag. On 4 January 1933 a meeting took place which led to the unholy alliance referred to by Jackson. Hitler, accompanied by Hess and Himmler, met Papen in the house of von Schroeder, the Cologne banker, and preparations were made to overthrow von Schleicher, the Chancellor who had been in office since 2 December 1932. The Schleicher government resigned on 28 January 1933 and on the 30th Hitler was appointed Reich Chancellor by Hindenburg.

6. IMT Vol. II, pp. 98ff.
7. Pflücker in *Waldeckische Landeszeitung*, 11 October 1952.
8. ibid., but date indecipherable. Pflücker says: 'Goring told Kaltenbrunner, for instance, that he need not worry about his future since he would certainly be hung.'
9. Pflücker in *Waldeckische Landeszeitung*, 16 October 1952.
10. ibid., 14 October 1952.
11. ibid., 11 October 1952.
12. ibid., Serial 20 1952 – date uncertain.
13. ibid., Serial 6 1952 – date uncertain.
14. ibid. – date uncertain (October 1952).
15. ibid.
16. ibid., 14 October 1952.
17. ibid.
18. ibid., 13 October 1952.

CHAPTER 7: THE EVIDENCE

1. The US Prosecutor's staff examined a total of 1,100 tons of files – information from the Head of the Document Division of the Military Tribunal to Wolfgang Mommsen (*Die Akten der Nürnberger Kriegsverbrecherprozesse*, p. 16). In November 1945 Storey did not yet know the full total.
2. Affidavit dated 19 November 1945 (001 A–PJ, US 1). See also IMT Vol. II, pp. 157ff.
3. In all the Prosecution selected 2,736 documents. See Hans-Günther Seraphim: 'Die Dokumentenedition der amtlichen deutschen Ausgabe des Verfahrens' in *Europa-archiv*, 5/17 of 5 September 1950, pp. 3307–10 (henceforth referred to as 'Seraphim–Dokumentenedition'). See also following Note.
4. Exhibit US–4, 2836–PS.
5. IMT Vol. II, pp. 156ff.
6. The reference is to Document 1809–PS.
7. p. 16 of Document Book GB–88, 1809–PS.
8. Document 1780–PS.
9. Document 1809–PS.
10. Document 1809–PS.
11. IMT Vol. XV, pp. 383ff.
12. Personal information from Otto Kranzbühler, 6 March 1972.
13. ibid.
14. IMT Vol. IX, p. 1.
15. ibid., IMT Vol. X, p. 182. See also Speer: *Inside the Third Reich*, p. 514.
16. See Speer, ibid.
17. Ribbentrop's defence counsel, for instance, knew nothing of foreign policy.
18. Personal information from Karl Dönitz.
19. Letter from Karl Dönitz, 6 April 1974.
20. Letter from Karl Dönitz, 6 April 1974 and letters from a source in Tahiti, whose name cannot be given for obvious reasons. His letters to the author are dated 26 March 1974, 27 May 1974, 25 June 1974, 1 July 1974, 11 July 1974 and 31 July 1974.

I asked Burton Andrus in writing to give a view on the accusation made against him that during the Nuremberg Trial he had permitted the removal of documents or had even done so himself. My letter read (extracts): 'During my researches I have established that before and during the Trial documents disappeared with the result that they could not be laid before the Court either by the German defence or by the prosecution. According to Colonel Storey's official statement documents were in safes under the care of US officers who ... were under your command ... It is stated that some of these documents were removed on your orders. If this is true, I would like to know how many documents there were and who selected them. I would also be interested to know where the documents were taken and who removed them.' Burton Andrus thought it best to say nothing.

21. Otto Meissner (born in Bischweiler, Alsace, in 1890) was appointed Head of the Presidential Chancellery (ranking as State Secretary) by President Friedrich Ebert in 1920; he continued in office under Hindenburg and, after Hindenburg's death on 2 August 1934, under Hitler at the latter's wish. Though never a member of the Nazi Party, he was appointed to the rank of Minister by Hitler in 1938, without thereby becoming a member of the Reich government. See affidavit by Otto Meissner dated 8 July 1946, quoted in IMT Vol. XLII, pp. 401ff.

22. Letter dated 19 September 1975 from Dr Hans-Otto Meissner, the Minister's son, who was German Consul in Milan until the end of the war; this says that the officers concerned were in some cases of the rank of Colonel.

23. Letter from Dr Hans-Otto Meissner, 19 September 1975. Although there was no case of any sort against him, Hans-Otto Meissner was placed under automatic arrest at the end of the war and, despite being declared innocent, was kept in the US 'Automatic Internment' Camp 74 at Ossweil near Ludwigsburg as a 'hold case'. On his release in October 1947 he applied to US Headquarters in Heidelberg asking for the return of his father's documents which had been confiscated, so that they might possibly be tabled in the Wilhelmstrasse Trial. He was asked sarcastically for the American search parties' 'receipts', which he could not produce. His father's documents were not returned to Hans-Otto Meissner even subsequently.

24. IMT Vol. II, pp. 254–5.

25. IMT Vol. II, p. 255.

26. ibid., p. 350.

27. ibid.

28. ibid., pp. 350–51.

29. ibid., p. 351.

30. ibid., pp. 351–2.

31. ibid., p. 352.

32. Count One, Section IV, sub-section E, IMT Vol. I, p. 35.

33. IMT Vol. II, pp. 178–9.

34. ibid., pp. 184–5.

35. ibid., p. 191.

36. ibid., p. 195.

37. ibid., p. 214.

38. Erwin Lahousen was a General, born in Vienna in 1897, whom the prosecution examined as a witness on the subject of the German invasion of Austria.

39. IMT Vol. II, p. 435.

40. ibid., pp. 435–6.

41. ibid.
42. ibid.
43. ibid.
44. ibid.
45. ibid.
46. ibid., p. 439.
47. The letter was kindly made available to me by Frau Jodl on 1 December 1975.
48. Speer, op. cit., p. 512.
49. ibid., p. 513.
50. Hildegard Springer: *Es sprach Hans Fritzsche. Nach Gesprächen, Briefen, Dokumenten*, Stuttgart, 1949, p. 63.
51. Rebecca West: *A Train of Powder*, London, 1955, p. 9. The diary entries of the British Member of the Tribunal, Sir Norman Birkett, from 28 January to 13 February 1946 speak for themselves. There are continuous references to 'repetitions', 'waste of time' and the crudity of Soviet procedure. See also Gerhard E. Gründler and Arnim von Manikowsky: *Das Gericht der Sieger*, pp. 143ff.
52. I M T Vol. V I I, p. 519. The application was tabled on 18 February 1946. See also the court's decision on 19 February 1946 (ibid., p. 562).
53. *Nürnberger Tagebuchnotizen, November 1945 bis Oktober 1946*, p. 132.
54. I M T Vol. V I I, pp. 146ff.
55. See following pages.
56. At this point it is superfluous to comment in greater detail on the secret supplementary agreement to the Non-Aggression Pact which has so frequently been quoted since Nuremberg. Suffice it to point out that this supplement set out the Russo-German agreement that, in the event of political and territorial changes in Eastern Europe, their mutual spheres of interest would be bounded by the line of the Rivers Narev, Vistula and San.
57. I M T Vol. X V, p. 374.
58. ibid.
59. U S House of Representatives, 'The Katyn Forest Massacre'. Hearings before the Select Committee to Conduct an Investigation of the Facts, Evidence and Circumstances of the Katyn Forest Massacre. 82nd Congress, 1st and 2nd Sessions, 1951–2, Washington, U S Government Printing Office, 1952 – 7 parts, 2,362 pages. The letter from the Polish politicians is in Part 7, pp. 1976ff. On 26 February 1946 Jackson received from the U S Secret Service documents labelled 'Secret' which contradicted one another – in Jackson's words: 'The German account blaming the Soviets, two Soviet documents blaming the Nazis and a file labelled "Extracts from conversations between Sikorski, Anders, Stalin and Molotov"' (Hearings, Part 7, p. 1948).
60. I M T Vol. V I I, pp. 425–8.
61. In 1951 the Select Committee formed in 1949 by the Americans for investigation of the Katyn massacre, after inquiries and taking of evidence in Washington, Chicago, London, Frankfurt, Berlin and Naples, concluded definitely and unanimously that the Polish prisoners had been murdered by the Russians. See Select Committee, 'The Katyn Forest Massacre' (Note 59 above) – henceforth referred to as 'Hearings'.
62. I M T Vol. X V, p. 289.
63. I M T Vol. X V I I, p. 275.
64. One of the defence witnesses, Colonel Friedrich Ahrens, reported voluntarily to

Nuremberg, where he declared in writing on 15 March 1946: 'I heard over the radio that Hermann Göring's defence counsel had cited me as a witness in the Katyn case ... I have ... come here of my own free will and have ... made myself available.' Typescript, seven DIN-A-4 pages, signed 'Friedrich Ahrens'. Document in the author's possession.

65. See also J. K. Zawodny: *Zum Beispiel Katyn. Klärung eines Kriegsverbrechens*, Munich, 1971, pp. 62ff.
66. ibid., p. 62.
67. IMT Vol. XVII, p. 340.
68. ibid., p. 343.
69. ibid., p. 347.
70. ibid., p. 286.
71. Roosevelt's letter is to be found in 'Hearings', Part 7, p. 1946.
72. 'Hearings', Part 7, pp. 2302ff.
73. 82nd Congress, Report A 1599 (1952).
74. *New York Post*, 20 March, 1946.
75. See Werner Bross: *Gespräche mit Hermann Göring während des Nürnberger Prozess*, Flensburg/Hamburg, 1950, p. 138.
76. Viktor Freiherr von Lippe: *Nürnberger Tagebuchnotizen*, op. cit., p. 178.
77. See IMT Vol. IX, p. 443 and elsewhere.
78. ibid., p. 445.
79. H. Montgomery Hyde: *The Life of Lord Birkett of Ulverston*, London, 1964, p. 510.
80. IMT Vol. IX, pp. 500ff.
81. See also statements by General Karl Bodenschatz, IMT Vol. IX, p. 10. As a witness for the defence Bodenschatz testified that Göring had known nothing about 'Kristallnacht' beforehand, which may well be right.
82. See also IMT Vol. I, p. 80, and Vol. II, pp. 217ff.
83. See also Field Marshal Milch's evidence when testifying for the defence on 8 March 1946 (IMT Vol. IX, p. 58). Milch said: 'All measures taken by Hitler (prior to 1939) beginning with the occupation of the Rhineland (apart from the "Polish affair") came very suddenly ... A complete surprise.'
84. IMT Vol. IX, p. 512. On the examination of Göring see IMT Vol. IX, pp. 236ff. The passages quoted here are on pp. 505–12.
85. Personal information from Dr Robert M. W. Kempner on 27 November 1975. When Jackson suddenly put a question touching on this subject, Göring referred to his agreement with Kempner, who confirmed it to Jackson, thus saving Göring from an embarrassing situation.
86. See Göring's closing address.
87. IMT Vol. IX, p. 580.
88. ibid.
89. ibid., pp. 580ff.
90. IMT Vol. IX, p. 647.
91. ibid., p. 648.
92. ibid.
93. ibid.
94. ibid.
95. ibid.
96. ibid.
97. IMT Vol. I, p. 282.

98. See IMT Vol. X, pp. 311ff.
99. ibid., pp. 312–13.
100. ibid., pp. 311–12.
101. IMT Vol. IX, p. 28.
102. ibid., p. 29.
103. ibid.
104. IMT Vol. IX, pp. 60ff.
105. ibid., p. 61.
106. ibid.
107. ibid.

CHAPTER 8: THE MILITARY UNDER CROSS-EXAMINATION

1. IMT Vol. XV, pp. 311ff.
2. See IMT Vol. XV, pp. 300, 308, 383 and elsewhere, also Vol. IX, pp. 102–3.
3. See IMT Vol. XV, pp. 318ff. and elsewhere.
4. IMT Vol. XV, p. 342.
5. Record of Case X, p. 13800, quoted from Kurt Heinze and Karl Schilling; *Die Rechtsprechung der Nürnberger Militärtribunale*, p. 83.
6. See H. Donnedieu de Vabres: 'Le Procès de Nuremberg' in *Revue de Science Criminelle et de Droit Pénal Comparé*, Paris, 1947, No. 2, p. 172.
7. On this subject see IMT Vol. II, pp. 262–73, Vol. XXV, pp. 404–13, PS-386 and Friedrich Hossbach: *Zwischen Wehrmacht und Hitler*, Göttingen, 1965, pp. 189ff.
8. See Werner Maser: *Hitler's Mein Kampf*, Faber & Faber, London, 1970, pp. 18ff.
9. IMT Vol. XXII, p. 468.
10. ibid., p. 469.
11. IMT Vol. I, p. 29, Vol. II, pp. 31ff.
12. IMT Vol. XV, pp. 345–6.
13. ibid., p. 301.
14. ibid., pp. 301–2.
15. See ibid., pp. 344ff.
16. On 5 June 1946 Jodl stated: 'The concentration along the West Wall was purely defensive. The forces in position there were so weak that we could not even occupy all the bunkers' (IMT Vol. XV, p. 372, also pp. 379–80).
17. IMT Vol. XV, pp. 347ff.
18. IMT Vol. I, p. 322.
19. ibid.
20. See Alan Bullock: 'Hitler and the Origins of the Second World War', Raleigh Lecture on History, 22 November 1967, pp. 259–87, published for the British Academy by Oxford University Press, London, 1968. Henceforth referred to as Bullock, 'Second World War'.
21. On the question of German rearmament see Alan S. Milward; *The German Economy at War*, London, 1965; Burton H. Klein: *Germany's Economic Preparations for War*, Cambridge, Mass., 1959; and Heinrich Stübel: 'Die Finanzierung der Aufrüstung im Dritten Reich' in *Europa-Archiv* No. 6 of 1951, pp. 4128ff.
22. Hitler's instruction to Göring. The documents were found after the war among Speer's papers. See *Documents on German Foreign Policy*, Series C, Vol. 5, No. 490; Gerhard Meinck: *Hitler und die deutsche Aufrüstung*, Wiesbaden, 1959, p. 164;

Georg Tessin: *Formationsgeschichte der Wehrmacht 1933–1939*, Schriften des Bundesarchivs, Boppard, 1959, Vol. 7.

23. Bullock, 'Second World War', p. 268.
24. See Hans Kehrl: 'Kriegswirtschaft und Rüstungsindustrie' in *Bilanz des Zweiten Weltkrieges*, p. 272.
25. Albert Speer: *Inside the Third Reich*, p. 548.
26. Hitler in a speech to the Reichstag, given in Max Domarus: *Hitler. Reden und Proklamationen*, Vol. II/3, pp. 1112ff.
27. See Andreas Hillgruber: *Hitlers Strategie, Politik und Kriegsführung 1940/41*, Frankfurt, 1965, p. 31.
28. On the Hitler–Stalin Pact in this context see F. Friedensburg: 'Die sowjetischen Kriegslieferungen an das Hitlerreich' in *Vierteljahreshefte für Wirtschaftsforschung*, 1962, pp. 331ff.; Ph. Faby: *Der Hitler–Stalin-Pakt 1939–1941*, Darmstadt, 1962, pp. 168ff.
29. See W. Treue: *Gummi in Deutschland*, Munich, 1955, and 'Gummi in Deutschland zwischen 1933 und 1945' in *Wehrwissenschaftliche Rundschau*, 1955, pp. 196ff.
30. See W. Birkenfeld: *Der synthetische Treibstoff 1933 bis 1945*, Göttingen, 1964.
31. See also Hillgruber, op. cit., p. 34.
32. See Alfred Weidemann: 'Der rechte Mann am rechten Platz' in *Bilanz des Zweiten Weltkrieges*, Oldenburg, 1953, pp. 215ff.
33. See Erich von Manstein: *Lost Victories*, Methuen, London, 1958, pp. 70ff.
34. See Hitler's speech on 8 November 1938 given in Domarus, op. cit., Vol. I/2, p. 968.
35. See among others Walter Warlimont: *Inside Hitler's Headquarters*, Weidenfeld & Nicolson, London, 1964, pp. 66, 70.
36. See Werner Maser: *Hitler*, Allen Lane, London, 1973, pp. 287ff.
37. Quoted from Walter Görlitz: *Keitel. Verbrecher oder Offizier?*, p. 381.
38. IMT Vol. XIV, pp. 225ff. See also Görlitz, op. cit., p. 382.
39. Görlitz, op. cit., p. 383.
40. IMT Vol. XL, p. 420.
41. Görlitz, op. cit., p. 395.
42. See IMT Vol. I, pp. 288ff. The IMT's judgement accused Keitel, among other things, of having been present with two other generals at Hitler's meeting in Berchtesgaden in February 1938 with Kurt von Schuschnigg, the Austrian Federal Chancellor, and that, seeing he was Chief of the High Command of the German Armed Forces, this constituted a 'military demonstration' intended to put pressure on Austria. He was further accused of having signed 'many directives and memoranda' concerning the occupation of Czechoslovakia ('Fall "Grün"'). The fact that Keitel was present (on Hitler's orders) at the meeting in 1939 between Hitler and Emil Hacha, the Czechoslovak President, which ended, under pressure from Hitler, in the rump of Czechoslovakia being declared the Protectorate of Bohemia and Moravia, was also held by the IMT to be a 'Crime against Peace' committed by Keitel, as also were his signatures to Hitler's directives for the invasion of Poland, Norway and Denmark and instructions to disregard the neutrality of Belgium and Holland. 'Formal planning for attacking Greece and Yugoslavia,' the judgement continues, 'had begun in November 1940. On 18 March 1941 Keitel heard Hitler tell Raeder that complete occupation of Greece was a prerequisite to settlement and he also heard Hitler decree on 27 March

that the destruction of Yugoslavia should take place with "unmerciful harshness"'
(IMT Vol. I, p. 289). The judgement under Count One concluded with a reference
to his signatures to Hitler's directives for 'Case Barbarossa' and his order of
16 June 1941 prescribing that army units should carry out Göring's economic
directives in the 'Green Folder' for the exploitation of Russian territory, food
and raw materials. Under Count Two, 'War Crimes and Crimes against
Humanity', Keitel was accused of having issued an order that enemy paratroopers
be turned over to the SD, of 'participation' in the Commando Order (see Appendix
2) and the Commissar Order; the case against him was of failure to oppose Hitler
when the latter issued criminal orders contrary to international law such as his
anti-partisan measures, his order of 1 October 1941 to commanders concerning
hostages (hostages to be held ready at all times so that they could be shot in
the event of attacks on German soldiers) and the 'Night and Fog' order of
7 December 1941 (proceedings against civilians accused of resistance to the occupying power only to be taken when death sentences were required, otherwise they
should be handed over to the Gestapo). The judgement on Keitel concludes:
'He was present on 4 January 1944 when Hitler directed Sauckel to obtain 4
million new workers from occupied territories. In face of these documents Keitel
does not deny his connection with these acts. Rather, his defense relies on the
fact that he is a soldier, and on the doctrine of "superior orders" prohibited
by Article 8 of the Charter as a defense. There is nothing in mitigation. Superior
orders, even to a soldier, cannot be considered in mitigation where crimes as shock-
ing and extensive have been committed consciously, ruthlessly and without military
excuse or justification' (IMT Vol. I, pp. 290–91).
43. See Görlitz, op. cit., pp. 312ff.
44. See Maser, *Hitler*, op. cit., pp. 267ff.
45. Görlitz, op. cit., pp. 27ff.
46. *Völkischer Beobachter*, 10 March 1941.
47. IMT Vol. X, p. 600.
48. ibid. Hitler, who had a great sense of mission, repeatedly emphasized (not only
in *Mein Kampf*) that he had only been a simple soldier during the First World
War, so it seems unlikely that he would have told Keitel that he had been promoted
Lieutenant after the end of the war. Hitler left the army as a corporal on 31
March 1920. After the revolution Hitler attended training courses at Munich
University – on orders from his military superiors – and thereafter acted as
'contact man' for military headquarters in Munich; he occasionally referred to
himself as an 'education officer' at this period. (See Maser, *Hitler*, pp. 103ff.)
In Nuremberg Keitel obviously thought that the appointment of 'Education
Officer' carried the rank of Lieutenant.
49. See also Jodl's statements on this subject.
50. IMT Vol. X, pp. 601–2.
51. IMT Vol. I, pp. 310ff.
52. ibid., pp. 315ff.
53. ibid., pp. 322ff.
54. IMT Vol. X, pp. 602ff.
55. In US Document Center, Berlin.
56. One of Himmler's main objects in this report was to impress Hitler with as many
inflated figures as possible. This is shown by the fact that he even included the
capture of a box of surgical instruments, two radios and similar relatively unim-

portant objects such as two bicycles, twelve hoppers and 200 spades, shovels and saws.

57. IMT Vol. X, p. 611.

58. ibid., pp. 613ff.

59. ibid., pp. 614–15.

60. Document in US Document Center, Berlin. According to a minute by Himmler dated 10 May 1943 (Top Secret document in US Document Center, Berlin) 12,900 men of the Ordnungspolizei and 2,000 men of the Sicherheitspolizei were employed on anti-bandit operations in 'South Russia'; this would mean that each of the Germans doing their 'duty' in the area referred to by Himmler would have been responsible for killing approximately 3,224 people (an average of twenty-seven a day). It should be mentioned, however, that in this connection Himmler points out that some 300,000 'foreigners' were on duty 'throughout Russia' at the time – Letts, Lithuanians, White Russians, Ukrainians, Tartars and Cossacks.

61. Typescript document of sixteen pages. The letter-heading on page 1 is: 'Inspector of Statistics attached to the Reichsführer-SS'. Himmler's initials are underneath the 'Top Secret' stamp. Document in Federal Archives, Koblenz, No. NS 19 neu/1570.

62. ibid., p. 10. Inmates of ghettos and concentration camps were not included in this figure.

63. ibid., p. 9.

64. ibid.

65. Top Secret document in US Document Center, Berlin. In this minute Himmler also stated: 'The most important thing to me still is that as many Jews should be deported to the East as is humanly possible. In the Sicherheitspolizei's monthly summary reports I merely wish to be informed how many have been deported each month and how many Jews still remain at the time in question.'

66. Document in US Document Center, Berlin.

67. Typescript document of nine pages. Heading: 'Top Secret. Eyes only. Führer Headquarters. March 1941.' Five copies. Document in Federal Archives, Koblenz.

68. ibid., p. 2. There is clear documentary evidence that, particularly in 1944 and 1945, Himmler opposed Keitel's moderating influence in the matter of judicial powers in the occupied eastern territories. On 21 August 1944, for instance, he protested to the Field Marshal in a most unusual way. He sent a teleprint to Keitel saying that he raised definite objection to the Army General Staff proposal to endow Commanders-in-Chief of Army Groups in the East with judicial authority over all persons in the area of their command. He stated pointedly: 'I am the judicial authority for these formations' (meaning units of the Waffen-SS and police and those Wehrmacht units placed under him by Hitler). Document in US Document Center, Berlin.

69. See Werner Maser: *Hitlers Briefe und Notizen*, pp. 223ff.

70. See also Andreas Hillgruber: 'Die "Endlösung" und das deutsche Ostproblem als Kernstück des rassenideologischen Programms des Nationalsozialismus' in *Vierteljahrshefte für Zeitgeschichte*, No. 2 1972, pp. 133ff.

71. Hitler's *Mein Kampf*, p. 620 (Manheim's translation).

72. Quoted from Domarus, op. cit., Vol. II/3, p. 1058. See also Hitler's speeches on 30 January 1942, ibid., pp. 1663 and 1829.

73. See Maser, *Hitler*, p. 245.

74. See Heinz Höhne: *The Order of the Death's Head*, Secker & Warburg, London, 1969, pp. 315ff.
75. IMT Vol. X, pp. 617ff.
76. Original document (four typewritten sheets on Hitler's typewriter) in private ownership in the USA. Copy in the author's possession.
77. IMT Vol. X, p. 621.
78. ibid., pp. 618ff. The troops did not adhere strictly to Hitler's decree of 13 May 1941 and some men were punished for things done during anti-bandit operations. Keitel accordingly had to sign and distribute a top secret document dated 16 December 1942 starting 'The Führer has commanded ...' and reiterating the order that no German 'employed on anti-bandit operations' was to be 'subjected to disciplinary or court martial measures' for his 'behaviour in battle against the bandits or their auxiliaries' and that no sentences contrary to this order were to be confirmed. Document in US Document Center, Berlin.

CHAPTER 9: KARL DÖNITZ

1. See IMT Vol. XIII, p. 443, also pp. 395ff.
2. Personal information from Otto Kranzbühler, 6 March 1972.
3. Personal information from Otto Kranzbühler, 6 March 1972. See also his article 'Der letzte Auftrag meines Admirals' in the German illustrated paper *Stern*, Hamburg, No. 2 of 1966, pp. 94ff.
4. Personal information from Otto Kranzbühler, 6 March 1972.
5. Gerhard E. Gründler and Arnim von Manikowsky: *Das Gericht der Sieger*, p. 181. See also IMT Vol. XIII, pp. 422ff.
6. See judgement on Dönitz, IMT Vol. I, p. 314.
7. IMT Vol. XIII, pp. 410ff.
8. ibid., p. 407.
9. ibid., p. 418.
10. ibid., pp. 418–19.
11. ibid., p. 411.
12. ibid.
13. ibid., pp. 253ff.
14. ibid., p. 412.
15. ibid.
16. ibid., p. 421.
17. ibid., p. 552.
18. Kranzbühler's questionnaire was submitted to Admiral Nimitz on behalf of the IMT on 11 May 1946. His declaration was laid before the Tribunal by Kranzbühler on 2 July 1946. See IMT Vol. XIII, pp. 237, 451, Vol. XIV, p. 350, Vol. XVII, pp. 378ff., Vol. XVIII, pp. 319, 333, Vol. XL, pp. 276ff.
19. IMT Vol. VIII, p. 549.
20. See Francis Biddle: *In Brief Authority*, New York, 1962, p. 452.
21. IMT Vol. I, p. 312.
22. Special care had been taken on the German side to ensure that U-boat action was not taken against United States merchant ships and this entailed action under the Prize Regulations. An entry in Naval Headquarters War Diary on 5 March 1940, for instance, is: 'With reference to the conduct of economic warfare, orders are given to the Naval Forces that US ships are not to be stopped, seized or

sunk ... All possibilities of difficulties arising between the USA and Germany as a result of economic warfare are thereby to be eliminated from the start' (IMT Vol. XIII, p. 420).

23. On 11 September 1941, eighty days before the German declaration of war on the USA, President Roosevelt had stated publicly: 'Hitler knows that he must win the mastery of the seas if he wants to win the mastery of the world. He knows that he must first tear down the bridge of ships which we are building over the Atlantic and over which we constantly transport the war material that will help, in the end, to destroy him and all his works. He has to destroy our patrols on the sea and in the air' (IMT Vol. XIII, p. 466). It must nevertheless be remembered that Hitler, who inevitably had to combat this transport of war material from the USA, had authorized action against US merchant ships in the blockade zone around England on 18 July 1941 (IMT Vol. XIII, p. 421).

24. IMT Vol. I, p. 313.

25. Information personally and in writing to the author from Karl Dönitz on several occasions between 1969 and 1975.

26. IMT Vol. I, p. 291.

27. See Chapter 10 below.

28. IMT Vol. XIII, p. 252.

29. ibid.

30. IMT Vol. I, p. 310.

31. ibid.

32. ibid., p. 314.

33. IMT Vol. XIII, p. 342. In conversation with the author in 1969 Dönitz, who had shielded naval officers of Jewish origin, repeated that prior to Nuremberg he had not known what took place in concentration camps nor where all the camps were located. From January 1943, when he became Commander-in-Chief of the Navy, Dönitz had increasingly been used as an adviser by Hitler, with whom he had relatively frequent talks until the end of January 1945 (Sir David Maxwell-Fyfe reckoned that Dönitz had had 119 interviews with Hitler but Dönitz thought he could recall only fifty-seven – see IMT Vol. XIII, p. 321); nevertheless Hitler had never told him of this aspect of his policy, which Dönitz was ultimately supposed to continue in May 1945. The 'functional' machine in this respect was that of Heinrich Himmler, whom Dönitz did not include in his government.

The figures produced by Himmler's Inspector of Statistics in March 1943 concerning Jewish inmates of concentration camps (Federal Archives, Koblenz, NS 19 Neu/1570, p. 12) speak for themselves:

Lublin: Men: 4,683 out of 23,409 inmates, 4,509 releases, 14,217 deaths. Women: 2,659 out of 2,849 inmates, 59 releases, 131 deaths.

Auschwitz: Men: 1,200 out of 4,917 inmates, 1 release, 3,716 deaths. Women: 212 out of 932 inmates, no releases, 720 deaths.

Buchenwald: 227 out of 16,827 inmates, 13,805 releases, 2,795 deaths.

Mauthausen: 79 out of 2,064 inmates, no releases, 1,985 deaths.

Sachsenhausen: 46 out of 7,960 inmates, 6,570 releases, 1,344 deaths.

Stutthof: Men: 15 out of 28 inmates, no releases, 13 deaths. Women: 3 out of 3 inmates.

Ravensbrück: Men: 0 out of 273 inmates, 44 releases, 229 deaths. Women: 3 out of 1,321 inmates, 531 releases, 787 deaths.

Dachau: 0 out of 12,026 inmates, 11,140 releases, 886 deaths.

Gross-Rosen: 0 out of 231 inmates, no releases, 231 deaths.

Lichtenberg: 0 out of 195 inmates, 195 releases.

Neuengamme: 0 out of 192 inmates, 2 releases, 190 deaths.

Flossenbürg: 0 out of 80 inmates, 2 releases, 78 deaths.

Sachsenburg: 0 out of 52 inmates, 52 releases.

Esterwegen: 0 out of 36 inmates, 33 releases, 3 deaths.

Niederhagen: 0 out of 12 inmates, 12 deaths.

Natzweiler: 0 out of 10 inmates, 10 deaths.

    According to this statistical report, therefore, which Himmler described on 9 April 1943 as 'potential material for later use and excellent for camouflage purposes' (Document S.368, US Document Center, Berlin), up to 31 March 1943 out of 73,417 Jews handed over to concentration camps 27,347 'deaths' had been reported.

34. German industry was under obligation to use not only foreign workers but also concentration camp inmates. A directive from the Armaments Ministry, for instance, says: 'Where obstacles exist to the employment of special groups of persons (... inmates of concentration camps), armaments agencies will use every available means to remove difficulties' (quoted from Tilo Freiherr von Wilmowsky: *Warum wurde Krupp verurteilt? Legende und Justizirrtum*, p. 191). Even before the war an instruction had been issued (on 13 February 1939) concerning 'guaranteeing provision of labour for tasks of special national political importance' (*Reichsgesetzblatt* I, p. 206); it laid down that all public and private concerns and agencies were obligated to meet the 'demands of labour offices' and in future to follow the instructions of the Reich Minister of Labour concerning 'labour law, protection of labour and national insurance' (p. 652).

35. IMT Vol. XIII, pp. 341ff.

36. IMT Vol. XVI, p. 442.

37. ibid., p. 588.

38. ibid., p. 441; see also Dönitz's statement on 10 May 1946, IMT Vol. XIII, p. 344.

39. IMT Vol. I, p. 314. This shows that the IMT relied on the evidence of an officer who testified to Dönitz's remark.

40. ibid., pp. 314–15. Dönitz repeated his statement of 1946 in personal conversation with the author in May 1969.

41. See also Albert Speer's statement on this subject on 20 June 1946 (IMT Vol. XVI, pp. 526ff.).

CHAPTER 10: CRIME BY ORDER

1. IMT Vol. XV, pp. 312–13.

2. See Luise Jodl: *Jenseits des Endes. Leben und Sterben des Generalobersts Alfred Jodl*, Vienna, Munich, Zurich, 1976, p. 281.

3. IMT Vol. I, p. 324.

4. See *Kriegstagebuch des Oberkommandos der Wehrmacht (Wehrmachtführungsstab)* (War Diary of OKW Operations Staff), Vol. 1, edited by Hans-Adolf Jacobsen, p. 341. According to the entry for 3 March 1941 Hitler's 'directions for the final version' of 'Instructions on Special Matters attached to Directive No. 21 (Operation Barbarossa)' laid down that German military courts were to have nothing to do with the liquidation of 'Bolshevist leaders or commissars'

by the Secret Field Security Police. Their province was legal matters internal to the armed forces. Employment of SS units was to be further discussed with Hitler.

5. Hitler on 30 March 1941. See Hellmuth Greiner: *Die Oberste Wehrmachtsführung 1939–1943*, Wiesbaden, 1951, p. 371. Greiner kept the OKW War Diary from 1939 to 1943. On 17 March 1941 Hitler had told the military that the most brutal force would be necessary.

6. See also Franz Halder: *Kriegstagebuch. Tägliche Aufzeichnungen des Chefs des Generalstabes des Heeres 1939–1942*, edited by Arbeitskreis für Wehrforschung, Stuttgart, 3 vols., Stuttgart, 1962–4, Vol. II, pp. 336ff.

7. IMT Vol. XV, p. 308.

8. ibid., pp. 308–9.

9. ibid., p. 309.

10. ibid., pp. 313–14. This cross-examination took place on 4 June 1946.

11. The document carries Eugen Müller's own signature.

12. Probably on 21 May 1941.

13. See Werner Maser: *Hitler's Mein Kampf. An Analysis*, Faber & Faber, London, 1970, p. 138ff.

14. Top Secret. Dated 16 August 1941.

15. The head of section was General Warlimont.

16. The draft referred to in Note 14 above.

17. Typescript dated 21 August 1951 and signed personally 'Adolf Heusinger'. Copy in the author's possession.

18. See *Kriegstagebuch des Oberkommandos der Wehrmacht* (*Wehrmachtführungsstab*), collated and annotated by Andreas Hillgruber (Frankfurt/Main), Vol. II, p. 341.

19. ibid.

20. IMT Vol. XV, p. 314.

21. ibid., pp. 314ff.

22. ibid., p. 318.

23. The Americans allowed the French General Staff only 20 per cent credibility and Reuter even gave them 0 per cent for truthfulness. See Erich Murawsko: *Der Deutsche Wehrmachtsbericht 1939–1945. Ein Beitrag zur Untersuchung der geistigen Kriegführung*, Boppard, 1962, p. 122.

24. IMT Vol. XV, pp. 317–18.

25. ibid., pp. 319–20.

26. See Cmd 3794, 1931.

27. During cross-examination on 4 June 1946 Jodl stated (IMT Vol. XV, p. 329) that he had informed Hitler about the shackling of German soldier prisoners but had concealed from him the fact that members of the non-military 'Todt Organization' had been similarly treated and that they had strangled themselves as a result.

28. IMT Vol. XV, pp. 321–2.

29. Written information from Frau Jodl, 1 December 1975.

30. IMT Vol. XV, p. 323.

31. In addition to the Geneva Convention and the Hague Convention on War on Land there was the *Militärstrafgesetzbuch* (Military Criminal Code) (...'in the wording of the decree of 10 October 1940') which was published in Berlin in 1943 by Walter de Gruyter. In this reference is made to Article 27 of the German *Militärgesetzbuch* 1872 (the oldest written and universally binding regulation on the question of compliance with orders) and it is pointed out that military orders

emanate from and are covered by the supreme command authority resident in the Führer (Hitler); it lays down:

' 1. If criminal law is infringed through execution of an order dealing with military duty, the superior authority issuing the order is solely responsible. A subordinate obeying the order may, however, be punished as an accessory: 1. If he exceeds the order given, or 2. If it is known to him that his superior's order concerns an action, the purpose of which is a common or military crime or misdemeanour.

2. If the subordinate's guilt is minor, punishment may be withheld.' (Para 47)

The Reich Court Martial regarded official orders as binding, even if illegal, starting from the assumption that the individual soldier had neither the right nor the duty to check whether his superior's orders were legal, illegal or merely expedient.

32. A motion by Admiral Lord Cork to re-establish the original paragraph 443 was rejected by the House of Lords on 19 July 1955 by twenty-one votes to eighteen.

33. It says, for instance, that persons 'may be punished' for infringement of military law, the fact that this was done in pursuance of orders being taken into account in deciding the degree of punishment for the actions concerned.

34. *Deutsche Allgemeine Zeitung*, 28 May 1944.

35. Indictment 13 January 1947, judgement 3 November 1947.

36. 'Landsberg. Ein dokumentarischer Bericht' issued by Information Service Division, Office of the US High Commissioner for Germany, Munich, 1951, p. 21.

37. Two-page manuscript letter – copy in the author's possession. Quoted with the addressee's kind permission.

38. Written evidence dated 1946 in the author's possession.

39. IMT Vol. XV, p. 323.

40. ibid.

41. Quoted from Thomas Erskine Holland: *The Laws of War on Land*, Clarendon Press, London, 1908, pp. 20ff.

42. IMT Vol. XV, p. 323.

43. ibid., p. 324.

44. ibid.

45. See Werner Maser: *Hitler*, Allen Lane, London, 1973, pp. 274ff.

46. See *Hitler's Table Talk*, 20 August 1942. Original in Federal Ministry of Justice, Ref. No. R 22 Fr. 5/112. See also *Vierteljahreshefte für Zeitgeschichte*, No. 12 of 1964, H 1, pp. 86ff.

47. IMT Vol. XXII, pp. 465–6.

48. See H. Lauterpracht: *Annual Digest and Reports of Public International Law Cases 1941/42*, Case No. 168, pp. 564ff.

49. *Ex Parte Quirin* 1942, 317 US 1. Quoted from IMT Vol. XXII, p. 465.

50. ibid., p. 466.

51. *Reichsgesetzblatt* I, p. 535. Quoted from *Gesetze des NS–Staates*, edited by Ingo von Münch, Bad Homburg, Berlin, Zurich, 1968, p. 115.

52. Maser, *Hitler*, op. cit., pp. 274ff.

53. Document in Federal Archives, Koblenz, No. LXIV B 26, folio 1–160.

54. Federal Archives, Koblenz, LXIV B 22, folios 1–72, p. 11.

55. Affidavit by Viktor Brack dated 12 October 1946. Federal Archives, Koblenz, LXIV B 22, folios 1–72, p. 18.

56. They included dive-bomber pilots and soldiers who, for instance, had lost both arms and legs.

57. Viktor Brack's statement of 12 October 1946 in first Nuremberg follow-up trial. Federal Archives, Koblenz, LXIV B 22, folios 1–72, p. 19.

CHAPTER 11: LIMITS OF RESPONSIBILITY: THE NON-MILITARY DEFENDANTS

1. IMT Vol. XVI, p. 430.
2. ibid., p. 563.
3. ibid.
4. ibid., p. 430.
5. ibid., pp. 563–4.
6. ibid., p. 564.
7. ibid., p. 431.
8. ibid.
9. ibid.
10. ibid., p. 565.
11. The record refers to Raginsky throughout as 'Mr Counsellor' but for brevity's sake the title has been omitted in the extract below.
12. IMT Vol. XVI, pp. 565–6.
13. ibid., p. 570.
14. ibid.
15. ibid., p. 573.
16. ibid., pp. 576–7.
17. ibid., p. 581.
18. ibid.
19. ibid., pp. 580–81.
20. See Werner Maser: *Hitler*, p. 69, and *Hitlers Briefe und Notizen*, pp. 133ff. See also Speer's interview in *Der Spiegel*, 38/69, p. 68.
21. *Der Spiegel* 38/69, p. 78; see also Maser, *Hitler*, op. cit., pp. 69 and 361.
22. *Der Spiegel* 16/75, p. 79.
23. Gerhard E. Gründer and Arnim von Manikowsky: *Das Gericht der Sieger*, p. 188.
24. Speer in *Welt am Sonntag*, 13 October 1976, and Maser in *Welt am Sonntag*, 14 November 1976.
25. David Irving: 'Nürnberg – Die letzte Schlacht' in *Welt am Sonntag*, 7 November 1976 and Note 24 above.
26. IMT Vol. XVI, p. 544.
27. ibid., p. 532.
28. ibid., p. 531.
29. ibid., pp. 532–3.
30. ibid., p. 561.
31. ibid., p. 563.
32. ibid. Raginsky then began his cross-examination.
33. ibid., p. 543.
34. See Maser, *Hitler*, op. cit., pp. 209ff., and in particular p. 221.
35. IMT Vol. XVI, p. 583.
36. ibid., pp. 582ff.
37. ibid. See also W. A. Boelke: 'Hitlers Befehle zur Zerstörung oder Lähmung des deutschen Industriepotentials 1944/45' in *Tradition* 13/68, pp. 301ff.
38. Albert Speer: *Inside the Third Reich*, p. 515.

39. ibid., p. 508. See also Speer in *Welt am Sonntag*, 31 October 1976, and Maser in *Welt am Sonntag*, 14 November 1976. On the conflict between Speer and Sauckel and the subject of forced labour see E. L. Homze: *Foreign Labor in Nazi Germany*, Princeton, N.J., 1967; H. Pfahlmann: *Fremdarbeiter und Kriegsgefangene in der deutschen Kriegswirtschaft 1939–1945*; Hans Kehrl: *Krisenmanager im Dritten Reich. 6 Jahre Frieden, 6 Jahre Krieg*.
40. Speer, *Inside the Third Reich*, op. cit., p. 517.
41. Stahl was Head of Speer's Main Munitions Committee.
42. IMT Vol. XVI, pp. 493ff.
43. IMT Vol. I, p. 330.
44. On Sauckel see pp. 210ff below.
45. IMT Vol. I, pp. 331ff.
46. Judgement on Ribbentrop, IMT Vol. I, pp. 285ff.
47. On this subject see IMT Vol. X, pp. 242ff.
48. *The Ribbentrop Memoirs*, Weidenfeld & Nicolson, 1954, p. 199.
49. IMT Vol. X, p. 225.
50. ibid., pp. 224–5.
51. ibid., pp. 226–7.
52. ibid., pp. 227–8.
53. Gustav M. Gilbert: *Nuremberg Diary*, Signet Books, 1961, p. 67.
54. IMT Vol. X, p. 228.
55. ibid., pp. 228–9.
56. ibid., p. 230.
57. In his memoirs he wrote: 'Some of the defendants in the dock have incriminated me. I could have said much but I desisted because the German cause always came, and still comes, first and foremost with me; mutual recriminations in such a situation could only harm the nation. The past year has been hard for me, not least because of the disputes with my counsels, to whom I had to explain at every conference that I could say nothing against Adolf Hitler before this enemy court' (*Ribbentrop Memoirs*, p. 195).
58. IMT Vol. X, pp. 322–3.
59. ibid., pp. 426ff.
60. ibid., pp. 415–16.
61. A letter to Ribbentrop from Heydrich dated 24 June 1940 is addressed: 'Reich Foreign Minister SS-Gruppenführer Joachim von Ribbentrop' (Israeli Police Document No. 464).
62. IMT Vol. X, pp. 386–7. On Ribbentrop's relations with Himmler and the SS see Heinz Höhne: *The Order of the Death's-Head*, Secker & Warburg, 1969, pp. 277ff.
63. On these two Ribbentrop wrote: 'During the years in which they worked with me they showed a very different side of themselves. However in the psychosis of these days any change of opinion seems possible ... I am sure that with only slight pressure from the prosecution almost any Foreign Office official will give the desired evidence against me. This is sad, but alas true' (*The Ribbentrop Memoirs*, pp. 181–2). Weizsäcker and Kordt did not give evidence under pressure, as Ribbentrop wished to imply; he did not know that they had been members of the Resistance and so had been opposed to him even before the end of the war.
64. On Gaus, Ribbentrop noted: 'Gaus is behaving so contemptibly ...' (*Memoirs*, p. 184). Anneliese von Ribbentrop expands on this, pointing out that it was proved during the Wilhelmstrasse Trial (Case 11 of the American follow-up trials in

Nuremberg) that the prosecution in Nuremberg had dictated this attitude on the part of Gaus 'by threatening to hand him over to the Russians' (Ribbentrop: *Erinnerungen*, p. 283 – not in English translation). On Weizsäcker see Hellmut Becker's plea in defence in H. Becker: *Quantität und Qualität – Grundfragen der Bildungspolitik*, Freiburg, 1962.

65. *The Ribbentrop Memoirs*, pp. 180ff.
66. ibid., pp. 182ff.
67. ibid., pp. 184ff.
68. ibid., p. 188.
69. IMT Vol. X, pp. 444.
70. ibid.
71. ibid., pp. 444–5.
72. *The Ribbentrop Memoirs*, p. 192.
73. Judgement on Ribbentrop (IMT Vol. I, p. 285).
74. Letter dated 25 March 1969 to the author from Anneliese von Ribbentrop forwarding certain documents. Among them were Ribbentrop's 'Conclusions' of 2 January 1938 in which he forecast to the Führer that a British declaration of war was certain if war broke out. See also Maser, *Hitler*, p. 148.
75. IMT Vol. I, pp. 285ff.
76. ibid., p. 287.
77. ibid., pp. 287–8.
78. *The Ribbentrop Memoirs*, p. 192. See also p. 180.
79. ibid., p. 194.
80. Israel Police Document No. 464 (copy in the author's possession). On the problems of 'emigration', the 'final territorial solution' and 'final solution' see Höhne, op. cit., pp. 324ff., for the 'final solution', in particular, pp. 353ff. See also Robert M. W. Kempner: *Eichmann und Komplizen* and Uwe Dietrich Adam: *Judenpolitik im Dritten Reich*.
81. *The Ribbentrop Memoirs*, pp. 193–4.
82. IMT Vol. XX, pp. 151–2. For some time there was discussion about which French general should be murdered. It was originally planned to kill General de Boisse (sometimes referred to as 'Deboisse') (IMT Vol. XX, p. 563).
83. IMT Vol. XII, p. 375. See also pp. 306ff.
84. ibid.
85. ibid., pp. 375–6.
86. ibid., pp. 376–7.
87. IMT Vol. I, p. 302.
88. ibid., p. 304.
89. Otto Kranzbühler: *Nürnberg als Rechtsproblem*. See pp. 226ff.
90. Wilhelm Frick (1877–1946) was a lawyer. From 1917 to 1925 he was District Attorney and Clerk of the Court to Munich Police Headquarters, where he remained until the Hitler *putsch* of 8/9 November 1923. From the outset he kept 'a protecting hand over the still youthful Nazi Party and Adolf Hitler'. On 24 April 1924 he was sentenced to fifteen months' fortress arrest for complicity in treason (the Hitler *putsch*) and incarcerated in Landsberg am Lech together with Hitler. In 1924 he became a Reichstag deputy of the National-Socialist Freedom Party and in 1927 a deputy of the Nazi Party; he was made leader of the Party in the Reichstag in 1930 and at the same time Minister of the Interior and Minister of Popular Education in Thuringia. In 1933 he became Reich Minister of the Interior

and in 1938 (after the incorporation of Austria into the Reich) General Pleni-potentiary for Reich Administration (apart from military and economic matters). In 1939 he was made minister for Civil Defence and in 1943 Protector of Bohemia and Moravia.

91. IMT Vol. I, pp. 299ff. It is interesting that Frick should have been acquitted under Count One (Common Plan or Conspiracy to wage aggressive war).
92. ibid., pp. 300ff.
93. IMT Vol. XIX, pp. 570ff.
94. ibid., pp. 509ff.
95. IMT Vol. I, pp. 291ff. Kaltenbrunner (1903–46) was pronounced guilty under Counts Three and Four. He joined the Austrian SS in 1932 and became leader of it in 1937. In 1938 (after the Austrian Anschluss) he became State Secretary for Public Security, in 1941 Higher SS and Police Leader and in 1943 (by which time he was an Obergruppenführer in the SS) Chief of the Security Police and SD and Head of the Reichssicherheitshauptamt (RSHA – Central Security Department of the SS) in succession to Reinhard Heydrich who had been murdered in June 1942. On Kaltenbrunner see also Robert M. W. Kempner: *SS im Kreuzverhör*, Munich, 1964, pp. 129, 138, 193ff., 248, 270.
96. See IMT Vol. III, p. 367, and Gilbert, *Nuremberg Diary*, pp. 63–4.
97. IMT Vol. XIX, p. 432.
98. ibid., p. 598.
99. ibid., p. 599.
100. IMT Vol. I, p. 321.
101. IMT Vol. XIX, p. 491.
102. IMT Vol. I, pp. 320ff.
103. Seyss-Inquart had been in contact with the Nazi Party, however, ever since 1931. In February 1938 he was appointed Austrian Minister of the Interior after pressure exerted by Hitler on Kurt von Schuschnigg, the Austrian Chancellor, during their meeting in Berchtesgaden on 12 February. After the arrest of Schuschnigg (he was first imprisoned and then kept in a concentration camp until 1945) Seyss-Inquart acted as Austrian Chancellor and organized the Austrian Anschluss. The day after his acceptance into the Nazi Party Seyss-Inquart took over from Wilhelm Miklas, the Austrian President, who had resigned because he refused to agree the Anschluss. See IMT Vol. I, pp. 327ff.
104. IMT Vol. I, p. 366.
105. IMT Vol. XIX, p. 417.
106. IMT Vol. I, pp. 328ff.
107. ibid., p. 329.
108. His legacies to his wife (Gertrud Seyss-Inquart) included four clocks, one leather overcoat, one leather jacket, leather jack-boots, trunks, bags, 1,210 marks and a copy of Goethe's *Faust* (manuscript will (one page) dated 13 October 1946 – privately owned in the USA, copy in the author's possession).
109. Judgement on Seyss-Inquart, IMT Vol. I, pp. 329ff.
110. Hans Frank (1900–1946) was a lawyer. He became a member of the Nazi Party in 1927 and a deputy in the Reichstag in 1930. In 1933 he was made Minister of Justice in Bavaria, Nazi Party Reichsleiter for Legal Matters and President of the German Law Academy (a post which he held until 1942). In 1934 he became Minister without Portfolio and in 1939 head of the civil administration in the occupied Polish territories and Governor General of Poland. In 1942 he quarrelled

with Himmler, and Hitler, primarily owing to a speech by Frank which he did not like, came down on Himmler's side; as a result Frank inevitably became less intimate with Hitler. See Frank's memoirs written in Nuremberg: *Im Angesicht des Galgens*, Munich Gräfelfing, 1953, pp. 430ff.

111. See IMT Vol. I, p. 298.
112. IMT Vol. XXII, pp. 384–5.
113. *Im Angesicht des Galgens*, pp. 402ff. Even these death-bed memoirs shed some light on Frank's real character. He always yearned for recognition by Hitler and from 1942 suffered almost physically at his exclusion from Hitler's immediate entourage.
114. In a minute dated 15 November Himmler reported a discussion on this subject with Alfred Rosenberg, who argued that Himmler's powers in this respect were not unlimited. 'I contested this,' Himmler noted (in US Document Center, Berlin). Himmler explicitly stated, however, that he needed Rosenberg's agreement.
115. In US Document Center, Berlin. Himmler's policy on this subject in 1941 was characterized by the following: 'To further this matter the subservience of the Poles and the Ukrainians to their church and the greed of their priests should be taken into account. An equally good guarantee is the self-interest of these priests and also of the better-off Poles and Ukrainians who can be made responsible with their lives for bringing in the harvest and providing labour ... I regard it as most important that ... this year the priesthood together with one or more large-scale farmers or influential landowners in each village, businessmen or teachers or other dignitaries should be recruited for this purpose. I most emphatically forbid any agency to bribe any such scalawags in any village by financial or other chicanery or underhand dealing. Anyone recruited in the first year we have captured for ever, since he will be afraid of retribution from his neighbours and fellow-inhabitants and in addition will be unwilling to let a nice fat profit slip through his fingers.' Himmler advised Krüger to pay special attention to harnessing 'the priests' into the programme and rewarding their services to the Reich with money or payment in kind. 'The priest,' he wrote, 'is our collecting point. He will be interested in the yield. Above all, from every yield over 100 per cent he will get 20 per cent or payment in kind ... I will have no stupid German bureaucratic pettifogging which, using normal methods, will be unable to collect even half the desired yield ... At the same time the priest and other village dignitaries can be turned into potential hostages ... to ensure that nothing goes astray. Schools, not churches, should be used as storage space since I think it important that at the collecting points our wholesalers should be able to address their flock in the name of God and, threatening them with all the pains of hell, present the gathering of the harvest and work in Germany to them as the dictate of heaven.'
116. *Im Angesicht des Galgens*, p. 404.
117. ibid.
118. IMT Vol. XIX, pp. 500–501. Shawcross was quoting from IMT Document 2233–PS.
119. IMT Vol. I, p. 298.
120. Alfred Rosenberg (1893–1946) studied architecture in Riga and Moscow, passing the Moscow examination in 1918. At the end of 1918 he moved first to Berlin and then to Munich where, as an 'expert on bolshevism', he made the acquaintance of Hitler's friend and mentor Dietrich Eckart and through him that of Hitler. He

joined the DAP (Deutsche Arbeiter Partei – German Workers' Party) at the end of 1919, some three months after Hitler; his membership number was 625. Early in 1920 the Party changed its name to NSDAP (National-Socialist German Workers' Party). In 1921 he became a sub-editor of the *Völkischer Beobachter*, of which Hitler maintained that he was the owner at that time (see Maser: *Der Sturm auf die Republik*, pp. 258ff.); Hitler also made him editor of the *National-sozialistische Monatshefte*. In 1923 he took part in Hitler's *putsch* of 8/9 November in Munich and thereafter, while the Party was banned, held it together while Hitler was under fortress arrest in Landsberg am Lech (where 255 of the war criminals sentenced at Nuremberg were hanged two decades later). In 1930 Rosenberg became a Nazi Reichstag deputy and in 1933 Head of the External Political Office of the Nazi Party and a Reichsleiter. In 1934 Hitler charged him with supervision of the 'ideological education' of the NSDAP, the German Labour Front and all assimilated organizations; in 1940 he was made responsible for setting up the 'Hohe Schule', the central research institution for National-Socialist ideology and education; in 1941 he became Reich Minister for the Occupied Eastern Territories. Rosenberg's whole career was governed by his early political experiences between 1918 and 1925. See Maser: *Der Sturm auf die Republik*, pp. 24ff., 89, 177ff., 181–4, 185, 209, 214, 237, 252, 268, 330ff., 336ff., 339, 342, 357, 376, 380, 382, 401ff., 405, 432, 472.

121. See *Völkischer Beobachter*, 4 November 1924, where Rosenberg denies this.

122. See *8 Uhr Abendblatt*, 28 October 1930. Rosenberg took the newspaper to court in Munich and won the case. See also *Vorwärts*, 14 November 1931, and *Berliner Volkszeitung*, 4 March 1932.

123. See *Völkischer Beobachter*, 4 November 1924. Rosenberg denied the 'charges' made against him and his wife of being Jewish. Franz Seel, a journalist living in Reval, sent large numbers of open letters to 'Alfred Rosenberg, Chief Editor of the *Völkischer Beobachter*'. These stated that Martin Rosenberg, Rosenberg's grandfather, was a Lett and his mother (Luise Karoline née Sire) a Frenchwoman, that Martin Rosenberg's grandmother, Saly Rosenberg, was a Jewess and the paternal grandmother's grandfather, H. Sram, a Mongol and a serf. In para. 4 of one letter Seel, who offered to appear before the Reich court in Leipzig and prove his statements, set out his sources and concluded '. . . accordingly you have not a drop of German blood in your veins'. The document, which is undated, is in US Document Center, Berlin. Seel's offer was not accepted.

124. Judgement on Rosenberg, IMT Vol. I, pp. 295ff.

125. Quoted from Rudenko's final address on 29 July 1946 (IMT Vol. XIX, p. 603). Shawcross, in his final address, stated that Erich Koch, the Gauleiter of East Prussia, had been designated as Commissar in Moscow by Rosenberg (IMT Vol. XIX, p. 500). According to the minute by Himmler of 15 November 1941 referred to below SA Obergruppenführer Siegfried and not Koch had been 'selected to occupy the Reich Commissariat, Moscow'. Himmler was opposed to this appointment, seeing in it 'a source of endless vexation' since, in his view, Kasche was 'a desk man', 'in no way energetic or strong' and 'a definite enemy of the SS'.

126. IMT Vol. XIX, p. 500.

127. US Document Center, Berlin.

128. IMT Vol. I, pp. 295–6.

CHAPTER 12: CLOSING ADDRESSES AND FINAL PLEAS

1. IMT Vol. XIX, p. 397. Four years later Jackson stated that he was not personally in favour of capital punishment but that the society he represented punished murder with death. See also Gerhard E. Gründler and Arnim von Manikowsky: *Das Gericht der Sieger*, p. 189.
2. IMT Vol. XIX, pp. 397–8. Jackson emphasized that he did not wish to 'labor the law of this case' since the British Prosecutor would deal with this aspect on behalf of all the Chief Prosecutors; he continued that he would 'rest upon the law of these crimes' as enshrined in the Charter.
3. IMT Vol. XIX, pp. 426–7.
4. ibid., p. 428.
5. ibid., p. 432. Jackson's address ended at 13.45. Sir Hartley Shawcross followed in the afternoon.
6. ibid., p. 529. Shawcross's quote from Goethe came, as the men of letters soon discovered, from Thomas Mann's *Lotte in Weimar*, published in 1939.
7. IMT Vol. XX, p. 14.
8. ibid., p. 179.
9. ibid., pp. 179–80.
10. ibid., pp. 180ff. This was the end of Hoffmann's cross-examination.
11. ibid., pp. 198–9.
12. IMT Vol. XXII, pp. 35–6.
13. IMT Vol. XX, pp. 205–6. Shortly before this the President had intervened in the cross-examination and asked Hoeppner whether he did not know that the Einsatzgruppen were composed of members of the SD, the Gestapo and the Criminal Police, which Hoeppner was forced to admit (IMT Vol. XX, pp. 201–2).
14. Heinz Höhne: *The Order of the Death's-Head*, Secker & Warburg, 1969, p. 358. Höhne gives details: 'Nevertheless by May 1941 Heydrich had assembled some 3,000 men whom he formed into four Einsatzgruppen. Stahlecker assumed command of Einsatzgruppe A which was to follow Army Group North through the Baltic States towards Leningrad; Nebe was in charge of Einsatzgruppe B attached to Army Group Centre, operating between the Baltic States and the Ukraine. Rasch commanded Einsatzgruppe C, operating in the west, north and east of Army Group South's area. Ohlendorf's Einsatzgruppe D was responsible for the southern part of Army Group South's zone between Bessarabia and the Crimea.'
15. IMT Vol. XXII, p. 365. In his closing address on 29 July 1946 Rudenko described the IMT as an international criminal court (IMT Vol. XIX, p. 570).
16. Reader's letter in *Frankfurter Allgemeine Zeitung*, 18 July 1975.
17. IMT Vol. XXII, p. 366.
18. ibid.
19. ibid.
20. IMT Vol. XXVIII, Document 1816–PS.
21. Confidential instruction to non-Prussian *Land* governments (including Austria) dated 10 January 1939. Document in US Document Center, Berlin.
22. Heydrich's papers, 19 November 1959. Document IF–0250, p. 21.
23. Hanged in Landsberg am Lech 7 June 1951.
24. See IMT Vol. IV, pp. 316ff. and Vol. XXXI, Document 2620–PS.

25. ibid.
26. IMT Vol. IX, p. 174.
27. ibid., pp. 10ff.
28. IMT Vol. XXII, p. 368.
29. ibid.
30. Dr Pflücker in *Waldeckische Landeszeitung*, October 1952. The date of the entry is indecipherable. Pflücker says: 'He (Göring) criticized Speer in sharp terms for having offloaded on to Sauckel all responsibility for forced labour by foreign workers.'
31. IMT Vol. IX, p. 100. Questioned by Jackson on 11 March 1946 Milch explained what was meant by the word 'slackers' as follows: '... those people who were compelled to work during the war' (IMT Vol. IX, p. 112).
32. IMT Vol. IX, p. 110.
33. ibid., p. 111.
34. IMT Vol. XXII, p. 372.
35. ibid., p. 373.
36. ibid., pp. 377–8.
37. Francis Biddle: *In Brief Authority*, New York, 1962, pp. 465ff.
38. Viktor Freiherr von Lippe: *Nürnberger Tagebuchnotizen. November 1945 bis Oktober 1946*, Frankfurt, 1951, p. 290. See also p. 373.
39. Woods, in the US soldiers' newspaper *Stars and Stripes*, 20 October 1946.
40. Pflücker, in *Waldeckische Landeszeitung*, 16 October 1952.
41. Quoted from *Der Spiegel* No. 50 of 1975, 8 December 1975, p. 166.
42. ibid., p. 167.
43. ibid., pp. 167ff.
44. ibid., p. 168.
45. Pflücker, in *Waldeckische Landeszeitung*, 16 October 1952.
46. See also *Der Spiegel*, 8 December 1975, p. 169.
47. Pflücker, in *Waldeckische Landeszeitung*, 16 October 1952.
48. Quoted by kind permission of Frau Luise Jodl.

CHAPTER 13: THE JUDGEMENT

1. In certain cases the figures differ from those given in 1976 by Luise Jodl in *Jenseits des Endes* (p. 176). According to Frau Jodl's 'list' 28 journalists regarded Seyss-Inquart as guilty but only 3 thought that he would be condemned to death. Journalists' bets on death sentences as given by Luise Jodl were: Raeder 13 (out of 32), Streicher 13 (out of 30), Speer 3 (out of 28) and Funk 5 (out of 30).
2. For composition of the Tribunal see IMT Vol. I, p. 1.
3. Dr Pflücker in *Waldeckische Landeszeitung*, October 1952, date indecipherable.
4. See Werner Maser: *Hitler*, Allen Lane, 1973, pp. 117ff.
5. IMT Vol. XII, pp. 450–51.
6. IMT Vol. IX, p. 440.
7. ibid., p. 370.
8. ibid., p. 400.
9. ibid., p. 615.
10. ibid., p. 614.
11. IMT Vol. XIII, p. 301.
12. ibid.

13. IMT Vol. XII, p. 13.
14. IMT Vol. X, p. 600.
15. ibid.
16. ibid., p. 485.
17. ibid., pp. 227–8.
18. IMT Vol. XXII, p. 405.
19. IMT Vol. XV, p. 302.
20. ibid.
21. ibid., p. 552.
22. ibid., p. 375.
23. IMT Vol. XVII, p. 93.
24. IMT Vol. XIII, p. 82.
25. IMT Vol. XII, p. 313.
26. IMT Vol. XII, p. 324.
27. Speer's estimate of Seyss-Inquart was surprisingly favourable – see Speer: *Inside the Third Reich*, pp. 457, 487, 497, 510ff.
28. Dr Pflücker in *Waldeckische Landeszeitung*, October 1952.
29. ibid.
30. Seyss-Inquart and Papen together with Frank and Kaltenbrunner had attempted to find peace within the bosom of the Catholic church while in Nuremberg. During the court's recess from 20 December 1945 to 2 January 1946 they had celebrated a Catholic Christmas in the prison chapel with Father Sixtus O'Connor, the American Army chaplain. At the same time Pastor Henry F. Gerecke, who came from St Louis, Missouri, and did not speak German particularly well, held a short Christmas service for the Protestant defendants in two cells converted into a chapel; he read them the Christmas story from the Bible and Sauckel thanked him warmly on behalf of his fellow-defendants.
31. Streicher had equally been baptized as a Catholic but he made fun of 'last-minute christians' like Frank and did not go to the 1945 Christmas service. On the gallows, however, he assured the chaplain: 'Father, I am with God.'
32. Sixtus O'Connor, the Catholic priest, was determined to remain to the end of the trial. Pastor Gerecke, the evangelical chaplain, on the other hand expressed a wish to return to his family and parish in St Louis at the end of 1945. The defendants were much downcast; they wrote a communal letter to Mrs Gerecke begging her to do without her husband for the time being. See Henry F. Gerecke: 'I walked to the gallows with the Nazi chiefs' in *Saturday Evening Post*, 1 September 1951, pp. 17–19 and 57ff.
33. *Waldeckische Landeszeitung*, October 1952.
34. Viktor Freiherr von Lippe: *Nürnberger Tagebuchnotizen*, p. 492.
35. Dr Pflücker in *Waldeckische Landeszeitung*, 21 October 1952.
36. ibid., October 1952 – date indecipherable.
37. ibid.
38. ibid.
39. Quoted from Jodl's letters by kind permission of Frau Luise Jodl.
40. Albert Speer: *Spandau. The Secret Diaries*, Collins, 1976, p. 6.
41. These and the comments immediately following are typical of Speer's usual fanciful descriptions. Since he was handcuffed to a guard, he could not have seen what was going on in the cells. His remarks on his fellow-defendants speak for themselves.

42. Speer, *Spandau*, op. cit., pp. 8ff.
43. Quoted from Walter Görlitz: *Keitel. Verbrecher oder Offizier?*, p. 385. Incomprehensibly Frau Lisa Keitel wrote to Dr Nelte on 1 October 1946: 'I have just written the last letter to my husband. I trust that the request to be executed as soldiers will be granted him and Jodl. Otherwise, please, no petition for clemency' (quoted from Görlitz, op. cit., p. 384). It is difficult to judge whether her attitude was dictated by pride or intuition. In a letter to his eldest son on 13 October 1946 Keitel complained that he had only had letters from the women of his family. 'How cowardly men are,' he said (quoted from Görlitz, op. cit., p. 384).
44. Quoted by kind permission of Luise Jodl.
45. Letter from Luise Jodl, 6 October 1975.
46. ibid.
47. ibid.
48. The letter to Montgomery was transmitted by Maxwell-Fyfe. Personal information from Luise Jodl in 1973.
49. See B. C. Andrus: *The Infamous of Nuremberg*, London, 1969.
50. Dr Pflücker in *Waldeckische Landeszeitung*, October 1952, Serial 16.
51. ibid., Serial 17.
52. ibid.
53. Letter from Dr Kempner, 28 November 1975.
54. Dr Pflücker in *Waldeckische Landeszeitung*, October 1952, Serial 17.
55. Letter is dated 11 October 1946. It is published here by permission of Dr Kempner, who kindly made it available to me for evaluation.
56. Information from Frau Göring to Dr Kempner – letter from Dr Kempner 28 November 1975.
57. The story spread by von dem Bach-Zelewsky, the ex-SS officer, that it was he who passed the poison to Göring cannot be proved.
58. *Waldeckische Landeszeitung*, October 1952, Serial 14.
59. Personally from Ernst Wilhelm Keitel, 21 July 1975.
60. *Stars and Stripes*, 28 July 1950.
61. A 'collector' from Havana telegraphed Woods offering $2,500 for a rope.
62. *Stars and Stripes*, 20 October 1946.
63. See Charles A. Duff: *A Handbook of Hanging*, London, 1961, p. 132.
64. Personal information from Helmut Kamphausen, May 1973.
65. In 1946 Germans were paying an average of RM 7,000 on the Berlin black market to anyone who would certify that they had a Jewish grandmother. See *Die Tat*, 17 April 1946.

CHAPTER 14: NUREMBERG IN HISTORY

1. IMT Vol. I, p. 170.
2. Article 3 of the Charter stipulated that: 'Neither the Tribunal, its members nor their alternates can be challenged by the Prosecution, or by the defendants or their counsel' (IMT Vol. I, p. 10).
3. IMT Vol. I, p. 168 (footnote).
4. The only instance of a differing opinion was in 'Case II' where the Tribunal declared that: 'Under the American concept of liberty as brought to us by our Anglo-Saxon heritage and the English Common Law every person accused of crime is presumed to be innocent until proof of his guilt is established' (*Trials of War*

Criminals before the Nuremberg Military Tribunals, Vol. II, p. 877).

5. Punishment of war criminals had been declared one of the most important Allied war aims in the St James's Declaration on 13 January 1942.

6. IMT Vol. I, pp. 168ff.

7. The Convention was signed on 4 November 1950 and was largely based on the United Nations 'Universal Declaration of Human Rights' of 10 December 1948. Article 7 of the Convention enunciated the principle of *Nullum crimen, nulla poena sine lege*: 'No one shall be held guilty of any penal offence on account of any action or omission which did not constitute a penal offence under national or international law at the time when it was committed. Nor shall a heavier penalty be imposed than the one that was applicable at the time the penal offence was committed.' The other rights guaranteed were: Right to Life (Article 2); Prohibition of Torture (Article 3); Prohibition of Slavery or Servitude (Article 4); Right to Freedom and Security of the Person (Article 5); Right to a Fair Hearing (Article 6); Right to Privacy (Article 8); Freedom of Thought, Conscience and Religion (Article 9); Freedom of Opinion and Expression (Article 10); Peaceful Assembly and Association (Article 11); Right of Marriage (Article 12); Right to Aid for persons whose Rights and Freedoms guaranteed by the Convention have been violated (Article 13).

8. Robert M. W. Kempner in *Mann in der Zeit*, October/November 1966.

9. IMT Vol. I, pp. 282ff.

10. Eugene E. K. Bird in German television programme *Augenzeugen berichten* on 22 August 1976. In England persons sentenced to life imprisonment are generally released after nine years and in the Soviet Union after ten years. See also Helga Einsele, Johannes Feige and Heinz Müller-Dietz: 'Die Reform der lebenslangen Freiheitsstrafe' in *Beiträge zur Strafvollzugswissenschaft*, No. 10, Stuttgart, 1972, p. 34.

   International law supersedes inter-state agreements; the Declaration on Human Rights of 10 December 1948 and the Human Rights Convention of 4 November 1950 take precedence over all inter-state treaties; nevertheless Hess has not been released. A. J. P. Taylor's view that he was only pronounced guilty by the Americans, the British and the French 'to please the Russians' (*Sunday Express* 27 April 1969) is probably fairly near the truth.

11. A letter in *The Times* of 2 January 1970 from Lord Shawcross, British Chief Prosecutor in Nuremberg, includes: 'His [Hess's] life sentence by the IMT at Nuremberg was, in comparison with others, by no means a lenient one. I suspect that all of us on the Western side took it for granted that it would be subject to the sort of commutation recognized in civilized systems of criminal justice and would not literally be for life. That he should continue to be imprisoned now seems to me an affront to all notions of justice.'

12. Taylor was nominated by President Truman to succeed Jackson as Chief Prosecutor of the IMT (Executive Order 9547, 2 May 1945). His official title was 'Chief Prosecutor for War Crimes' (Truman's order 9679, 16 January 1946). See Taylor: *War Crimes and International Law*, pp. 44ff. On 2 October 1946, the day after the IMT had pronounced judgement, Taylor and Kempner flew back to the US and there worked on preparations for the 'follow-up' trials until February 1947. They returned to Nuremberg in March 1947 (personal information from Dr Kempner, 8 March 1974). See also Taylor: 'The Nuremberg Trials' in *International Conciliation* (Carnegie Endowment for International Peace), 1949, p. 450.

13. Telford Taylor: *Nuremberg and Vietnam*, Quadrangle Books, Chicago, 1970, pp. 84ff.
14. *International Conference on Military Trials*, Department of State Publication, 3080, p. 328.
15. UNO Document A/CN 425, 26 April 1950.
16. Taylor, op. cit., p. 99.
17. ibid., pp. 102–3.
18. ibid., p. 103.
19. IMT Vol. I, p. 276. See also p. 356.
20. On security measures to protect Hitler see Peter Hoffmann: *Die Sicherheit des Diktators*, Munich, 1975.
21. Taylor, op. cit., p. 12.
22. IMT Vol. I, p. 317.
23. The Pact to Outlaw War was signed in Paris on 27 August 1928 by representatives of Germany (Stresemann), the United States (Kellogg), France (Briand), Belgium (Hymans), Czechoslovakia (Benesh), Great Britain including Ireland and the British Dominions overseas (Mackenzie King, McLashlan, Parr, Smith, Cosgrave, Cushenden), Italy (Manzoni), Japan (Ushida) and Poland (Zaleski). Articles 1 and 2 stated:
    'The High Contracting Parties solemnly declare in the names of their respective peoples that they condemn recourse to war for the solution of international controversies and renounce it as an instrument of national policy in their relations with one another.
    'The High Contracting Parties agree that the settlement or solution of all disputes or conflicts, of whatever nature or of whatever origin they may be, which may arise among them, shall never be sought except by pacific means.'
    Great Britain, France and Poland had reservations; Great Britain stipulated that self-defence remained an inalienable right and demanded freedom of action in certain specific areas (the Suez Canal, for instance); all three demanded the right of unilateral decision on self-defence. Any signatory power which attempted thereafter to 'promote its national interests by war' was to forfeit all advantages offered by the treaty. See K. Schwendmann: *Abrüstung und Sicherheit* (2nd edition 1933), Vol. 1, Annex 7, pp. 550ff. There was no mention of punishment of individuals in the Pact so that it could hardly be regarded as a part of criminal law in the legal sense.
24. Significantly, in the Weizsäcker Trial (Case XI) the court declared in its judgement: 'We hold that aggressive wars and invasions have, since time immemorial, been a violation of international law' (*Trials of War Criminals before the Nuremberg Military Tribunals*, Vol. XIV, p. 319).
25. As the defence pointed out, justice in Nuremberg was based on a new concept of criminal law, particularly as regards Crimes against Peace and Crimes against Humanity. Until the Nuremberg Trial, Oppenheim's interpretation had been generally held to be valid; under this violations of the rules of war were only regarded as war crimes 'if they were committed without an order from the belligerent government concerned'. Oppenheim also stated that, if committed by members of the armed forces on orders from their government, they were 'not war crimes and could not be punished by the enemy'. Quoted from Gerhard Brennecke: *Die Nürnberger Geschichtsentstellung*, Tübingen, 1970, p. 48.
26. In the IMT's view (IMT Vol. XXII, p. 461) the London Charter was 'an

expression of international law existing at the time of its creation'. The defence was particularly critical of the Charter for the fact that it was not confined to laying down rules of procedure but contained provisions laying down criminal law to be applied by the court.

27. IMT Vol. XXII, p. 85.
28. Quoted from Otto Kranzbühler: *Rückblick auf Nürnberg*, p. 16.
29. IMT Vol. XXII, pp. 465–6.
30. ibid., p. 461.
31. Robert M. W. Kempner in *Mann in der Zeit*, October/ November 1966.
32. Article 51 of the Hague Agreement, for instance, laid down: 'For every contribution [levied by an occupying power on the people of an occupied territory] a receipt shall be given to the payer.' Article 52 prescribed: 'Supplies in kind shall, as far as possible, be paid for on the spot; if not ... payment of the sums due shall be made as soon as possible.' It is superfluous to point out that such provisions were in no way regarded as binding by any of the belligerents even in 1914–18.
33. Article 43. See Thomas Erskine Holland: *The Laws of War on Land* Clarendon Press, 1908, p. 52.
34. Article 23h, ibid., p. 104.
35. IMT Vol. XXII, p. 461.
36. Kempner in *Mann in der Zeit*, op. cit.
37. ibid.
38. Smith is referring here to the Charter of the International Court, on the interpretation of which, however, prominent international lawyers are by no means agreed. Under Article 38 the International Court is charged with deciding disputes submitted to it in accordance with international law ('without prejudice to the provisions of Article 59, using judicial decisions and the doctrines of the most highly qualified experts from the various nations as guides for establishing the rules of law'). The Soviet international lawyer G. O. Tunkin objected that: 'It does not at all follow from this that the International Court's decisions ... set a precedent in law. This idea ... is not applicable to international law. To ascribe such a role to the International Court is go beyond the provisions of its Charter' (quoted from *Modernes Völkerrecht. Form oder Mittel der Aussenpolitik*, Berlin, 1965, p. 296). Sir Hersch Lauterpracht, on the other hand, regarded the International Court's decisions as carrying the same weight as international treaties and common law; in his view, therefore, they were international law. See H. Lauterpracht: The *Development of International Law. The International Court*, London, 1958, p. 22.
39. *Freies Europa*, Vol. 13, No. 162, July 1946.
40. *Hitler's Table Talk*, Weidenfeld & Nicolson, 1953, pp. 641ff.
41. Precise figures cannot be established. Telford Taylor says (*Nuremberg and Vietnam*, p. 28) that by the beginning of 1948 3,500 war crimes trials had been concluded in Europe and 2,800 in the Far East. In addition numerous trials ending in death sentences had been conducted in the Soviet Union and in China.
42. In addition to the eleven death sentences pronounced by the IMT, American judges awarded thirty-six death sentences in the twelve 'follow-up' trials. Numerous death sentences were also pronounced by Army Military Commissions in the so-called concentration-camp trials and by administrative military courts. Of those condemned to death 255 were hanged in Landsberg am Lech, where Hitler had written the first volume of *Mein Kampf* in 1925.
43. Article 19 of the IMT Charter, IMT Vol. I, p. 15.

44. Article 21 of the IMT Charter, ibid.
45. IMT Vol. X, p. 6 and Vol. XIX, p. 113. For procedure prejudicial to the defence see also IMT Vol. XIX, p. 221.
46. Article 20 of the IMT Charter, IMT Vol. I, p. 15.
47. IMT Vol. XII, pp. 222–3.
48. See Hans-Günther Seraphim: 'Erschliessung der Nürnberger Prozessakten' in *Der Archivar*, No. 28 of 1975, pp. 418ff.
49. IMT Vol. I, p. 172.
50. See *Exchange Telegraph*, 11 January 1946. Of the witnesses heard by the IMT thirty-three testified orally for the prosecution and eighty for the defence. A further 143 witnesses gave written evidence for the defence. Twenty-two witnesses were heard on behalf of the 'criminal organizations'. 101 witnesses for the defence were heard by specially appointed 'Commissioners'. 1,809 affidavits from other witnesses were submitted by the defence. (IMT Vol. I, p. 172.)
51. IMT Vol. I, p. 2.
52. ibid., pp. 3ff.
53. Kranzbühler, op. cit., p. 13.
54. Among the critics was Liddell Hart, the well-known British military historian. He was acting as adviser to the British prosecuting team and thought Alfred Jodl's sentence in particular to be unjust. See also J. R. Evenhuis: 'Pflicht und Dilemma der deutschen Militärs' in *Elseviers Weekblad*, 24 July 1948.
55. On 22 July 1946 Gaston Oulman, the radio commentator, said: 'The opinion has been expressed, not only in German circles, that the soldiers should not be held responsible. We refer in this instance to Jackson's statement that the case is directed against certain aspects and not against the military profession as such. The prosecution is not prepared to abandon this point of view, particularly not where violations of obligations under international law are concerned' (transcript by a secretary of the US prosecuting team; document in the author's possession).
56. In Nuremberg Biddle quoted from the IMT judgement: 'A plan in the execution of which a number of persons participate, is still a plan even though conceived by only one of them and those who execute the plan do not avoid responsibility by showing that they acted under the direction of the man who conceived it ... They are not to be deemed innocent ... if they knew what they were doing' (IMT Vol. XXII, pp. 468–9).
57. Merle Miller: *Plain Speaking. An Oral Biography of Harry S. Truman*, Gollancz, 1974, p. 227.
58. When his biographer asked him whether he was prepared to go to Hiroshima and talk to certain people there in front of a film camera, he replied: 'I'll go to Japan if that's what you want, but I won't kiss their arse' (ibid., p. 230).
59. P. W. Tibbets, the commander, was a Colonel in 1945. He left the US Air Force as a Brigadier-General in 1969. Thirty years after dropping the atom bomb he was Vice-President of an air taxi company in Columbus, Ohio.
60. Tibbets, in an interview with the German illustrated paper *Stern*, No. 32 of 1975, p. 41.
61. ibid.
62. In a personal statement, which Judge Elliott attached to his decision. Calley was permitted to say: 'War is war and it is by no means unusual for innocent civilians like the victims of My Lai to get killed.' His statement even quoted the Bible, continuing: 'It was so throughout recorded history. It was so when Joshua took

Jericho. But Joshua was not accused of the murder of Jericho's civilian population. Moreover, so we are told, God was on Joshua's side.' Judge Elliott stated significantly: 'War is hell. If we take a young man into the army and train him to kill, if we teach him to obey orders and send him to a foreign country and if then, in the heat of battle, he does something which, long after the event, leads to an accusation of capital crime, then justice demands ... that he be given fair treatment by the press, by his government and by the arm in which he served' (quoted from *Frankfurter Allgemeine Zeitung*, 27 September 1974).

63. Castro – Cuba; Lumumba – Congo (Zaire); Trujillo – Dominican Republic; Schneider – Chile; Diem – South Vietnam.

64. *Der Spiegel*, No. 48 of 1975, p. 114. Certain instructions were signed by Allen Dulles, head of the CIA (ibid.). Lumumba was murdered by his Congolese rivals early in 1961. Diem was killed in 1963 during a generals' *putsch* supported by the US government.

65. Letter from Dr Kempner, 8 October 1975 and verbally from Dr Kempner, 13 October 1975.

66. In accordance with these provisions of international law the Potsdam Agreement of 2 August 1945 explicitly stated that the German eastern territories were only provisionally ('without prejudice to ultimate decisions on territorial questions in the peace settlement') placed under Russian (City of Königsberg and adjacent area) and Polish administration; the ultimate boundaries were only to be decided in a peace treaty with Germany.

67. Under Article 8 of the Geneva Convention of 1949 'protected persons' (in other words the civil population) in occupied territories were not to be deprived of these rights. In the light of West Germany's treaties with the Soviet Union, Poland and Czechoslovakia this is worth remembering.

68. British Parliamentary Miscellaneous Papers 1814–15, Vol. XIII, p. 191.

69. Personally from Frau Emmy Göring (1953).

70. See W. J. Bosch: *Judgement on Nuremberg. American Attitudes towards the Major War Crime Trials*, University of Carolina Press, 1970.

71. Karl Dönitz in an interview on German television, Programme 1, 12 March 1973.

72. During the IG-Farben trial the opinion was expressed that Trainin, the Russian legal expert who was a co-signatory with Nikitchenko of the London Four-Power Agreement of 8 August 1945 (IMT Vol. I, pp. 9ff.), had exerted an extraordinary and negative influence on Jackson and the content of the London Charter; he was held responsible for injecting Russian-influenced politics into the proceedings. His critics also named him as the man responsible for acceptance into the Indictment of the Count of 'Crimes against Peace'. In fact on several important points Jackson's views were identical with those openly championed by the Russian, who was not inhibited by 'traditional legalisms'. Some unimportant differences aside, both held the view that the 'legalisms' developed during the era of imperialism obscured the legal position and restricted the possibilities of punishing the defendants, so that it was better to ignore them.

73. In this same article Jackson Junior accused George Schuster, the former President of Hunter College, of unjustified bias in favour of Göring.

74. W. E. Jackson: 'War Nürnberg gerechtfertigt?' in *Collier*, 19 May 1947.

75. Taylor: *Nuremberg and Vietnam*, op. cit., p. 86.

76. From Kranzbühler op. cit., p. 25.

77. ibid., p. 24. Kranzbühler himself heard Jackson say this.

78. ibid., p. 25.
79. ibid.
80. Quoted from *Arbeitskreis für Wahrheit und Gerechtigkeit*, Wuppertal-Elberfeld, 23 January 1951, p. 4.
81. *New York Times*, 6 November 1950.
82. Quoted from *Arbeitskreis für Wahrheit und Gerechtigkeit*, 23 January 1951, p. 5.
83. Lord Shawcross in the foreword to Gründler and Manikowsky: *Das Gericht der Sieger*, pp. 19ff.
84. H. Montgomery Hyde: *The Life of Lord Birkett of Ulverston*, p. 515.
85. Francis Biddle: *In Brief Authority*, New York, 1962, pp. 452ff., 473.
86. Donnedieu de Vabres: 'Le Procès ...' in *Revue de Science Criminelle et de Droit Pénal Comparé*, Paris, 1947, No. 2, p. 179.
87. Telford Taylor: 'War Crimes and International Law' in *International Conciliation*, April 1949, p. 352.
88. ibid., p. 353.
89. Taylor: *Nuremberg and Vietnam*, op. cit., p. 207.
90. The phrase is that of the historians John Fried and Martin Broszat during discussions on the Nuremberg trials held in Washington in 1975.
91. Sir David Maxwell-Fyfe: Foreword to *The Peleus Trial, War Crimes Trials*, London, 1958, Vol. 1, p. xv.
92. Gründler and Manikowsky, op. cit., p. 245.
93. In course of time these have led to really absurd theories. Hayo Uthoff, for instance, in *Rollenkonforme Verbrechen unter einem totalitären System* (Berlin, 1975) maintains that many crimes were both legally and morally permissible judged by the standards and functions of the Hitler period. This would appear to make punishment of those condemned as criminals unjustified. There is no need to prove that many of the Nazi crimes were punishable even under pre-1945 German law.
94. On the East German constitution see Siegfried Mampel: *Die Entwicklung der Verfassungsordnung in der sowjetisch besetzten Zone Deutschlands von 1945 bis 1963*, Tübingen, 1964.
95. The judgement in the 'Justice Case', for instance, states: 'Hitler's decrees were a protection neither to himself nor his subordinates' (*Trials of War Criminals before the Nuremberg Military Tribunals*, Vol. III, p. 1011).
96. In the same trial the court stated in its judgement on Lautz, a Nazi Public Prosecutor: 'If German law were a defence, which it is not, many of his acts would be excusable' (ibid., p. 1128).
97. Kranzbühler: *Nürnberg als Rechtsproblem*, p. 232.
98. Judgement in OKW trial, *Trials of War Criminals ...* Vol. XI, p. 489.
99. The preamble to this treaty, dated 26 September 1815, for instance, states that 'it is essential that the attitude adopted by the Powers in their mutual relationships be based on the sublime truths taught us by the eternal religion of God, our Saviour'. It is then solemnly declared that 'the present instrument has no other purpose than to proclaim to the world their unshakable determination that the commandments of this sacred religion alone shall govern their behaviour both in the governance of their own countries and in their political relationships to any other government; these commandments are justice, human friendship and peace which, far from being applicable only to private life, should directly influence the decisions of Princes and guide their every step, since they are the sole means of consolidating human institutions and alleviating their imperfections.'

Article 1 lays down: 'In accordance with the words of Holy Writ, which enjoin all men to regard each other as brothers, the three contracting Monarchs remain linked by the ties of a true and indissoluble fraternity and, seeing they have a common Fatherland, will afford each other assistance and support at every opportunity and in every place; since they regard themselves as fathers to their subjects and their armies, they will direct them in the same spirit of brotherhood as that which inspires them to protect religion, peace and justice.'

In Article 2 the partners and signatories to the Alliance assured each other: 'Consequently the sole principle governing relationships between both the said governments and their subjects is that of mutual service, mutual affection and mutual goodwill; all consider themselves solely as members of one and the same christian nation, in consideration whereof the three Allied Princes consider themselves charged by Providence with the governance of three branches of one and the same family, namely Austria, Prussia and Russia. They therefore acknowledge that this christian nation, of which they and their peoples form part, in fact has no other sovereign than He to whom all power belongs and is due, because in Him alone are to be found all the treasures of love, knowledge and eternal wisdom, namely God, our heavenly Saviour Jesus Christ, the Word of the All-Highest, the Word of Life.'

See F. W. Ghillany: *Diplomatisches Handbuch 1648–1867*, 3 vols., Nördlingen, 1855–68, Vol. 1, pp. 386ff.; and F. W. von Rohrscheidt: *Preussens Staatsverträge*, Berlin, 1852, p. 485.

100. On this problem in general see Yehezkel Dror: *Verrückte Welt. Politische Wahnsinn und seine Bekämpfung*, Stuttgart, 1975.

101. On the history of the 'Axis' alliance between Hitler and Mussolini: see Jens Petersen: *Hitler–Mussolini. Die Entstehung der Achse Berlin–Rom 1933–1936*, Tübingen, 1974.

102. The politicians are the people who should give careful study to the change in some of the Nuremberg defendants – a suggestion which should not really be buried in the last footnote in this book. At the beginning of the trial all had pleaded 'not guilty'. Yet Hans Frank, for instance, soon came to look upon the IMT as a god-given world court. Albert Speer and Baldur von Schirach talked of a share of responsibility even under a totalitarian dictatorship. Wilhelm Keitel declared that, were he to stand again on the threshold of a career so fateful to him, he would rather choose death than tread the same road again. In the light of this Walter Funk's remark that his complicity was a 'human tragedy' but not a crime needs no comment.

Bibliography

ADAM, UWE DIETRICH: *Judenpolitik im Dritten Reich*, Düsseldorf, 1972.

ALDERMAN, S. S.: 'Background and Highlights of the Nuremberg Trial' in *I.C.C. Practitioners' Journal*, 1946/7.

ALEXANDER, CH. W., and KEESHAN, A.: *Justice at Nuremberg*, Chicago, 1945.

ALLARD, SVEN: *Stalin und Hitler. Die sowjetrussische Aussenpolitik 1930 bis 1941*, Berne and Munich, 1974.

AMAUDRUZ, G. A.: *UBU justicier au premier procès de Nuremberg*, Paris, 1949.

ANDRUS, B. C.: *The Infamous of Nuremberg*, London, 1969.

APRIL, N.: 'An Inquiry into the Juridical Basis for the Nuremberg War Crimes Trial' in *Minnesota Law Review*, 1946.

ARONEANU, EUGÈNE: *Das Verbrechen gegen die Menschlichkeit*, Baden-Baden, 1947.

ASCHENAUER, RUDOLF: *Zur Frage einer Revision der Kriegsverbrecherprozesse*, Nuremberg, 1949; *Landsberg*, Munich, 1951.

ATKIN, LORD: 'The Trial of the Nazis' in *Law Journal*, 1945.

BADER, KARL: 'Der Nürnberger Ärzteprozess' in *Deutsche Rechtszeitschrift*, 1947, and 'Zum Nürnberger Urteil', ibid., 1946.

BAER, MARCEL DE: 'The Treatment of War Crimes incidental to the War' in *Bulletin of International News*, February/March, 1945.

BALAZS, ANDRÉ: 'Die rechtliche Begründung des Nürnberger Urteils' in *Friedenswarte*, 1946.

BALMER-BASILIUS, H. R.: 'Nürnberg und das Weltgewissen' in *Friedenswarte*, 1946.

BARCIKOWSKI, WACLAW: 'Les Nations Unies et l'Organisation de la Répression des Crimes de Guerre' in *Revue Internationale de Droit Pénal*, 1946.

BARDÈCHE, MAURICE: *Nuremberg ou la terre promise*, Paris, 1948.

BAUER, FRITZ: *Die Kriegsverbrecher vor Gericht*, Zurich, 1945.

BAUM, WALTER: 'Der Zusammenbruch der obersten deutschen militärischen Führung 1945' in *Wehrwissenschaftliche Rundschau* No. 5, Frankfurt, 1960.

BECKER, HELLMUTH: 'Gericht der Politik' in *Merkur*, 1950.

BECKER, H.: *Quantität und Qualität – Grundfragen der Bildungspolitik*, Freiburg, 1962.

BEHLING, KURT: 'Die Schuldaussprüche im Nürnberger Juristenurteil vom 4/5 Dezember 1947' in *Archiv des Völkerrechts*, 1949; 'Nürnberger Lehren' in *Juristische Rundschau*, 1949.

BELGION, MONTGOMERY: *Epitaph on Nuremberg*, London, 1946; *Victor's Justice*, Chicago, 1949.

BELLONI, G. A.: 'Criminalità di guerra' in *Giustizia Penale*, 1946.

BERGAMINI, DAVID: *Japan's Imperial Conspiracy. How Emperor Hirohito Led Japan into War against the West*, New York, 1971.

BERGER, JAKOB: 'The Legal Nature of War Crimes and the Problem of Superior Command' in *American Political Science Review*, 1944.

BERNAYS, M. C.: 'The Legal Basis of the Nuremberg Trials' in *Survey Graphic*, 1946.

BERNSTEIN, O. H.: *Final Judgement. The Story of Nuremberg*, New York, 1947.

BEZYMENSKI, LEW: *The Death of Adolf Hitler*, London and New York, 1968.

BIAL, L. C.: 'The Nuremberg Judgement and International Law' in *Brooklyn Law Review*, 1947.

BIDDLE, FRANCIS: *In Brief Authority*, New York, 1962; 'Report to President Truman' in *Department of State Bulletin*, 1946; 'The Nuremberg Trial' in *Proceedings of the American Philosophical Society*, 1947, and *Virginia Law Review*, 1947.

BIRKENFELD, W.: *Der synthetische Treibstoff 1933 bis 1945*, Göttingen, 1964.

BIRKETT, LORD JUSTICE: 'International Legal Theories Evolved at Nuremberg' in *International Affairs*, 1947.

BLAKENEY, B. B.: 'International Military Tribunal' in *American Bar Association Journal*, 1946.

BOELKE, W. A.: 'Hitlers Befehle zur Zerstörung oder Lähmung des deutschen Industriepotentials 1944/45' in *Tradition* 13 of 1968.

BOISSARIE, A.: 'La Définition du crime contre l'humanité'and 'La Répression des crimes nazis contre l'humanité et la protection des libertés démocratiques' in *Revue Internationale de Droit Pénal*, 1947.

BOSCH, W. J.: *Judgement on Nuremberg. American Attitudes toward the Major War Crime Trials*, University of Carolina Press, 1970.

BOVERI, MARGRET: *Der Diplomat vor Gericht*, Berlin and Hannover, 1948.

BRAND, G.: 'The War Crimes Trials and the Law of War' in *The British Yearbook of International Law*, 1949.

BRAND, J. T.: 'Crimes against Humanity and the Nuremberg Trials' in *Oregon Law Review*, 1949.

BRENNECKE, GERHARD: *Die Nürnberger Geschichtsentstellung*, Tübingen, 1970.

BROSS, WERNER: *Gespräche mit Hermann Göring während des Nürnberger Prozesses*, Flensburg and Hamburg, 1950.

BROSZAT, MARTIN: *Nationalsozialistische Polenpolitik 1939–1945*, Stuttgart, 1961.

BUCHHEIM, HANS, BROSZAT, MARTIN, JACOBSEN, HANS-ADOLF, and KRAUSNICK, HELMUT: *Anatomy of the SS State*, London, 1968.

BULLOCK, ALAN: 'Hitler and the Origins of the Second World War', Raleigh Lecture on History, 22 November 1967, published for the British Academy by Oxford University Press, London, 1968.

CALOYANNI, M.: 'Le Procès de Nuremberg et l'avenir de la justice pénale internationale' in *Revue Internationale de Droit Pénal*, 1946.

CALVOCORESSI, PETER: *Nuremberg. The Facts, the Law and the Consequences*, London, 1947.

CARTER, E. F.: 'The Nuremberg Trials. A Turning Point in the Enforcement of International Law' in *Nebraska Law Review*, 1949.

Charter and Judgement of the Nuremberg Tribunal. History and Analysis. Memorandum by the Secretary-General, New York, 1949.

CHASE, J. L.: 'The Development of the Morgenthau Plan through the Quebec Conference' in *Journal of Politics*, Vol. 16, No. 2, May 1954.

CHURCHILL, WINSTON S.: *The Second World War*, London, 1948ff.

'Common Cause', Chicago University Press, special issue, January 1950.

COMTESSE, M. A.: 'Betrachtungen zum Nürnberger Prozess' in *Schweizer Monatshefte*, 1946.

Consolidated Treaty Series, edited by Clive Perry, Oceana Publications Inc., New York, 1969.

Corpus Juris Secundum, Vol. 19, 1940.

COWLES, W. B.: 'High Government Officials as War Criminals' in *Proceedings of the American Society of International Law*, 1945; 'Universality of Jurisdiction over War Crimes' in *California Law Review*, 1945.

CREEL, G.: *War Criminals and Punishment*, London, 1945.

CZAPSKI, SUZANNE: 'Rechtsanwälte in Nürnberg', DANA report, 8 June 1946.

DANIEL, J.: *Le Problème du châtiment des crimes de guerre d'après les enseignements de la deuxième guerre mondiale*, Cairo, 1946.

Das Urteil von Nürnberg 1946, foreword by Herbert Kraus, Munich, 1961.

DESCHEEMAEKER, J.: *Le Tribunal militaire international des grands criminels de guerre*, Paris, 1947.

'Die andere Seite', monthly information service of *Arbeitsgemeinschaft für Recht und Wirtschaft*, from May 1950.

'Die Beziehungen zwischen Deutschland und der Sowjetunion 1939–1941' – Documents of German Foreign Office, edited by Alfred Seidl, Tübingen, 1949.

DIX, HELLMUTH: 'Die Urteile in den Nürnberger Wirtschaftsprozessen' in *Neue Juristische Wochenschrift*, 1949.

DODD, T. J.: 'The Nuremberg Trials' in *Journal of Criminal Law and Criminology*, 1946/7.

DOMARUS, MAX: *Hitler. Reden und Proklamationen 1932–1945*, 4 vols., Munich, 1965.

DONNEDIEU DE VABRES, H.: 'Le Jugement de Nuremberg et le principe de la légalité des délits et des peines' in *Revue de Droit Pénal et de Criminologie*, 1946/7; 'Le Procès de Nuremberg' in *Revue de Science Criminelle et de Droit Pénal Comparé*, No. 2, Paris, 1947; 'Le Procès de Nuremberg devant les principes modernes du droit pénal international' in *Receuil des Cours de l'Académie de Droit International*, Vol. 70.

DROR, YEHEZKEL: *Verrückte Welt. Politischer Wahnsinn und seine Bekämpfung*, Stuttgart, 1975.

DUBOST, CHARLES. 'Les Crimes des États et la coutume pénale internationale' in *Politique Étrangère*, December 1946.

DUFF, CHARLES: *A Handbook of Hanging*, London, 1961.

DULLES, J. F.: 'International Criminal Law and Individuals' in *American Bar Association, Proceedings of the Section of International and Comparative Law*, 1949.

ECCARD, F.: 'La Signification suprême du Procès de Nuremberg' in *Revue de Droit International, de Sciences Diplomatiques, Politiques et Sociales*, 1946.

EHARD, HANS: 'Der Nürnberger Prozess gegen die Hauptkriegsverbrecher und das Völkerrecht' in *Süddeutsche Juristenzeitung*, 1948 (English translation in *American Journal of International Law*, 1949).

EINSELE, HELGA, FEIGE, JOHANNES, and MÜLLER-DIETZ, HEINZ: 'Die Reform der lebenslangen Freiheitsstrafe' in *Beiträge zur Strafvollzugswissenschaft*, No. 10, Stuttgart, 1972.

FABY, PH.: *Der Hitler–Stalin Pakt 1939–1941*, Darmstadt, 1962.

FELDMANN, HORST: *Das Verbrechen gegen die Menschlichkeit*, Essen, 1948.

FERENCZ, B. B.: 'Nuremberg Trial Procedure and the Rights of the Accused' in *Journal of Criminal Law and Criminology*, 1948.

FINCH, G. A.: 'The Nuremberg Trial and International Law' in *American Journal of International Law*, 1947.

Foreign Relations of the United States. Diplomatic Papers. The Conferences at Cairo and Teheran 1943, Washington, 1961.

FRANK, HANS: *Im Angesicht des Galgens*, Munich Gräfelfing, 1953.

FREEMAN, ALWYN V.: 'War Crimes by Enemy Nationals Administering Justice in Occupied Territory' in *American Journal of International Law*, 1947.

Freies Europa, Vol. 13, No. 162, July 1946.

FRIEDENSBURG, F.: 'Die sowjetischen Kriegslieferungen an das Hitlerreich' in *Vierteljahreshefte für Wirtschaftsforschung*, 1962.

GERHARD, EUGENE C.: *America's Advocate: Robert H. Jackson*, Indianapolis and New York, 1958.

GHILLANY, F. W.: *Diplomatisches Handbuch 1648–1867*, 3 vols., Nördlingen, 1855–68; *Europäische Chronik von 1492 bis Ende April 1877*, 5 vols., Leipzig, 1865–78.

GILBERT, G. M.: *Nuremberg Diary*, Signet Books, New York, 1961; *The Psychology of Dictatorship*, New York, 1950.

GLASER, STÉPHANE: 'La Charte du Tribunal de Nuremberg et les nouveaux principes du droit international' in *Schweizerische Zeitschrift für Strafrecht*, 63rd year; 'Les Principes de la légalité des délits et des peines et les procès des criminels de guerre' in *Revue de Droit Pénal et de Criminologie*, 1947.

GLUECK, SHELDON: 'Ist der Nürnberger Prozess illegal?' in *Amerikanische Rundschau*, 1946, No. 9; *The Nuremberg Trial and Aggressive War*, New York, 1946; *War Criminals, their Prosecution and Punishment*, New York, 1944.

GÖRLITZ, WALTER: *Keitel. Verbrecher oder Offizier?*, Göttingen, 1961.

GOODHART, A. L.: 'Questions and Answers concerning the Nuremberg Trials' in *International Law Quarterly*, 1947; 'The Legality of the Nuremberg Trials' in *The Juridical Review*, April 1946.

GRAVEN, JEAN: 'De la justice internationale à la paix; les enseignements de Nuremberg' in *Revue de Droit international, de Sciences Diplomatiques, Politiques et Sociales*, 1946 and 1947; 'Les Châtiments des crimes de guerre' in *Alma mater*, No. 31, 1947.

GRAVESON, R. H.: 'Der Grundsatz "nulla poena sine lege" und Kontrollratsgesetz Nr 10' in *Monatsschrift für Deutsches Recht*, December 1947.

GREEN, L. C.: *International Law through the Cases*, London, 1951.

GREINER, HELLMUTH: *Die Oberste Wehrmachtsführung 1939–1943*, Wiesbaden, 1951.

GREWE, WILHELM, and KÜSTER, OTTO: *Nürnberg als Rechtsfrage*, Stuttgart, 1947.

GROSS, LEO: 'The Criminality of Aggressive War' in *American Political Science Review*, 1947.

GRÜNDLER, GERHARD E., and MANIKOWSKY, ARNIM VON: *Das Gericht der Sieger*, Oldenburg and Hamburg, 1967.

GÜDE: 'Zur Deutung des Organisationsverbrechens' in *Deutsche Rechtzeitshrift*, 1948.

GUGGENHEIM, PAUL: 'Der völkerrechtliche Schutz der Menschenrechte' in *Friedenswarte*, 1949.

Gutachten und Denkschriften über das I M T und die Nürnberger Nachfolgeprozesse by Donnedieu de Vabres (25 June 1949), Franz Exner (4 January 1946), Gilbert Gidel (18 August 1949), Carl Haensel (5 August 1947), Erhard Heinke (28 January 1947), Eric Kaufmann (27 October 1948, 15/20 July 1949), Theodor Klefisch (5 June 1946, August 1947), Herbert Kraus (24 May 1946, 15 June 1946, 10 May 1947, 8 June 1947, 10 January 1948, 10 April 1948, 18 June 1949), Günther Lummert (July 1947), Hermann Mosler (15 February 1946, 2 March 1946, 7 May 1947), Ch. Rousseau (27 July 1949), Eberhard Schmidt (1 November 1946), Robert Servatius (15 February 1946), Eduard Wahl (21 May 1948) – all, and others, in Institut für Völkerrecht, University of Göttingen.

Habeas-Corpus in Kriegsverbrecherprozessen in Archiv des öffentlichen Rechts, 1949.

HAENSEL, CARL: *Das Gericht vertagt sich. Aus dem Tagebuch eines Nürnberger Verteidigers*, Hamburg, 1950; *Das Organisationsverbrechen. Nürnberger Betrachtungen zum Kontrollratsgesetz Nr 10*, Munich, 1947; 'Das Urteil im Nürnberger Juristenprozess' in *Deutsche Rechtszeitschrift*, 1948; 'Der Ausklang von Nürnberg' in *Neue Juristische Wochenschrift*, 1949; 'Nürnberger Probleme' in *Deutsche Rechtszeitschrift*, 1946; 'Schuldprinzip und Gruppenkriminalität' in *Süddeutsche Juristenzeitung*, 1947.

HALDER, FRANZ: *Kriegstagebuch*, edited by *Arbeitskreis für Wehrforschung*, Stuttgart, 3 vols., Stuttgart 1962-4.

HANKEY, LORD: *Politics, Trials and Errors*, Oxford, 1950.

HARTLMAYR, F.: 'Nürnberger Kriegsverbrecherprozess und Völkerrecht' in *Österreichische Monatshefte*, 1946.

HAZAN, E.: 'Étude critique du Jugement de Nuremberg' in *Revue de Droit International pour le Moyen-Orient*, No. 1, 1951.

HEINZE, KURT, and SCHILLING, KARL: *Die Rechtssprechung der Nürnberger Militärtribunale*, Bonn, 1951.

HERZOG, J. B.: 'Les Organisations national-socialistes devant le Tribunal de Nuremberg' in *Revue International de Droit Pénal*, 1946; 'Les Principes juridiques de la répression des crimes de guerre' in *Schwizerische Zeitschrift für Strafrecht*, 1946.

HEYDECKER, JOE J., and LEEB, JOHANNES: *The Nuremberg Trials*, translated E. A. Downie, London, Melbourne, Toronto, 1962.

HILLGRUBER, ANDREAS: *Hitlers Strategie, Politik und Kriegführung 1940/41* Frankfurt/Main, 1965; 'Die "Endlösung" und das deutsche Ostproblem als Kernstück des rassenideologischen Programms des Nationalsozialismus' in *Vierteljahrshefte für Zeitgeschichte*, No. 2, 1972.

History of the United Nations War Crimes Commission and the Development of Laws of War, London, 1948.

Hitler's Table Talk, London, 1953.

HODENBERG, HODO FREIHERR VON: 'Zur Anwendung des Kontrollratsgesetz Nr 10 durch die deutschen Gerichte' in *Süddeutsche Juristenzeitung*, special issue, 1947.

HÖHNE, HEINZ: *The Order of the Death's Head*, translated Richard Barry, London, 1969; *Canaris. Patriot im Zwielicht*, Munich, 1976.

HOFFMANN, PETER: *Die Sicherheit des Diktators. Hitlers Leibwache, Schutz-massnahmen, Residenzen, Hauptquartiere*, Munich, 1975.

HOFMANNSTHAL, E. VON: 'War Crimes Not Tried under Retroactive Law' in *New York University Law Quarterly Review*, 1947.

HOLBORN, LOUISE W.: *War and Peace. Aims of the United Nations*, World Peace Foundation, Boston, 1943, 1948, Vol. II.

HOLTMANN, GÜNTER: *Amerikas Deutschlandpolitik im Zweiten Weltkrieg, Kriegs-und Friedensziele 1941-1945*, Heidelberg, 1958.

HOMZE, E. L.: *Foreign Labor in Nazi Germany*, Princeton, N.J., 1967.

HONIG, F.: 'Nuremberg – Justice or Vengeance' in *World Affairs*, London, 1947.

HOSSBACH, FRIEDRICH: *Zwischen Wehrmacht und Hitler*, Göttingen, 1965.

HUBATSCH, WALTER: *Die deutsche Besetzung von Dänemark und Norwegen 1940*, Göttingen, 1952; *Hitlers Weisungen für die Kriegsführung 1939-1945*, Munich, 1952 (slightly abridged translation: *Hitler's War Directives*, London, 1964).

HUGUENEY, L.: 'Le Procès de Nuremberg devant les principes modernes du droit pénal international' in *Revue Internationale de Droit Pénal*, 1948.

HYDE, H. MONTGOMERY: *The Life of Lord Birkett of Ulverston*, London, 1964.

Instrumentum Pacis Caesaro-Gallicum Monasteriense, Quellen zur neueren Geschichte, Introduction, Berne, 1949, Nos. 12/13.

International Conference on Military Trials, London, 1945, Washington, 1949.

JACKSON, ROBERT H.: 'Angriffskrieg und Kriegsrecht' in *Amerikanische Rundschau*, 1945; opening speech before the IMT in Nuremberg, Frankfurt/Main, 1946; 'Nuremberg in Retrospect' in *Canadian Bar Review*, 1949; speech in Buffalo on the Nuremberg judgements, *New York Herald Tribune*, 6 October 1946; report to International Conference on Military Trials, London, 1945, Washington, 1949; 'The Law under which Nazi Organizations Are Accused of Being "Criminal"' in *Temple Law Quarterly*, 1946; *The Nuremberg Case*, New York, 1947; 'Trial of the Trials: Nuremberg' in *Common Cause*, 1950.

JACKSON, W. W.: 'Putting the Nuremberg Law to Work', in *Foreign Affairs*, 1947.

JACOBSEN, HANS-ADOLF: *Fall 'Gelb'. Der Kampf um den deutschen Operationsplan zur Westoffensive*, Wiesbaden, 1957; *1939-1945. Der Zweite Weltkrieg in Chronik und Dokumenten*, Darmstadt, 1959; *Deutsche Kriegführung 1939-1945*, Hanover, 1961; *The Diplomacy of the Winter War. An Account of the Russo-Finnish War 1939/40*, Cambridge, Mass., 1961; *Der Zweite Weltkrieg. Grundzüge der Politik und Strategie in Dokumenten*, Frankfurt/Main, 1964; *Der Zweite Weltkrieg in Dokumenten*, Frankfurt/Main, 1965; *Nationalsozialistiche Aussenpolitik 1933-1938*, Frankfurt/Main, 1968.

JACOBSEN, HANS-ADOLF, and DOLLINGER, H.: *Der Zweite Weltkrieg in Bildern und Dokumenten*, 3 vols., Munich, Vienna, Basle, 1962/3.

JAHRREISS, HERMANN: 'Die Fortentwicklung des Völkerrechts' in *Jahrbuch für internationales und ausländisches Recht*, 1949.

JANECZEK, EDWARD JOHN: *Nuremberg Judgement in the Light of International Law*, Geneva, 1949.

JASPERS, K.: 'The Significance of the Nuremberg Trials for Germany and the World' in *Notre Dame Lawyer* 1946/7.

JESSUP, PHILIP C.: 'The Crime of Aggression and the Future of International Law' in *Political Science Quarterly*, 1947.

JODL, LUISE: *Jenseits des Endes. Leben und Sterben des Generaloberst Alfred Jodl*, Vienna, Munich, Zurich, 1976.

The Katyn Forest Massacre. Hearings before the Select Committee to Conduct an Investigation of the Facts, Evidence and Circumstances of the Katyn Forest Massacre, 82nd Congress, 1st and 2nd sessions 1951/2, 7 vols., Washington, 1952.

KATZENBERGER, K.: 'Das Korps der Politischen Leiter im Urteil von Nürnberg' in *Neue Juristische Wochenschrift*, 1947/8.

KEHRIG, MANFRED: *Stalingrad*, Stuttgart, 1973.

KEHRL, HANS: *Krisenmanager im Dritten Reich, 6 Jahre Frieden, 6 Jahre Krieg*, Düsseldorf, 1973.

KEITEL, WILHELM: *The Memoirs of Field Marshal Keitel*, introduction by Walter Görlitz, translated by David Irving, London, 1965.

KELLEY, DOUGLAS M.: *22 Cells in Nuremberg*, New York, 1947.

KELSEN, HANS: 'Collective and Individual Responsibility for Acts of State in International Law' in *The Jewish Yearbook of International Law*, 1948; *Peace through Law*, Chapel Hill, 1944; 'The Rule against ex post facto Laws and the Prosecution of the Axis War Criminals' in *The Judge Advocate Journal*, Vol. 2; 'Will the Judgement in the Nuremberg Trials Constitute a Precedent in International Law?' in *The International Law Quarterly*, 1947.

KEMPNER, ROBERT M. W.: 'The Nuremberg Trials as Sources of Recent German Political and Historical Material' in *American Political Science Review*, 1950; *Eichmann und Komplizen*, Zurich, Stuttgart, Vienna, 1961; *SS im Kreuzverhör*, Munich, 1964; *Das Dritte Reich im Kreuzverhör*, Munich, Esslingen, 1969.

KEMPSKI, JÜRGEN VON: 'Krieg als Straftat' in *Merkur*, No. 1 of 1947.

KENNY, JOHN P.: *Moral Aspects of Nuremberg*, Washington, 1950.

KIESSELBACH, WILHELM: 'Zwei Probleme aus dem Gesetz Nr 10 des Allierten Kontrollrats' in *Monatsschrift für Deutsches Recht*, 1947.

KLEFISCH, THEODOR: 'Gedanken über Inhalt und Wirkung des Nürnberger Urteils' in *Juristische Rundschau*, 1947.

KLEIN, BURTON H.: *Germany's Economic Preparation for War*, Cambridge, Mass., 1959.

KOLLER, KARL: *Der letzte Monat. Die Tagebuchaufzeichnungen des Chefs des Generalstabes der deutschen Luftwaffe vom 14 April bis 27 Mai 1945*, Mannheim, 1949.

KOTZE, HILDEGARD (ed.): *Heeresadjutant bei Hitler 1938–1943; Aufzeichnungen des Majors Engels*, Stuttgart, 1974.

KRANZBÜHLER, OTTO: *Rückblick auf Nürnberg*, Hamburg, 1949.

KRAUS, HERBERT: *Gerichtstag in Nürnberg*, Hamburg, 1948; *Kontrollratsgesetz Nr 10*, Hamburg, 1948.

KUHN, ARTHUR: 'International Criminal Jurisdiction' in *American Journal of International Law*, 1947.

LACHS, MANFRED: 'Le Jugement de Nuremberg' in *Revue International de Droit Pénal*, 1946; *War Crimes. An Attempt to Define the Issues*, London, 1945.

LA FOLETTE, CHARLES M.: *Der Nürnberger Prozess gegen führende Juristen des Dritten Reiches*, Stuttgart, 1948.

LANDE, A.: *The Legal Basis of the Nuremberg Trials*, New York, 1945.

Landsberg – documentary report issued by Information Services Division, Office of the US High Commissioner for Germany, 1951.

LASERSON, MAX: *Russia and the Western World*, New York, 1945.

LATERNSER, HANS: *Verteidigung deutscher Soldaten*, Bonn, 1950.

LAUTERPRACHT, H.: *Annual Digest and Reports of Public International Law Cases 1941/42, Case no. 168*; *The Development of International Law: The International Court*, London, 1958; 'The Law of Nations and Punishment of War Crimes' in *British Yearbook of International Law*, 1944.

Law Reports of Trials and War Criminals: Selected and prepared by the United Nations War Crimes Commission, 15 vols., London, 1947–9.

LAZARD, DIDIER: *Le Procès de Nuremberg. Récit d'un témoin*, Paris, 1947.

LEMKIN, RAPHAEL: *Axis Rule in Occupied Europe*, Washington, 1944; 'Responsibility of Persons Acting on Behalf of States in the Crime of Genocide' in *The American Scholar*, 1946.

LENER, S.: 'Diritto e politica nel processo di Norimberga' in *Civiltà Cattolica*, 1946.

LEONHARDT, HANS: 'The Nuremberg Trial: A Legal Analysis' in *Review of Politics*, 1949.

Le Procès de Nuremberg: Paris, undated.

Le Procès de Nuremberg: 'La Responsibilité individuelle dans la perpétration des crimes contre la paix', brochure No. 3 of 1946, *Société Egyptienne de Droit International*.

LEVENTAL, HAROLD, HARRIS, SAM, and OTHERS: 'The Nuremberg Verdict' in *Harvard Law Review*, 1947.

LEVY, A. G. D.: 'Criminal Responsibility of Individuals in International Law' in *University of Chicago Law Review*, 1944/5.

LEYRAT, P. DE: 'Crime de la guerre et crimes de guerre' in *Cahiers du Monde Nouveau*, 1945.

LIDDELL, HART, SIR BASIL: *History of the Second World War*, London, 1970.

LIPPE, VIKTOR FREIHERR VON: *Nürnberger Tagebuch-Notizen, November 1945 bis Oktober 1946*, Frankfurt, 1951.

LÜDDE-NEURATH, WALTER: *Regierung Dönitz. Die letzten Tage des Dritten Reiches*, Göttingen, 1953.

LÜDERS, KARL-HEINZ: 'Strafgerichtsbarkeit über Angehörige des Feindstaates' in *Süddeutsche Juristenzeitung*, 1946.

LUMMERT, GÜNTHER: *Die Strafverfahren gegen Deutsche im Ausland wegen 'Kriegsverbrechens'*, Hamburg, 1949.

LUNAU, HEINZ: *The Germans on Trial*, New York, 1948.

MANGOLDT, HERMANN VON: 'Das Kriegsverbrechen und seine Verfolgung in Vergangenheit und Gegenwart' in *Jahrbuch für internationales und ausländisches öffentliches Recht*, 1948.

MANSTEIN, ERICH VON: *Lost Victories*, London, 1958.

MAPEL, SIEGFRIED: *Die Entwicklung der Verfassungsordnung in der sowjetisch besetzten Zone Deutschlands von 1945 bis 1963*, Tübingen, 1964.

MARTIN, BERND: *Friedensinitiativen und Machtpolitik im Zweiten Weltkrieg 1939–42*, Vol. 6, Düsseldorf, 1974.

MARTIUS, GEORG: 'Das Nürnberger Urteil in völkerrechtliche Beziehung' in *Neue Justiz*, 1947, No. 4/5.

MASCHKE, HERMANN M.: *Das Krupp-Urteil und das Problem der 'Plünderung'*, Göttingen, 1951.

MASER, WERNER: *Adolf Hitler. Legende – Mythos – Wirklichkeit*, Munich and Esslingen, 1971 (*Hitler*, translated Peter and Betty Ross, London and New York, 1973); *Der Sturm auf der Republik. Frühgeschichte der NSDAP*, Stuttgart, 1973; *Hitlers Briefe und Notizen. Sein Weltbild in handschriftlichen Dokumenten*, Düsseldorf and Vienna, 1973; *Adolf Hitler. Mein Kampf. Fahrplan eines Welteroberers. Eine Analyse*, Munich, 1974.

MAXWELL-FYFE, SIR DAVID: Foreword to 'The Peleus Trial', *War Crimes Trials*, Vol. I.

MAYNARD. J. A.: 'Crimes et criminels de guerre, problème étudié par un groupe de juristes aux États-Unis' in *Revue Internationale de Droit Pénal*, 1946.

MEINCK, GERHARD: *Hitler und die deutsche Aufrüstung*, Wiesbaden, 1959.

MENTHON, FRANÇOIS DE: 'France demands justice in the name of humanity' speech before the IMT, Neustadt, 1946.

MERLE, MARCEL: *Le Procès de Nuremberg et le châtiment des criminels de guerre*, Paris, 1949.

MIALE, FLORENCE R., and SELZER, MICHAEL: *The Nuremberg Mind. The Psychology of the Nazi Leaders*, New York, 1975.

Militärstrafgesetzbuch (version of 10 October 1940), Berlin, 1943.

MILLER, MERLE: *Plain Speaking. An Oral Biography of Harry S. Truman*, New York and London, 1974.

MILWARD, ALAN S.: *The German Economy at War*, London, 1965.

MITSCHERLICH, ALEXANDER, and MIELKE, FRED: *Das Diktat der Menschenverachtung, Eine Dokumentation*, Heidelberg, 1947.

MOMMSEN, WOLFGANG: 'Die Akten der Nürnberger Kriegsverbrecherprozesse und die Möglichkeit ihrer historischen Auswertung', *Der Archivar. Mitteilungsblatt für deutsches Archivwesen*, Düsseldorf, 3rd year, No. 1.

MONTERO, MARIO: 'El Tribunal de Nuremberg' in *Revista Peruana de derecho internacional*, 1948.

MORGAN, J. H.: 'Nuremberg and After' in *The Quarterly Review*, 1947; *The Great Assize. An Examination of the Law of the Nuremberg Trials*, 1948.

MOSLER, HERMANN: 'Die Kriegshandlung im rechtswidrigen Kriege' in *Jahrbuch für internationales und ausländisches öffentliches Recht*, 1948.

MOSLEY, LEONARD: *The Reich Marshal*, London, 1974.

MURAWSKO, ERICH: *Der deutsche Wehrmachtsbericht 1939–1945. Ein Beitrag zur Untersuchung der geistigen Kriegführung. Mit einer Dokumentation der Wehrmachtsberichte vom 1.7.1944–9.5.1945*, Boppard, 1966.

MYERSON, M. G.: *Germany's War Crimes and Punishment*, New York, 1945.

Nazi Conspiracy and Aggression, 8 vols., Washington, 1947ff.

NEAVE, A. M. S.: 'The Trial of the SS at Nuremberg' in *Revue Internationale de Droit Pénal*, 1946; 'Final Report on the Evidence of Witnesses for the Defence of Organisations Alleged to be Criminal', IMT Vol. XLII.

NELTE, OTTO: *Die Generale. Das Nürnberger Urteil und die Schuld der Generale*, Hannover, 1947.

NEUMANN, FRANZ: 'The War Crimes Trials' in *World Politics*, 1949.

'Neurenberg en de Geschiedenes' in *Nederland in Oorlogstijd*, Year 4, No. 4, 1949.

'The Nuernberg Confusion' in *Fortune*, No. 6, December 1946.

Das Nürnberger Juristenurteil, complete edition, Hamburg, 1948.

344 *Bibliography*

OAKSEY, LORD (formerly Lawrence): 'The Nuremberg Trial' in *International Affairs*, 1947; *The Nuremberg Trials and the Progress of International Law*, Birmingham, 1947.

PASTON, D. G.: *Superior Orders as Affecting Responsibility for War Crimes*, New York, 1946.

PELLA, V. V.: *Fonctions pacificatrices du droit pénal supranational et fin du système traditional des traités de paix*, Paris, 1947; *La Guerre-crime et les criminels de guerre*, Paris, Geneva, 1946.

PETERSEN, JENS: *Hitler–Mussolini. Die Entstehung der Achse Berlin–Rom 1933–1936*, Tübingen, 1974.

PFAHLMANN, H.: *Fremdarbeiter und Kriegsgefangene in der deutschen Kriegswirtschaft 1939–1945*, Darmstadt, 1968.

Potsdam 1945. Quellen zur Konferenz der Grossen Drei, edited by Ernst Deuerlein, Munich, 1963.

The Public Papers and Addresses of Franklin Delano Roosevelt, edited by Samuel Rosenman, Vol. 1944–5, New York, 1950.

Punishment for War Crimes, Inter-Allied Declaration signed at St James's Palace, London, 13 January 1942.

RADBRUCH, GUSTAV: 'Das Reichsjustizministeriums Ruhm und Ende. Zum Nürnberger Juristenprozess' in *Süddeutsche Juristenzeitung*, 1948, coln 57; 'Zur Diskussion über die Verbrechen gegen die Menschlichkeit', ibid., special number, 1947, coln 131.

RADIN, M.: 'International Crimes' in *Iowa Law Review* 1946/7; 'Justice at Nuremberg' in *Foreign Affairs*, 1946, No. 3.

RAWLS, JOHN: *Eine Theorie der Gerechtigkeit*, Frankfurt, 1975.

'Recht im Dienst des Friedens', Festschrift für Eberhard Menzel, eds. Jost Delbrück, Knut Ipsen and Dieter Rauschning, Berlin, 1975.

'Relative Documents' issued by Inter-Allied Information Committee, London, 1942.

'Report of Robert H. Jackson, United States Representative to the International Conference on Military Trials, London 1945', Department of State Publication 3080, Washington, 1949.

Report on the International Juridical Status of Individuals as 'War Criminals', Washington, 1945.

RIBBENTROP, JOACHIM VON: *The Ribbentrop Memoirs*, introduction Alan Bullock, translated Oliver Watson, London, 1954.

RITTLER: 'Kampf gegen das politische Verbrechen seit dem Zweiten Weltkrieg' in *Schweizerische Zeitschrift für Strafrecht*, 1949.

ROHRSCHEIDT, F. W. VON: *Preussens Staatsverträge*, Berlin, 1852, p. 485.

ROOSEVELT, ELLIOTT: *Wie er es sah*, Zurich, 1947.

RUDENKO, R. A.: 'Let justice take its course', speeches by the Soviet Chief Prosecutor during the Nuremberg Trial, Berlin, 1946.

SACK, A. N.: 'War Criminals and the Defense of Superior Orders in International Law' in *Lawyers Guild Review*, 1945.

SAUER, WILHELM: 'Zum Begriff der Kollektivschuld' in *Deutsche Rechtszeitschrift*, 1947.

SCELLE, G.: *Manuel de droit international public*, Paris, 1948.

SCHEUNER, ULRICH: 'Die Annexion im modernen Völkerrecht' in *Friedenswarte*, 1949.

SCHICK, FRANZ B.: 'Crimes against Peace' in *Journal of Criminal Law*, 1948; 'The Nuremberg Trial and the International Law of the Future' in *American Journal of International Law*, 1947; 'The Nuremberg Trial and the Development of an International Criminal Law' in *Juridical Review*, Vol. 59, 1947; 'War Criminals and the Law of the United Nations' in *University of Toronto Law Journal*, 1947/8.

SCHIRACH, BALDUR VON: *Ich glaubte an Hitler*, Hamburg, 1967.

SCHMIDT, K. L.: 'Satzung der Vereinten Nationen' in series *Welt- und Friedensprobleme*, Offenbach, 1947.

SCHNEEBERGER, E.: 'The Responsibility of the Individual under International Law' in *The Georgetown Law Journal*, 1946/7.

Schriften des Bundesarchivs, Vol. 7, Boppard, 1959.

SCHULTZ, JOACHIM: *Die letzten 30 Tage. Aus dem Kriegstagebuch des OKW*, Stuttgart, 1951.

SCHWARZENBERGER, G.: 'The Judgement of Nuremberg' in *Tulane Law Review*, 1947, p. 329; also in *Yearbook of World Affairs*, 1948.

SCHWELB, EGON: 'The Work of the War Crimes Commission' in *British Yearbook of International Law*, 1946.

SERAPHIM, HANS-GÜNTHER: 'Erschliessung der Nürnberger Prozessakten' in *Der Archivar*, No. 28/75; 'Quellen zur Erforschung der Geschichte des Dritten Reiches. 1. Der Index der amtlichen deutschen Ausgabe des Prozesses gegen die Hauptkriegsverbrecher. 2. Die Dokumentenedition der amtlichen deutschen Ausgabe des Verfahrens gegen die Hauptkriegsverbrecher' in *Europa-Archiv*, 1950.

SHAWCROSS, SIR HARTLEY: Speech by the British Chief Prosecutor during the Nuremberg Trial, Hamburg, 1946.

SMITH, H.: 'The Nuremberg Trials' in *Free Europe*, 1946.

SOTTILE, ANTOINE: 'Les Criminels de guerre et le nouveau droit international, seul moyen efficace pour assurer la paix du monde' in *Revue de Droit International, de Sciences Diplomatiques, Politiques et Sociales*, 1945, No. 4.

SPEER, ALBERT: *Inside the Third Reich*, translated Richard and Clara Winston, London, 1970; *Spandau. The Secret Diaries*, translated Richard and Clara Winston, London, 1976.

SPIROPOULOS, J.: 'Draft Code of Offences against the Peace and Security of Mankind. Report of the International Law Commission' in *Revue Hellénique de Droit International*, 1950.

SPRINGER, HILDEGARD: *Es sprach Hans Fritzsche. Nach Gesprächen, Briefen, Dokumenten*, Stuttgart, 1940.

STEINBAUER, GUSTAV: *Ich war Verteidiger in Nürnberg*, Klagenfurt, 1950.

ST GEORGE and LAWRENCE, DENNIS: *A Trial on Trial*, Chicago, 1946.

STILLSCHWEIG, KURT: 'Das Abkommen zur Bekämpfung von Genocide' in *Friedenswarte*, 1949.

STÖCKER, JAKOB: *Vor dem Tribunal des Weltgerichts*, Hanover, 1946.

STÜBEL, HEINRICH: 'Die Finanzierung der Aufrüstung im Dritten Reich' in *Europa-Archiv*, 6th year, 1951.

TAYLOR, TELFORD: *Report on the Conduct and Current Status of the Nuremberg War Crime Trials* (12 May 1948); *Final Report to the Secretary of the Army on the Nuremberg War Crimes Trials under Control Council Law No. 10*, Washington, 1949; 'Nuremberg Trials. War Crimes and International Law' in *International*

Conciliation, April 1949; *Nuremberg and Vietnam*, Chicago, 1970; 'The Use of Captured German and Related Records in the Nuremberg War Crimes Trial' in *Captured German and Related Records. A National Archive Conference* (editor Robert Wolfe), Athens, Ohio, 1974.

The Teheran, Yalta and Potsdam Conferences, Progress Publishers, Moscow, 1969.

TEITGEN, M.: 'Le jugement de Nuremberg' in *Revue de Droit International, de Sciences Diplomatiques, Politiques et Sociales*, 1946.

TESSIN, GEORG: *Formationsgeschichte der Wehrmacht 1933–39. Stäbe und Truppenteile des Heeres und der Luftwaffe*, Boppard, 1959.

The Conferences at Cairo and Teheran 1943, Foreign Relations of the United States, Diplomatic Papers, World War II Conferences, Vol. 3, Washington, 1961.

The Conferences at Malta and Yalta 1945, Foreign Relations of the United States, Diplomatic Papers, World War II Conferences, Vol. 1, Washington, 1955.

The Conference of Berlin 1945, Foreign Relations of the United States, Diplomatic Papers, World War II Conferences, Vols. 1 & 2, Washington, 1960.

THIELE-FREDERSDORF, HERBERT: 'Das Urteil des Militärgerichtshof Nr III im Nürnberger Juristenprozess' in *Neue Juristische Wochenschrift*, 1947/8.

Times, 27 January, 2 December, 7 December, 1943.

TOLSTOY, COUNT NIKOLAI: *The Victims of Yalta*, London, 1978.

TORGERSEN, R. N.: 'Nürnberg processen' in *Tidsskrit for Rettvitenskap*, 1946.

TRAININ, A. N.: 'Le tribunal militaire international et le procès de Nuremberg' in *Revue International de Droit Pénal*, 1946; *The Criminal Responsibility of the Hitlerites*, Moscow, 1944.

TREUE, W.: *Gummi in Deutschland*, Munich, 1955.

Trial of the Major War Criminals before the International Military Tribunal, 40 vols., Nuremberg, 1947 – the IMT.

Trials of War Criminals before the Nuremberg Military Tribunals, October 1946–April 1949, 15 vols., Washington, 1949–53.

UNITED NATIONS: 'Plans for the Formulation of the Principles of the Nuremberg Charter and Judgement' in *Yearbook of the United Nations 1947–8* (p. 214) and 1948–9, Lake Success, 1949, 1950.

UNITED NATIONS: 'International Law Commission, Draft Code of Offences against the Peace and Security of Mankind', Report by Spiropoulos, A/CN 4/25, 26 April 1950.

UNITED NATIONS: *Reports of the International Law Commission*, General Assembly, Official Records, Suppl. No. 10 (A/925), No. 12 (A/1316), Lake Success, 1949, 1950.

UNITED NATIONS: 'Report of the International Law Commission Covering its Third Session 16 May–27 July 1951, with Draft Code of Offences against the Peace and Security of Mankind', A/CN 4/48, 30 July 1951.

UNITED NATIONS: 'Committee of International Criminal Jurisdiction, Draft Statute for an International Criminal Court' in *Report to the General Assembly on the Session held 1 August–31 August 1951*, with Annex I, A/AC48/4, 5 September 1951.

UNITED NATIONS: 'International Law Commission, Bibliography on International Criminal Law and International Criminal Courts', A/CN 4/28, 6 June 1950.

United States Court of Appeal, No. 9883, Brief for Appellees and Petition for Writ of Habeas Corpus, 1 April 1948.

UTHOFF, HAYO: *Rollenkonforme Verbrechen unter einem totalitären System*, Berlin, 1975.

UTLEY, FREDA: 'Nuremberg Judgements' in her book *The High Cost of Vengeance*, Chicago, 1949.

VALTERS, NIKOLAUS: 'Neue Bahnen des Völkerrechts. Die völkerrechtliche Haftung' in *Friedenswarte*, 1949.

VOIGT, F. A.: 'Nuremberg' in *Nineteenth Century and After*, 1949.

Waldeckische Landeszeitung, October 1952.

WALL, E.: *Il processo di Norimberga*, Milan, 1946.

War Crimes Trials Series, edited Sir David Maxwell-Fyfe, London, 1948ff.

WARLIMONT, WALTER: *Inside Hitler's Headquarters*, translated Richard Barry, London, 1964.

WEBER, HELMUTH VON: 'Die strafrechtliche Verantwortlichkeit für Handeln auf Befehl' and 'Das Verbrechen gegen die Menschlichkeit in der Rechtsprechung 1949' in *Monatsschrift für Deutsches Recht*, 1948 and 1949.

WEBER, WERNER, and JAHN, WERNER: *Synopse zur Deutschlandpolitik 1941–1973*, Göttingen, 1975.

WECHSLER, HERBERT: 'The Issues of the Nuremberg Trial' in *Political Science Quarterly*, 1947.

WEIDEMANN, ALFRED: 'Der rechte Mann am rechten Platz' in *Bilanz des Zweiten Weltkrieges*, Oldenburg, 1953.

WEST, REBECCA: *A Train of Powder*, London, 1955.

WILDNING-WHITE, A. M.: 'Punishing War Criminals' in *Law Journal*, 1945.

WILLE, SIEGFRIED: 'Grundsätze des Nürnberger Ärzteprozesses' in *Neue Juristische Wochenschrift*, 1949.

WILMOWSKY, TILO FREIHERR VON: *Warum wurde Krupp verurteilt? Legende und Justizirrtum*, Stuttgart, 1950.

WIMMER, AUGUST: 'Die Bestrafung von Humanitätsverbrechen und der Grundsatz *nullum crimen sine lege*' in *Süddeutsche Juristenzeitung*, special issue, 1947.

WINKLER, EMIL: *Die Kosaken. Herkunft, Leben, Untergang*, Lienz, 1971.

WITTENBERG, J. C.: 'De Grotius à Nuremberg. Quelques réflexions' in *Revue Générale de Droit International Publique*, 1947.

WOODWARD, LLEWELLYN: *British Foreign Policy in the Second World War*, Vol. 3, HMSO, London, 1971.

WRIGHT, QUINCY: 'Against the rule of Law. The International Court' in *Free World*, 1947; 'The Crime of "War-mongering"' in *American Journal of International Law*, 1948; 'The Law of the Nuremberg Trial' in *American Journal of International Law*, 1947.

WYZANSKI, CHARLES E.: 'Nuremberg – a Fair Trial?' and 'Nuremberg in Retrospect' in *The Atlantic Monthly*, April and December 1946.

ZAWODNY, J. K.: *Zum Beispiel Katyn. Klärung eines Kriegsverbrechens*, Munich, 1971.

ZEUMER, K.: *Quellensammlung zur Geschichte des deutschen Reichsverfassung*, Tübingen, 1913.

Index

Admiralty, the (UK), and merchant ship attacks on U-boats, 155; orders sinking of all vessels in Skagerrak, 159

Ahrens, Col. Friedrich, voluntary witness in Katyn case, 308

Albrecht, Counsellor, 201

Alderman, Sidney S., US Associate Trial Counsel, 77; reads the Indictment, 77–8; favours use of affidavits, 100–102

Allied Control Commission, dissolves Dönitz's government, 56

Allied Control Council, 22

Allies, the, and future of war criminals, 17, 18; war aims, 18; ideas for future of Third Reich, 19; Tripartite dinner meeting, 25; gulf between USSR and US/UK, 25; and capitulation of Germany, 27, 28, 56–7, 287; absence of agreed plans on war crimes trials, 27; agreed policy towards defeated Germany, 30–31; anti-Nazi propaganda, 52; and surrender of Wehrmacht, 53–6; ignorant of German armaments in 1939, 138; restrictions on reporting of IMT trials, 229; maintain silence over execution blunders, 255; demand punishment of war criminals, 269; aerial bombardment of Germany, 271n; commission of indictable crimes, 277–8

Amann, Max, in Nuremberg Prison, 59n

Amen, Col. John, Associate Trial counsel, 80, 196, 230–31

American press, assesses war communiqué credibility, 170

Americans, souvenir hunters of executed Germans, 14; treatment of Nuremberg prisoners, 57, 68; secret service informers, 61; regard war against US as a crime, 279

André, Maj. John, executed for espionage, 279

Andrus, (US) Col. Burton C., in control of Bad Mondorf, 57; Prison Commandant Nuremberg, 57, 61–4, 66, 68, 245;

security precautions, 61; attitude towards prisoners, 69, 75; hands them copy of Indictment, 71, 74; in control of documentary evidence, 98; and Göring's suicide, 251; and the executions, 252–3

Anglo-American-Soviet Protocol, 1942, 18

Antonescu, Ion, pro-German, 20

Armaments and aircraft industries, employment of foreign workers, 232

Atlantic Charter, 17; USSR violations, 278

Attlee, Clement (later Lord), succeeds Churchill at Potsdam, 31; wants Hitler named as war criminal, 33

Auschwitz, annihilation of Jews; see Concentration camps

Austria, Anschluss, 208, 212

Babel, Dr Ludwig, defence counsel, 74

Bach-Zelewsky, Erich von dem, in Nuremberg Prison, 59n, 327

Bad Mondorf, 'Palace Hotel', detention of Nuremberg defendants, 29, 35, 46, 52, 53n, 56, 57

Bailey, Maj., head of Administration Section, 274

Balkans, the, 96, 127

Barrett, Lt, and original documents, 96

Basic Field Manual on Rules of Land Warfare, 174

Basilevsky, Prof., USSR prosecution witness, 111

Bavaria, hiding place of German records, 93

Berchtesgaden, arrest of Göring, 43–4; RAF raid, 44–5; detention of prisoners of war, 46–7; processing of records, 93

Berger, Gottlieb, Himmler's amanuensis, 48

Bergold, Dr Friedrich, defence counsel, 73

Berlin, signing of Instrument of Surrender, 53–5; IMT sessions, 71, 77; German prisoners, 72

Laconia, U-boat rescue of survivors, 153–4

Lahousen, Gen. Erwin, prosecution witness, 60 and n, 105–6

Laird, Melvin, U S Defence Minister, never indicted for My Lai massacres, 277

Lammers, Reichsleiter Dr, 48, 218

Landsberg am Lech, site of hanging of war criminals, 175, 249; execution blunders by hangman, 255n

Laternser, Dr Hans, defence counsel, 74; questions Milch on Luftwaffe's preparedness for war, 128–30

Laval, Pierre, 28

Law, the, 270 and n; Nazi concept, 271–2; *see also* International law

Lawrence, Lord Justice, President of the Nuremberg Court, 71, 72; opening speech, 76–7; deems Hess fit to plead, 79; answers questions from the defence, 81–2; and 'guilty' or 'not guilty' pleas, 83; and possession of briefs by defence counsel, 103–4; clashes with Dr Nelte, 106; and Katyn case, 112; intervenes in Jackson/Göring dispute, 114; and disclosure of documents before cross-examination, 114–16 *passim*; and supply of documents in German, 116; and the answering of questions by defendants, 116–17, 119, 120–22, 166–7; disallows legal formalism, 122; and Rudenko's documentary evidence, 125; intervenes in interrogation of Dönitz, 159

Leadership Corps of the Nazi Party, named criminal organization, 37, 78; defence counsel, 74

League of Nations, 1927 declaration on aggressive war, 195; omission of Crimes against Peace, 259, 260; expulsion of USSR, 261

Leahy, Admiral, 296

Lebanon, US 'aggression', 265, 266

Lehmann, Dr, Head of Wehrmacht Legal Service, on Keitel, 140

Leistner, Public Prosecutor, 252

Lersner, Freiherr von, and post-First World War criminals, 20–21

Ley, Robert, 36, 49, 78, 163, 183; search for, 43; discovery and arrest, 47; eventual suicide, 47–8, 72; reaction to Indictment, 71–2; and intensification of the struggle, 190; with Hitler in his shelter,

190; use of 'slackers' from industry, 232

Lippe, Viktor Freiherr von der, 109; and death sentences, 235

Lloyd George, David Lloyd George, Earl, and German war criminals, 297

Lohse, Reich Commissar, 218

London (Four Power) Agreement 1945, governments of US, UK, USSR and French Republic, 77; and methods of trial of major war criminals, 31; becomes IMT Charter, 33, 34; signatories, 34, 77; designation of war crimes and envisaged punishment, 33–4; a transition in international law, 221; IMT and its decisions, 267; and right of resistance, 267

London Charter, 33; and plea in mitigation of punishment, 17, 35; foundation of Nuremberg Trial, 34, 71, 74, 77, 88, 220, 272–3, 280; criticized by defence counsel, 34, 267; appears a form of retribution rather than court of justice, 34–35; and final designation of major war criminals, 35, 77; and defence plea of 'obedience to orders', 178; demands no specific degree of punishment, 220; Jackson and, 220, 221; states IMT cannot be challenged by prosecution, 259; and 'no punishment without corresponding penal law', 260; acknowledged as binding by IMT, 263, 264; influence of Jackson on its drafting, 280; influence on major political developments, 284

London Naval Agreement, 1930; Kranzbühler on its invalidity, 158

Lorenz, Heinz, gives Hitler news of Pearl Harbor, 304

Lossberg, Col., OKW Operations Staff, 167 and n

Ludendorff, General, designated war criminal, 296

Lüdinghausen, Dr Otto Freiherr von, defence counsel, 73

Lumumba, Patrice, CIA-planned elimination, 277

Mann, Thomas, quotation from attributed to Goethe, 223

Manual of Military Law (UK), 174

Manstein, Erich, Field Marshal von, 59n; trial, 275